The Analytical Engine

The Analytical Engine

An Introduction to Computer Science Using the Internet

Rick Decker
Stuart Hirshfield
Hamilton College

PWS Publishing Company
I(T)P An International Thomson Publishing Company
Boston ▪ Albany ▪ Bonn ▪ Cincinnati ▪ London ▪ Madrid ▪ Melbourne ▪ Mexico City
New York ▪ Paris ▪ San Francisco ▪ Singapore ▪ Tokyo ▪ Toronto ▪ Washington

PWS Publishing Company
20 Park Plaza, Boston, MA 02116-4324

I(T)P®
International Thomson Publishing
The trademark ITP is used under license.

Sponsoring Editor: *Michael J. Sugarman*
Editorial Assistant: *Kathryn Schooling*
Developmental/Technology Editor: *Leslie Bondaryk*
Marketing Manager: *Nathan Wilbur*
Production Manager: *Elise S. Kaiser*
Cover/Interior Designer: *Julia Gecha*
Website Designer: *Interactive Factory*
Compositor/Interior Illustrator: *Argosy*
Manufacturing Buyer: *Andrew Christensen*
Cover Printer: *Phoenix Color Corp.*
CD-ROM Duplicator: *Inser-Tec*
Text Printer/Binder: *R. R. Donnelley/Crawfordsville*

This text is printed on recycled, acid free paper.

Printed and bound in the United States of America.
98 99 00 01 02 — 10 9 8 7 6 5 4 3 2 1
FREE COPY ISBN: 0-534-95375-1

Library of Congress Cataloging-in-Publication Data

Decker, Rick.
The analytical engine: an introduction to computer science using the Internet / Rick Decker, Stuart Hirshfield.
p. cm.
ISBN 0-534-95365-4 (alk. paper)
1. Computer science. 2. Internet (Computer network)
I. Hirshfield, Stuart. II. Title.
QA76.D33344 1998 97-46811
004--dc21 CIP

For more information, contact:
PWS Publishing Company
20 Park Plaza
Boston, MA 02116

International Thomson Publishing Europe
Berkshire House 168-173
High Holborn
London WC1V 7AA
England

Thomas Nelson Australia
102 Dodds Street
South Melbourne, 3205
Victoria, Australia

Nelson Canada
1120 Birchmont Road
Scarborough, Ontario
Canada M1K 5G4

International Thomson Publishing GmbH
Königswinterer Strasse 418
53227 Bonn, Germany

International Thomson Editores
Campos Eliseos 385, Piso 7
Col. Polanco
11560 Mexico D.F., Mexico

International Thomson Publishing Asia
221 Henderson Road
#05-10 Henderson Building
Singapore 0315

International Thomson Publishing Japan
Hirakawacho Kyowa Building, 31
2-2-1 Hirakawacho
Chiyoda-ku, Tokyo 102
Japan

To Bubba

For getting us started down this road and
giving us enough gu* to make the trip worthwhile

*__gu__ (goo), *n* The feeling that results from sitting on a tropical beach, holding a drink with a paper umbrella in it; as in, "Now that's he's finished writing the book, he's gotten his *gu* back."

Contents

MODULE 5 *Cordon Bleu* Computer Science 126

Preface

ÆVOLUTION

Our first proposal for this project, written ten years and three versions ago, described a package much like this one. We wanted to design a "CS 0" course that was a true survey course, reflecting a serious disciplinary point of view, firmly grounded in a liberal arts tradition, and we wanted the course to be lab based. In effect, we wanted the computer to serve as both the message and the medium. We regard this package, *Æ Online,* as an altogether new effort, as opposed to another edition of *The Analytical Engine,* because the medium has changed so dramatically in the past ten years that it has altered the message.

During the past decade, the Internet and the World Wide Web have changed forever the face of computing. Sitting down in front of a computer is no longer an inherently private event—there is a sense of connectedness that did not apply to the average user even a few years ago. This global aspect of computing has already changed the way we use machines and what we use them for, and is bringing many of the social implications of computing that have been debated in academic circles for decades into sharp and immediate focus. This globalization of computing explains the two most obvious differences between this version of *The Analytical Engine* and previous ones.

First, we have divided what was a single module on applications into two modules, one focusing on "local" applications (like word processors and spreadsheets), and one focusing on "global" applications, like those that support the World Wide Web (WWW). Next, the Web is now serving the role that HyperCard/HyperTalk and Toolbook/OpenScript had served in previous incarnations of this package. That is, it provides an integrated environment within which we can directly address the full range of computer science activities. It does so with two distinct advantages over its predecessors. From a practical standpoint, it allows us to present material in a machine- and system-independent way. Any machine with Web access and a browser (or a CD drive and a browser to work "locally" on the disk bound with the book) is capable of supporting these exercises. Conceptually, the WWW and its attendant technologies serve as an effective and contemporary metaphor for computer science as a whole. It affords teachers the luxury of using a medium that is as pedagogically sound as it is engaging and meaningful for today's students.

The third fundamental distinction, also explained by the new medium, is the degree of dependence between the text and lab components. Indeed, we refer to this collection of materials as a *package* (as opposed, say, to a text with a lab manual) because we view the text and the online or CD materials as inseparable. The text supports the lab component by providing background and explanatory material that is better read on paper than on a monitor. The labs provide the interactive, illustrative experiences that bring the material in the text to life in ways that were previously unattainable. The online and CD materials contain, among other things, hyperlinks across and within modules (concept links) so that students can see recurring themes, and external hyperlinks (reference links) to related materials.

These differences notwithstanding, the goals for this package are exactly the same as they were for previous versions. It describes our discipline from a variety of perspectives, and gives students—majors and nonmajors—a broad and realistic feeling for what computer scientists do and how they do it. It does so in a hands-on, lab-oriented way, providing students with both directed and open-ended exercises that allow them to consider a variety of global issues. The course encourages students to make connections between specific modules and other disciplines (Module 1 with history; Module 2 with art, English, and economics; Module 3 with communications; Module 4 with the art of creative writing; Module 5 with programming and problem solving; Module 6 with linguistics and anthropology; Module 7 with physics; Module 8 with mathematics; Module 9 with philosophy and psychology; and Module 10 with sociology, economics, and ethics). In short, it serves as an excellent model for a contemporary "CS 0" course.

So, all it took was ten years of classroom experience and a paradigm shift to produce what in many ways is very close to the version of *The Analytical Engine* that we always wanted to write.

THE Æ TEXT

This isn't to say that our previous efforts were wasted. In writing the original text we had hoped that most of the material would be resistant to changes in technology, and that has proven to be the case. Much of the course content is the same, and the arrangement of the topics proceeds essentially as before: first downward, to increasingly concrete points of view, and then up, returning to increasingly more general levels of abstraction—a kind of *Divine Comedy* itinerary.

Module 1 provides a historical orientation, describing the technological history of computers in the context of the increasing use of technology, beginning with the Industrial Revolution. The lab portion of this module is devoted to an introduction to the World Wide Web and to using a browser. **Module 2** discusses some local computer applications, both familiar—word processors, spreadsheets, and graphics processors—as well as some more specialized and less familiar ones in medicine, the sciences, and education. This module concludes with an introduction to some of the social implications of computer use, a theme that will be continued in Module 10. The lab part of this module asks students to solve a variety of problems using these tools. **Module 3** discusses computers and applications from a more global, connected perspective, concentrating on the Internet and the World Wide Web. In lab, students, still in the role of users of technology, work with search engines, downloading and compression tools, e-mail, and newsgroups to experience a virtual community.

Modules 4 through 7 lead the students ever deeper into the inner circles of the abyss. **Module 4** discusses system design using the example of the user interface. At this level, the focus is on combining components with fully developed functionalities into a smoothly functioning system. The lab part of Module 4 is devoted to the HyperText Markup Language (HTML), which serves as an example of a design language, and allows students to build their own Web pages.

In **Module 5** the gray box becomes a clear box—the students are introduced to programming by inspecting scripts of existing Web pages and writing programs of their own. We discuss most of the canonical programming constructs, discuss algorithm design, and take the students through a simple software life cycle using an "adventure game" program as an example. Students inspect the JavaScript code that implements the game, and extend the program to incorporate features of their own devising.

Module 6 deals with program translation. The important idea here is that since a computer can only execute programs in its own machine language, a source program in JavaScript must be translated into machine language to be executed. We discuss the problem of representing text in binary form and provide both an assembler and a simulator for a hypothetical computer, which the students use in lab to visualize the principles of language translation.

Module 7 concludes the progress toward the concrete by describing how the hardware of a computer works. Starting with switches, we construct gates, which we combine to construct logic, arithmetic, and memory circuits. Finally, we use the circuits to build the small computer that was only hypothetical in Module 6. The lab for this module is a simulated breadboard that the students can use to design and test circuits of their own.

Modules 8, 9, and 10 ascend from the most concrete, physical level to the most abstract and general. In **Module 8** we make two points. First, before there were physical realizations of computers, there were abstract, mathematical ones. Second, the physical machine is in some sense inessential when thinking about the nature of programs and computation. We introduce the Turing Machine, discuss the ideas of encoding strings and programs, and show that there are infinitely many tasks that computers cannot do—not only because there are an infinite number of input/output matchings and only a finite number of programs, but also because there are tasks, like the Halting Problem, that seem to be natural candidates for computer solution but are simply impossible to program. The lab exercises in Module 8 revolve around a Turing Machine simulator.

Module 9 is a segue, via Turing, from questions of what computers cannot do to what they might do. We use Arthur C. Clarke's HAL 9000 computer as a standard against which we view the current state of affairs in artificial intelligence research. In lab, students experiment with and modify a poetry generator and an expert system shell.

Finally, in **Module 10** we look at things to come. We identify the major trends in computer use and try to see what the implications of these trends might be, guided at all times by a knowledge of how difficult it is to predict the future. The "lab activities" here involve investigating an issue of social significance (freedom of expression, intellectual property, gender and identity in cyberspace) as it relates to the Web and to these trends.

THE Æ SITE

The lab component of the package takes the form of the Æ Site—a collection of World Wide Web pages or CD files that contain both the exercises and the software that are central to the course. In the process of working on the exercises, students will experience first-hand the World Wide Web and its supporting tools; a variety of local applications (word processors, spreadsheet programs, and graphics processors); the hypertext markup language (HTML) as a design medium; JavaScript as a programming tool; a parser, assembler, and simulator for a simple programming language; a logic breadboard; a Turing Machine simulator; a poetry generator; an inference engine; and more, all of which were designed to support the text directly. While some of these software titles are familiar to those who used previous versions of this package, the software has all been rewritten and enhanced, dramatically in many cases. Also, as mentioned earlier, the fact that these labs are now in the form of WWW pages allows us link them to one another and to other online resources, so as to better illustrate basic concepts.

With the online Web site and the bound-in CD, we have provided both global and local forms of the labs. The online and local versions are identical. In either form the labs are platform independent—all they require is a Java-aware Web browser. With a suitable browser, a student could work on the online material in a lab with Internet connection or could use the CD on a computer with no connection. In addition, if connection time and speed are troublesome issues, instructors might elect to network the labs locally by installing the software from the CD on their own intranet. Even though the lab materials can be used on a computer with no Internet connection, we would still urge all readers to connect to our online site or run the CD while connected to the Web whenever possible. Doing so will not only provide access to the off-site links we have included, but—especially in Modules 3 and 10—will also give access to the world of Æ users at other schools.

SCOPE AND ORDER OF TOPICS

We have made some very deliberate choices in choosing material for and organizing this package. Even a casual review of the table of contents gives the impression that it covers a great deal of material. It does! We have included what we regard as the core material of the discipline—material that is principled and resistant to change—and there is a lot of it. To be sure, there is more material in our text than can be covered in detail in a semester course at most schools, including our own. Our version of the course pays only casual attention to some of the topics (Module 8, for example, and the PIP material in Modules 6 and 7). This reflects both the interests of our audience and our curriculum.

The order of presentation of the topics reflects the lab orientation of the course. We want students to learn by doing, as well as by reading and thinking. The progression in Modules 2 to 7 from a black box, to a gray box, to a microscopic clear box, gives students experience with a computer at a particular level of abstraction before taking them down to the next level. Having just used a variety of local and global applications, students can evaluate the user interfaces of these programs and design their own. Having just designed a Web page, they can choose a menu item and see the programs that underlie it. After using JavaScript, students wonder how it is that the computer understands such a high-level language. The "language" that the machine understands is logic, and students eventually become convinced that logical devices can be built to accomplish a number of interesting tasks. Having seen how the machine does what it does, and with a base of practical experience, it is then appropriate to question, as we do in Modules 8 to 10, the machine's theoretical limitations, the current boundaries of the discipline, and the social implications of the technology.

Also as a result of the lab orientation, this package is more tightly structured than many others. Using "depends on the material from" as a relation on the set of modules in this package, we find that it is linearly ordered. We know that our order of presentation is not the one everyone would use, and we make no apologies about that. You can teach program translation after hardware, or reverse the order of presentation of the entire text, if you wish, but be aware that in doing so you run the risk of dangling forward references. If you have good luck with a different order, let us know.

PERORATION

Although this project was in many ways our creation, it would not exist in its present form without the contributions of many talented and dedicated people, each of whom influenced the final product—and in some cases, the authors—in some significant and positive way. Our thanks go out to the following people for their insightful reviews of both the text and online components of this package:

Anselm Blumer
Tufts University

Alyce Brady
Kalamazoo College

Dawn Cizmar
St. Edward's University

Will Dover
Georgia Institute of Technology

Robert G. Ford
Massachusetts Bay Community College

Masoud Ghyam
University of Southern California

Gordon Goodman
Rochester Institute of Technology

John A. N. Lee
Virginia Tech

David Levine
Gettysburg College

Barbara Boucher Owens
St. Edward's University

Bob Roos
Allegheny College

Kelly Schultz
Kalamazoo College

Larry K. Smith
Snow College

Richard Tenney
University of Massachusetts-Boston

Cornelia van Mourik
University of Detroit-Mercy

Dave Wonnacott
Haverford College

David B. Wood
Nebraska Wesleyan University

We are also deeply indebted to those enthusiastic and faithful instructors who over the past eight years have shared their Æ experiences and insights with us, none more valuable than those of our colleague, Anita Bhat. Our students have also been our colleagues throughout the evolution of the package. We appreciate their sense of adventure and, in the cases of Jeff Raab and Shawn Swistak, their tangible contributions. Speaking of tangible contributions, we offer special thanks to our real-world colleagues at the Interactive Factory who brought our software dreams to life. Finally, we have been blessed with a remarkably talented and supportive publication team that includes Mike Sugarman, David Dietz, Leslie Bondaryk, Elise Kaiser, Nathan Wilbur, and Liz Clayton—we are equally grateful for their trust and their friendship.

Rick Decker
Stuart Hirshfield
Hamilton College
February 1998

The Analytical Engine

MODULE 1

A History of Computing

1.1 INTRODUCTION

If you look at the table of contents, you'll see that we've divided this course into ten modules. Each module corresponds to one aspect of the nature and impact of computers and will take a week or two to cover. Each module has a text component and an online lab component; in both text and lab portions we begin with a map of the territory we'll cover in the module.

MODULE OBJECTIVES

The intention of Module 1 is to orient you, both historically and practically, to what you'll be studying and working on for the remainder of this course. We want to impress upon you that modern computer science is the result of over a century of evolution shaped by a confluence of forces—technological, social, political, commercial, and personal. We also want you to experience firsthand a state-of-the-art result of this evolution, the World Wide Web, since it is the medium through which we deliver all subsequent messages.

Toward these ends, we will

- Describe the machine, designed over a hundred years ago, that could be considered the first true computer.
- Discuss some of the historical currents that led to the development of modern computers.
- Describe the explosive growth of computers during the last three decades.
- Provide you with an opportunity to develop your surfing skills using a browser program and the World Wide Web.

Metaphor: The Analytical Engine

The metaphor for this first module shares the title of the book—the Analytical Engine, obviously a quaint name for a computer. What you might not realize is that the term *computer* originally applied exclusively to human beings—specifically, humans engaged in the task of arithmetic calculations. Arithmetic, particularly the arithmetic necessary to solve real-world problems, has been with us for a long time—at least 5000 years—and has always been difficult, tedious, time consuming, but necessary. Precisely because arithmetic is difficult, tedious, time consuming, and necessary, mechanical aids to calculation have also been with us for a long time. The origin of the abacus, which uses beads strung on wires to serve as an aid for human memory and to increase the accuracy of calculations, is lost in antiquity, but as early as 1642 Blaise Pascal (after whom the programming language Pascal was named) invented a mechanical adder that used a collection of rotating numbered wheels, much like the odometers in today's cars. The Analytical Engine was another mechanical aid to calculation, one that could properly be called the first nonhuman computer, in the sense in which we use the word *computer* today.

We tend to think of computers as electrical devices, but you will see that a computer depends on electricity only by happenstance. We have a considerable amount of experience with electronic technology, so it is convenient today to build computers out of electronic components. When Charles Babbage designed the Analytical Engine in the middle of the nineteenth century, the technology of choice was mechanical, so his Analytical Engine used gears and shafts, like a gigantic clock, to store and process information. The Analytical Engine was never completed, partly because of engineering problems but mostly because Babbage ran out of money, and the working drawings and some parts of the Analytical Engine languished in the British Museum for more than a century.

As is often the case, however, ideas may prove to be more important than objects. We have in the writings of Babbage and his chronicler Augusta Ada, Countess Lovelace, the seeds of modern computer science. What Babbage intended was a mechanical device to process information, but more important, he envisioned a *general-purpose* information processor that stored the instructions that it was intended to execute. In essence, instead of performing one task, like Pascal's adding machine, the Analytical Engine would be given a list of tasks to perform—a recipe, if you will—and would perform those tasks in sequence. Rather than having to stop and rebuild the machine for each operation, the Analytical Engine would be capable of performing any number of operations, governed by the program stored in its memory.

In this respect, the Analytical Engine is no different from the computers of today. It is in homage to Babbage and his machine that we choose our first metaphor: a physical device capable of processing information in the most general and flexible way possible.

Æ Online

This module's set of lab exercises addresses the dual tasks of providing an introduction to the online tools that you will be using to conduct the lab exercises for all subsequent modules and asking you to use these tools to browse through some related pages on the World Wide Web.

The related pages in this case are those that constitute the online component of this package as well as a number of interesting external resources about, not surprisingly, the history of computing.

1.2 ORIGINS

A continuing theme that runs through Western intellectual history over the past 400 years is the steady displacement of humanity from the central role in creation. In 1543, Nicholas Copernicus figurativley moved the earth from the center of creation. He hypothesized a vast universe with all humankind inhabiting an insignificant planet rotating about what we now know to be a perfectly ordinary star in the hinterlands of a perfectly ordinary galaxy consisting of millions upon millions of other stars, spread so widely in the heavens that light itself takes a hundred thousand years to cross from one end of the galaxy to another.

Not only did we lose our central role in space, but we lost our central role in time as well. As the eighteenth and nineteenth centuries passed, growing evidence demonstrated that we humans were very recent arrivals on a planet whose history extended more than 4 billion years into the past (unimaginably earlier than October 24, 4004 B.C., which was established as the date of Creation by Bishop Ussher in 1611). While geologists were assigning to us an insignificant slice of the earth's history, Charles Darwin and those who followed in his footsteps dealt what many considered the final blow by removing us from our special role in creation and showing that we, like all other living things, are part of a natural process of evolution, extending in an unbroken chain of changes over thousands of millennia. Each change in humanity's perception of its role was (and continues to be) resisted fiercely, of course. It is always hard to leave center stage and become one among many members of the cast in a vast, often frightening, and confusing play.

Still, throughout history, we could always take comfort in our unique nature as thinking beings. The horse may be faster and stronger, birds may take to the air while we can only imagine what unaided flight must be, dogs may hear and smell more acutely than we can, but, as far as we knew, humans alone among all living things had the unique gifts of thought, language, and creativity. Throughout history, horses, birds, and dogs have served humanity, augmenting our limited abilities with theirs, because we could think and learned to domesticate at least some of the beasts of land, sea, and air.

The Industrial Revolution extended our mastery to machines, increasing our power even further. Through the eighteenth and nineteenth centuries the engine—powerful, tireless, self-regulating, and completely under humanity's control—became one of the central metaphors of society. The steam engine, and later the internal combustion engine, replaced the horse and the ox as primary sources of power. This itself was an important step, but the Industrial Revolution marked the beginning of a much more important trend: the replacement of human skills by the machine.

■ Skilled Machines

The factories and mills of the eighteenth and nineteenth centuries represented a fundamental change in the process of manufacturing. During this time, the nature of production shifted from small shops with a few workers producing goods largely by hand to factories employing hundreds of workers using steam- or water-powered machines. The result was an unprecedented increase in production, due in no small measure to a completely new idea: building the skill of the worker into the machine.

For example, weaving a fabric with an intricate pattern was a complex task that for centuries had been the sole province of master weavers. Typically, the pattern in a woven cloth was made by stretching many threads in parallel on a loom and attaching these *warp* threads to several harnesses that could be raised by the weaver. In the simplest fabric, the structure of the cloth is produced by weaving the crossways *weft* thread over and under alternating warp threads. This was achieved on a loom by attaching warp threads 1, 3, 5, and so on to one harness, and the remaining even-numbered threads to another harness. Then, by raising one harness, the weaver raised half of the warp threads so that the weft thread could be passed between the two warp layers, in effect passing the weft under half of the warp and over the other half. The weft was then beaten into place, the first harness was lowered, and the other harness raised so the weft could be passed between the layers again, locking the previous row in place. In this way, the cloth was formed.

By increasing the number of harnesses, weavers could make more complex patterns. Weaving had been done this way for 3000 years or more, and for all that time it was the master weaver alone who knew how to thread the loom's many harnesses and raise them in just the right way to produce complex brocades with intricate floral patterns, a skill that took decades to learn. As a result he was the only one who could do this work; the production of complex fabrics was thus limited to the amount that the master weavers could produce. In other words, production was limited by the knowledge bound in the heads of a small number of people. That began to change as the eighteenth century gave way to the nineteenth.

In 1801, the Frenchman Joseph Jacquard invented a loom in which the raising of the warp threads was controlled by punched cards (Figure 1.1). Each harness was replaced by a collection of hooks attached to the warp threads, and each collection of hooks could be raised or lowered as a group. This in itself was nothing new—such *draw looms* had existed for hundreds of years. Typically, such looms had two operators: the master weaver, who sat at the front of the loom, and the drawboy, who was an apprentice weaver and sat within the loom itself, raising the hooks at the command of the master weaver. What Jacquard did, though, was to mechanize not only the physical power of the drawboy but also the skill of the master. Instead of the drawboy raising and lowering the groups of hooks, this process was controlled by cards of wood or paper with holes punched in them. Each card in turn passed into a box containing many small wires that were connected to the hooks. The tips of the wires were pressed onto the punched card, and where there was a hole for a wire to pass through the card, the corresponding warp thread would be raised, thus forming the pattern, row by row—and card by card.

The Jacquard loom was a genius stroke, removing the bottleneck of productivity by storing in the machine itself the knowledge of the master weaver. Having made the cards, the master weaver was no longer necessary. The drawboy, or anyone else with a minimum of training, could produce cloth on the Jacquard loom faster than the most skilled expert using traditional methods. In much the same way as a book can be regarded as a device that stores knowledge, the cards and the loom stored the expertise of the master weaver. Just as the invention of printing allowed a vast increase in the amount of available knowledge, the Jacquard loom allowed a vast increase in the production of fine fabrics. Not only could the new loom weave faster and more accurately than any human, but this information could be spread by simply making more looms and more cards.

FIGURE 1.1
The Jacquard loom (© Corbis-Bettmann)

The implications of this new information technology were not lost on the French, and they quickly enacted strict laws in an attempt to halt the spread of this new machine's secrets to competing countries. Of course, the attempt was doomed to failure. As has been the case throughout history, even if such secrets could not be bought or stolen, the knowledge that such a device could be built was sufficient in itself, and within a few years the technology had spread throughout the world, carrying with it the seeds of social change.

The notion of storing expertise in a machine was not confined to the weaving industry. An automatic lathe could make flawless chair legs by the thousands by duplicating a single pattern made by a master woodworker. Again, such a machine could be tended by an inexperienced factory worker who had received a day or two of training. In Europe at the time there was an abundance of unskilled labor. A simple fact was obvious to factory owners from the outset: Unskilled labor, merely by virtue of its abundance, was far less expensive than skilled. As a result, thousands of skilled craftsmen found themselves without work and with the prospect that their expertise would never be valuable again. In 1811, these people took action. Angered and frightened by this change in their lives, many of them banded together, calling themselves Luddites,[1] and reacted by breaking into their former factories and mills, destroying any of the new machines on which they could lay their hands.

Technological progress, however, has a nearly irresistible momentum, especially when the march of progress benefits the wealthy and powerful. Within two years, the Luddites were broken, their leaders either hanged, deported, or imprisoned. This was neither the first nor the last time that technological change brought with it social change. We will have much more to say about the social implications of technology in later modules.

The Weaver of Algebra

Although little note was made of the fact at the time, the Industrial Revolution planted the seeds of the Information Revolution. We can now see that not only could the new skilled machines produce and manipulate objects, but there was also the possibility that machines could produce and manipulate information. Machines could augment the powers of the human brain, as well as the powers of arm and leg.

Calculating machines were in existence long before the Industrial Revolution. The abacus and Pascal's calculator had been developed years before, and mechanical calculators were in widespread use by the early part of the nineteenth century. The increasingly complex worlds of science and commerce demanded increasingly complex calculations, however, and by the early 1800s the time was ripe for a new, more powerful machine.

Charles Babbage, a gifted British inventor and mathematician, was born in 1791. As a mathematician, he was well acquainted with the drudgery that many human calculators endured in their jobs of solving equations and producing tables of logarithms. Babbage had both the funds and the talent to do something about this problem, and he bent his skills and much of his inherited wealth to devising a machine that would automate the tedious tasks of calculation. In 1821 he proposed his *Difference Engine,* and in 1822 he demonstrated a pilot model to the Royal Astronomical Society. In its individual parts, the Difference Engine was similar to mechanical calculators of the time, representing numbers by the positions of wheels connected by shafts, cogs, and ratchets. This clockwork technology was well developed by then, and indeed had produced not only clocks, but also mechanical birds and dancing mannequins of astonishing complexity, largely as toys for the very rich.

The Difference Engine was to be vastly more complex than any calculator or automaton yet built, but it was still a special-purpose machine. To find the solutions of a polynomial equation, such as $3.56x^7 - 7.6x^3 + 2.39x - 8.94 = 0$, a human calculator of the time would perform a long series of additions, subtractions, multiplications, and so on, dictated by his or her knowledge of the steps needed to find the solutions. These individual calculations could be performed with the help of existing mechanical calculators, but the important part of the process was the human calculator's knowledge of which steps to perform, in which order. Babbage, in

[1] Named after Edward "Ned" Ludd, who may or may not have been a real person. The term *Luddite* is used today to refer to someone with a hostility to technology.

designing the Difference Engine, built his mathematician's knowledge of the steps to be performed directly into his machine, in effect eliminating the need for mathematical skills by the way he connected the cams and shafts. In the pilot model, the operator had only to set the wheels to correspond to the equation to be solved and turn a crank until the answer appeared.

◆ To celebrate the sesquicentennial of the Difference Engine in 1991, a working model was made from Babbage's plans. It resides today in the Science Museum, London.

The idea of the Difference Engine was received enthusiastically, and Babbage immediately built a workshop on his property, hired machinists, and set to work. Eleven years later, after having spent tens of thousands of pounds of his own money and grants from the British government, Babbage had still not completed the Difference Engine. The fault lay not in Babbage's plans, but in part in the technology with which he was forced to implement his plans. The inescapable fact is that gears, shafts, and other mechanical parts require energy to turn them, and this energy must be smoothly transmitted from each part to the next. This presents few problems in a watch (or in Babbage's pilot model), since any slight binding or failure to mesh smoothly would be unnoticed in the overall working of the machine. Such small irregularities, however, tend to accumulate and be passed from one part to the next; in a machine with thousands of parts, these irregularities grow to such a degree that the machine invariably jams or breaks during operation. In short, Babbage's conception was plagued by what we today call the *problem of scale:* An idea that works perfectly well at one size may fail in entirely unpredicted ways at a size ten or a hundred times larger. The modern version of the Difference Engine, though, demonstrates that Babbage's technical problems, while difficult, could have been solved (Figure 1.2). Unfortunately, on top of his technical problems, Babbage was by all accounts also a notoriously difficult person to work with and wound up alienating not only his chief engineer but also his sources of funding.

Babbage's vision, clearly far beyond the production of windup finches that could sing and hop about their cages, went further still, beyond the capabilities of his uncompleted Difference Engine. Just as the Jacquard loom contained in its cards the knowledge of the master weaver and contained in its structure the ability to perform the instructions on any series of cards, Babbage envisioned a much grander machine, capable of performing any series of mathematical instructions given to it. This *Analytical Engine* would be composed of several smaller devices: one to receive the list of instructions (on punched cards, as it happened), one to perform the instructions coded on the cards, one to store the results of intermediate calculations, and one to print out the information on paper. The entire device was to be powered by a steam engine, much as the power looms of the time were. As Lady Ada was to remark in her writings about Babbage, "The Analytical Engine weaves algebraical patterns just as the Jacquard loom weaves flowers and leaves."

There must certainly be other instances of an idea being a hundred years ahead of its time but probably none so compelling. The organization of the Analytical Engine is in its broad outlines virtually identical to that of modern computers. Almost universally, the architecture of a computer today consists of an *input* section, a *central processor* that performs arithmetic and logical operations dictated by a program of instructions, a *memory* unit to store information, and an *output* section to make the results available to the user, exactly as described by Babbage a century ago. It is poignant to imagine the completed Analytical Engine as Babbage must have, this vast and certainly deafening machine with its thousands of gears and levers turning

FIGURE 1.2
The Difference Engine (© IBM)

smoothly, glistening with machine oil in the light streaming through the windows of a large brick building, the punched cards clacking through the receiver one by one, the paper rolling out of the printing press at one side, all against the background of a chugging steam engine—a perfectly fitting Victorian vision of a machine that we all consider a quintessential part of the late twentieth century.

Review Questions

1. What were the roles played in our story by Nicholas Copernicus, Charles Darwin, Charles Babbage, and Augusta Ada?
2. What were the differences between the Difference Engine and the Analytical Engine?
3. Why was the Analytical Engine never completed?
4. Why do we call the Analytical Engine the first true computer?

LAB 1.1

It's Browsing Time Again

It is slightly ironic that in order to start our exercises dealing with the history of computing, you need to make use of what is perhaps the most contemporary combination of hardware and software available—the World Wide Web (WWW) and a browser. The WWW is an increasingly vast combination of computers, connections, programs, and information (including all of the lab exercises we have developed for this course) that has evolved from the Internet. You need a browser program running on your computer in order to use the network to access it all in a user-friendly fashion. "Starting a lab," in the context of this course, means using your browser and your WWW connection to go to the associated pages in our online materials. The goals of this set of exercises are to provide you with experience in doing so, and to develop your basic WWW navigation skills.

Since we want all of our materials to be useful to you no matter which browser program you are using, we are not going to describe any particular version of any particular browser. Instead, we'll point out some common features of the most popular browsers, and introduce you to them in very basic terms. Your instructor will provide you with more detailed instructions on how the browser you will use works on the computer you'll be using. To start, then, you need access to a computer and a browser. Once you have your browser running, do the following exercises.

◆ **URL: Uniform Resource Locator – the address of a page on the World Wide Web.**

1. The most direct—and perhaps least convenient—way to move to a new page is to type the page's URL in the browser's Go To window. The inconvenience stems from the need to remember an often lengthy and cryptic URL and to type it correctly. There are certainly better ways to navigate around the Web, but for now we must resort to using the Go To box. Type `http://www.pws.com/aeonline.html` in the Go To box that appears near the top of your browser screen, and then hit Enter or Return. This should display the Analytical Engine home page.

2. Bookmark this page. That is, mark it so that you can return to it directly by using your Bookmarks menu. The Bookmarks menu in your browser should have an Add Bookmark (or some similar) command. Selecting that menu command will add the current page to your list of bookmarks; selecting that bookmark from the list will return you to the AE home page from wherever you are.

3. Notice how certain text and icons are highlighted, specially colored, or underlined. This usually indicates that they are clickable (or *hot,* in the vernacular), and that clicking on them will cause a new page to be displayed. You can, on many browsers, confirm that a part of a page is clickable by simply dragging (but not clicking!) the mouse over it. Place the mouse over any of the text or icons that refer to Module 1, and watch the status bar near the bottom of the browser screen

change to contain the URL for the start of Module 1 lab exercises. Click on any Module 1 reference now.

4. You should now be looking at the page entitled "Module 1: The History of Computing." Read the abstract, the Module Objectives, and the chapter summary. Then, click on Lab 1.2, listed under "Activities." You are now ready to continue with the remaining lab exercises (which, like those for all subsequent chapters, are completely online) for Module 1. Follow the instructions on that page to complete the lab activities.

1.3 HANDLING THE INFORMATION EXPLOSION

Charles Babbage died in 1871 and his work passed into obscurity. Mechanical calculators were gradually improved over the following years, but the idea of the computer had died, temporarily. In 1887, Verdi's *Otello* premiered in Milan, Sir Arthur Conan Doyle wrote the first Sherlock Holmes story, the telephone was eleven years old, the phonograph ten, and the 1880 United States census was seven years behind schedule. This latter was a serious problem, since the census is mandated by law. Article 1, Section 2 of the United States Constitution states that, for the purposes of assigning congressional districts:

> The actual Enumeration [of the population] shall be made within three Years after the first meeting of the Congress of the United States, and within every subsequent Term of ten Years, in such Manner as [the House of Representatives] shall by Law direct.

When the Constitution was written, the population of the new United States stood at slightly under 4 million, a figure well within the abilities of statisticians of the day to tabulate. A century later, in 1887, the U.S. population, as near as anyone could figure, numbered about 57,217,000, and it was clear to the officials at the Census Bureau that, at the rate things were going, the 1890 census could not be completed by the end of the century. Fortunately, Herman Hollerith, a young mathematician-inventor in the spirit of Babbage, combined the old technology of punched cards with the new electrical technology to produce a sorting and tabulating machine. With the help of his machine, the 1890 census was completed in six weeks.

Hollerith founded the Tabulating Machine Company to produce and sell his machines, and his company did remarkably well. The machines his company produced were used to store time records and inventory and accounting data, and for sorting, tabulating, and collating this information. They were not computers in the sense we know, but they were ideal servants in an age that increasingly felt the need for accurate and timely management of large quantities of data. If time travel were possible, it would be worth the price of a trip to go back a hundred years or so and invest in Hollerith's fledgling venture, which today is known as IBM.

The Birth of Computers, From A to Z

Beginning in the 1930s, events began to move much more rapidly than before, not only in the world in general, but particularly in the world of information processing. In 1932, Franklin Roosevelt was elected president by a landslide; Adolf Hitler refused an offer to become vice chancellor of Germany; Aldous Huxley wrote *Brave New World;* Amelia Earhart became the first woman to make a solo flight across the Atlantic; and at the Massachusetts Institute of Technology, Vannevar Bush completed a mechanical calculator called the *Differential Analyzer,* which solved calculus problems. Like the Difference Engine, the Differential Analyzer was a purely mechanical device with essentially a single purpose. The promise of the Analytical Engine remained unfulfilled, though not for much longer.

John V. Atanasoff received his doctorate in physics from the University of Wisconsin in 1930. Part of the research for his dissertation involved months of laborious calculations on a mechanical desk calculator. Like Babbage, he became interested in finding a way to eliminate the drudgery of computation. Unlike Babbage, Atanasoff lived in a world with a well-developed electronics technology, and that made all the difference. In 1939 Atanasoff began work on a machine that used currents of electricity to represent information.

The idea of encoding information electrically was not new. Samuel F. B. Morse had demonstrated the practicality of the idea with his telegraph in 1838, only five years after Babbage began research on the Analytical Engine. Hollerith's card-reading machine used electrical signals as well. By 1939, though, the technology of controlling, switching, and amplifying electrical signals had reached a level comparable to the technology of mechanical devices in Babbage's time. Atanasoff and his assistant, Clifford Berry, were as comfortable with their technology as Babbage had been with his.

As far as we need to be concerned, the chief difference between mechanical and electrical technologies is that electrons are very light and easy to shove around, moving through wires at about a billion feet per second, well over a million times faster than most mechanical devices can move. A vacuum tube that Atanasoff could buy off the shelf for a few dollars could switch a signal on or off thousands of times faster, far more reliably, and at far less cost than it would take to perform the same function with rods, gears, and levers.

Like the Difference Engine and the Differential Analyzer, the Atanasoff-Berry Computer (ABC, for short) was a single-purpose machine, designed to find solutions to systems of linear equations. An example of such a problem is to find values of x and y that satisfy both $2x - 3y = 1$ and $x + 5y = 20$. You may recall enough algebra to find that $x = 5$ and $y = 3$ is a solution (and, indeed, is the only solution). Whether or not you know how to solve such a system, you can imagine that solving a system of 29 such equations, each with 29 unknowns, would be a daunting task to do by hand. The ABC was built for just such a task. Atanasoff estimated it would produce the answer five times faster than a person could, even with the aid of a desk calculator.

At about the same time, Konrad Zuse, a German engineer, and his assistant, Helmut Schreyer, were working on a machine similar in principle to the ABC, though grander in conception. It is here, almost exactly a century after the conception of the

Analytical Engine, that we see the notion of a *general-purpose* computer reborn. The machines of Zuse and Schreyer—Z1, and later versions Z2, Z3, and Z4—used electrical signals to represent information, just as in the ABC, but while Atanasoff's machine could do only one thing, Zuse's, from the beginning, was intended to perform its tasks under the control of a program of instructions. Zuse, in other words, had become the intellectual heir of Babbage.

◆ The airplane and the telegraph are other examples of this phenomenon. The Wright brothers and Morse weren't the only ones working on these inventions – they just finished first.

This simultaneous and independent development of electronic calculation by Atanasoff and Zuse, including Zuse's unwitting rediscovery of Babbage's ideas, is an example of a recurrent theme in the history of technology. Often the time just seems right for an idea, the necessary technology and the right way to look at a problem providing fertile ground for independent discoveries of the same principle or device. Sadly, though, the time was also wrong for both Atanasoff and Zuse. Their governments were locked in a deadly war and called for their efforts elsewhere. Neither Atanasoff nor Zuse was able to complete his machine, and by the end of World War II, the march of progress had passed them by, fueled by the same war that interrupted their separate projects.

Military Computers

At about the same time that Atanasoff and Zuse were working on their machines, a third such project was going on, independent of the others, under the direction of Howard Aiken, an applied mathematician and physicist at Harvard University. While Atanasoff and Zuse were struggling with extremely limited funds, Aiken went to IBM with his idea for a computer and returned to Harvard with a million dollars. Unlike Atanasoff's ABC, Aiken's machine (like Zuse's), was an *electromechanical* device, a hybrid of electrical and mechanical components. Switching in the ABC was controlled by vacuum tubes, whereas the other two devices relied on relays, components much like contemporary light switches except that the switch arm was moved by a magnet controlled by another electrical circuit. Although about a thousand times slower than vacuum tubes, relays were reliable (vacuum tubes burn out, much like light bulbs), used very little power (vacuum tubes have a filament that must be kept glowing at all times), and were cheap (the telephone company used relays by the hundreds of thousands).

Far from being halted by the war, Aiken's project was encouraged by the U.S. Navy, which quickly clamped a lid of secrecy on the entire operation. By 1944, the International Business Machines' Automatic Sequence Controlled Calculator, also known as the Harvard Mark I (certainly a more euphonious name than the corporate version), was completed, the first true working computer. Babbage's dream was finally a reality, a fact that was not lost on Aiken, since he alone of the three pioneers had read the reports on the Analytical Engine (albeit three years after he had begun thinking about the Mark I).

A useful perspective on of the history of computers is to place them against the background of a world that needed to handle increasingly large and complex sets of information. Warfare, throughout history, has always demanded accurate and timely information. The global war of the 1930s and 1940s, with its huge armies and new machinery, demanded computational power on a scale undreamed of before. This insistent demand for powerful computing was met, again independently, by two machines: the British Colossus and the American ENIAC.

Sending military information via coded messages has been a common practice since Caesar's time and was indispensable during World War II, when radio messages could be heard by anyone with the proper equipment. The German military relied on a machine called Enigma, a mechanical device that looked like a large typewriter. By setting the dials of the Enigma machine, the code could be changed daily. Through Polish secret agents, the British managed to obtain an Enigma, but while that told the British the principles behind the German encoding schemes, the coded messages still could not be deciphered without the correct dial settings. In theory, of course, all one had to do was run the coded message through the captured Enigma while trying all possible dial settings, much as one would open a safe by trying all possible combinations. The number of different settings was so large, though, that the information would be cold and useless long before the right combination was found. What was needed was a way to simulate the action of the Enigma on a much faster device.[2]

The British were fortunate to have the services of Alan Turing, a mathematician who, in 1936, had published a paper with the forbidding title "On Computable Numbers with an Application to the *Entscheidungsproblem*." In this remarkable work, written *before* there was a working computer of any kind, Turing laid the theoretical groundwork for all of modern computer science. We will return to Turing's contribution in Module 8; for now, he is of interest to us for his wartime work in code breaking. Turing and a group of British scientists, mathematicians, and engineers, working in the tightest possible secrecy at a country estate known as Bletchley Park, managed to build a completely electronic computer by 1943, like Atanasoff's ABC but vastly more powerful. Colossus was designed for code breaking, and it worked spectacularly well. It is not too farfetched to suggest that the efforts of the Bletchley Park group in breaking the Enigma codes significantly shortened the war. It is chilling to speculate what the result would have been if Zuse, who had considered using tubes but discarded the idea because of their expense, had been allowed to complete a similar machine for the Axis.

Meanwhile, on the other side of the Atlantic, John Mauchley and J. Presper Eckert were working on a similar machine, the Electronic Numerical Integrator and Computer, or ENIAC (Figure 1.3). Mauchley and Atanasoff had communicated extensively during 1941 about the possibilities of electronic computation, and many of the principles of ENIAC are similar to those of the ABC. ENIAC was designed to produce ballistic firing tables for artillery, a forbiddingly complex computational task, and was completely operational by the end of the war. Along the way, the ENIAC project was lucky enough to acquire the considerable talents of John Von Neumann, who first proposed the idea of storing the program of a computer in the computer's memory, along with the data. The importance of this idea cannot be overestimated, since it led to the eventual practical use of the new technology. Without a stored program, ENIAC could still be "instructed" to perform different tasks, but the instruction took the form of essentially rewiring most of the machine. The scene was set for a technological explosion that dwarfed anything seen during the Industrial Revolution.

[2] We're simplifying the code-breaking process quite a bit here, but the fundamental idea remains the same—finding a way of rapidly testing a large number of possible combinations.

FIGURE 1.3
ENIAC, an early computer (Courtesy of IBM)

Review Questions

1. Arrange the following machines in chronological order, and associate them with the names below:
   ABC, Colossus, Differential Analyzer, ENIAC, Mark I, Z1
   Aiken, Atanasoff, Bush, Eckert, Mauchley, Turing, Zuse
2. What did Hollerith's tabulating machine and the Jacquard loom have in common?
3. What advantage does electrical technology have over mechanical?
4. What advantages do tubes have over relays? Relays over tubes?
5. In what ways did World War II spur the development of computers?

LAB 1.2

Our Analytical Engine

In the first lab, you learned how to navigate through the World Wide Web using your browser's Go To box and a few hot links. There are other simple ways to change the page you are viewing, including the Back and Forward buttons and the history list. Open your browser now and go to the page for Lab 1.2, where you'll explore some of these other navigation features.

As their names imply, these features are related in that the first two use the third. Most browsers keep a list of which pages you visit and the order in which you visit them. This list of pages is usually referred to as the *history list*. Any time you want to return to a page that you have previously viewed (since last opening the browser program—unlike bookmarks, the history list may not persist between uses!), you can look at the history list and simply select (by clicking) any of the pages listed therein. Clicking on the Back button takes you to the page you visited immediately before the page you are currently viewing; clicking the Forward button opens the page (if one exists) that you visited after first visiting the current page.

1. Use all these standard navigation techniques (hot text and icons, the Go To window, the Back and Forward buttons, and the history list) to browse through (hence the terms *browser*) the materials that compose the Analytical Engine Online. In the interest of guiding (ever so gently) your efforts, navigate your way through the AE online materials to answer the following questions, which you should do on a separate sheet of paper.

a) What is the URL of Lab 8.3? Can you determine it without visiting that page?
b) How many lab activities are provided for Module 7?
c) What is the title of Lab 9.4?
d) What happens when you click on the Back button when you are viewing the introduction page for Module 6, "Program Translation"?
e) Which lab activities have programs (Java applets or JavaScript programs) included with them? How can you tell?
f) "Spreading the Wealth" is the name of a lab activity in which module?
g) List three ways to return to the AE home page from the introductory page for Module 3.

1.4 GENERATIONS

Colossus was aptly named—the first computers were physically titanic by today's standards. The Mark I was over 50 feet long, and ENIAC completely filled a 30- by 50-foot room with its 18,000 vacuum tubes and miles of wiring. The technical side of the rest of computer science history takes us from the "giant brains" of the post-war years to the microcomputer on which this text was written, and can be summarized in one word: size. Without the invention of a simple device made largely from common sand, there would be no Information Revolution, and the world would be profoundly different from the one we know.

◆ **First Generation** computers used vacuum tubes.

The computers of the 1950s were huge machines, requiring enormous power to heat their thousands of tubes—a typical computer of the time used as much power as an entire block of single-family homes. Vacuum tubes could switch electrical signals quickly (the electronic ENIAC was a thousand times faster than the electromechanical Mark I), but most of the energy to run a tube goes to make heat, which is useless to the function of the computer and in fact must be disposed of by cooling systems lest the computer bake itself into scrap. Although they were large, expensive (typically costing a million dollars or more), and required an extensive maintenance staff, the early commercial computers found a ready market in large corporations, research institutes, the military, and the government. The impact of the computer, though, was not felt by the average citizen, and analysts of the time estimated that the computing needs of the entire world could easily be met by a few dozen large machines. All this was changed by a very small but important device.

◆ Second Generation computers were based on transistors.

The transistor was invented at Bell Telephone Labs in 1947. The transistor, like the vacuum tube, is essentially an electric switch, made of a bit of silicon with small impurities added. The first transistor was a can about the size of your thumbnail with three wires running into it. In simple terms, a current applied to one wire determined whether or not another current could pass between the other two wires. The transistor used much less power than a tube and could be switched much more quickly. More important, though, transistors could be made very small, much smaller than a tube. The First Generation vacuum tube computers gave way in 1957 to the Second Generation—transistorized machines that were faster, smaller, more reliable, and cheaper than their ancestors.

In the late 1950s and the 1960s small businesses could for the first time afford computing power previously available only to those with a spare million dollars or two. From another point of view, for prices similar to those of their old machines, large companies could purchase ten times the computing power they could before. As was the case with earlier emergent technologies, uses were found for computers that had not been dreamed of by their inventors. Airline reservations were automated, billing and inventory were done by machines, and complex tasks such as air defense were computerized.

New programming techniques eased the job of instructing the machines to perform their tasks, and new programming languages were developed: FORTRAN, for scientific calculation; COBOL, tailored for business use; and BASIC, for teaching programming. No longer was it necessary to write programs in the forbidding binary language of the computer—these new languages were closer to human languages than to the dialect of the machine.

◆ Third Generation computers used integrated circuits.

While computer companies were riding an exponential sales curve, scientists and engineers were developing circuits of a completely new design. In these *integrated circuits,* the transistors, wires, and other components of the computer were all fabricated on a single chip of silicon (Figure 1.4). In much the same way that a color print is made by photographically depositing layers of dye, integrated circuits can be made by "printing" a picture of the circuit on a silicon base, adding one chemical layer after another. Because it is easy to photographically reduce such a circuit, a typical Third Generation computer might pack a thousand transistors into the same space occupied by a single transistor a decade before. Also, just as the printing press allowed many books to be made from the same master type, dozens of integrated circuits could be made simultaneously out of a single wafer of silicon a few inches across.

FIGURE 1.4
An integrated circuit (© Richard T. Nowitz/ Corbis)

Again, computers became cheaper, smaller, and faster (largely because the signals had less distance to travel—electrons move quickly, but not instantaneously). More power was available for the same price; the same power cost less than it did before. At this time, we began to see the first *embedded computers,* small, special-purpose computers that could run traffic signals, elevators, and pocket calculators—miniature descendants of the Difference Engine. To give you an idea of the progress made in 30 years, in the mid 1970s one could purchase a hand-held programmable calculator, weighing perhaps half a pound, that was faster than the room-sized ENIAC at about one ten-thousandth the cost.

◆ Fourth Generation computers rely on large-scale integrated circuits.

The pace of technological progress showed no sign of slackening; indeed, it continued to accelerate. In 1971, the Vietnam war was grinding to its conclusion; Erich Segal published *Love Story;* the Baltimore Colts defeated Dallas, 16–3, to win the Super Bowl; and the first microprocessor went on sale. A *microprocessor* is an entire computer on a single chip, a Fourth Generation machine based on the technology of *large-scale integration,* that is, a Third Generation machine with many more circuit elements, on a much smaller scale. For $300 (the price today is under $3, purchased in quantity), you could buy a single chip and program it for your needs, be it a calculator, a traffic control mechanism, an ignition control in a car, or a general-purpose computer. When your computer broke down, all you had to do was throw it out and buy another. The Analytical Engine had shrunk to a size that Babbage could have used as a shirt button, and was similarly disposable.

Within a few years, microcomputers based on these new chips were available to everyone with a few hundred dollars. At first, the computer giants (such as IBM, Digital Equipment, and Hewlett-Packard) had no interest in this new "micro" market, not imagining that any money was to be made by selling small computers for people to use at home. Dozens of new microcomputer companies sprang up, competing for spaces in this new ecological niche.

Steve Jobs and Steve Wozniak were not the first to produce microcomputers, but they are certainly among the most successful. Beginning in 1976 with 50 machines assembled in Jobs's parents' garage in Los Altos, California, the two began their own computer company. In the next six years, their sales were $2.5 million, then $15 million, $70 million, $117 million, $335 million, and $583 million. By 1982, their company, Apple Computer, Inc., was listed among the largest 500 companies in the United States. If you can't afford the price of a time machine ticket to invest in Herman Hollerith's company, you might consider two shorter trips—one to 1978 to invest in Apple at nine cents a share, and one to late 1980, when the stock was first offered to the general public at $22 per share, a tidy return of 24,444 percent on your investment in just two years.

■ Today

◆ This annual doubling was observed by Gordon Moore and is known as *Moore's Law.*

No technology in the history of the world has progressed as fast as computer technology. To take just one aspect of computer hardware as an example, since 1960 the information capacity of an integrated circuit chip of a given area has doubled each year, at no increase in cost. We could, for instance, compare advances in computer technology with those in the automotive industry: If automotive technology had progressed as fast as computer technology between 1960 and today, the car of today would have an engine less than one tenth of an inch across, would get 120,000 miles to a gallon of gas, have a top speed of 240,000 miles per hour, and would cost $4. This is the stuff of fantasy, not science fiction.

◆ The closest description of modern computational ubiquity, in fact, can be found in a much earlier isolated instance, E. M. Forster's short story "The Machine Stops," published in 1909.

While we're on the subject, science fiction authors have a reputation for accurate prognostication (the first description of the atomic bomb appeared before the first bomb was even tested), but the computer revolution took them completely by surprise. You can search the literature of the 1940s and 1950s in vain looking for any mention of a society that has computational powers in every household appliance. In computer science in particular, we see reason to believe what we might call the First Law of Futurology: *Any reasonable prediction of future technology is almost certain to be too conservative.*

While you're doing the labs for this course, try to bear in mind that the computer you're using, no matter what it is, has powers beyond the wildest imaginings of Atanasoff, Zuse, Aiken, Turing, Von Neumann, Mauchley, Eckert, and the rest of the pioneers. As for how father Babbage would have viewed your computer, we can only recall the dictum of Arthur C. Clarke, who we'll meet again in Module 9: "Any sufficiently advanced technology is indistinguishable from magic."

Review Questions

1. Define First, Second, Third, and Fourth Generation computer technology.
2. In simple terms, what is a transistor?
3. What advantages do transistors have over tubes?
4. What is an integrated circuit, and why is it important to computer technology?
5. What theme best describes the advances in computer technology over the past 40 years?

LAB 1.3

Let's Get Historical

Now let's use your browsing skills to explore pages of interest from all around the WWW. In keeping with the theme of this module, we'll concentrate on pages like those listed below that describe some aspect of the history of computing. Open your browser, go to Lab 1.3 and explore these Web pages:

50 Years In Computing
Charles Babbage Institute
British National Museum of Science and Industry
Alan Turing Home page
The History of Computing

Your job is to examine these sites, and any others you come across in your browsing travels, to produce a list of ten historical facts about computers, computing, or the people involved in advancing the discipline. Each fact should be something you didn't know before you began this exercise, and something that isn't described in Module 1 of our text.

1.5 EXERCISES

1. There is a chance that there could have been a working computer by 1850, if Babbage had employed Morse's electrical technology. Assuming he had done so, speculate on how pervasive the computer would have been and its likely uses between 1850 and 1900. You might want to take a look at the fictional work *The Difference Engine,* by Gibson and Sterling, listed in the sources at the end of this module.

2. What were some of the social consequences of the widespread use of the automobile? You might want to investigate the traction industry (interurban trolleys, streetcars, and the like) in the period 1900–1920, or the effects of the automobile on dating patterns, mobility, urban growth, and so on.

3. Society and technology interact in complicated ways. For example, explain why the introduction of the railroad to the American frontier in the early nineteenth century reduced the rate of alcohol abuse in those regions.

4. List three professions that are likely to become obsolete (or nearly so) as a result of the spread of computers, and explain your answer.

5. Report on the background of the October 19, 1973, court decision that the ENIAC patent was invalid.

6. Find three good John Von Neumann anecdotes. This is an easy question once you find a contemporary account of Von Neumann's life.

7. An *analog* device, such as the Differential Analyzer or the volume control on a radio, stores information by representing it as the continuous position of an object. The number 17.56, for

example, might have been represented in the Differential Analyzer by a shaft that was rotated 17.56 degrees from its starting position. A *digital* computer, such as the abacus, represents each digit (ones, tens, hundreds, and so on) by a separate unit. What are the limiting factors to the accuracy of an analog computer, and how does this differ from the accuracy of a digital computer? In particular, is it easier to increase the accuracy of an analog or a digital computer?

8. We don't have to think of embedded computers solely as parts of machines such as microwave ovens or automobile ignition systems. Give some existing uses for computers embedded in or attached to living bodies, human or otherwise, and speculate about possible future uses for such devices.

9. Why does making an integrated circuit smaller make it cheaper? Speculate on whether a desire for small computers or economic reasons led to smaller chips.

10. Assuming that the capacity of a modern computer chip is equivalent to a million bits of information (however we define *bits*) and that the information capacity of a human brain is the equivalent of ten trillion bits, how many years will it take for chips to exceed brains in capacity, assuming Moore's Law continues to hold?

11. Bearing in mind the First Law of Futurology, speculate on one use of computers in the year 2010. Don't be boring—give your imagination free rein.

12. There are connections between Charles Babbage and his legacy and Victor Frankenstein and his. Both concern man's creations run wild, but there is also a literary connection, through Countess Lovelace. Write on both.

13. In the period since 1900, which has increased more—humankind's computing power or destructive power? Provide figures to support your answer, and be careful to explain what you mean by *power.*

14. What is a computer? Are you a computer by your definition? Be careful in using the words *inorganic* or *living,* especially in light of recent advances in building specialized computers from DNA molecules.

15. Take one more trip in our time machine, and give a modern computer (equipped with a CD drive, just to make things interesting) to Atanasoff or Zuse, with no explanation, manuals, or supporting information. What would scientists of the time have been able to discover about its workings? Needless to say, you'll have to read up on the science of the 1930s.

Additional Readings

Bernstein, J. *The Analytical Engine.* New York: Random House, 1963.

Bowden, B. V. *Faster Than Thought.* London: Sir Isaac Pitman, 1953.

Engelbourg, S. *International Business Machines: A Business History.* Salem, NH: Ayer, 1976.

Evans, C. *The Micro Millennium.* New York: Washington Square Press, 1979.

Gassée, J.-L. *The Third Apple: Personal Computers and the Cultural Revolution.* New York: Harcourt Brace Jovanovich, 1987.

Gibson, W., and Sterling, B. *The Difference Engine.* New York: Bantam Books, 1991.

Goldstein, H. *The Computer from Pascal to Von Neumann.* Princeton, NJ: Princeton University Press, 1972.

IEEE Annals of the History of Computing. Los Alamitos, CA: Institute of Electrical and Electronics Engineers.

Kranzberg, M., and Pursell, C. W., Jr., eds. *Technology in Western Civilization.* New York: Oxford University Press, 1967.

Leebart, D., ed. *Technology 2001.* Cambridge, MA: MIT Press, 1994.

Mackintosh, A. R. "Dr. Atanasoff's Computer." *Scientific American* 258, no. 2 (Aug. 1988): 90–96.

Martin, J. D. *Inside Big Blue: Will the Real IBM Please Stand Up?* New York: Vantage, 1988.

Moritz, M. *The Little Kingdom: The Private Story of Apple Computer.* New York: William Morrow, 1984.

Morrison, P., and Morrison, E. *Charles Babbage and His Calculating Engines.* New York: Dover Publications, Inc., 1961.

Rogers, E. M., and Larson, J. K. *Silicon Valley Fever.* New York: Basic Books, 1984.

Singer, C. J., et al. *A History of Technology.* 7 vols. Oxford: Clarendon Press, 1954–1978.

Shurken, J., *Engines of the Mind.* New York: W. W. Norton, 1996.

Stein, D. *Ada: A Life and Legacy.* Cambridge, MA.: MIT Press, 1987.

———. *Ada Lovelace and the Thinking Machine.* Cambridge, MA: MIT Press, 1985.

Turing, S. *Alan Turing.* Cambridge: W. Heffer and Sons, 1959.

Wilkes, M. W. *Computing Perspectives.* San Francisco: Morgan Kauffman, 1995.

Winterbotham, F. W. *The Ultra Secret.* New York: Harper and Row, 1974.

MODULE 2

Local Applications

2.1 INTRODUCTION

You've seen that microelectronic technology—computer technology in particular—has undergone a rate of growth that can, without any exaggeration, be called explosive. In terms of both technical sophistication and number of uses, the growth of computers cannot be matched by anything in the history of technology. In this module, we will explore this growth in more detail, focusing mainly on the past decade and looking at the uses to which this marvelous machine has been put.

MODULE OBJECTIVES

This module is intended to convert you from a casual observer of computing technology to a more accomplished *user* of the machine, at least at a local software level. We want you to appreciate that you don't have to be a "power user nerd" to get the computer to work effectively and productively for you. You will see that, thanks to the evolution and proliferation of task-oriented application programs, everyone can be a typesetter, an accountant, and a graphic designer.

Toward these ends, we will

- Describe four common "microworlds" and their realizations as modern software applications.
- Present an inventory of some computer applications in business, technology, the professions, and entertainment.
- Provide you with an opportunity to develop (or demonstrate) your skills with a word processor, a spreadsheet program, a graphics processor, and a page layout program.

The Computer as a Tool

In Module 1 we concentrated almost entirely on the computer itself, that collection of microcircuitry and wires that you can pick up and hold in your hand. We'll come back to the hardware in Module 7; in this module we will adopt a point of view that is at the same time more abstract and more personal, namely, the user's view of computers and their programs. In our efforts to peel away the layers of mystery that surround the computer, we will begin with a black box approach, by discussing computers as seen through their programs. Computer hardware is universal in that it can perform a virtually unlimited collection of tasks, given the right collection of instructions.

We could call a computer by itself a *data processor*, manipulating electrical signals that we think of as zeros and ones. People generally have little use for data, however; the real power of the computer appears when, combined with a program, it acts as an *information processor*. Consider, for example, the number 102.7. As a rational number—as data, that is—102.7 has little intrinsic meaning and is of little interest to us. A program, however, can invest that number with a context: either innocent as the frequency of an FM radio station, enviable as an hourly wage in dollars, deplorable as an hourly wage in lire, worrisome as a child's temperature in degrees Fahrenheit, or impossible as a child's temperature in degrees Celsius, depending on the intentions of the programmer. In this module, we will concentrate on the combination of computer and program as a single machine, a powerful black box.

The natural question to ask here is: Now that we have all this power, what can we do with it? The answer, as we will see here and in Modules 4 and 5, is: (Almost) anything that we can write a program to do. We will see in later modules that there are limits to the power of computers—some tasks are inappropriate for computers because of purely physical limitations on speed and storage, and there are logical limitations in the sense that some tasks can be proven impossible to perform by their very nature. However, within the boundaries set by these limitations, we have an immense field in which to work.

Computer applications are commonplace today and likely will be ubiquitous tomorrow. Why are there so many uses for computers? One answer is that computers, properly programmed, can perform tasks that would be either infeasible or downright impossible otherwise. This, in turn, stems from the fact that the computer is both fast enough to do otherwise impossible tasks in a reasonable amount of time and flexible enough to be applied to a wide variety of problems.

The most visible computer applications today are those for personal computers. Even restricting our attention just to programs written for microcomputers, we can comb through popular computing magazines and easily come up with several thousand programs, ranging from those for serious word processing and file management to those that perform astrological readings. Using microcomputer applications as our starting point, we will begin by exploring some of the most popular programs, then go on to look at some commercial and industrial applications generally written for larger machines. Along the way, we will lay the groundwork for Module 10 by beginning our discussion of the social and personal implications of the computerization of the modern world.

Metaphor: The Calculator

The portable electronic calculator is a program and computer in a box; it serves as the fundamental paradigm of a computer application, as well as the guiding example of this module. Unlike what we generally call a computer, you cannot get inside the box and change the program that controls the calculator. The + key will always perform an addition, no matter what you do. In many cases, modern calculators do indeed contain fully functional, programmable microcomputers, but the programming to make the computer act as a calculator is done once and for all at the factory. From the user's point of view, a calculator is like all the other computer/program combinations we will discuss here—a black box designed to perform one complex and open-ended task, the internal workings of which need be of no concern to the user.

The calculator and the digital watch were the first major commercial and practical successes of microelectronic, integrated circuit technology. Of course, calculating devices existed long before the development of electronic technology. Mechanical calculating devices consisting of gears and wheels had been around for centuries. A bronze astronomical calculator dating from the first century B.C. was discovered by sponge divers in a shipwreck off the Greek island of Antikythera, for example. By the 1930s, a century after the Analytical Engine, it was possible to buy a mechanical desktop calculator for about $1000 that could add, subtract, multiply, and divide ten-digit numbers much faster and more accurately than is possible with pencil and paper (see Figure 2.1).

Despite the speed and accuracy of mechanical calculators, their sales were sparse, due in large part to their cost and limited capabilities. Of course, other options were available. Until very recently, most scientific calculations were per-

FIGURE 2.1
A mechanical calculator (© Super Stock, Inc.)

formed with the aid of slide rules and mathematical tables (see Figure 2.2). We might be inclined to dismiss these calculating aids as hopelessly neolithic, but we should also keep in mind that the atom bomb, the most ambitious engineering project in history at the time, was developed almost entirely without the aid of electronic computers. Still, it is a measure of the astonishing success of electronic calculators that the slide rule, once standard equipment for every college student in a science course, has almost completely vanished from the scene, to the extent that the odds are excellent that you've never seen a slide rule, much less used one. We take the calculator so much for granted today that it is worth our time to consider briefly its rise to prominence.

There are conflicting claims concerning the origin of the first electronic calculator, but we can say that the first such device was developed around 1963. Texas Instruments marketed an electronic calculator in 1967, without much commercial success at first. The calculator market blossomed in the late 1960s and early 1970s, however—annual sales went from zero to millions of units in less than a decade, and the price of a typical calculator dropped from $100 to $5 in less than five years. The industry was stunned at first; analysts who had projected demands for integrated circuits in the tens of thousands found that their predictions were a thousandfold too low. Almost overnight, the microelectronics industry changed from a producer of scientific specialty items to a major producer of consumer goods. Now, of course, electronic calculators are cheap enough to be given away as premiums, and there are about 190 million calculators in the United States alone, according to an estimate by Texas Instruments.

If we think of the calculator as a *microworld,* that is, as a model of one aspect of the world, it's clear that the calculator is based on the model of a person performing numeric calculations. Indeed, the design of most calculators is a direct reflection of this model: To add 345 and 720, one presses, in order, the 3, 4, 5, +, 7, 2, and 0 keys and then presses the = key to display the result. If we extend the model slightly, we can consider the calculator as an electronic assistant, capable of performing not just a single operation but a series of calculations at blinding speed. For instance,

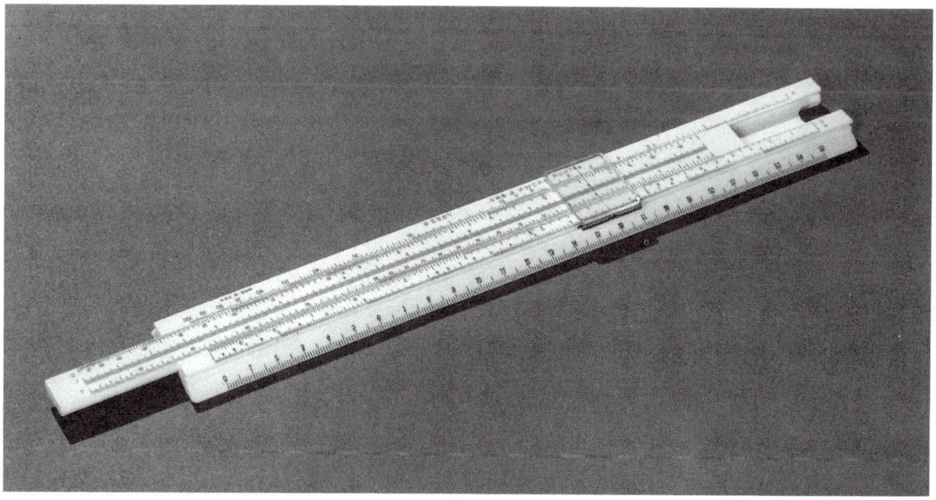

FIGURE 2.2
A Slide Rule
(© Super Stock, Inc.)

one way to compute the square root of a positive number, n, is to perform the following steps:

1. Begin with a guess, say 1, for the square root of n.
2. Repeat the following process until you are as close to the square root as you wish to be:
   Replace the original guess by $(n + guess^2)/(2 \times guess)$.

For example, to compute the square root of 5, we have the following guesses:

$$1.000000000 \rightarrow (5 + 1.000000000^2)/(2 \times 1.000000000) = 3.000000000$$

$$3.000000000 \rightarrow (5 + 3.000000000^2)/(2 \times 3.000000000) = 2.333333333$$

$$2.333333333 \rightarrow (5 + 2.333333333^2)/(2 \times 2.333333333) = 2.238095238$$

$$2.238095238 \rightarrow (5 + 2.238095238^2)/(2 \times 2.238095238) = 2.236068896$$

$$2.236068896 \rightarrow (5 + 2.236068896^2)/(2 \times 2.236068896) = 2.236067977$$

The last guess, after only five steps, is correct to nine decimal places. This technique, known as *Newton's Method,* is our first example of an *algorithm,* a finite collection of simple instructions that can be performed by a computer and is guaranteed to halt in a finite amount of time. We've all used algorithms before, perhaps without knowing the name—think, for instance, of the elementary-school algorithms for multiplication or long division.

At any rate, if we wanted our hypothetical calculator to be able to compute square roots, we would need only to include a small program, activated by the square root key, to perform the algorithm above until, say, the guesses didn't change. Notice, by the way, that the only operations required by the square root program are addition, multiplication, division, and moving and storing numbers. This feature is common to almost all areas of computer science, where, as we will see over and over again, complex objects with sophisticated behavior are built by combining simpler parts.

◆ **Hoff remarked that at one time he had a great deal of difficulty explaining to a reporter that although the small size of the microchip would indeed make it difficult to repair, that wasn't the right question to ask. The philosophy of "when it breaks, just throw it away" brought the computer to a position much like the modern ballpoint pen.**

One might wonder how many people actually need to compute square roots, but including this extra functionality adds effectively nothing to the cost of a calculator. In terms of chip area, we can pack so much computational power into a microchip that adding a few more circuits to compute square roots adds far less than a square millimeter. In terms of speed, the extra hardware comes up with the answer so fast that there's almost no reason not to include this extra functionality, whether or not the consumer ever uses it. We thus have a technology in the unprecedented position of being able to provide consumers with more than they need at no increase in price.

The electronic calculator is the direct ancestor of today's microcomputer. The first computer on a single chip was designed in 1971 by Ted Hoff for the Intel Corporation in response to a request from the Busicom Company of Japan, which wanted to develop a calculator of its own. At the time, a typical calculator consisted of several chips wired together on a printed circuit board. The resulting circuit was a single-purpose machine, designed with the sole purpose of driving the calculator. To design a different calculator, one would have to replace the chips with others, in effect rebuilding the entire circuit. Hoff's clever idea was to design a single chip that could be programmed by the manufacturer, so that changing the design of the calculator required no hardware changes at all. It didn't take Hoff and others long to realize that this chip, the Intel 4004, could be put to many uses beyond mere numeric calculations, and thus was born the microcomputer.

Æ Online

The Module 2 lab exercises provide you with opportunities to develop your expertise with four local (and increasingly commonplace) applications: a word processor, a spreadsheet, a graphics processor, and a page layout program. Although we don't provide detailed instruction in the use of any of these programs (your instructor can help you there), we set out some general tasks for you (like preparing a resume, entering simple data and performing basic calculations, and recreating – or just creating – graphic art) that will help you to learn by hands-on experience.

You will appreciate the longer-term benefit of completing these exercises when you realize that many of the basic concepts and operations that are used in standard local applications have made their way into the more global, Web-based technologies that you will be working with throughout the remainder of this course.

2.2 FAMILIAR MICROWORLDS

You've already seen that the modern computer owes its existence to electronic technology. That's true enough, but in a sense it is not particularly relevant to the nature of the computer, particularly when viewed as a black box. Although we cannot do it yet, it is at least theoretically possible to build a computer using *photonic* technology, in which information is transferred by light rather than electricity. As another example, it is not only theoretically possible to construct an information processor using carbon, rather than silicon, chemistry, it is also eminently practical today—one only has to look at our own brains and those of our pets. What a computer is made of and how it works is just an enabling technology; the important notion is what J. David Bolter calls a *defining technology*. Just as the steam engine could be viewed as the defining technology of the Industrial Revolution—the technology of power, of manipulating the physical world—Bolter views the computer as the defining technology of our time—the technology of information, of manipulating the world of ideas.

Revolutionary technologies never spring forth from a social vacuum. New devices always owe their existence to older ideas, and the computer is no exception. In particular, the computer and its programs are a natural step in an evolutionary process that began more than 5000 years ago with what are the most important of all technological innovations to date—writing and (much later in history) mechanical printing. Both of these technologies can be viewed as the representation of ideas in physical form: "petrified truth," as Mark Twain said. In the case of this book, for instance, when we wrote down our ideas about Module 2, we could put the pages away and come back to them years later, and they would still be there, unchanged, for us to read again. We could give the pages to others, for them to read at their leisure, even if we were no longer around to communicate the ideas contained therein. You are holding a printed copy of our ideas, one of many identical copies owned by many other people, yet we can speak to you through these pages just as if you were sitting in a class listening to us—better, in some ways, since the book is not constrained by time. You can read the same passage again and again: A book never cuts you off because it is impatient or its feet hurt. Also, you can write your own additions to our ideas in the margins, thereby customizing our ideas to suit your own purposes.

What you now hold in your hands or your lap, though, is a comfortable old technology. The subject matter might be new, but the idea of a physical embodiment of ideas on paper would be familiar to a scribe in the time of the Pharaohs. The lab portion of this module, however, represents a new way of thinking about information in physical form. Except for the comments you add in the margin, the information in this text, like all written and printed matter, is essentially static. The lab programs, however, contain not only representations of information, but also instructions to the computer to manipulate this information. The computer can perform arithmetic calculations, sort lists of numbers, solve algebraic equations, and, by treating the data as characters rather than numbers, handle mailing lists of names and addresses. Furthermore, if the bits of data are considered to be graphical rather than textual, the computer can use these data to display pictures on the screen.

In all these examples, the computer and its program together take on the nature of an active metaphor, a microworld if you will, having its own natural laws that govern its behavior. These microworlds are frequently models of a portion of the real world, either in an attempt to imitate the physical world or to create the environment of the job to be done. As we will see shortly, computer microworlds may begin by modeling familiar tasks, but often they evolve to include behavior far beyond the ranges of the tasks they originally imitated.

■ The Word Processor

At first, people thought of the computer solely as the apotheosis of the adding machine, a glorified supercalculator. It didn't take long to realize, though, that any information that could be expressed in numeric code could be grist for the computer's mill. By assigning a code number to each letter, digit, and punctuation mark, for instance, a text document could be stored in a computer's memory and hence manipulated by a program. This, in simplest form, is all that a word processor really does.

Word processors began as models of typewriters. Indeed, one of the first word processors, the IBM magnetic tape Selectric of 1964, actually was a typewriter, with a way of storing electrically a coded version of what had been typed. In these early, paper-based word processors, the typist used special code sequences or keys to type a chosen range of lines and to enter or modify text in those lines. To produce a perfectly typed document, then, the typist made a draft copy that was stored electrically, then edited the paper copy, returned to the tape to make the corrections, and finally printed the finished version. A master copy of a commonly used letter, for example, could be made and slightly modified for each name and address, so it was no longer necessary to retype the entire letter to make just a few changes.

As useful as early word processors were, they were of limited commercial impact until they were combined with display screens in the 1970s. Still, they didn't really take off until personal computers became popular in the late 1970s and early 1980s. With these WYSIWYG (for "What You See Is What You Get," pronounced *whizzy-wig*) word processors, the user didn't have to insert special control codes (or *tags,* as they are known in World Wide Web documents) while typing to produce special printed effects. Instead of having a document that looked like this:

```
{ \ bf 1.} Some of the { \ it invisible benefits} of this plan
      include: \ cr
\ tab \ bullet Reduced { \ ul downtime} for the \ Sigma -7 units
      \ cr
```

The user could see on the screen exactly what the finished document would look like:

1. Some of the *invisible benefits* of this plan include:
   - Reduced <u>downtime</u> for the Σ-7 units

If you've ever used a word processor, you know that control of the typefaces, styles, and special characters is achieved by pressing certain key combinations or making selections from a menu. These are translated in turn into invisible control characters that are translated by the word processing program into instructions to the screen display. The internal representation of the document in the computer's memory still looks very much like the first example above—the difference is that the screen display is sophisticated enough to show the letters in many forms, when instructed by the word processor to do so.

Notice that by this time the microworld that began as a model of the typewriter had evolved to include features that were difficult or even impossible to achieve with the typewriter, such as the mixing of fonts and typestyles in the example above. This evolution beyond the original model also included such features as the ability to cut a selection of text and paste it elsewhere in the document (something that would have to be accomplished with scissors and tape or glue in the typewriter world, hence the terms *cut* and *paste*), as well as the ability to replace every occurrence in a document of a nonword such as *alot* with the correct version *a lot* at the stroke of a key (or click of a mouse). A program that instructed the computer to perform simple reading of a text file also led to features that were undreamed of in the typewriter model, such as automatic spelling checkers.

We have noted before that paper and ink provide a physical embodiment of the world of ideas. You can pick up a paper and smudge the ink with greasy fingers. In a sense, the word processor is even closer to the world of ideas than the typewriter or pen, since the words cannot be touched. They are fleeting electrical currents internally, and patterns of light and dark dots on a screen externally. This "light writing," to use the words of Jack Harris, provides a flexibility impossible with paper and ink, by dispensing (at least from the user's point of view) with the need to produce and manipulate physical objects. The power and utility of the computer comes in large part from the fact that computer programs are *plastic*—they can be constructed and modified far more easily than physical devices.

LAB 2.1

Words on Your Behalf

This set of exercises will help you to appreciate (if you don't already) the power of one of the most pervasive computer applications, the word processor. If you are already familiar with basic word processing concepts, you can skip over the following material and proceed directly to the last exercise in this section (Exercise 4, below).

Word processing programs have evolved from simple automated versions of typewriters to full-blown WYSIWYG editing tools, and in the process have become increasingly standardized. The microworld that these programs reflect is simply an (effectively infinite) roll of paper, represented by a scrollable field on the screen.

Simply clicking in the field changes the cursor to an *insertion bar,* which marks the spot where typed characters will be inserted into the field. You need not concern yourself with carriage returns as you type, unless you want text broken at specific points. Your word processor knows the size of the field and adjusts your text to fit into it. For the moment, you can use the Delete or Backspace key to erase individual characters. Note, too, that you can reposition the insertion bar within the field by moving and clicking the mouse. Subsequent insertions and deletions are made relative to the new spot.

If inserting and deleting text were the only operations available, word processors would be little more than automated typewriters. Most, though, offer a wide range of editing features. Before reviewing these standard operations, we must first describe how one selects the text to be operated upon.

The standard pattern for describing a text-editing operation is first to select the thing to be operated upon, and then to choose an operation from the appropriate menu. Selecting text is the process whereby you specify which part of the text is to be edited (moved, removed, revised, and so on). To select a point for inserting or removing text, simply click the mouse at any point within the field. To choose a group of characters, click at the start of the group (immediately before the first character desired) and drag the mouse (with the button held down) until the entire group is highlighted. Dragging the mouse down or up within the field selects entire lines. The operation chosen (even pressing Backspace or Delete) then applies to the entire selection. Each command in the menu applies to whatever text has been selected when the menu item is chosen.

The Undo command undoes the most recent editing operation. If, for example, you inadvertently delete some text, choosing Undo immediately after doing so will restore it. Note that this operation works only for the operation immediately preceding it. Choosing Undo many times in a row accomplishes nothing more.

The Clipboard is a special place used to save information from the immediately preceding operation. Cutting a portion of text removes it from the field and saves it (temporarily!) on the Clipboard. The cut text can then be pasted into another location within the same or even another field. Copying text works just like cutting text—the copied text is saved on the Clipboard so that it can be pasted—except that the selected text is not removed from the original field. Once copied to the Clipboard, text can be pasted into any field. Pasting inserts the current contents of the Clipboard at the current insertion point in a field. The Clipboard remains unchanged by pasting. The normal method for moving text from one location to another (even across pages and documents) is to cut or copy the text to be moved, click where it is to be inserted, and choose Paste from the Edit menu.

Clear removes the current selection from its field. It is equivalent to hitting the Delete or Backspace key. Note that clearing a portion of text does not place it on the Clipboard and cannot be undone.

1. Enter the memo below into your word processor now.

```
    Friday, January 13, 1998
    To:    Professor Decker
    From: Ben Realbusy Re: Homework
    I regret to report that do to an extremely full calendar these
past two weaks (my new car broke down, I've been trying to maintain
my tan, and I have had to prepare for an outrageous Super Bowl
party-you're invited!), I will not be handing in assignment #1 on
thyme. I amsurethatyou appreciate the pressure I have been under
and, since you have nothing to do but sit in your office anyway, I
feel certain that you will accept my assugnemtn whenever I get
around to handing it in. If there is any problema, please leave a
massage on my answering machine.
    Chow,
    Ben
```

2. Use the keyboard and the Edit menu to

   a) Correct all misspelled words.
   b) Fix the spacing in the memo (use the space bar and the Return key to add spaces, the Backspace or Delete keys to remove them).
   c) Customize the memo to include your name and that of your favorite instructor.

Another essential ingredient of today's word processors is their ability to save and retrieve documents as files on disks. This allows not only for documents to be revised at any time after they have been created, but also for them to be revised as often as necessary (which, in the case of a form letter, may be often indeed). The file-handling capabilities of most word processors are embodied in the File menu at the top of the screen. The commands therein use standard parlance for describing common storage and retrieval operations.

Selecting New from the File menu, appropriately enough, creates a new document named "Untitled" or "Document." If a document already appears in the application window when New is selected, you may be asked if you want to save it before creating a new blank document.

The Open... command allows you to retrieve an existing document from a file and to have it appear in the application window. The ellipses following the word "Open" in the File menu are significant. Ellipses are commonly used in command names (whether on buttons or in menus) to indicate that there is more to invoking the command than a single click of the mouse. In this case, after selecting Open... we must specify which file is to be opened. We do so by means of a standard input-output dialog box.

Selecting the Save command stores the contents of the text field using the current file name. The Save As... command also stores the text field, but first presents you with a dialog box (as indicated by the ellipses) that asks you to name the file and to specify where the file is to be saved.

3. Edit your memo so that it is a generic excuse letter. That is, fix it so that it can be used for any instructor, any assignment, and any excuses. Then, save the memo as "Excuse Me."

4. Use your word processor to create your resume. Include headings and information for biographical data, education, work experience, professional and personal goals, and references. Be sure to include your e-mail address!

The Spreadsheet

A spreadsheet combines the attributes of a calculator and a word processor. Represented as a rectangular array of *cells,* the spreadsheet is modeled after an accountant's ledger sheet. Figure 2.3 illustrates a typical spreadsheet with six columns (one for the row title, one for each quarter of the year, plus one for the year to date) and four rows (the column titles, and the sales, costs, and profits for each quarter).

Each cell of the spreadsheet contains not only visible information, but also codes representing how the information is to be displayed. In the example figure, the numeric information is displayed with two decimal places of accuracy, right justified, with any negative values enclosed in parentheses, while the textual information in each cell of row 1 is centered. In this sense, the spreadsheet is very much like a modern word processor. The display of information (which can be regarded simply as a collection of strings of characters) can be edited by typing, cutting, copying, and pasting, while each piece of information carries with it a hidden collection of formatting information, as specified by the user. In a modern spreadsheet, this format information can be applied to each row or column. For example, to change the format of

FIGURE 2.3
A sample spreadsheet

	1	2	3	4	5	6
1		Spring	Summer	Fall	Winter	YTD
2	Sales	2275.91	1120.65			3396.56
3	Cost	1480.03	1289.98			2770.01
4	Profit	795.88	(169.33)			626.55

a column from integers to decimal numbers with two-place accuracy requires changing the format of only a single cell and issuing a command to extend the characteristics of that cell to its entire column, in much the same way that the margins of a paragraph can be made to apply to an entire document in a word processor.

This by itself would be useful to accountants, saving the trouble of having to redo a ledger sheet to adapt to a client's wishes, but the true power of the spreadsheet goes much further than mere pretty formatting. When Daniel Bricklin and Robert Frankston designed VisiCalc, the first spreadsheet, they began with a microworld that was dynamic rather than static. Along with numeric or textual data and display format information, each cell of a spreadsheet can communicate with every other via a user-defined rule that describes the information to be stored in the cell. Look at the YTD (for Year To Date) column in Figure 2.4, for example. We know that the total cost to date is the sum of the costs that have been entered so far, and the spreadsheet allows us to specify that the value in row 3 of column 6 will be the sum of the values in columns 2 through 5 of that row. When setting up the spreadsheet, then, the user enters a rule in row 2, column 6, and then enters the command to make that rule apply to all the cells in column 6. After all the formulas have been properly entered (including the "profit = sales – cost" rule for the cells in row 4), the user need only enter the numbers to be operated upon. As each number is entered in a cell, any other cell that uses that number is immediately recalculated. Of course, some cells, such as the title cells in the first row and column, may have empty rules that say, in effect, "display just the information in this cell."

In a manner similar to the way in which the word processor quickly evolved beyond its original typewriter model, the spreadsheet was from the first recognized by its users as not only a powerful and efficient tool for managing existing data, but also as a simulator, a "what if" tool. Every faculty member, for instance, has had a student who comes in with the plaintive cry, "What grade do I need on the final to pass this course?" If the course records have been kept in an electronic spreadsheet, the instructor can use the spreadsheet, saying "Well, let's see . . . suppose you got a 65 on the final [types in "65" in the column for final exam and the spreadsheet recalculates the course grade]. That'll give you a 59 average in the course, so maybe we'll try a 75 on the final . . . ," and so on, until the student is satisfied. In fact, even this process can be automated in a

FIGURE 2.4
Spreadsheet formulas

	1	2	3	4	5	6
1		Spring	Summer	Fall	Winter	YTD
2	Sales	2275.91	1120.65			3396.56
3	Cost	1480.03	1289.98			2770.01
4	Profit	795.88	(169.33)			626.55

row 2 – row 3 of this column

sum of (column 2 to column of this row)

modern spreadsheet. For example, the cells in a spreadsheet could be programmed with the rules for computing income tax, and the operator could use the spreadsheet program's *solving* capability to instruct the spreadsheet to perform tasks such as the following: Assuming that my gross income next year is $45,788, compute how large my charitable deductions should be to make my tax liability no larger than it is this year.

LAB 2.2

Spreading the Wealth

Although there is some variation across spreadsheet programs as to how they specify information, all modern spreadsheets are capable of processing the relatively simple kinds of data and formulas described in the examples below. Also, all spreadsheet programs reflect a microworld consisting of an unformatted ledger sheet. Your job in using such a program is to decide what and how information is to be entered, and then describe in formula form what calculations are to be performed. Most spreadsheets also provide a set of tools for presenting the results of the calculations in graphical and tabular forms.

As before, the first of the exercises below focuses on the most basic spreadsheet questions, and can be skipped if you are already familiar with your spreadsheet program. If that is the case, go directly to Exercise 2.

1. Open your spreadsheet program now and follow the steps below to define a ledger to keep track of a bowling team's weekly scores. Imagine a team of five players, each of whom bowls three games per week.

   a) Enter three scores for player 1 into cells A1, B1, and C1.
   b) Enter a formula for player 1's total score (A1 + B1 + C1) into cell D1.
   c) Enter the formula for player 1's average score (D1 / 3) into cell E1.
   d) Change one of player 1's scores and verify that the total and average values change correspondingly.
   e) Enter the scores for players 2 through 5 into columns A, B, and C of rows 2 to 5, respectively.
   f) Enter appropriate formulas for each player's total and average scores into columns D and E. (Note: You may want to copy and paste formulas from player 1, or use a Fill command for copying and pasting the formula).
   g) Enter formulas that calculate the team's total score for all games in cell D6 and the team's overall average in cell E6.
   h) Change some of the players' scores. Once you are convinced that the totals and averages are being calculated correctly, use the Save As... command from the File menu to save the spreadsheet in its current form. A dialog box will appear on the screen that will allow you to name the file and to decide where it should be stored. After saving the spreadsheet, clear the ledger by selecting New from the File menu.

2. Use your spreadsheet to define a ledger that acts as a grade book for a class of ten students. Each student is to complete two homework assignments (each receiving a numeric grade out of 25 points), one midterm exam (50 points), and one final exam (100 points). The spreadsheet should calculate the numeric class average for each assignment and exam. Each student's weighted average is also to be calculated, given that the homework constitutes 50 percent of the grade, the midterm 15 percent, and the final exam 35 percent.

3. Finally, use your spreadsheet program to create a bar graph displaying the weighted averages for each of the ten students in the class.

Graphics Processing

Once you understand that a computer can store and manipulate numeric information, it's not difficult to imagine using a computer as a calculator. From there, it's a small leap to assigning each letter a numeric code and using similar codes for formatting information and hence making a program that allows the computer to act as a word processor. Combine the two concepts and you can build a spreadsheet. We don't have to limit ourselves to letters and numbers, though—any information that can be represented as a suitable collection of numbers can be processed by a computer.

One of the most visible computer applications today comes from representing and manipulating pictorial information. This use of the computer is so commonplace today that not only do we scarcely notice it, we can scarcely avoid it. Every time you open a newspaper, turn on the television, or go to the movies, there's a good chance you'll see the results of a computer graphics program.

How might we represent a picture in the memory of a computer? There are two basic approaches. In a *painting* program, we decompose an image into a collection of small dots, known as *pixels,*[1] assign a numeric code for the color of each pixel, and represent the collection of pixels as a collection of numbers. This is the form of information you see if you look closely at a newspaper photograph or a TV screen (see Figure 2.5). In a *drawing* program, an image is represented as a collection of predefined figure codes (6 for circle, 7 for rectangle, 2 for a line, for example), along with codes for radius, height, width, border color, and so on.

Generally, a painted image will take up more space in memory (compare the representations in Figure 2.6, for example), but will have greater flexibility than a corresponding drawing. Each approach has its merits—a paint program would be better suited for manipulating photographs, while a drawing program would be a natural choice for architectural and mechanical drawings.

Computer graphics programs have been around almost as long as computers, but their widespread use had to wait for sufficient hardware capacity, in terms of both speed and storage. This is because all but the simplest picture is worth vastly

[1] For *pic*ture *el*ements.

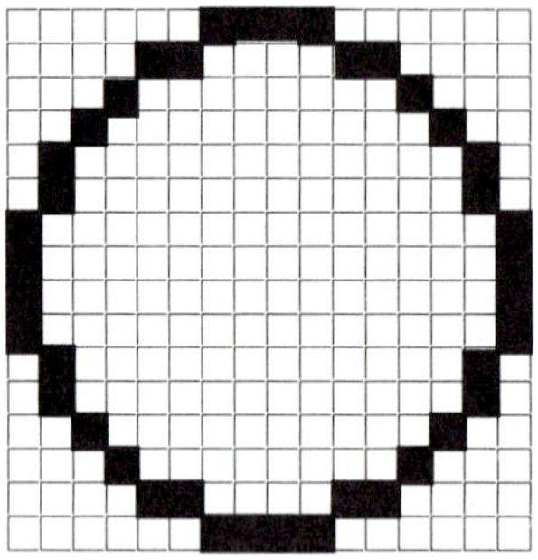

FIGURE 2.5
A circle, as it appears on the screen

FIGURE 2.6
A circle, represented in a painting program (left) and a drawing program (right)

```
0000001111000000
0000110000110000
0001000000001000
0010000000000100
0100000000000010
0100000000000010
1000000000000001
1000000000000001
1000000000000001
1000000000000001
0100000000000010
0100000000000010
0010000000000100
0001000000001000
0000110000110000
0000001111000000
```

```
6 (code for circle)
8 (radius)
8 (x-coordinate of center)
8 (y-coordinate of center)
1 (border width)
0 (fill color = white)
1 (border color = black)
```

more than the proverbial thousand words. A three-by-five-inch color image, for instance, may contain as many as 75,000 pixels and might take as much memory as 60,000 words of plain text. Once hardware caught up with the demands of graphics software, in the late 1980s, the results achieved were nothing short of amazing. The original King Kong was a fur-covered flexible doll and life-sized models of a head and a hand, and however terrifying he was to audiences in the 1930s, to our modern eyes he appears as a quaint and obvious fake. The *Jurassic Park* dinosaurs existed only in a computer's memory and for all practical purposes are as faithfully represented in the movie as they would be had they actually been photographed from living creatures. The capabilities of computer graphics are such, in fact, that feature-length movies can be made with no live actors at all, using only computer-generated animated images of people and objects.

Another consequence of the success of digital manipulation of images is that photographs are no longer valuable as records of reality. Since the invention of photography (at about the same time as the invention of the Jacquard loom), photographs had stood as reliable depictions of their subjects—so faithful, in fact, that they have often been accepted as evidence in courts of law. In the past, it was fairly easy for an expert to tell when a photograph had been doctored. With current image processing technology, though, it is now possible to take a photograph, convert it to a digital image, manipulate the image in a graphics program, and convert the image back to a photograph. Done with care, the resulting manipulated photograph is utterly indistinguishable from an original, even by the most expert tests. There are many commercial services today that will do this manipulation for you. Would you like your wedding pictures without tacky Uncle George? No problem—for a few dollars, Uncle George can be expunged without a trace. Do you need a photograph of the president shaking hands with an alien? Equally easy, and a good way to pump up circulation of a tabloid newspaper. This is yet another example of a theme that runs through this book: Technological changes can have surprising and unexpected social implications. Sad to say, you can no longer believe everything you see in newspapers, magazines, television, or movies.

LAB 2.3

No-Mess Painting

There are many local applications devoted to processing images, or picture data. These programs may be called *illustrators, painters,* or *graphics programs,* but all are intended to provide basic facilities for creating, editing, and manipulating pictures. The range of operations available in such programs varies, but all support the types of operations we need to accomplish the following. The intention is to gain a basic familiarity with the tools available in your paint application.

1. Use your paint program to draw a picture of the computer you are using. Include the screen, the keyboard, the processor, and the mouse, and display as many details as you can (like corporate icons, lights, and wires). Leave the monitor on your drawing of the computer blank for now.

2. Find an image to put on the monitor screen you drew in the previous exercise. Import the image, and resize it to fit onto the screen of your computer drawing.

Review Questions

1. Explain the distinction between data and information.

2. What is an algorithm? Give an example other than those mentioned in the text. What is the difference between an algorithm and a program?

3. List at least four ways in which the word processor has transcended the model of a typewriter.

4. What are the three kinds of information that are stored in a cell of a spreadsheet?

5. Explain the two ways of representing graphical images in a computer.

2.3 THE STATE OF THE ART

Word processors, spreadsheets, and graphics programs are some of the most visible computer applications today, due in large part to their accessibility and general utility. Each is applicable to a variety of common tasks in a wide range of settings. Most important, these programs have evolved so that they are genuinely useful to nonspecialists, a fact that has a great deal to do with their appeal. One need no longer be a whiz at arithmetic (or even, as we shall see, other aspects of mathematics) to solve numeric problems. Neither does one have to be an expert typist to produce polished-looking documents. Whereas standard high-school graduation gifts were once typewriters and slide rules, today's graduates come to college with calculators and, in increasing numbers, word processors and spreadsheets in hand.

These applications, though, represent the tip of the iceberg. Far more numerous and pervasive are the highly specialized programs that solve domain-dependent problems, or help humans to do so, in virtually every profession. The number of such off-the-shelf, task-specific applications grows daily as software developers respond to acknowledged professional needs. Still, this market goes largely unnoticed by most of us, who have little use for or appreciation of, say, a program that helps to determine the best mix of components to be used in the casings of an oil well. This is not to say that such specialized applications don't affect us in our everyday lives. On the contrary, it is safe to say that there would be no telephone service, space program, nuclear power plants, or computers as we know them without applications programs used by specialists in related fields.

The fields that rely heavily on applications software are not limited to the highly technical ones you might expect. Programs are now available at your local computer store and through the mail to assist specialists in business, the sciences, industry, the professions, the arts, entertainment, and education. The following pages review applications programs in use today. The list is by no means comprehensive, and provides no details about most of the specific programs. We do not even mention embedded applications (those that are an indistinguishable part of some larger system or machine, such as a car or a microwave oven), and we similarly disregard applications related directly to computer science (for example, programs that control touch-sensitive screens or produce computer speech). Rather, we provide the list to expose you to the breadth of applications software. The common thread relating all of these programs is that, despite the magnitude of the problem the application addresses, each can be regarded by those who use it as a black box.

■ Business Applications

It is no coincidence that two of our three standard computer applications, word processors and spreadsheets, grew essentially out of the business world. Business or data processing needs that exploit the computer's facility for storing and processing vast amounts of information were among the first addressed by commercial computers. The general accounting processes of governments, insurance companies, banks, and other businesses have long since been implemented as computer applications, which are now available and affordable for small businesses using personal computers. Individual and integrated applications can be purchased off the shelf for, among other functions, general ledger, accounts receivable, accounts payable, payroll, inventory, and tracking and billing of professional services. These programs typically provide features for recording information similar to those in word processors; features for accomplishing standard calculations similar to those in spreadsheets; and functions for storing, retrieving, sorting, and organizing information similar to those in databases. Many allow their users to print standard forms such as checks and W-2 forms, and some even allow users to design their own forms and reports.

Similar programs have been developed for personal use and customized for use in specific businesses. There are programs for maintaining checkbooks, for home budgeting, for individual tax preparation (complete with printable federal and state tax forms), and for portfolio management. Small and large businesses, ranging from restaurants to pharmacies and publishing houses, similarly benefit from applications programs that take into account the specifics of those businesses. For example, inventory programs of restaurant management applications incorporate food spoilage rates into their algorithms for ordering food stock. Programs that print labels on prescription drugs typically check a patient's chart to make sure that a newly prescribed medication will not interact in harmful ways with any other of the patient's prescribed medicines. Desktop publishing systems provide full text and graphic layout facilities that go far beyond conventional word processors.

Perhaps the most common business application is the database program, used to organize and classify information for convenient access. In a common form of database, information is classified as a *relation,* which may be regarded as a table describing the attributes possessed by the elements in the database. Figure 2.7 illustrates a sample relation for a database consisting of student information.

The relation of Figure 2.7 consists of five records, each of which has five attributes or fields identified by the labels Name, Year, GPA, Financial Aid, and Meal Plan. The information stored in the fields may be strings of characters, integers, real numbers, logical values, and so on. Viewing a computer application as a

FIGURE 2.7
A simple database

Attributes

Name	Year	GPA	Financial Aid	Meal Plan
Andrews, P. W.	1	2.34	3450	true
Barton, F. McG.	3	3.67	0	true
Cicci, R. T.	2	3.08	750	false
Dorzhinski, Y. I.	1	2.50	5600	true
Fu, J. H.	3	3.87	1250	false

A record

model of a real-world situation, it would be appropriate to think of a database program as a fast, efficient, and tireless records clerk or inventory manager.

The advantage of a database program is that it allows one to query the program to search and manipulate the database. In the example of Figure 2.7, for instance, we could enter the query

```
LIST Year = 2 AND FinancialAid > 1000
```

to obtain a list of all student records for sophomores whose financial aid is greater than $1000. The query language might also have commands such as

```
SORT FinancialAid
```

to sort the relation in order of increasing financial aid amounts. Other commands add new fields or new records, or format reports for printing or screen display, as follows:

```
EXPAND TABLE Student ADD FIELD Id (INTEGER 9)
DEFINE VIEW StudentFinancialView AS
  SELECT Name, Id, FinancialAid
  FROM Student
```

The tabular nature of our sample database makes it look very much like a spreadsheet, and indeed there are considerable overlaps between the two types of programs. The principal differences are not between what they can and cannot do, but rather between what they can and cannot do easily. A typical database lacks some of the simple "what if" features of a spreadsheet, but includes the ability to store large numbers of records for fast access and allows complicated interdependencies between the records.

Numerical Applications

Historically, the main beneficiaries of the computer's numerical prowess have been the sciences. Scientists and engineers use application programs based on numerical techniques to design aircraft and space vehicles; to design and test camera lenses and other optical systems; to launch and track vehicles in space; to enhance photographs taken from space; to analyze aerial and satellite images for weather prediction, pollution patterns, crop assessment, and military reconnaissance; and to simulate the formation of galaxies. As other disciplines become increasingly quantitative, they too benefit from similar applications. Economists and social psychologists, for example, make use of programs that allow them to describe models and test their theories. Image processing programs are used in archaeological studies to restore and analyze blurred pictures, and by geographers in developing maps. Linguists use programs that record and analyze speech and text. As tools for writers and literary critics, certain programs even help to analyze text for stylistic tendencies. Anthropologists and historians use statistical programs to analyze cultural data in an effort to better understand our past.

Our first standard application, the calculator, embodies the computer's facility in performing efficient numerical calculations. As useful numerical techniques were implemented on computers, they were incorporated, first, into the computer's circuits (we'll see how this is accomplished in Module 7), then into programming languages, and subsequently into software libraries that could be used conveniently by programmers. These techniques are now incorporated into stand-alone applications that can solve a remarkable variety of mathematical problems.

How remarkable? Suffice it to say that many—if not most—of the problems one encounters in college courses in algebra, calculus, linear algebra, numerical analysis, and differential equations can be solved by entering them into a program and pushing a button. Results can be expressed numerically and graphically (in two or three dimensions) with equal facility. The programs that solve such problems have been written, encapsulated, made accessible to nonprogrammers, and, thanks to advances in hardware technology, can now be run on personal computers. Consider, for example, the *Mathematica* program, designed by Stephen Wolfram. Mathematica is a recent example of a class of programs that act as intelligent mathematical assistants. In this program, the operative metaphor is a notebook of the kind mathematicians use to keep the results of their investigations, but the notebook is unlike the conventional type in that it is active, like a word processing document or a spreadsheet.

To illustrate some of the simplest features of Mathematica, consider a session one of us had with the program recently. In analyzing the running time of a program we had written to sort lists of numbers in increasing order, we had accumulated data on the time the program took to sort lists of 250, 500, 750, . . . , 2000 numbers. Entering the running times and identifying them by name required only the line

```
bData = [0.45, 1.85, 4.18, 7.45, 11.67, 16.8, 23.06, 29.99]
```

The command

```
Plot [%]
```

then displayed a plot of the data, as follows:

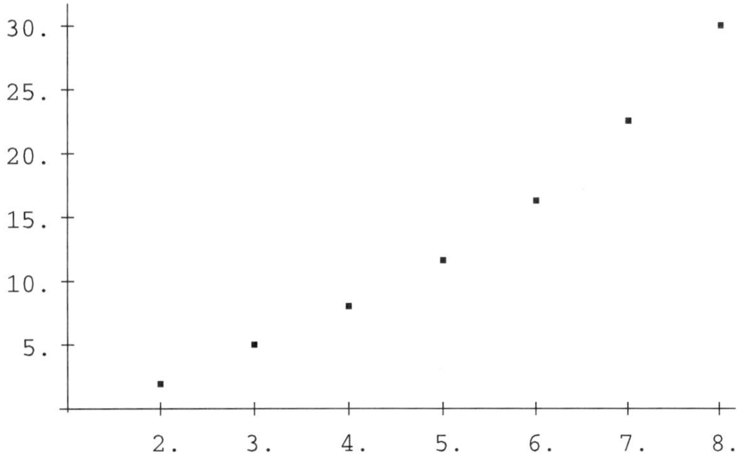

At this stage, we had good reason to believe that the data could be modeled as a quadratic curve, so we requested Mathematica to find the quadratic curve that best fitted the data by the command

```
bCurve = Fit[bData, (1, x, x^2), x]
```

which yielded the approximation

```
0.0119643 - 0.031131 x + 0.472917 x^2
```

which we could then plot, along with the data, to obtain the following graph:

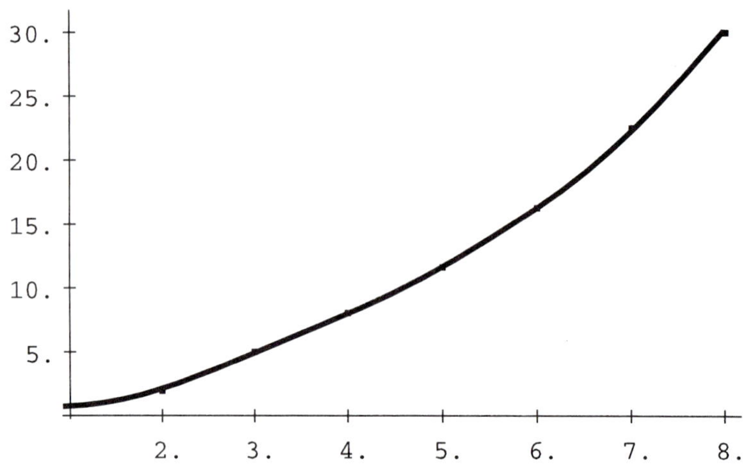

This is a very simple Mathematica exercise, one that hardly begins to draw upon the program's full functionality. Except for fitting the data to a quadratic curve, it is not hard to imagine how Mathematica must have worked in the example. Far more sophisticated, however, is the ability of programs such as Mathematica to perform symbolic algebra, as, for instance, when it factors

$$x^2 - y^2 + x^3 y - x^2 y^2 - x y^3 + y^4$$

into

$$(x + y) (x - y) (1 + x y - y^2)$$

The point, however, is that even in our simple example Mathematica can do in seconds the data plotting, curve fitting, and graphing that would have taken the better part of an hour to do manually. As with all applications, Mathematica and its cousins are not intended to substitute for the working knowledge of the user they are designed to assist. Let's look at a simple example: The equations $x + y = 3$, $2x + 2.0001y = 6.2$ have the common solution $x = -1997$, $y = 2000$, as you could verify by substituting these values into each of the equations. If a mathematics assistant program stored numbers to only four digits of accuracy, however, the two equations would be represented internally as $x + y = 3$, $2x + 2y = 6.2$, and these equations have *no* common solutions at all. The moral, of course, is that any computer application is an assistant to human experience and judgment, not a replacement. Like any other tool, applications must be used wisely.

■ Applications for the Professions

Many of the professions suffer from information overload and make extensive use of specialized applications software to manage the information. Doctors have for years relied on imaging equipment (such as X rays and sonograms) that is controlled by software. Now, medical consultation programs can advise doctors on pulmonary dysfunction, infectious diseases, glaucoma, renal disease, internal medicine, Hodgkin's disease, and psychopharmacology. Other programs monitor patients being treated by experimental drugs. There are even programs that run on personal computers and serve as family health care consultants. A variety of programs have similarly been developed for the offices of lawyers (for preparing and analyzing contracts, doing literature searches, and preparing briefs), law enforcement agencies (for maintaining driving records and automatic fingerprint matching), and architects (for producing drawings and three-dimensional renderings).

The programs used by architects and industrial designers exploit the computer's relatively newfound facility with pictures. While computers have been used to print graphs and tables for many years, only recently have they become sophisticated enough to display arbitrary shapes on their screens. Indeed, just as we saw a proliferation of word processing software a few years ago, we are now seeing graphics processing programs, that is, applications that let a user create, edit, refine, and print graphics at the computer. These stand-alone graphics applications have already evolved to the extent that they produce colored, three-dimensional pictures with shadings and perspectives that are controlled by the user. Light sources can be varied and the picture changes accordingly, and the picture can be moved, rotated, or translated in any dimension. Equally fascinating are the ways in which graphics programs are being incorporated into other specialized applications. Desktop publishing systems, which operate on pictures as well as text, would not exist today without graphics applications programs. Spreadsheet programs can now represent tabular data in a variety of graphical forms at the click of a mouse, thanks to graphics programs.

The medical CAT scan (for computerized axial tomography) is a good example of an application used in the professions. While X rays allow a physician to obtain information about the internal structure of a patient—to find tumors, for example—traditional X-ray images are difficult to interpret. Consider the example in Figure 2.8. In a conventional X-ray picture, the X rays pass through the body much like light rays to make a photograph, one slice of which we illustrate in the figure.

In the figure, the tumor is obscured by the large dark mass in front of it (a bone, perhaps). To find the tumor, several pictures might be necessary from different

FIGURE 2.8
Constructing a conventional X-ray image

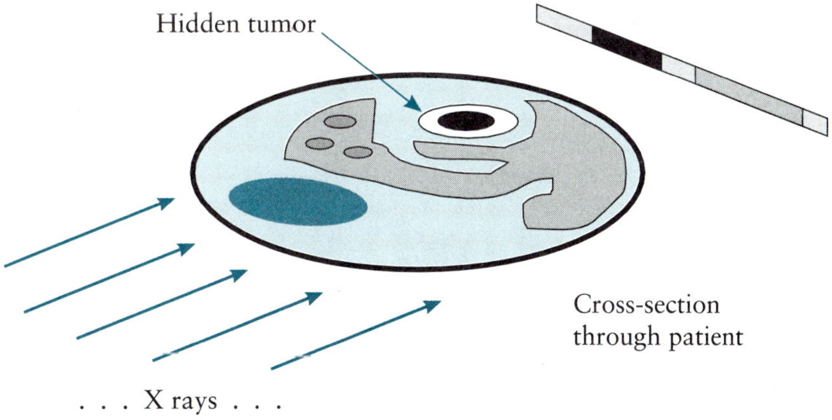

directions, but the images would still be difficult to interpret, not to mention that excessive exposure to X rays can injure the patient.

In a CAT scan, however, the scanning X ray is a single thin beam that is rotated to pass through a section of the patient in many different directions, as shown in Figure 2.9. For each direction, the computer stores the intensity of the beam after the beam has passed through the patient, and a program uses that information to reconstruct the internal structure of the patient. The process of reconstructing the cross-section from the data requires prodigious computing resources, as you might well imagine; it would be quite impossible to generate the resulting image without the aid of a computer. The result of a CAT scan is a much clearer image than could be achieved by conventional means and requires less exposure to the potentially damaging X rays.

Applications in Education

Applications have been developed to meet the needs of educators as well. Programs to assist in course scheduling, generating and grading exams, and maintaining computerized grade books are available for many computers. *Authoring* systems, programs that help instructors to develop interactive lessons for use by students on the computer (your lab modules, for example), are becoming commonplace. Intelligent tutoring systems designed to diagnose and respond to student errors as a teacher would can help students learn the alphabet, U.S. geography, or the principles of running a small business.

A typical authoring system is DISCUSS, used to help an instructor develop computerized lessons. Not too long ago, an instructor needed to know his or her own discipline as well as be an expert programmer to produce a package of computer-assisted instruction (CAI). As a result, most CAI was simplistic, boring to use, and time-consuming to construct. Recent applications such as DISCUSS, however, embody a high-level approach in which the authoring program does the work of producing the end product seen by the student, freeing the instructor from the need to know how to write a program.

In DISCUSS, the student sees a screen like the one in Figure 2.10, with two independently scrollable panels, the top one for the question text and the bottom

FIGURE 2.9
A CAT scan

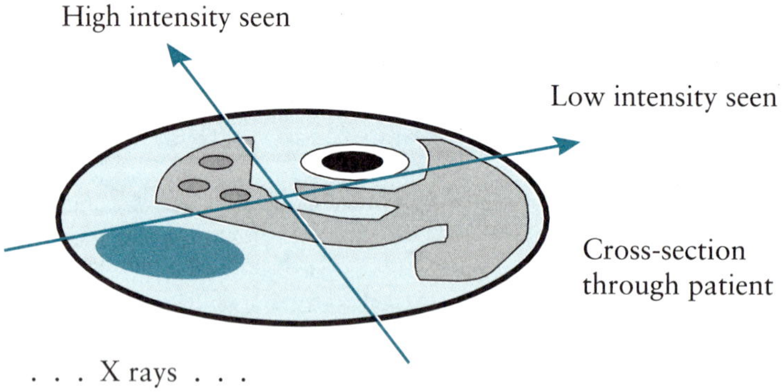

FIGURE 2.10
What the student sees in DISCUSS

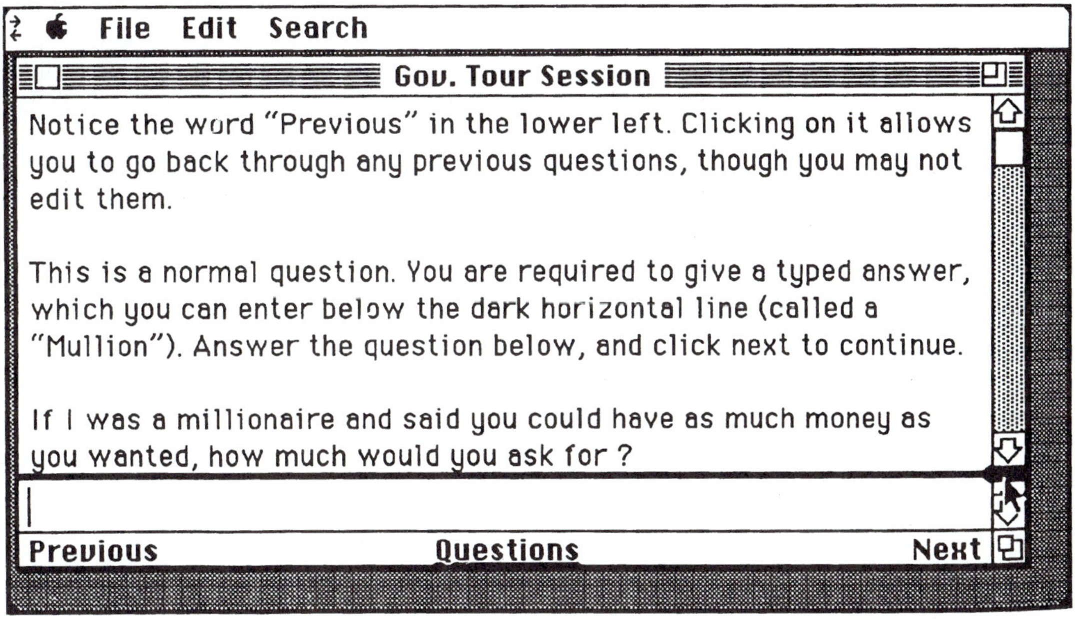

FIGURE 2.11
What the author sees in DISCUSS

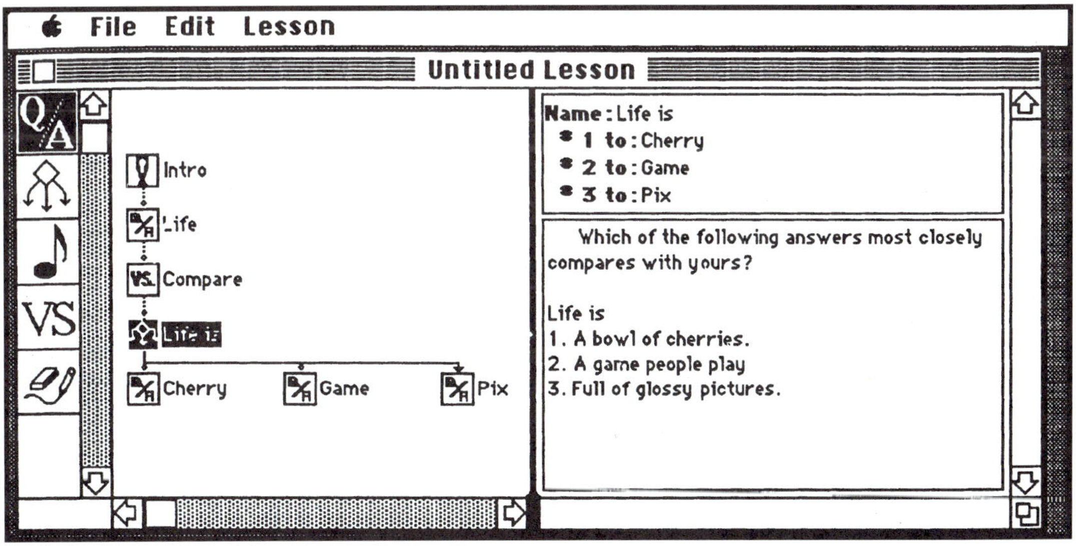

one for the student's response. The student user reads the question, types a response, and then clicks on a button in the lower bar to move to the next question or to review an earlier question.

There are several different forms for student screens—multiple choice, a look at other students' responses to questions, and so on—providing a flexible environment for the student sessions. The best part of the DISCUSS system, though, is that—like other courseware packages—the mechanics of building a lesson are made relatively easy for the author. The design of the lesson, which is the creative and important part, now becomes the primary issue rather than the programming.

The author creates a lesson by manipulating schematic representations of the screens the student will see, adding text in a separate panel, as shown in Figure 2.11. The authoring program then uses this schematic representation, along with the text, to construct the lessons for the student.

LAB 2.4

Tools of the Trade

Spurred on equally by the evolution of commercial image processing, the demand for multimedia documents, and the explosive growth of the WWW, applications now abound that are, essentially, integrated media processors. Some are described as page layout programs, others as presentation graphics software. All are intended to incorporate into a single program the tools needed to manipulate and coordinate text, images, and even sounds.

If you have access to such a program, you can use it to accomplish the tasks below. If not, don't worry. Modern word and image processors have been expanding toward each others' domains for years now. You can include (or *import*) images into word processing documents as easily as you can add text to an image. The exercises below can be accomplished using any combination of applications that you have at your disposal.

1. Pick any page from the *Analytical Engine* text that contains both text and graphics. Use your application programs to recreate the page as nearly as you can. Save the resulting document as a file.
2. Pick any WWW page that you have come across that contains interesting text and graphics. Use your application programs to recreate that page as nearly as you can. It is permissible to download or otherwise copy any complex images for your own labwork (this falls under what is known as "fair use"), though such copying wouldn't be acceptable if you used the result on your own Web page.

Review Questions

1. Describe two uses that an automobile manufacturer might have for a database program.
2. Consider a database program, a program such as Mathematica, a CAT scanner, and a program such as DISCUSS. For each of these, would it be better described as a faster and more efficient way of performing a traditional task or as a way to perform a task that was not possible prior to the development of computers?
3. In what ways is an application such as Mathematica significantly different from a high-powered calculator?
4. DISCUSS and similar programs may be regarded as intelligent assistants. List some other programs that may also be so regarded.

2.4 IMPLICATIONS

Will the calculator destroy the ability of the next generation's children to do even the most elementary arithmetic? What will the word processor do to the skill of handwriting? These are just two of the more obvious questions about the impact of the computer on our way of life. We mentioned earlier that new technologies do not develop in a vacuum; nor do they exist in one. The history of technology is inextricably bound to the historical forces that shape human society. A machine may be value-neutral, but the uses to which the machine is put are most emphatically not. Being able to do something does not necessarily mean that we should do it—a point made by the Luddites as they destroyed factory machines. Of course, the Luddites failed to halt the mechanization of factory work; in many cases, the introduction of a new technology simply proves to be irresistible. We will talk about the effects of the computerization of society in more detail in Module 10. In this section, we will merely pave the way by discussing some of the obvious consequences of this tidal wave of computerization.

■ Diminishing Skills

We probably do not need to concern ourselves overly with the decline of arithmetic and handwriting skills. In the large scale, social forces tend to maintain the level of skills deemed necessary for the functioning of society. We may deplore the deemphasis of certain skills for nostalgic reasons, but there is little evidence that today's world has suffered from a lack of skilled drivers who can handle a team of mules or people who know how to cut a quill so that it can be used as a pen.

As long as arithmetic is a valued skill, it will continue to be part of the primary school curriculum. If, somehow, calculators become as common as pencils, we might then see an actual decline of arithmetic skills. True, someone who forgets to bring a calculator to the store may then be unable to decide whether it is better to buy the three-for-a-dollar items than those selling for thirty-five cents apiece, but then many people today are in the same predicament. Most people have few qualms about asking a stranger if they may borrow a pen; the same would probably hold for calculators in our hypothetical future.

A similar argument holds for other simple skills, such as handwriting. As long as there is a need for a skill, and as long as there is no universal replacement for that skill, it will not be allowed to vanish. Most of us could not live off the land unassisted for an extended period of time, a complex collection of skills quite common (and vitally necessary) 10,000 years ago, and society is, arguably, none the worse for this loss.

Productivity

The computer and its applications are often touted as means of enhancing productivity by accomplishing more in less time. This is unquestionably true in some cases, particularly in those tasks involving intensive calculations or massive amounts of information. We have seen that mechanized information processing arrived just in time to save the census from being hopelessly delayed, and it is certainly true that many large corporations and government agencies could not operate as they do today without the aid of computers. We see the computer as an agent of social change, as indeed it is, but to view the computer solely as an agent of change is to ignore the subtler view of the computer as an agent of stabilization. In *Computer Power and Human Reason,* Joseph Weizenbaum compellingly argues the opposing view:

> Yes, the computer did arrive "just in time." But in time for what? In time to save—and save very nearly intact, indeed, to entrench and stabilize—social and political structures that otherwise might have been either radically renovated or allowed to totter under the demands that were sure to be made on them. The computer, then, was allowed to conserve America's social and political institutions. It buttressed them and immunized them, at least temporarily, against enormous pressures for change. Its influence has been substantially the same in other societies that have allowed the computer to make substantial inroads upon their institutions: Japan and Germany come immediately to mind. (Weizenbaum, p. 31. See Additional Readings at the end of this chapter.)

Weizenbaum's point, that the computer is often just another tool for doing the same things that were done before, holds equally well on the small scale as in the large. The word processor, for instance, has from its inception been marketed as a device that can lead to great increases in office productivity. The processes of proofreading, editing, and revising a document are certainly easier and faster with a word processor than with a typewriter. With a word processor, multiple copies of a form letter can easily be customized for its recipients, and it is increasingly common for a disk containing a document produced on a word processor to be used directly by a mechanical typesetter, saving weeks or months of time in publishing books and articles. We must keep in mind, though, that it is often easier to change technology than it is to adapt the new technology smoothly into the workplace.

The production of the text you are holding is a good example of the effect—or lack thereof—of the word processor on productivity. Prior to the word processor, we would have written this text by hand (or dictated it), then given it to a secretary to type. After editing it by cutting sections out with a pair of scissors and taping them elsewhere, we might have had the secretary make a clean—but not necessarily perfect—copy, perhaps retyping some of the pages. Finally, we would have gone through the manuscript, underlining the words to be italicized, putting wavy underlines under the words to be boldface, and so on. The publisher would have been perfectly content with a few handwritten corrections, a necessary compromise in a time when changing a single letter would otherwise involve 15 minutes to retype the entire page.

The word processor allows us to send a manuscript to the publisher that could almost be copied directly and bound between covers. Running heads and page numbers are handled automatically, italicized and bold words are displayed rather than indicated, paragraphs are left and right justified, and headings and subheadings are displayed in a typeface that is different from that of the body of the text. The manuscript, we admit with justifiable pride, is lovely, almost as nice-looking as what you're holding, but at what cost? To begin, our secretary is out of the loop, free to work on other projects for the department. That's a benefit, but the downside is that we have to do the typing ourselves, and neither of us can even come close to her speed at the keyboard. By doing the typing ourselves, we can make the manuscript look pretty and not have to worry about conflicting demands on secretarial time, but the time required to produce the manuscript is at least as long as it would have been without the word processor. Finally, for good reasons or not, our time costs our college much more than a secretary's, not to mention the fact that we have to arrange typing sessions so that they don't conflict with classes, office hours, faculty and committee meetings, and all the other duties of a faculty member.

The bottom line is that using a word processor to produce this text is not significantly better than the old-fashioned way and may be less cost-effective, all things considered. Why, then, did we produce the manuscript that way? Because it looks so darned good, that's why. Designed originally to fill a need for efficient editing, the word processor evolved so many attractive features that instead of filling a need, it created one. Because it can do so many things, we use an application to the hilt and take time doing things we wouldn't have even considered doing before. We might call this the "power user's syndrome" and note that it appears with many applications.

In fairness to an emerging technology, we should close by mentioning that the overall situation is not as bleak as it might appear. If we imagine writing a book of this size a few years in the future, the picture is considerably rosier. We would still type the manuscript ourselves, if only because we have a better idea of the format we want than does our secretary, but after having produced the manuscript we could then send the disks to the publisher (or transmit the document directly over the phone lines) and receive in turn an edited copy that, when loaded into our computers, would appear on our screens exactly as it would when typeset between covers. Major changes in format at this stage could be made by a few keystrokes, rather than resetting the entire book in type. In short, the publication time could be reduced to a small fraction of its present amount.

In presenting our personal example of the use of word processors, we have been harder on this new technology than many authors would be. We are certainly not Luddites—we would never want to go back to the typewriter, and we realize that there certainly are applications in other areas that would simply be impossible without computers. We took as long on this example as we did, however, because it is important to underscore the point that *new* is not necessarily a synonym for *better,* and that a new technology often requires changes in the patterns of its use.

Information Technology

Mozart was said to produce his manuscripts complete on the first draft, without corrections. Robert Frost said that "Stopping by Woods on a Snowy Evening" came to him all of a piece, without any preliminary versions. Most authors don't work that way, though. Any major library has collections of manuscripts with authors' corrections liberally sprinkled throughout. Indeed, scholars of literature can often gain valuable insights into the creative process by studying these steps along the way to the finished product. Even in the highly unlikely event that scholars of the future would be interested in the collected works of Decker and Hirshfield, there will be no preliminary versions of this text for them to study. It is so easy to make corrections on disk that the final version of this text, or any work made with a word processor, will be the only version available. Of course, as information storage technology improves, we might be able to store a complete transcript of all work on a document, from the first keystroke to the last change, but at least for the immediate future we see that the new technology has introduced a change that may not be for the better.

Libraries are the repositories of our written culture. Often the information we need to answer a particular question is available, but only to those who know exactly where to look. Automated search and retrieval programs promise to make finding information far easier than it has been in the past. It seems that here, as in the detailed study of the works of an author, we are in a difficult period of transition. A computerized database allows the user to select a topic and browse through all of the references stored in the database in much less time than it would take to track down the citations in thousands of indices and bibliographies. We mentioned earlier, for example, that there are 190 million electronic calculators in the United States. That information took a reference librarian the better part of two days to track down. How much more efficient it would have been to have a program to search for such data in the mountains of reference guides available. The problem, though, is that until such time—if ever—when the entire written output of society is available for computer search, there will be problems of omission. These problems will not become pressing until computerized searches become the primary way of doing research. Then we will be faced with the real danger of assuming, incorrectly, that information that is not online does not exist. To take another example, the work of anthropologists today is considerably simplified by a standard database of 186 cultures, broken down by categories such as methods of food distribution, social structure, attitudes toward conflict resolution, and so on. As useful as this database is, it would obviously be very risky for an anthropologist to use it as the only source of information about human culture. New technologies are often almost irresistibly seductive, leading us to assume that the new way of doing things is better, and, eventually, to believe that the new way is the only way.

Review Questions

1. Should we worry about a decline in arithmetic skills due to increasing use of computers and calculators? Explain.

2. Give an example of an area in which introduction of computers has led to significant increases in productivity, and another in which significant gains in productivity have yet to be felt.

3. Give two reasons for concern about the near-term effects of computerized information storage. Explain whether you expect these concerns to be important in the distant future.

2.5 EXERCISES

1. What contributes to making a computer application successful? That is, what are the common ingredients in calculators, word processors, and spreadsheet programs?

2. In your opinion, are computers really labor-saving or time-saving devices? If you think they are, how do you explain the fact that we still seem to be working as hard as ever? If you think they aren't, then why are computer applications so popular?

3. Spreadsheet programs, word processors, the Mathematica program, and JavaScript can all be viewed as active extensions of former static entities, where the computerization of a task allows a document to act on its data. Think of a currently static entity and speculate on the effects of making it active through computerization.

4. Which computer application do you use most often, and for what task? How has the application affected how you would otherwise have accomplished the task?

5. If you were designing a spreadsheet program, what operations would you like cells to be able to perform? If you can, find a spreadsheet program such as Microsoft's Excel and see if your list of operations agrees with its list.

6. In the course of your normal activities, how might you make use of a spreadsheet's "what if" capabilities?

7. If you have used a word processor, are there any features that it does not have that you would like included?

8. Two of the classic three R's of education—writing and arithmetic—have been addressed quite successfully by computer applications. What about the third R, reading? Can computers help us to read?

9. Choose a business, a profession, or an industry that you are interested in or know something about. Find three specialized applications for it.

10. List some of the commands that should be in the query language of a database program.

11. How does Mathematica factor algebraic expressions? Describe at least two specific problems that must be solved for a program to be able to factor (for example, reading the input and keeping track of what the variables are).

12. To give you an idea of how much computational effort a CAT scan requires, consider a simple problem of determining the composition of a two-by-two grid, in which each cell can be filled or empty. The 16 possibilities are shown below:

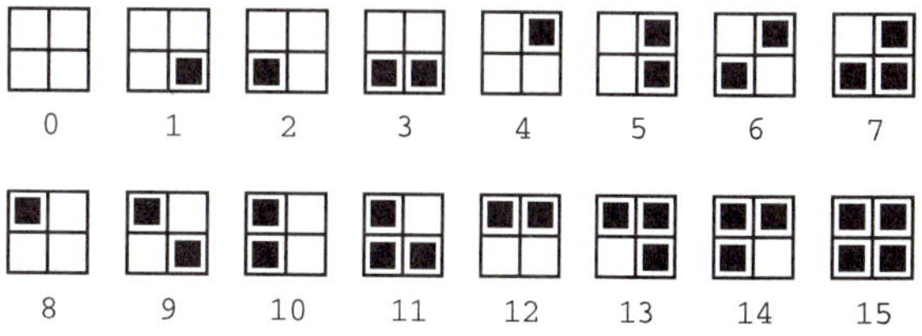

Your scanner can send a beam through the grid in one of six ways (along the bottom row, the top row, the left column, the right column, or either of the two diagonals) and record the number of filled cells. Scanning just the bottom row and the top row is not sufficient to distinguish all possible patterns, since those two scans cannot tell the difference between patterns 1 and 2, or among patterns 5, 6, 9, and 10.

a) Show that no two scans can distinguish all possible patterns. Hint: Compare the number of possible values for the two scans with the number of possible patterns.

b) Find a collection of four scans that will suffice.

c) Prove or disprove: There is a collection of three scans that will distinguish all patterns.

13. Is the introduction of a new technology really irresistible? Why are certain societies relatively immune to technological advances whereas others (such as ours) tend to embrace them all?

14. It has been said that the value of any tool lies in its ability to change how we think about certain tasks. Which computer application has had the most dramatic effect on your way of thinking? Why?

Additional Readings

Bell, D. *Using Applications Software.* New York: McGraw-Hill, 1986.

Bylinsky, G. "Here Comes the Second Computer Revolution." In *The Microelectronics Revolution,* edited by Tom Forester. Cambridge, MA: MIT Press, 1982.

"Computer Software." Theme issue, *Scientific American* 251, no. 3 (Sept. 1984).

Marx, L. *Machine in the Garden.* New York: Oxford University Press, 1964.

Miller, R. K., and Walker, T. *Artificial Intelligence Applications in Manufacturing.* Madison, GA: SEAI Technical Publishers, 1988.

O'Shea, T., Self, J., and Thomas, G., eds. *Intelligent Knowledge-Based Systems: An Introduction.* London: Harper and Row, 1987.

Price, D. J. de S. "An Ancient Greek Computer." *Scientific American* 201, no. 6 (June 1959): 60–67.

Rogers, E. M., and Larsen, J. *Silicon Valley Fever.* New York: Basic Books, 1984.

Sanders, D. H. *Computers in Society.* New York: McGraw-Hill, 1977.

Weizenbaum, J. *Computer Power and Human Reason.* San Francisco: W. H. Freeman, 1976.

MODULE 3

Global Applications

3.1 INTRODUCTION

The entity we now know as the Internet is just over 25 years old. From a collection of four linked computers in 1969, the Net has grown into what some people consider to be a global "hive mind," containing millions of computers used by tens of millions of people worldwide. We have already explored the important local applications, that is, programs used by individuals for financial analysis, word processing, personal record keeping, graphic arts, and the like. Perhaps even more important then these programs, though, are applications of a more global nature, that is, programs that connect a computer user to this expanding global information network.

MODULE OBJECTIVES

Our intention in this module is to help you make the leap from local, user-controlled, essentially private applications to a global network of machines and programs controlled by and participated in by millions of user-operators. Using these programs and machines means communicating and interacting with a virtual community. Our goal is to bring you up to speed on the tools, techniques, and responsibilities that come with using the World Wide Web.

In particular, we will

- Explore the historical background and technology of the Internet.
- Discuss some of the important applications of the Internet, including electronic mail, newsgroups, and the WWW.
- Encourage you to use these applications in conventional ways.
- Consider some consequences and implications of these ever-more-pervasive uses of the WWW.

Surprises Within Surprises

As we saw in Module 1, the growth in computer speed, power, and pervasiveness took even the experts by surprise. If you search early pronouncements about the nature and importance of computers, you can find statements that seem laughable in hindsight:[1]

> I think there is a world market for maybe five computers.
>
> —Thomas Watson, chairman of IBM, 1943

> Where a calculator like the ENIAC is equipped with 18,000 vacuum tubes and weighs 30 tons, computers in the future may have only 1,000 vacuum tubes and perhaps weigh 1 1/2 tons.
>
> —*Popular Mechanics,* ca. 1947

> There is no reason anyone would want a computer in their home.
>
> —Ken Olson, president, chairman, and founder of Digital Equipment Corp., 1977

As odd as these pronouncements seem today, they at least mention developments we see today, however wrong the predictions turned out to be. However, if you were to search the literature of the 1930s and 1940s, or even if you extended your search to the 1960s, one glaring absence would stand out clearly: You would find almost no mention whatsoever of the situation we find ourselves in today, with millions of personal computers connected into a gigantic whole.

Metaphor: The Global Village

The Internet is a globe-spanning network of computer networks, a community of users, a collection of shared resources, and an increasingly important social, political, legal, and ethical phenomenon. As surprisingly rapid as the growth of computing technology is, the growth of a global network of computers has been even more rapid. If the community of Internet users was a country, it would certainly qualify for membership in the United Nations, having grown from zero to a population larger than that of Spain or Poland in under three decades. With the exception of disasters like plagues and global wars, one would be hard-pressed to find a phenomenon that has involved so many people in such a short period of time.

Æ Online

In the online exercises for this module we begin the process of developing your Web skills in earnest. Ultimately, you will see how WWW pages are designed and programmed, and will do some page design and programming of your own. Here, though, we start with the basics, concentrating on the tools you need to navigate around this rich and complex source of information. You will gain firsthand experience with these tools (including downloading and unpacking utilities, e-mail, newsgroups, and search engines), some of which are available from right within your browser.

[1] From the business section of the *Kansas City Star,* January 17, 1995.

3.2 HISTORY AND TECHNOLOGY

In the Cold War days of the 1960s, the U.S. Department of Defense decided the country needed a national network connecting the scores of government and research computers, for what is known in the jargon as Command, Control, and Communications (C^3, if you prefer acronyms). This proposed network was to be resistant to point-of-failure attacks, which is to say that a nuclear attack on Boston would not bring the network crashing down, and it had to be fault tolerant, in the sense that it would still work as expected, even if—as often happens, even today—a computer broke down or a transmission line between computers was full of static, or accidentally cut by a backhoe.

■ Design

These requirements dictated certain design decisions. First, it was clear that the proposed network had to be decentralized. Unlike the telephone system, the proposed network could not include any vulnerable hubs controlling the switching and routing of messages. Control had to be distributed among each of the networked computers, so that each computer would receive messages and would pass them on to others on the route to their destinations. Thus, if one computer went down, the rest of the system could adapt by passing messages around the inactive site. We can think of the network of computers as similar to the interstate highway system, with cars representing messages—if a bridge were washed out by a flood or a city became impassable because of an earthquake, the traffic could always find alternate routes to its destinations.

◆ There's a historical connection here, too. The interstate highway system was also a federally funded program with military justifications. A decade before the proposal that led to the Internet, the U.S. government decided that a national network of high-capacity highways would be vital for defense in the event of an invasion by a foreign military force.

If we continue our highway metaphor, we run into some problems, as we always do when we push a metaphor beyond its limits. First, we have to take all the cars, trucks, and busses off the roads and replace them with motorcycles. Given that the connections won't always be reliable, we would want to limit the amount of information lost or delayed by traffic jams or breakdowns. Rather than pile the whole family in a car, we'll put each member on a bike and let them find their own way to Grandma's house. Finally, we'll put a traffic control station at each junction, and require each motorist to check in upon arrival to find out which roads out are still reliable.

What we have, then, is a fairly accurate description of what the national computer network was to be. What resulted is known as the *Internet Protocol* (IP), a collection of rules to be used for governing the transmission of information from one computer to another.

- Each computer on the network would be given a unique address (a number, known as the *IP address*). In human-readable form, these addresses are broken down into four numbers (each from 1 to 256), and the result is known as a *dotted quad*, for example, 202.47.104.3.
- Each message, whether it was text, a picture, a sound file, or anything else that could be represented in digital form, would be broken up into *packets* of a size equivalent to about 1500 characters.

- Each packet would be addressed with its source and destination IP address, along with a number indicating which portion of the whole message it represented, roughly like this:

FROM: 202.47.104.3	*The source's IP address*
TO: 101.78.44.19	*The destination's IP address*
NUMBER: 14 of 27	*The packet number*

- As a packet arrived at one of the computers on the network (known as a *router* or *host*), the computer would read its destination address and determine how best to pass the message along to its destination.
- Finally, when the packet arrived at the destination computer, that computer would use another set of rules, the *Transmission Control Protocol* (TCP) to reassemble all the packets back into a message, perhaps sending a retransmit message of its own back to the source if any packets had gotten lost or garbled along the way.

◆ The ARP part of ARPANET came from the Advanced Research Projects arm of the Department of Defense, under whose jurisdiction the project fell.

What later became known as the Internet was born as ARPANET on Labor Day, 1969, connecting four host computers at the University of California at Los Angeles, the University of California at Santa Barbara, the University of Utah, and the Stanford Research Institute. At roughly the same time, we find the beginning of civilian networks, independent of ARPANET, at least at first. These were often the result of collaboration between colleges and universities, using protocols of their own to transmit information between computers, typically using existing telephone lines.

Consequences

A visitor from another planet might quite reasonably deduce that the sole purpose of the design of ARPANET was to guarantee its growth. Though the original plans didn't include a requirement for rapid growth, it turned out that the resulting system could scarcely have been better designed if growth had been the sole criterion. First, and most difficult for many people to grasp, the distributed nature of the Internet means that there is no central control. There is no board of governors, no central committee, no regents, no Internet Police. There's nothing, in fact, but a collection of autonomous computers and a largely volunteer group of people who get together to decide on protocols and share the task of administering the technical details.

In consequence, it's exceedingly easy to become part of the Internet. If you were an administrator of the computer at a university research site in the 1970s, for instance, and the users of your computer started to clamor for access to this new network, all you had to do was get permission from a neighboring institution with an Internet host to connect your machine to theirs, find the money to pay for a connection to them, either by wire, microwave, or satellite, get the right TCP/IP software, get assigned an IP address, and—presto!—your computer was part of the Net. There would be some startup costs and a monthly fee for the connection lines, but otherwise it would cost the system administrators, and hence the users, essentially nothing once things were up and running.

Another design consequence is that distance is irrelevant. An early test of the network involved sending a message from a van in San Francisco to a computer at the University of Southern California, via satellite to Norway, over land lines and undersea cables to London, up to a satellite again to West Virginia, and finally to southern California by land lines and microwave repeaters, a distance of 94,000 miles. Because of the way packets are transferred over the Net, there is essentially no way to measure the distance of a transmission. Depending on which transmission paths were busy and which happened to be lightly used at the time, it might happen that at a particular time a message between two sites 20 miles apart might very well go halfway around the world and back, all without any action whatsoever by the sender and recipient. In simple terms, every call is local.

Of course, having the world's best, fastest, and cheapest new means of communication is worthless if nobody out there has any interest in using it. In the case of the Internet, though, it turned out that millions of people eventually wanted to use it. Although the real justification for the network was to provide a wartime backup communications system, the Department of Defense quite intelligently pushed the idea as a way for research scientists to collaborate on shared projects, connect to remote computers, and converse with each other, an entirely different kind of C^3. This suite of features had an immediate appeal—why update your co-investigators by mail, why travel to their sites to use their computers, why pick up the phone to talk to a colleague when you could do all these things almost instantly and practically for free simply by walking down the hall to the nearest terminal?

◆ There are actually several interconnected backbones: some, like NSFNET, maintained by the government, and some, like MCI's, maintained by organizations in the corporate sphere.

As time went by, more and more researchers had powerful microcomputers on their desks, connected by local networks to their host computer, and the topology of the national network changed from a collection of a few big computers to an *internet* of smaller networks connected to each other via their routers. To return to our highway metaphor, we can think of the Internet *backbone* as the fast, high-capacity interstate highway system connected by access ramps to the smaller, slower county roads that compose the smaller networks.

As it was with computers, the growth of the Internet was entirely unanticipated. From 4 host machines in 1969, the number grew to 23 in April 1971, to 62 in June 1974, and to over a thousand in 1984 (the original plans assumed an absolute maximum of 256 hosts). Thereafter, the number of Internet host computers more than doubled each year, passing ten thousand in 1987, one hundred thousand in 1989, and one million in 1992. The size of the Internet grows so rapidly that it is

FIGURE 3.1
The Internet is a network of networks

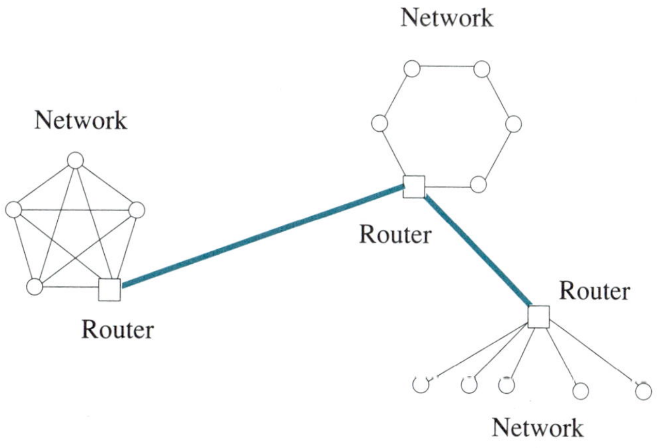

almost impossible to get reliable figures, but at the time of this writing, it's estimated that there are

- over 40 million people with Internet access,
- in 100,000 networks,
- in 150 countries,
- transferring the equivalent of over 20 trillion characters of information each month (which is considerably larger than the information content of the entire Library of Congress).

Since at the time of this writing the traffic on the Internet is increasing at 30 percent per month and the number of hosts doubles each year, the numbers above will be guaranteed to be woeful underestimates by the time you read this. We've moved at warp speed into a global information structure of almost unimaginable size in two decades, all because of a few lucky design decisions and an apparently insatiable demand.

LAB 3.1

Down and Out

One of the most interesting aspects of the WWW is the seemingly unlimited freedom one has in viewing pages. While there are many sites that require membership or the securing of some access privileges (like these AE Online materials, for example!), many are free for the viewing. The same is true for the content of WWW pages. The words and images that appear on pages are sometimes restricted by copyright laws and the like, but often are available for easy download to your computer so that you can use them for your own purposes.

Downloading an image, for example, is simply a matter of clicking the right combination of mouse buttons in most modern browsers. Doing so will provide you with your own copy of the file describing the image. Sound files can also be borrowed (that is, you can save the name of the file so that it can be referenced from one of your pages), but doing so typically does not give you a local copy. Ask your instructor how these downloading operations are accomplished on your machine and browser, and do the following.

1. Download two images that you think you might like to incorporate into a personal home page. (We'll show you how to do this incorporation in the lab exercises for Module 4. For now, just collect the images, and save them on one of your disks.)

2. Copy and save a link to a sound file that can be added to any page of your own devising.

As you may have noticed, files describing things such as images and sounds—exactly the types of files that one often wants to download—tend to be huge.

Indeed, the noticeable delays that you may have encountered in the exercises above stem from the sizes of the files involved and the time it takes to transmit them.

To facilitate all types of file transfer, programs have been developed that effectively shrinkwrap a file (compress, stuff, or zip it) so that it takes up as little space as possible. Complementary programs are, of course, available for expanding, unstuffing, or unzipping files once they have arrived at their destination machines. You will, again, have to rely on your instructor (or you can refer to our list of online resources for this module) to determine how best to expand a compressed file once it is delivered to your machine. When you are ready to try it out, do the following.

3. Click on the link in the lab exercise to download a single file containing a collection of images and sounds that we will use in subsequent lab exercises. Once the file is on your machine, you will have to expand it to view and use the individual files therein. Expand the file now, and save the images on a personal disk for later use.

Review Questions

1. What was the original purpose of the Internet?
2. Where is the central governing body of the Internet located?
3. Describe how a file of information is transmitted over the Internet.
4. What factors contributed to the rapid growth of the Internet?
5. Define *TCP/IP* and explain what it does.

3.3 APPLICATIONS 1: E-MAIL

As we mentioned, the early development of the Internet brought several surprises, such as the number of interested participants. Electronic mail, or *e-mail,* was another. Originally it was thought that the ability to send and receive electronic mail was going to be nothing more than a minor feature, but e-mail grew to be the single largest source of traffic on the Net until the coming of the World Wide Web in the 1990s.

Like many of the applications we'll discuss, electronic mail is larger than the Internet. While a lot of e-mail is carried on the Net backbone, a considerable amount may never leave the confines of the sender's network, whether it's a local network such as the one at a college or university or a much larger, national service such as America Online. The technical details of e-mail are simple enough: An electronic mail message over the Internet is transmitted by a store-and-forward process, very much like the way letters are sent through the postal service. The sender types his or her message and ships it to the local *mail server* computer. The local server holds all outgoing messages and periodically ships them out to one or more remote servers, which likewise hold the messages until a convenient time comes to pass them along. This process continues until, assuming everything is going right, the original message winds up on the recipient's mail server. This means, of course, that an e-mail message may very well pass through a dozen computers, following a path that is determined without any input from the sender or recipient.

Part of the ease of use of e-mail, and the rest of the features of the Internet as well, stems from the fact that it is no longer necessary to remember that the address of your friend's computer in Kansas or Kiev is 38.166.98.10. In the mid-1980s, the Internet community saw the introduction of a system of *domain names* that made the address system far more palatable for users. In this system, there is a hierarchical system of names, arranged so that each computer on the Internet has a unique description. For example, the domain name `vega.astro.usndh.edu` might refer to the computer named `vega`, which is part of the astronomy department's domain, `astro`, within the University of Southern North Dakota at Hoople (`usndh`), in the top-level `edu` domain of all connected educational institutions. The top-level domains are `edu`, as we just said; `mil`, which includes all military installations; `gov`, for government; `com`, for commercial organizations; `net`, for those sites devoted to Internet concerns; and `org`, which includes pretty much everything else, such as nonprofit organizations. Along with these six, there are also top-level domains for countries, such as `fr` for France, `jp` for Japan, and `au` for Australia.

When you use a name such as `vega.astro.usndh.edu`, it is the job of a *domain name server* (DNS) program, either within your local network or somewhere else out there, to look up the dotted quad IP address in its database (or to pass the request on to another DNS that will know) and send it back to your computer. All this is done invisibly to the user, so there is no need for the user to ever know that `vega.astro.usndh.edu` really represents 17.98.102.67.

◆ **Don't try to register sony.com or macdonalds.com with the intent of selling the domain name to a big corporation. First, these two are already taken, and, sadly for domain name arbitrageurs, such a practice has been declared by the courts to constitute "trademark dilution" and could get you sued by some corporation with pockets far deeper than yours.**

New domain names are introduced by registering them with the appropriate-level domain administrator. In the above example, if the astronomy department wanted to add a new computer named `sirius` to their network, creating `sirius.astro.usndh.edu`, the addition could be handled internally by simply adding the new name to the local DNS. The Spiveyville branch campus of the university, though, would have to go further up the hierarchy, to the `edu` level, to see whether the domain name `spiveyu` had been used.

The Nature of Electronic Mail

Electronic mail shares many features with ordinary postal mail (often referred to as *snailmail*), telephone conversations, and face-to-face communication. While this new form of communication is similar in many ways to traditional forms, it is also a fundamentally different medium in several important respects. For example, e-mail communication is faster than snailmail but slower than talking over the phone or conversing in person. Like the post, an e-mail message provides a permanent record of what was said. An electronic message does not have the immediacy of an oral communication; as with a message on a telephone answering machine, e-mail messages may be *time-shifted*, to be answered at the recipient's convenience.

As we will see many times, any new technology brings with it a set of social consequences that are determined by the nature of the technology itself. When we receive e-mail about this book, for instance, we have almost no clues about the identity of the sender except what she or he chooses to reveal. We can't see the person or hear a voice to determine age or gender, so we have no way of verifying whether the sender is indeed the Nobel Prize–winning senior professor she is claiming to be, or whether "she" is really a thirteen-year-old boy just putting us on. We can't get any clues from the stationery on which the message was written, because every e-mail message looks the same when it appears in the window of our mail reading software.

Humans have hundreds of thousands of years of experience in talking to other people, and have been writing for millennia and conversing on the telephone for around a century; however, we have just a few decades of experience with electronic mail. With the other media, we have had time to formulate hundreds of common rules about communication, most of which we follow without ever giving them any conscious thought: When talking to someone, observe the appropriate conventions for social distance, Answer your mail, or When you answer the phone, say something to indicate you're there. We are still evolving the rules for electronic communication, in much the same way that we are learning how to deal with other consequences brought about by the new technology of the Internet.

As always, social consequences eventually bring about laws governing acceptable and unacceptable behavior. For example, every country has laws governing communications with the potential to cause harm. You can be sued for slandering someone if you say something with the intention to cause harm to their reputation, and libel laws exist to protect people from potentially damaging written communications. Laws have evolved defining harassment over the telephone and providing appropriate legal recourse. In many countries, if you tell a telephone solicitor "Please don't call me again," they are legally obligated to obey, and, similarly, you can protect yourself from being deluged by junk mail by requesting the sender to remove your name from their mailing list. As yet, there are few such protections for e-mail.

In spite of society's limited experience with electronic communication, some formal and informal rules have already evolved. As we would expect, these rules are derived from the nature of e-mail technology, as well as from analogies to other media.

The permanence and accountability of e-mail (it's much harder to make a valid case for "I never said that" in e-mail than it is in oral communication, for example) dictate some obvious guidelines:

- "Never say anything in an electronic message that you wouldn't want appearing, and attributed to you, in tomorrow morning's front-page headline in the *New York Times*" (David Russell).
- Reread your message before sending it.
- Cool down, take a coffee break, or wait until tomorrow before responding in anger (which is known as *flaming*).

There are very few nuancing cues in e-mail. When talking to someone, you can often get away with saying something outrageous or sarcastic if you accompany it with body language like a wink. That kind of *para-language* is much harder to do when typing.

- Be very careful with humor, irony, and sarcasm. What might seem completely innocuous to you may very well be interpreted as a violently offensive utterance by someone reading your message.

- If you type something that might be misinterpreted, consider adding a cue like a *smiley* (also known as an *emoticon*). The symbols :-) indicate a smile, ;-) a wry wink, and <g> is shorthand for "grin." Get the picture, dimwit? ;-)
- DON'T SHOUT. All-caps text is conventionally interpreted as shouting by most experienced netizens, so use it with care. (It's also much harder to read than the conventional mixture of capital and lowercase letters.)
- Reread a message before firing off a flaming response. Ask yourself, "Could I possibly be misinterpreting the sender's intent?" Even if you're convinced that the sender's intent was to be offensive, it's far better to capture the moral high ground in your response by being reasonable and mild than it is to answer offense with offense. Flame wars get tediously boring very quickly.

It costs essentially nothing to send e-mail. That's certainly a good thing, but you have to keep in mind the fact that every e-mail message takes up space on a number of servers, not to mention the fact that, strictly speaking, each e-mail message belongs to the originator by copyright law.

- While it's easy to send a copy of a message to a friend, there are many times when you should think twice before entering someone's name in the CC: or Forward To: line. An excellent example of this happened to us a few years ago, when a group of our friends were charged with preparing a position paper on a topic. Each revision was forwarded to the dozen or so members of the committee, and all responses were likewise broadcast, resulting in every message appearing twelve times on the server. There are better ways of collaboration, as you'll see in the lab exercises for this module.
- E-mail is intended to be a one-to-one communication. Don't broadcast e-mail you receive unless you first have the sender's permission. As we'll see when we talk about intellectual property on the Net, retransmitting someone's e-mail without permission is a violation of copyright law.

Review Questions

1. What was one of the early surprises of e-mail use on the Net?
2. What is a dotted quad? What has more or less replaced it?
3. In what ways is e-mail like conventional mail, telephone conversations, and face-to-face communication? In what ways does e-mail differ from these older forms of communications?

3.4 APPLICATIONS II: USENET NEWS

Newsgroups are Internet discussion groups devoted to a particular subject. Participants *post* messages that can then be read by any other participant. Unlike e-mail, which is usually one to one, newsgroup posts are often read by thousands of people.

You can think of a newsgroup as a large room, with perhaps thousands of people arriving, listening, and departing. Every so often, one person may stand up and say something, and their remarks are immediately placed on a wall full of other messages, for everyone to read.

As with e-mail, to participate in Usenet you need a special program, like Newswatcher, or a program with news-reading facilities, like Netscape Navigator or Microsoft's Internet Explorer. The newsreader gives you access to your local news server, a petty tyrant that keeps a database of some (but not all) of the newsgroups available. The news server keeps track of its own "local" groups, along with messages in other groups, which it receives from neighboring news servers (which are forwarded from their neighbors, and so on). Similarly, if you post an article, it propagates outward from your server to its neighbors, their neighbors, and so on.

■ How Usenet Works

Newsgroup names are arranged hierarchically, in order of increasing specialization. Notice that this is exactly the reverse of the situation with Internet addresses, where the domain names are arranged in increasing order of size. For example, `rec.arts.drwho` is the group in the major domain `rec`, the domain of newsgroups devoted to topics of recreational interest. Within that domain, the `arts` subdomain includes all the groups related to the arts, and within that group we find the drwho newsgroup, devoted to discussions about the TV series *Doctor Who*. The main top-level categories are `alt` and the "big 8": `comp`, `humanities`, `misc`, `news`, `rec`, `sci`, `soc`, and `talk`.

This "ill-defined distributed machine," in the words of Thomas Briedbart, is known as *Usenet*. At the time of this writing, there are somewhere around ten million regular Usenet participants, reading and posting messages to something like 18,000 newsgroups. There are groups devoted to cats, video games, beer, ballet, HIV, bicycles, NIN, jokes, erotic pictures, comic books, polymer chemistry, alien visitations, cooking, Scientology, Turkish politics—virtually any subject you might be interested in (and lots you wouldn't be). Like the Internet, Usenet has experienced explosive growth, from 3 groups in 1979 to about 18,000 today. To give you an idea of the nature of Usenet, consider the following facts, the interpretation of which we leave up to you.

- The top newsgroups by number of readers:

1. `news.announce.newusers`, containing useful information for Usenet "newbies" (with about 600,000 readers at any given time).
2. `alt.sex`, devoted to general discussions of sexual subjects (500,000 readers).
3. The list continues with `alt.sex.stories` and `alt.binaries.pictures.erotica`. Nine of the top twenty groups by number of readers are sex-related. The most popular nonnews, nonsex group is `misc.jobs.offered`.

- The top newsgroups by volume of information transferred: All but one of these fall in the category `alt.binaries`, which makes sense when you consider that pictures, program code, sounds, and such take far more storage space than plain text. Again, the overwhelming majority of these are sex-related, usually consisting of archives of pictures.

- The top newsgroups by number of postings:

1. `misc.jobs.offered`
2. `rec.games.trading-cards.marketplace`
3. `alt.binaries.warez.ibm-pc`

What Usenet Is; What Usenet Isn't

A newsgroup is a community—a group of people with shared interests communicating. In a newsgroup you can decide to sit back and listen to the conversations (known as *lurking*), you can participate in a discussion by posting your own messages, you can get help or help someone else, or you can get support or furnish support and comfort to someone else. It's not like most communities you know, though—a fact that takes a bit of getting used to. First, a particular newsgroup is open to anyone, but (except in the rare cases of moderated newsgroups) not controlled by anyone. You don't have to sign up; there are no membership requirements except an interest in the group's subject. A newsgroup (NG, for short) is somewhat like a club, except there's no one around to greet you and explain the rules and customs when you come in the door.

As in other communities, inappropriate behavior in a newsgroup is discouraged by both formal and informal means. Language that is offensive or inappropriate will often lead to responses ranging from gentle reminders to vitriolic flames. Off-topic posts—messages that have nothing to do with the group's stated purpose—may be followed by requests to move the discussion elsewhere. Depending on the newsgroup, responses to inappropriate behavior might be mild and forgiving or might be devastatingly harsh. Complicating the confusion for newcomers, the rules of behavior vary considerably from one group to another: Posts that are common and acceptable in `alt.tasteless`, for instance, might be considered wildly out of line in `rec.pets.cats`.

In addition to responses from newsgroup members, there are more formal methods of discouraging inappropriate behavior, just as there are in other communities. Severe cases of *spamming*—posting duplicate messages to many newsgroups simultaneously—may result in automatic cancellation of messages (so that they don't propagate through the Net) by programs known as *cancelbots*. A cancelbot is programmed to look for messages that exceed a threshold number of recipient newsgroups and issue a cancel request. Cancelbots are tolerated by the Usenet community because spamming is generally agreed to be improper: It wastes huge amounts of space on hundreds of news servers, the messages are almost always off-topic for most of the recipient groups (even though the originator might feel differently), and they waste the time of the readers who have to read at least the first few lines before quitting with a snort of disgust. It's important to realize that spam cancelations are not made on the basis of content, only on the amount of cross-posting. You are free to say anything you want—almost—in a newsgroup, but you have to bear in mind that this freedom extends to others, too. In the words of an oft-cited anonymous quote, "Anarchy means having to put up with things that really piss you off."

This is not to say that anything goes in the Usenet community. Chronic and acute offensive behavior can, in severe cases, result in the sender having his or her access to the local news server terminated, the electronic equivalent of banishment. Many news servers are run by colleges and universities and if the administrators (newsadmins) receive enough e-mail about one of their user's offensive behavior, they might decide not to have that individual associated with their organization's electronic communications. Access to Usenet is not a right; rather it is a privilege extended to members using the local server. Even more formal remedies exist, of course, for controlling inappropriate behavior. Libel laws have repeatedly been held to apply to electronic communications. "Make Money Fast" pyramid scams, where the victim sends money to the top few names on a list and then adds his or her name to the list and passes it on to a number of others, are a clear violation of the laws of many countries. Despite comforting assurances like "This is completely legal, since you are only being added to a mailing list," the fact is that a pyramid scam is illegal in most countries; if any money changes hands, it can result in criminal prosecution.

Virtual Communities

Participation in the community of a Usenet newsgroup can be deeply satisfying. You may develop lasting friendships with people in other countries who you may never meet in person. Your age, gender, race, disability, and religious or ethnic background are only as public as you wish them to be. In a newsgroup, it is truly the case that you are what you write. To a large extent, you are judged by the community of your group solely on the basis of what you say. Where else can you say something—almost anything you wish, really—and know that what you say will be heard by thousands of people?

On the other hand, this liberating freedom to say what you want comes with a price. You are entering a potentially vast community whose rules are generally never made explicit. If you innocently step over the bounds of appropriate behavior, you may discover you've made a fool of yourself in front of thousands of people all over the world. This, as we can attest from personal experience, can be immensely humiliating.

A common problem is "clueless newbie" behavior, which is to say behavior that demonstrates ignorance of Usenet behavior. A clueless newbie might, for example, test his or her newsreader by posting a message consisting solely of the phrase "This is a test." This is quite common and is an obvious violation of netiquette: It is of no interest to anyone in the group, it wastes space on hundreds of news servers, and takes up the readers' valuable time. The newsgroups `alt.test` and `misc.test` are made for just these kinds of tests.

Another sign of clueless newbie-ism is asking a question that is so central to the topic of the group that it has been seen dozens of times already by the seasoned readers. Participants in `alt.folklore.urban` will groan with dismay when they see "I heard from a friend that a local [Chinese, Thai, Cuban—pick your favorite ethnic group] restaurant serves cat disguised as lamb," just as readers of `sci.math` will respond to "Why [is or isn't] .99999999... equal to 1?" Many newsgroups have a few kindly regulars who have compiled a list of answers to frequently asked questions (FAQ) that cover just these commonly heard questions.

The best advice for newbies who wish to avoid appearing clueless is to lurk for a while, looking for the limits of acceptable behavior and getting a feel for the kinds of questions that evoke helpful responses and the kinds that garner quick directions to the appropriate FAQ. As with e-mail, there are some commonly agreed on rules of netiquette that hold in most groups:

- You are participating in a community whose rules are not obvious at the start. Lurk for a while before jumping in.
- Think about your audience. Some questions or discussions are better continued via e-mail, especially if they're of no interest to the rest of the group or are something the group has heard dozens of times already.
- Some participants are paying for Net access by the minute: Keep your responses short, to the point, and clearly identified in the subject header, and only quote the parts of the original message that are absolutely necessary to give others a clue about the context of your response. Don't quote 350 lines of a message only to add "Me too."
- Usenet is characterized by the same lack of nuancing as e-mail. Use the same care we mentioned earlier.
- Remember, it will take three to five days for your message to propagate to all the readers of a group. Sometimes responses will arrive at your news server before the original message. Live with it and cultivate patience.
- Don't advertise. Usenet has a long tradition of being noncommercial. The common analogy is walking into a club and shouting out that you have a car for sale. Count yourself lucky if you don't get tossed out on the street.
- Keep in mind the common purpose of the group. There's nothing to be gained by going into `comp.sys.mac.advocacy` and saying "PCs rule; Macs are crap!" just as there's nothing to be gained by posting an antigun diatribe on `rec.hunting`.

LAB 3.2

You Never Write

One of the forces that helped to popularize the Internet, and ultimately led to the development of the WWW, was the interest in and demand for electronic mail. Today, e-mail is an accepted and useful means for communication between computers located in peoples' homes, businesses, and dorm rooms. In fact, public forums have even been developed so that e-mailers can be in touch with large groups of people all at once and can participate in virtual, online, group discussions through newsgroups, discussion groups, interest groups, and the like. Since WWW users tend to be people who are predisposed to using e-mail, it is not surprising that the lines between these communication services (Web servers, mail servers, and newsgroups) have already blurred. Indeed, many browsers have built-in mail and newsgroup facilities.

Use whatever e-mail service is available to you to do the following:

1. Send an e-mail message to your instructor telling her or him how much you are enjoying this course (it doesn't hurt!).
2. We have established a discussion group for AE Online. To get to the discussion group simply follow the link in the lab exercise. Then, do Exercises 3 and 4.
3. Read some of the postings from other AE Online users.
4. Post a message of your own to the group describing your experience to date in using AE Online.

Note that the discussion group uses WWW forms, instead of e-mail, to post your message to a central repository on the server instead of sending the message once and having it inaccessible to future readers.

Review Questions

1. What is Usenet?
2. How do newsgroup postings differ from e-mail?
3. What are the top level domains of Usenet? What domain would you try first to find a newsgroup devoted to skiing?
4. What is the most popular topic of discussion on Usenet?
5. What's *lurking*? Is it a good thing? Why or why not?

3.5 APPLICATIONS III: THE WORLD WIDE WEB

◆ CERN is the acronym for the *Conseil Européen pour la Recherche Nucléaire*, a major European particle physics lab.

The newest (and hottest) addition to the Internet family, the World Wide Web (WWW, or the Web, for short) dates back just to 1989, with a proposal by researchers at CERN. The Web consists of a collection of computers, most of which are on the Internet. A significant number, however, are connected to purely local *intranets,* which may be completely disconnected from any machines in the wider world. These computers all have software, known as *browsers,* that allow them to send and receive documents according to a particular collection of standards, known as the *hypertext transfer protocol* (HTTP).

Web documents are quite different from the rest of digital information in that they are what is known as *distributed hypermedia.* A hypermedia document is not limited to a certain type of information; it may contain text, but mingled with the text there might also be graphic images, sounds, movies, and anything else that can be digitally encoded, shipped to another computer, and reconstituted at the receiving end. All of this information is melded together in a seamless whole. Thus, a *hypertext* document (as it is also known) about colobus monkeys might contain a textual description of their habitat, physical characteristics, social behavior, and the like, along with pictures of a family group, the sounds of their calls, and an animated clip of their threat behavior.

Of course, the concept of hypermedia originated long before 1989; what made the CERN proposal so important was that it included the idea of having a hypertext document include *links* to other documents, even those stored at other computers. This is why we use the term *distributed* hypermedia: A Web page may appear as a single visual entity, but the information it contains may come from a number of files, stored on computers spread across the globe. The microworld of hypermedia began as a model of printed literature, but as with all microworlds it rapidly acquired features that weren't present in the original. The presence of links to other documents allows the reader to explore a topic in a nonlinear fashion. Rather than reading a document from start to finish in the traditional way, users of hypermedia such as the World Wide Web are free to explore side paths and follow links to topics that might be only distantly related to the main topic.

◆ If this growth were to continue, there would be more Web sites than people on earth by 2006. By comparison, it is estimated that the number of Internet sites as a whole is increasing by a mere 10 percent a month.

Such a project clearly required a considerable amount of work: Not only did standards have to be developed for the way text, pictures, sounds, and the like were to be represented in binary, but browsers had to be invented to support the display of all this information and to handle the process of calling up hypertext documents from other computers on the Internet. By 1993 the first browsers had been developed and the World Wide Web was born, with some 50 sites supporting these linked hypertext documents by January of that year. Within just nine months, Web messages represented one percent of all Internet traffic. By June 1994 there were about 1500 Web sites; by April of 1995 Web traffic moved to the top of Net use, representing 26 percent of all traffic on the Internet and surpassing e-mail. Today the number of Web sites is approaching one hundred thousand, and according to one estimate, the number currently doubles every 53 days. It's important to realize that the World Wide Web is not a physical entity, like the Internet or a purely local intranet. Rather, it is a concept we use to refer to the documents, their links, and the browsers used to view and interact with this collection. If we think of the Internet as a village, we observe that every building has an address, but some of the buildings also have fancy signs and display windows indicating who lives there and enticing you to visit. These are the Web sites.

Factors in Web Growth

You've already seen that the growth of computer use, by any reasonable measure, has been amazing. As fast as the use of computers increased, though, this growth was completely eclipsed by the rapidity of the development of the Internet. As the most recent in a chain of surprises, the Web has exploded even faster than the Internet. What's the explanation?

First, the Web is *easy to use*. There is an almost unimaginable amount of information available on the Internet, but finding it used to be hard. Back in the ancient days of the 1980s, if you wanted to find some information you needed to know what computer it was on, what the address of the computer was, and which file in the machine contained it. There were some programs, like Fetch, Gopher, and Archie, that allowed you to look for the information you wanted and then get it, but they weren't all that easy to use.

Because a Web document can have links to other documents, the collection of Web documents is extremely dense logically, if not physically. Let's assume for the sake of argument that each Web document has an average of five links to other documents. If you can find one document even remotely close to your topic, it is then likely to be linked to five others. Two links away, then, there are 25 sites, and 125 within three links, and so on. The odds are good that if you can find even one entry point to a particular topic, following a few links will quickly provide you with all the information you could ever want. Notice that you never have to know the address (the *URL,* as it's called, for Uniform Resource Locator) of the other documents—all you have to do is navigate through the links provided for you.

A second reason for the growth of the Web is that *it's easy to search*. Even if you don't know where to start, *search engines* will do the searching for you. A *spider* is a program that spends all its time following links from one Web document to another, recording the keywords it finds in each document. These keywords are stored in databases connected to other Web pages, such as the ones run by Yahoo!, Lycos, Infoseek, Alta Vista, or Excite, to name a few. All you have to do is get to one of these search engine pages, submit the words or topics you're interested in, and the search engine will return a collection of links to related pages found by its spider. To find information on colobus monkeys, for instance, you would no longer need to know where the information was located. Instead, you could point your browser to one of these search engines and tell it to look for the keyword "colobus." The engine would then look in its database and return the Net addresses of all the locations where it had found the word "colobus." Just for fun, we tried this with several search engines and the results ranged from a low of 50 sites to a high of 709. We found enough text, photographs, video clips, and sounds in the space of a few minutes to satisfy anyone's curiosity about *colobus abyssinicus*.

Third, *it's easy to make a Web page*. As we'll see, a Web page is just a text document with some special features. You can learn how to make a simple Web page in half an hour. In two weeks you can be a very good Page Maker. In a month, you can be an expert, though it might take longer to learn the difference between getting the job done and producing something beautiful and useful. Learning how to make Web pages is facilitated by the fact that there's nothing hidden on the Web: If you see a nifty page, you can always inspect the underlying document to see how it was done.

◆ See for yourself: Pick a company and see if there's a page at `http://www.company_name.com/`

Finally, unlike much of the rest of the Internet, which reflects its academic origins in a diligent avoidance of anything that smacks of filthy lucre, there are *no commercial restrictions on the Web*. With millions of potential viewers, commercial enterprises see the Web as cheap advertising—making a Web site costs a small fraction of an ad on television. As a result, the `com` domain passed `edu` in number of sites in October 1994, due in no small measure to the presence of the Web. Some Web documents have the ability to obtain information from a visitor and send it to the files on the host machine, a very useful feature for "electronic mail-order." In addition, a business can place their advertising links on other people's pages, paying for the number of times their link is accessed. At present, lots of people are drooling over the potential of making huge bucks on the Web; by and large, it hasn't happened yet. As we'll see later, one of the things stumping the business world is how to pry any money out of a medium that is, for all practical purposes, free and uncontrolled.

Technical Details

However complicated the actual details are, the basic idea the people at CERN came up with is really quite simple. We begin with yet another protocol, HTML, which stands for *hypertext markup language.* A Web page is described as an ordinary text document, of the kind that even the simplest word processor can produce, containing one or more *tags,* which are collections of characters that are interpreted in special ways as indicators of text formatting, links to other Web documents, graphic images, and so on. For example, here is a snippet of HTML:

```
<H2>Web Growth</H2>
There are four main factors that contributed to the
growth of the World Wide Web.
<OL>
        <LI>It's <I>easy to use.</I>
        <LI>It's <I>easy to search.</I>
        <LI>It's <I>easy to make a Web page.</I>
        <LI>There are <B>no commercial restrictions.</B>
</OL>
```

When the browser has completed the task of interpreting the HTML tags, such as <I>, the document will be displayed on the screen as a Web page that might look like the one in Figure 3.2.

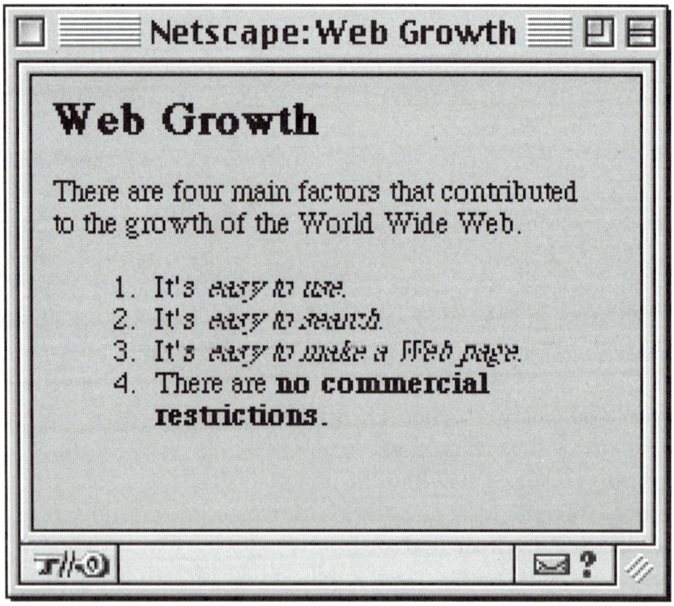

FIGURE 3.2
An HTML document displayed by a browser

We'll have much more to say about HTML and Web page design in Module 4, but even knowing nothing yet about the meaning of the tags, it should be pretty easy to deduce what the ones in this example do: `<H2>` and `</H2>` cause the enclosed text to be displayed in some sort of header format, `<I>` and `</I>` enclose text to be italicized, and `<B>` and `</B>` enclose text that is to be displayed in boldface. The `<OL>` and `</OL>` tags indicate the start and end of an ordered list, with list items indicated by `<LI>`.

When you point your browser at a page, or go to a new page by following a link, the browser first finds the computer indicated by the HTML link code. It then requests the remote computer to send it a copy of the required HTML document, along with any necessary graphics, sound, and movie files. The browser then collects all these pieces together and displays them on its own computer as dictated by the HTML document it just received (Figure 3.3).

In simple terms, then, to build a Web page of your own all you need is a computer, a text editor, and a browser, so you can look at your results. To make your Web page available to others, the only extra thing you need to do is get permission to put your documents on a computer that already has the extra software to serve requests for your documents, or purchase the software yourself, if your computer is already connected to the Internet or a local intranet. It's precisely this ease and transparency that has opened the way for an avalanche of grassroots electronic self-publication—making a page of your own that can be seen by a potential audience of millions is so easy almost anyone can do it

FIGURE 3.3
The browser handles the display of HTML documents

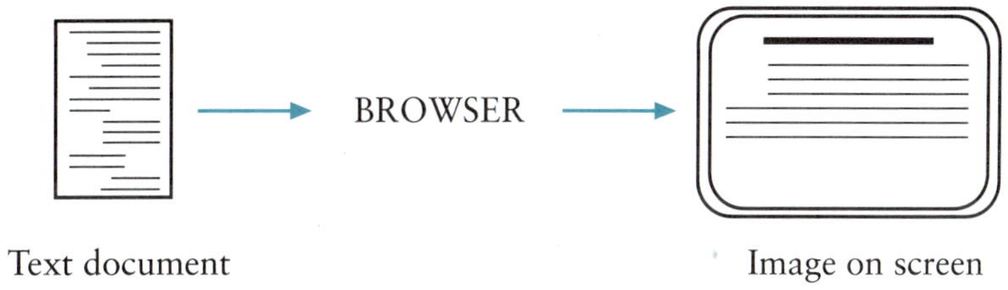

LAB 3.3

Been Searchin'

Given the vast amount of information on the WWW, it only makes sense that *search engines,* programs that help us to look through all of the available resources for keywords, have become important tools to WWW users. In this set of exercises, we help you to become familiar with a few search engines, both simple and industrial strength, so that you can use them to locate some very valuable information.

1. You may have noticed that every page for every AE Online module has a Search icon near its top. Clicking on this takes you to a simple search engine that we have

embedded in our pages. This search engine is simple in the sense that it searches only for keywords in the AE Online materials, and so is not useful for doing general Web-wide searches. But it will show you what is possible with a general search engine on a smaller scale. It does a pretty good job as an automated index for our online materials. To use it, click on the Search icon from any AE Online page. Then enter a word or a phrase into the text field and click the AE Online Search button.

Click the Search icon now, and search the AE Online pages to answer the following questions:

a) How many references are there to Alan Turing in AE Online?
b) What is JavaScript, and which module concentrates on it?
c) Are there any references in AE Online to poetry?
d) What does "MUD" stand for?

Now it's time to use the search engines that are associated with the WWW at large. Your browser may come with its own built-in search engine, or it may provide you with direct links to one or more of the many that are readily available from their own WWW pages. Links to some of the better-known search engines are available in the Resources for this lab. You are free to use these, or any of your choice, to perform the following exercise.

2. Locate each of the items below on the WWW. List on a piece of paper the URL at which you found it, and the keywords or phrase you used to initiate the search. If you are using your own machine and browser, you can bookmark any of the pages you wish.

a) A full-page rendering of the portrait of Mona Lisa by Leonardo da Vinci
b) An index of employment opportunities in your chosen (or anticipated) career field
c) The theme song from *The Rocky and Bullwinkle Show*
d) Information about your favorite actor or actress
e) A position statement by a U.S. representative or senator regarding the Communications Decency Amendment of the 1996 Telecommunications Act
f) Prehistoric caveman drawings
g) A current weather radar report for Tokyo, Japan
h) Product information page for the kind of car you would most want to own
i) An estimation of the current number of WWW sites

Review Questions

1. How much younger is the WWW than the Internet?

2. Define *hypermedia*.

3. What is a spider? How are spiders related to search engines?

4. What factors contributed to the rapid growth of the WWW?

3.6 IMPLICATIONS: AN OVERVIEW OF INTERNET ISSUES

As we've said several times in this book (and will repeat later), technological changes never occur in a vacuum. As soon as a new technology becomes widely used, it spurs a cascade of societal changes, sometimes minor, as in the case of a better mousetrap, and sometimes of vast dimensions, as was the case with railroads, the telephone, and the automobile. It often takes some time for the precise nature of change to be recognized and analyzed. In the case of the Internet, the technology has become pervasive so quickly that we find ourselves as a society in the position of not yet knowing what the eventual effects will be. The social, anthropological, legal, political, and ethical implications of the Internet are at present a moving target. While we certainly can't claim to provide answers to the question "How will the Internet affect me, in particular, and society in general?" we can at least provide some examples of changes that have already taken place and begin a discussion of some of the questions we, and society, will have to answer.

Freedom of Speech

Swayed in part by fear of children having access to pornography on the Internet, the U.S. House and Senate proposed the Communications Decency Act and the president signed it into law in February 1996. This act (blocked by a restraining order almost immediately, later overturned by a panel of federal judges, and finally declared unconstitutional by the Supreme Court) would have imposed severe criminal penalties on anyone providing "indecent" material over the Internet in a fashion such that the material might be seen by children, and might have been interpreted to apply equally well to the owners and operators of any computer through which indecent material was transmitted.

There is a long-standing series of legal precedents that hold that for material to be judged "obscene," and hence not eligible for First Amendment protections, the material must be offensive by local community standards. A couple in California were tried and convicted in a Tennessee court for providing electronic access to pictures that were judged to be obscene by Tennessee standards, even though the material was not deemed to be offensive by Los Angeles community standards.

There are controls on mail and telephone messages: Collection agencies are limited to the times and frequency of their calls, a telephone solicitor is obligated to obey when you say "Please don't call me in the future," and a request for a company to remove you from their mailing list is legally enforceable. No such remedies exist for e-mail.

These are just some instances of society's efforts to understand how traditional safeguards to freedom of expression should be applied to the Internet. Here are a few relevant questions to consider:

- Courts have established different degrees of First Amendment protection for speech, newspapers, books, radio, and television. Where in the spectrum should utterances on the Internet fall?
- Is it the responsibility of state or federal governments to limit the content of information on the Internet, or should this responsibility be left to parents, perhaps aided by blocking software?

- The global nature of the Net transcends state and national boundaries. What sort of control should we expect when, in the words of John Barlow, "the First Amendment is a local ordinance?"
- Should the protection of law be extended to provide a remedy from junk e-mail?

Privacy

Beta versions of Windows 95 contained a company-installed viruslike program, Registration Wizard, that searched the directory structure of each machine on the host computer's local network, recorded what software was installed, and reported the information back to Microsoft. Company officials said that the Registration Wizard was nothing more than an electronic version of the traditional paper registration card. Critics held that such a program represented an unwarranted attack on the privacy of users.

In 1990 the Secret Service raided the home of Steve Jackson and seized his computers, files on disks, papers, and business records. The stated reason was that Steve Jackson Games, a small producer of computer role-playing games, was about to release Gurps Cyberpunk, a game set in a future world with the players' objective being the invasion of other computers to steal data. The Secret Service said that such a game manual provided a "handbook on computer crime." Eventually, all charges against Jackson were dropped, but he claimed that his business had suffered irreparable harm as a result of the raid.

It is simple for the operator of a Web site to acquire programs that keep a log of the Internet addresses of each computer that accesses the site. There are a number of proposals for programs that will use this information to "push" advertising of related (or completely unrelated) materials to visitors of the site, in much the same way that companies keep mailing lists of their customers and sell these lists to other advertisers.

The next example is almost too good to be true. Rather than have you read a paraphrase, we'll quote the entire story as it came off the Internet.

Judge Rules on E-mail Privacy Case

Tulsa, OK—The Oklahoma Supreme Court has ruled on a case that many legal experts believe clearly delineates the e-mail privacy rights of computer users in the workplace. Judge Stan Musing declared that employees have a right to expect that their employers will refrain from monitoring e-mail messages transmitted on company systems.

The case went to court after programmer Augustus Lindsey's supervisor monitored his e-mail and intercepted a message from Lindsey to a colleague. The message read: "That little sex kitten has been driving me wild. She's moaning and begging for it every minute. Last night I was afraid someone would hear, and we'd be thrown out of the building. But don't worry—all is arranged. Wednesday she gets the knife."

Lindsey's supervisor alerted authorities, suspecting that a crime was in the making. Lindsey was arrested on the spot and spent an uncomfortable night discussing the situation with the police. However, he was released in

> the morning, just in time to get his female cat to the vet for spaying. Lindsey sued his boss for invasion of privacy and sought punitive damages as well.

The only problem is that the story almost certainly *is* too good to be true. Repeated searches by skeptics have failed to turn up any mention of this case in Oklahoma court records. Too bad—like so many urban legends, it has the feel of truth, but not the substance. Still, surveys indicate that one out of every fourteen businesses conduct random surveys of employee e-mail.

Here are some privacy-related questions to ponder:

- Should there be limits on the information a remote site can gather about you or your computer system?
- How are Fourth Amendment protections against unreasonable search and seizure applied in cyberspace?
- Since e-mail and Usenet messages pass through many computers, should there be security controls on snooping on your messages or, for example, credit card numbers?
- Does an employer have any right, legally or ethically, to determine or monitor the content of messages generated on company computers?
- Should an employer have the right to monitor an employee's use of company systems? For example, can an employer monitor use on company computers to determine if employees are playing games on company time?

Separating the Wheat from the Chaff

The Internet, and especially the World Wide Web, provides quick and easy access to an almost unimaginably vast store of information. We might think of the Web as a global library, with its search engines acting like our own personal research librarians. The Web differs from a library in one important respect, though. Because it's so easy for people to put their own pages on the Web, we have to modify the image of our global library somewhat. Along with the clients interested in looking up information, we also have to imagine a steady stream of people coming in, adding their own books to the shelves, modifying their books, and removing them or moving them to different locations.

As you can well imagine, this is an image that would give most librarians a screaming fit. Though you may not have considered it, an important underlying assumption about the nature of libraries is that they are, for the most part, repositories of reliable information. Librarians control the content of libraries by deciding what books to purchase, how to catalogue them, and where to place them on the shelves. In addition, books are for the most part produced under editorial direction, to ensure that they are factually correct. Such controls are by no means guaranteed for World Wide Web documents.

Look, for example, at the e-mail privacy article we quoted above. A quick search turned up nearly a dozen Web pages that contained either the article itself or a link to it. With that many appearances, one might reasonably believe the article was indeed factually correct. We tend not to question everything we read—not only would it take more time than we possess to verify each assertion we read, but we're also accustomed to assume, justifiably, that newspaper articles and books from reputable publishers are more or less reliable sources of information. Someone once asked Theodore Sturgeon, a science fiction author, "Isn't ninety percent of all science fiction nothing but junk?" After thinking a moment, Sturgeon admitted that was true, but added what has come to be known as *Sturgeon's Law:* "Ninety percent of everything is junk." While this law isn't correct when applied to Sturgeon's own writings, it certainly should be kept in mind when mining the Web for information.

Because the Internet allows information to be disseminated so rapidly, it serves as a fertile breeding ground for gossip, rumor, innuendo, and hoaxes. For example, one recent piece of misinformation concerns the Goodtimes virus. The story, usually circulated via e-mail, reads like this: "The FCC has discovered a virus which infects your computer if you read a message with 'Good Times' written in the subject line. Simply reading the message will destroy your computer's processor by setting it into an 'n-th complexity infinite loop.'" This sounds truly frightening, and many well-intentioned people read the alert and passed it along to their friends and colleagues. The problem, though, is that the message had utterly no basis in fact. As with other urban legends, it sounds reasonable, though. Few people have the expertise to realize that the Federal Communications Commission has nothing to do with identifying computer viruses and fewer still know enough computer science to realize that "n-th complexity infinite loop" is nothing but meaningless jargon, and that an e-mail message is no more likely to destroy the circuitry of a computer than harsh language is to curdle milk. There is indeed a virus here, spreading insidiously from one host to another, but it's a virus of ideas, not the computer variety.

◆ Ironically, many people circulated this warning with "Good Times" in the subject line of their message.

- Just how useful is the World Wide Web as a source of information?
- When looking at a Web page, how can we determine the difference between fact, opinion, well-intentioned misinformation, and deliberate lies?

■ Weapons in the Library

The Internet is far from being a secure medium. Packets sent over the Net are easy to intercept and decipher, a fact you might want to keep in mind when sending sensitive e-mail or posting an order with a credit card. Fortunately, there is—in theory, at least—an easy solution. One way to ensure the security of our electronic communications is to adopt a solution that dates back at least 2000 years: Code the message before you send it. Computers are particularly good at encrypting outgoing messages and decrypting the messages at the receiving end. It's very easy to write a program to produce a code that is, for all practical purposes, unbreakable, and such programs are in daily use to provide secure transmission of electronic funds transfer messages between banks, for example. Each day, hundreds of millions of dollars worth of such messages are sent over what are essentially unsecure channels, like phone lines and microwave transmitters.

Traditionally, much work in cryptography has been motivated by the military and intelligence arms of national governments, as we saw in Module 1 when we discussed the use of the Colossus computer to break the Enigma code. The U.S. government is sufficiently interested in control over cryptographic technology that the International Traffic in Arms Regulations (ITAR) defines cryptographic programs, articles, and books on cryptography as "munitions" and places controls on their export and use by foreign nationals residing in the United States. Under a strict interpretation of ITAR, then, most large libraries and bookstores have munitions on their shelves.

Restrictions on cryptographic technology weren't particularly noteworthy as long as the necessary computer equipment was so costly as to be unavailable to private and corporate users. Now, however, such computer power is available to anyone with enough money to purchase a personal computer. Programs such as Phil Zimmerman's Pretty Good Privacy (PGP) place effectively unbreakable cryptography within the reach of anyone using the Internet, and this development has caused considerable consternation in some circles in recent years. The government justifies limitations on the use of cryptography in part by the argument that allowing free use of encryption resources would make it virtually impossible to intercept messages sent by criminals, terrorists, and foreign agents. Pro-crypto critics, on the other hand, argue that the needs of the citizenry for privacy override the state's need for security.

This tension between individual liberty and community security is not new, by any means. It was an issue that was on the minds of the founding fathers of this country when they added protections against unreasonable search and seizure to the Constitution, deciding to limit the powers of law enforcement agencies in the interest of individual privacy. As we've seen before in this module, the new technology of computers and, particularly, the Internet forces us to evaluate our assumptions about law and social behavior in a new context.

- Is it even feasible to restrict cryptographic technology when information can be broadcast worldwide over the Internet?
- The courts have repeatedly upheld the government's right to limit free speech when such free speech clearly poses danger to others. Is there such an identifiable danger in the case of cryptographic information and programs?
- Should we be swayed by arguments from business and academia that such restrictions have a chilling effect on commerce and research in some areas?
- How reasonable, from a practical point of view, are the government's arguments in favor of restrictions on cryptography?

Intellectual Property

Most countries are signatories to the Berne Convention, which gives creators of original works rights of ownership of their creations. Copyright is, in the United States at least, intended to promote the creation of original works, such as novels, term papers, sculptures, paintings, and photographs, by giving the creators legal control over how these works are reproduced, disseminated, and modified. If you see a representation of Mickey Mouse or hear Homer Simpson's "D'ooh!" on someone's Web page, it is almost certain that the creator of the page is in violation of copyright law.

In most cases, it is the work of a mouse click and a few minutes of time to copy Microsoft Excel or a game such as Marathon or Quake. If you have your own computer, does your hard drive contain any software that you copied? If, as is probably the case, your answer is yes, the producer of the software is entitled to sue you.

- Should the same penalties be employed for taking a two-second sample from a U2 song as for placing the whole song on a Web page?
- It would be impractically expensive for Disney to go after every Web page producer who has used an image of Ariel or Cinderella. Does that make copying legal in these cases? Does that make it morally right?
- Does the legal framework depend on whether the copied material is on a publicly available Web page or on a page that is intended solely for the viewing of the producer?
- A common rationalization for software piracy is "I wouldn't have paid for the software anyway, so the producer isn't losing any money from my copying." Is this position morally justifiable? What about the argument "Bill Gates has too much money already; I'm copying Word as a protest!"
- Should we admit that the whole issue of ownership of intellectual property should be rethought for the Internet, given the ease and inevitability of copying? How would you redesign the machinery of intellectual property to be fair to both producers and consumers?

Feeding Frenzy

The large telecommunications companies, the ones who provide telephone and cable TV service, look at the Internet and drool over the potential vast audience, who are presently getting all their information for free, or at most for the cost of a local call and a monthly service fee. The problem is not only that they want to fill their coffers from Internet service charges, but that they are happiest thinking of the old model of information that is transferred in one direction—from the station into the home. Right now, the telecom lobbyists have the ear of the legislature and the executive branch of the government. With few exceptions, there are no voices for the grassroots, anarchic, organic Internet we've come to enjoy. If the telecom companies have their way, some people worry that you can kiss your own Web pages goodbye.

In an attempt to access a potential $2.5 trillion market of people who currently do not own computers, a number of industry heavy hitters, including Sun and Oracle, are betting heavily on the Network Computer (NC), a stripped-down computer without hard disk, keyboard, or monitor. Designed to be sold for about $500, this device would attach to a television and would provide Net access. If a user needed a spreadsheet, one could be downloaded off the Net, for example. This package would include a SmartCard, somewhat like an ATM card, that would allow a user to access their files from any NC (and, of course, would provide convenient billing).

- Should the Internet become nothing more than a box attached to the top of your TV with a single button, labeled Buy This?
- One of the stipulations of the original Communications Act of 1934 was that in exchange for a monopoly on telephone service, phone companies had to provide "universal access" to their services. Should there be similar universal access to the Internet; if so, how should it be implemented?
- How practical is the Network Computer concept? Is it currently a viable choice, considering speed of access to the Net, pricing, and user preferences? Would you buy one?

Review Questions

1. What is the Communications Decency Act? What is its current legal status?

2. Give two examples of the tension between privacy and the needs of others for information about an individual.

3. In what ways is the WWW like, and unlike, a library?

4. What do PGP and NC stand for?

3.7 EXERCISES

1. Try an experiment: Send e-mail to a friend and record how long it takes for your message to arrive. Does the delay time stay pretty much the same for several messages? Does the time of day have anything to do with the delay? Try the same experiment with several friends in different locations and see whether the delay time is influenced in any significant way by the geographic distance.

2. What is the dotted quad IP address of your local Internet connection?

3. If you could put a dollar in an investment that grows as fast as the number of hosts on the Internet, how much money would you have in ten years?

4. How does one go about registering domain names? This will require a bit of research on your part—search for "InterNIC" as a starting point.

5. Who owns the `apple.com` domain: Apple Computer, Apple Records, or someone else? Come up with a set of possible reasons that explain the ownership.

6. Make up a table in which the columns are headed *Face-to-face, Snailmail, Telephone,* and *e-mail.* Label the rows with the following characteristics of communication:

   - *Speed* of communication, from the time a message is sent to the time it is received.
   - *Synchronization,* measuring how fast the interval between a message and its response is.
   - *Permanence* of messages.
   - *Formality* of conversation in each medium.
   - *Accountability,* measuring how easy it is to refute a claim of "I never said that."
   - *Cost* of using this medium.
   - *Accessibility* of this medium to all members of society.
   - *Security* of a conversation against being overheard by others.
   - *Nuancing,* measuring how much information can be sent in addition to the words of the conversation.

   Fill in each of the resulting 36 cells with a rating one of High, Medium, or Low.

7. Some people are disturbed by the apparently heavy concentration of sex-related sites on the Internet in general and Usenet in particular, but that's just a fact of life. More interesting, though, is to ask why such a concentration exists. Speculate, perhaps after doing some research into the videocasette market.

8. If you have access to a newsreader (or to DejaNews, an archive of Usenet posts), find a flame war in some newsgroup and report on what the disagreement is, the nature of the flames (personal attacks, insults, illogical arguments, and so on), and what the other posters in the group seem to feel about the conflict.

9. Find an example of hypermedia that is not Net-related.

10. We've mentioned that technology always carries with it the possibility of social, legal, political, economic, and ethical changes. Let's take a hypothetical example: Suppose someone were to come up with a proposal for a device that would allow communications to follow a person

no matter where he or she went. In other words, with this device in my pocket (or, perhaps, surgically embedded), someone could call my number and the call would be automatically transferred to the phone nearest to where I was. List several pros and cons of such a proposal, and argue for or against its adoption. Would your position change if the proposal were presented as a requirement for everyone?

MODULE 4

Designing for Use

4.1 INTRODUCTION

You've seen a brief technological history of computers and some state-of-the-art applications, but you probably have almost no idea about what goes into constructing such local and global applications. Your WWW experience up till now has been limited to using the mouse to navigate through pages and using some of the basic services that are supported by your browser. We have designed these next two modules, both the text and the lab exercises, so that your Web experience and your knowledge of computer science will increase together—in parallel, if you will. In a sense, we are using the WWW both as a model of and as a medium for experimentation with the principles of program design.

MODULE OBJECTIVES

Up to this point, the computer, its programs, and the Web have been black boxes—perhaps fascinating, perhaps complicated, and probably incomprehensible in their details. In this module, we will explore the design process, showing you how complicated systems are constructed. By the end of this module, the black box will have become a gray box, and you will be ready for the next module, on programming, in which we make the box transparent, exposing even more of its inner workings.

Toward that end, we will

- Examine the evolution of the user interface.
- Discuss the desirable features of a user interface.
- Explore the composition of a WWW page.
- Demonstrate how to use the HyperText Markup Language (HTML) to design a variety of sample pages.
- Use the techniques illustrated in our sample pages to develop your own home page.

The User Interface

This module will introduce you to the principles of system design. We will concentrate on an important part of the design of any system, the *user interface*. The user interface is the aspect of a program or machine that is visible to the user. We will explore some of the desirable features of a user interface and speculate on the ways in which people might interact with computers in the future.

Along the way, we will introduce you to the HyperText Markup Language (HTML, for short) that is used to define all WWW pages. Every Web page has a style, format, and organization—a design—that provides an interface to everyone who visits that page. HTML was developed specifically for the purpose of describing such interfaces. You will see that it provides commands to describe the kinds of text, links, images, lists, tables, and frames that you have seen and used on many WWW pages. You will also see that HTML is easy to use in its own right, as you apply it to the task of creating your own home page in the associated lab exercises.

Although we will pay particular attention to the look and feel of a page, bear in mind that the principles we discuss apply to other aspects of a computer system as well. Just remember that at the system level, we are interested mainly in the smooth interaction of the major pieces, not the details of how they work.

Metaphor: Architectural Drawings

One of many continuing themes in this book and the labs is the importance of levels of abstraction when viewing a subject as complex as computer science. The notion of concentrating on the big picture to avoid being bogged down by details is important in all disciplines, but especially it is so in computer science.

In designing a user interface level, we want the freedom to concentrate on what information is to be presented and how it can be presented in the most useful and natural form for the intended audience. We don't want to concern ourselves with the details of how a specific computer indicates bold or emphasized text, what it takes to display an image on a certain part of the screen, or how to make a new page come up when we click on some "hot text."

The combination of HTML and your browser affords you this freedom of expression. The HyperText Markup Language was designed to allow us to describe directly all of the features and functionality that we have come to expect from WWW pages. Not only is it easy to define pages in terms of formatted text, images, sounds, tables, lists, frames, backgrounds, colors, and links to a variety of Internet resources, but we do so in a generic, text-based manner that can be interpreted by any browser program. Indeed, all of the gory details about how best to display a given page on a given machine are left to the browser program, as it reads through our HTML document.

In this sense, we function much like an architect might in designing a building. We think about the space we have to work with and how it can best be used to accommodate all of the features that are to be included. We are careful to include any navigational tools that will facilitate the flow of traffic in and around the site. We do our best to organize the site so that it fits the patterns of use and the expectations of those who will use it. Finally, we try to accomplish all of this with an artistic flair, so that our building is beautiful as well as functional. From this top-level design perspective, we can lay out our building (or our Web page, or a computer application) without having to deal with any of the low-level details. Just as the architect can leave to the builders decisions like what size screws to use to insert a window into a wall, Web page designers can let the browser decide how much white space to leave around a centered title.

Æ Online

In the lab exercises for this module, we walk you through the development of a typical Web page, in this case a hypothetical home page for your authors. Each exercise concentrates on a few basic HTML features, illustrating in side-by-side fashion how one uses the feature in an HTML document and how that part of the document is displayed by your browser. We then have you apply these techniques to the task of developing your own home page.

Finally, you'll subject your page to review – by a classmate, your instructor, and yourself – in terms of the stylistic criteria we describe in the text. While our coverage is necessarily limited to the most useful and basic HTML features, you'll see more than enough by the end of this module to create an interesting and nice-looking home page of your own. You'll also understand the HTML language well enough to use more comprehensive resources (we provide links to many of them) to develop both your language and design skills even further.

4.2 PEOPLE AND MACHINES

We will begin by talking about the good old days, which weren't so long ago and weren't always good. In the very early days of computers, the only users were the specialists—the programmers who had written the programs and who were intimately acquainted with their quirks and foibles. The very first user interface was wires and plugs: To change ENIAC's program, the operator literally had to rebuild the computer by reconnecting the components.

Evolution of the User Interface

It didn't take long for the programmers/designers/engineers of computers (often the same person held all three titles) to realize that rebuilding the computer for each new task took entirely too much time. Even the earliest efforts of Atanasoff, Zuse, and Mauchley and Eckert soon came equipped with devices (switches or a keyboard) to control the connections between the functional units of the computer. How these devices controlled the action of these computers is a subject we will cover later; for now it is enough to assert that they did indeed allow the operator to instruct the machine so that the computer carried out the instructions with a minimum of supervision. One turned on the machine, set the right switches or pushed the right key, and let 'er rip. Although the Analytical Engine was never completed, Babbage had much the same idea a century before, when he envisioned storing the sequence of instructions on Jacquard-like cards, to be executed one after another. Even the first hobby computers of the 1970s, some 30 or more years after the pioneer computers and almost a century after Babbage, had to be programmed by setting switches on the front panel.

When the user of a computer was the designer, or a programmer, the user interface wasn't too important. Suppose, for instance, you had an intimate knowledge of the workings of a computer, and the only way of communicating with the computer was at the very lowest machine level. First, you might never consider that there could be a more user-efficient way to get the machine to do what you wanted. In fact, while many of the earliest programs were computationally complex, the demands they placed on the user were very simple, requiring little more than a mass of numeric input along with a command to run the program on that input. Second, you might prefer to program at the machine level. After all, whether one believes or disbelieves that the accepted way of doing things is the best way, there is still a heady feeling of superiority that comes from being privy to great mysteries—the secrets of Egyptian hieroglyphics were the sole province of a handful of scribes for nearly 2000 years for what we suspect was partly this reason.

The computer scribes quickly lost their exclusive claims to the machine, largely for economic reasons. As computers made their way into commercial applications, it became clear that their hunger for data could not be appeased by having the operators set switches. To speed input, data were stored on paper tape or punched cards, prepared on a machine much like a typewriter, and read mechanically. The user was in effect being separated from the machine. A typical session consisted of entering a program and its input on cards, and carrying the completed deck of cards to the operator, who would place the cards in a mechanical card reader, wait for the computer to run the program, and, five minutes to several hours later, return the cards and the printed output to the user.

This *batch mode* of operation was slow at best. The computer operator controlled the scheduling of jobs, running job 1 until completion, then running job 2, then job 3, and so on. In effect, the user interface was the counter at the operator's window, with an in basket for the user to deposit his or her cards and an out basket where the user would get a printout of the results. Not only was this process slow, it was anything but user friendly. In addition to the program and the data, the user had to include in the deck certain cards that told the computer how to handle the job, so that the full deck of cards for a job might look like the following (taken from G. Struble, *Assembler Language Programming: The IBM System/360,* Reading, MA: Addison-Wesley, 1969]):

```
//QUESTNARJOB 204121,MARCO.POLO,MSGLEVEL=1
//     EXEC ASMFCLG
//ASM.SYSINDD *
```

(Some of your program cards would go here.)

```
/*
//LKED.SYSLIBDD DSNAME=USERLIB,DISP=OLD
//LKED.SYSINDD *
```

(Some more of your program cards would go here.)

```
/*
//GO.SYSPRINTDD SYSOUT=A,DCB=(BLKSIZE=133)
```

```
//GO.INDATADD DISP=OLD,UNIT=TAPE9,DSNAME
       QUEST215,VOLUME=SER=102139
//GO.SYSINDD *
```

(Your data cards would go here.)

```
/*
```

With the advent of *time-sharing* in the late 1960s, control was returned to the user—or at least the illusion of control. In such an arrangement, a computer would be connected to several terminals, each of which looked like an electric typewriter with a roll of paper attached (called a *TTY*, in the jargon, for *teletype*). Unlike batch mode, the computer would divide its attention among the terminals, running each job for a fraction of a second in turn. Since the computer could perform its operations vastly faster than either the user could type or the TTY could print, each user could act as if he or she had complete control of the computer.

Time-sharing was a considerable improvement in the user interface. Not only could the user see what he or she had typed without having to leaf through a deck of punched cards, but the interaction with the machine was in real time, so that the interval between making an error and being informed of the error could be measured in seconds, rather than hours. One could run a program, find an error, edit the program to fix the error, and try again, all in the space of a few minutes.

Of course, editing a program—or any text, for that matter—was still somewhat cumbersome. Text editors of the time were generally *line oriented*, meaning that the basic unit of text was a single line. Lines were identified by number, and a typical session might consist of typing the following editing commands:

`p 125:450`	Print lines 125 through 450
`i 220`	Insert a new line before line 220
`d 245:350`	Delete lines 245 through 350
`stotal$sum$340:#`	Substitute "sum" for every instance of "total" in all lines from 340 to the end

The video display terminal (VDT for short, or *glass TTY* to insiders) replaced the roll of paper with a video screen. This user interface should be familiar to you if you have ever looked behind the scenes at an airline ticket counter or the Department of Motor Vehicles. With such an arrangement, the user can move to any location on the screen by pressing the right combination of keys (the up arrow might move the text insertion bar up one line, for instance) and modify the text at that location by typing. For example, in a simple system to handle airline reservations the screen might contain several lines of text. To make a reservation, the clerk would first type a code for the departure airport, then press the tab key, type the code for the destination airport, tab once more to move to the flight number field, and enter the flight number. At that time, the screen would display the available seats on that flight, and the clerk could enter the chosen seat number. The rest of the process, such as payment method and so on, would be handled similarly. While this process is a smoother version of what would happen with a typewriter terminal, it is still text oriented and essentially line based. Using any modern computer as an example, we can imagine what the reservation system would look like on a machine that supports graphics and has a mouse attached.

The process whereby computers came to be able to represent, display, and manipulate graphical images was a long and gradual one (long, at least, in the brief history of computers). Image processing programs were developed in the early 1960s to enhance satellite images. Bit-mapped screens (monitors that could be controlled on a pixel-by-pixel basis, as opposed to line by line, or character by character) were available toward the end of the decade. These developments were followed, in pretty rapid succession, by simple paint programs, the mouse, fonts, specialized file formats for pictures, scanners, page layout programs, and, of course, the World Wide Web.

It is interesting that some of these developments represent innovations in computer hardware, whereas others are more software related. We see this pattern throughout the history of computer science, and in many different guises. Hardware advances provide more powerful, more useful machines, which in turn spur the development of software that exploits the hardware. Eventually, the demands on the hardware by the software (such as the memory required to hold the program or the processor speed needed to make the program respond to its user in a timely manner) necessitate new advances in hardware, and so the process continues.

It is also interesting that despite the availability of all these technologies and what, in hindsight, seem to be the obvious synergies between them (for example, bit-mapped screens allow for the possibility of different fonts; the mouse provides a means for pointing at images), it took a small, upstart computer company to see their applications and implications for personal computers.

Indeed, what amounts to today's standard iconic, window- and menu-based, point-and-click interface has been around since the early 1970s. It was developed originally at Xerox Corporation, and was installed on the in-house workstation computers used by the members of the research staff. Despite urgings from the staff to consider marketing the machine and its operating system as a "personal computer," the corporate powers-that-be decided not to do so. None of the other big players in the computer market at that time acted on these ideas either, perhaps because they didn't see computers as "personal," in the marketing sense of that term.

At any rate, after visiting one of the Xerox research facilities, Steve Jobs took these ideas (and a number of key Xerox personnel) with him back to his fledgling company, Apple Computer. The introduction of the Apple Macintosh in 1984 signaled a major event in the history of user interfaces. In fact, it is pretty much with that machine that the phrase "user interface" was expanded to "graphical user interface" (or GUI). When soon thereafter Microsoft and Sun developed operating systems with the same look and feel to run on different hardware, the standardization process had begun in earnest.

The standard GUI of today is already expanding to incorporate other media forms. High-resolution color monitors and printers have simultaneously raised our expectations of interfaces and increased the artistic and image-handling demands on interface designers. Since audio files can be used in HTML pages just as easily as image data, it is no surprise that many computers today include speakers as a standard part of their interface hardware. Microphones and speakers are also becoming commonplace so that spoken and recorded sounds can be processed. When combined with remote-control mice and keyboards, and satellite-based (as opposed to phone-line-based) communications systems, it seems certain that the next generation will interact with their computers according to a very different user interface than most of us do today.

We should make the point here that there is a considerable chronological overlap among the varieties of user interface we have described. All types we have mentioned, with the possible exception of rewiring, are in use today and will almost certainly continue into the future. After all, the horse wasn't replaced overnight by the automobile, and for a variety of reasons it will never be completely eliminated.

Guidelines for System Design

We have presented the user interface as a model of system design. It might seem that the evolution of the user interface was driven by changes in technology, and while this is partly true, it ignores a parallel theme in the evolution of computer systems. As computers became more pervasive, they were used increasingly by operators with little or no computer experience. It seems reasonable that one way to increase sales of a piece of hardware or software is to make it simpler and more pleasant to use, assuming that its functionality is roughly the same as that of competing products. We have already mentioned the parallel between computer and automotive technologies, and we can see another example here. The exotic sports cars of the 1950s and early 1960s (which would include almost all sports cars of the time) were exciting and fun to drive, especially compared with the conventional products then available. However, since they were quirky, not particularly reliable, and notoriously difficult to maintain (facts to which both your authors can attest, based on bitter experience), their sales were limited to a few aficionados.

What, then, do we mean by "easy to use" in regard to hardware and software? What are some of the desirable features that a system designer should use as guidelines? These questions are examples of the engineering aspect of computer science, where there isn't a single "right" answer, but rather there are "better" answers. Drawing on years of experience observing and questioning users, we have identified three very general guidelines for user-friendly systems (we'll offer much more specific advice after you've learned some HTML).

1. A system should be *transparent;* that is, the technology should not intrude excessively between the user and the task. The operator should be able to use a program or a computer, at least at the novice level, without having to master the entire user's manual.

This is an area in which computer technology lags behind automotive technology. We have to learn how to drive a car first, but having mastered that task, we can sit behind the wheel of an unfamiliar vehicle and drive to Buffalo without ever looking at the manual. At the very least, a transparent system should be easy to use—the commands should be as simple and logical as possible. For example, saving a document should be the result of choosing Save from the File menu, rather than having to type something like `V$=SYS(CHR$(6%) + CHR$(G0%) + 0$)`.

In this respect, computer technology is still at the stage where the machine drives the user's behavior, rather than the user's expectations driving the design of the machine. The situation is improving in software, though, as the common and popular features across programs emerge as de facto standards at a number of levels. For example, knowing how to use any modern word processor prepares you quite well to use another. Many such programs project the same basic interface and range of behavior to the user. Indeed, we are at the point where certain keystroke combinations retain their meanings across different word processors, graphics programs, e-mail systems, and operating systems.

2 In addition, a system should be *forgiving,* so that there is usually a way to avoid or recover from potentially disastrous actions. Avoidance might take the form of alerts after some actions, like this somewhat frivolous example:

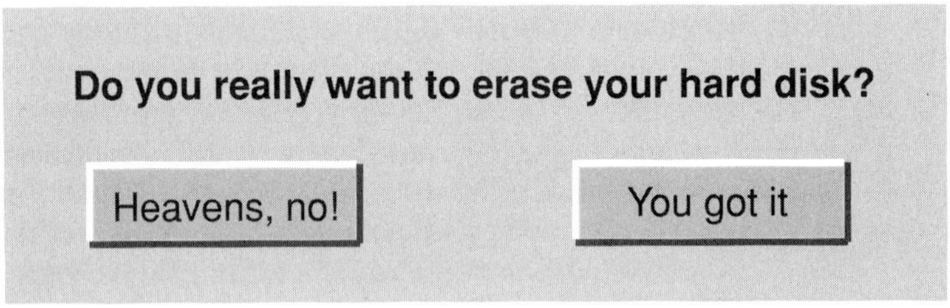

On a more mundane level, a forgiving program will not crash if the user enters numbers that would entail division by zero, but rather will either alert the user to the fact or handle the error without intervention, perhaps by printing "Division by zero!" where the answer might have gone.

Recovery means the ability to return to a previous state after taking one or more actions. Some programs for instance, have a File menu item such as Revert to Saved, which changes the current document back to the state in which it was the last time it was saved. Similarly, it has become an expected part of a program's interface to include an Undo command, which undoes the effects of the most recent editing action. In fact, many modern programming languages (including the one you will work with in Module 5) include statements that make it easy to present and control alert boxes like the one above.

3 A system should be *visually oriented*, since most people are. It's for good reason that we say a picture is worth a thousand words, and it is no accident that most modern computer systems have highly visual interfaces, with icons such as scroll bars and buttons. In technical terms, visual data has a higher *bandwidth* than textual, meaning that you can pack more information in a similar space.

This visual versus textual orientation was a source of some controversy only a few years ago, primarily because there is still a large installed base of computers and programs that use what is essentially a TTY mode of operation. It is natural for people to resist the new, especially if they have become accustomed to the old ways, and, to be honest, it is also much easier to design a text-based program than it is to design one that must deal with mice, menus, windows, and icons. In spite of this, these factions have essentially agreed to disagree. The installed base of text-based software remains, while the mainstream—the truly "personal" personal computers—embraces and evolves the graphical user interface.

Data and Programs

Until fairly recently, most computer applications presented a clear conceptual boundary between data and programs. In the conventional way of thinking, data were purely raw material: inert stuff that was acted on by programs. A text file, in this view, was like a lump of clay, with a word processing program serving as a potter's wheel. As we saw in Module 2, this paradigm was broken by the invention of the spreadsheet. A document produced by a spreadsheet program contained raw data, of course, but could also contain within itself formulas for manipulating the data. The spreadsheet program still controlled the action of any spreadsheet, but in the background, as it were. To the user, it appeared as if the spreadsheet were acting on itself, so that entering or changing the value of a cell could cause recalculation of the average of all the cells in that row, for example, with no further intervention on the part of the user.

The spreadsheet is a *user-configurable* object, whose functionality can be designed to suit its purpose. When we use a spreadsheet to design a grade book for one of our classes, we can construct a column of cells, each one of which will compute and display the weighted average of the exam scores in its row. Having built the spreadsheet, we need only enter the scores as they arrive, and the spreadsheet itself calculates the averages for us. Not only does this save us the trouble of calculating the averages anew for each entry, but, even better, if we need a similar average for another class, we can copy the formulas from the existing spreadsheet to a new one or even duplicate the entire spreadsheet for use in the other course. The spreadsheet contains not only data, but also mini-programs to manipulate the data, and these mini-programs can be cut, copied, pasted, and edited just as the data can be. We might call such a document *smart data*; in its most advanced form, computer scientists call the marriage of data and methods to manipulate the data *object-oriented programming*.

HTML is a powerful extension of this notion of combining data and program into a single unit. An HTML page can be defined to present a variety of data forms (text and images, for example), to respond to user input (using forms), and to link the page to other pages and Internet resources. The data items themselves are represented as commands that are, in turn, interpreted by a browser as a program for displaying the page. We'll see in the next module that we can even write program code of our own directly into HTML pages. In the following sections, though, we'll concentrate on the data aspects of HTML. That is, we'll show you how to define an HTML page so that it projects an effective and stylish user interface.

Review Questions

1. Trace the evolution of the user interface.
2. What are the three guidelines for good system design? Can you think of any other desirable features for an easy-to-use system?
3. Give some examples of good and not-so-good system design in the lab exercises you've seen so far.
4. What do we mean by *smart data*?

4.3 ANATOMY OF A PAGE

Earlier in this module, we likened the process of WWW page development to that of designing a new building. We noted that, from a design perspective, both the page designer and the architect have the freedom, thanks respectively to the browsers and construction workers of the world, to design their artifacts without worrying too much about the details that go into implementing them. This freedom, though, comes at a modest cost.

Good architects are not oblivious to the fact that creations must ultimately be built. They know enough about the implementation process to take into account basic techniques and guidelines that will help the builders accomplish their jobs. When it comes time to communicate their designs to the builders, they do so by means of a set of drawings in a standardized notation that specifies the design to the level of detail necessary for completing the job. This process of communication between the designer and the builders is often an interactive one, wherein the plan may get modified because either the builder doesn't understand the design or certain things just don't look right to the designer.

All of this is equally true for the designers of Web pages. In designing a user interface we have a well-defined collection of tools (like text, links, and images) and guidelines (file formats and the like) that we can be confident that any browser understands. And, you'll see in doing the lab exercises that the process of designing, building, and reviewing usually requires a few passes before we get a page to look just the way we want. In this section and the next, though, we concentrate on the standardized notation—the language—that we use to communicate our design to the browser.

Our design language is called the *HyperText Markup Language* (HTML), and it satisfies the two overriding demands of such a language. First, HTML provides a simple but formal notation for representing and describing nearly all of the features we would want to incorporate into the design of a page. Second, it does so in a logical, rather than a physical, manner. That is, an HTML document describes the components of a Web page and their interrelationships without specifying the exact details of their physical properties.

For example, if we want a piece of text or an image to be displayed in the center of a page, we simply indicate that we want it centered, and leave it to each browser to determine the width and resolution of the user's screen, the width of the window displaying the page, and the size of the item to be centered. Similarly, HTML specifies fonts, colors, widgets (such as buttons, checkboxes, and menus), links, tables, and the like, in terms that allow each browser to interpret them in its own physical style.

The phrase "hypertext markup language" not only names our design language, but also describes its essential characteristics. HTML is *text* based in the sense that it describes a Web page as a text document, and one embeds the text to be displayed on the page directly into the HTML code. It is *hyper* in that it directly supports the notion of hypertext by providing a text-based notation for links within and across pages. HTML is a *markup* language; that is, we describe the items that are to constitute our page and their relationships using a notation in which we embed instructions for the browser directly within our text description of the pages' items. We mark up the page to describe how it is to be displayed.

Finally, and perhaps most important, HTML is a language in the formal, computer science sense. It has a syntax (grammar rules to which we must conform when we write our HTML code), a semantics prescribing the meaning and interpretations of every one of the embedded commands, and a standardized vocabulary of commands[1] for describing the content and style of a page. To learn HTML one must master all of these linguistic features. While we can't provide you with a complete and detailed description of all of these features in a single module, we can show you the basic structure of an HTML document, describe the essential commands, and point you (or, better yet, link you) to a number of more complete references.

Elements, Tags, and Attributes

We start with the basic terminology used to describe an HTML document. An HTML document is a text file that describes not only the text that is to appear on the page, but also the nontextual and stylistic features of the page. These features are described by HTML *elements*, most of which mark off regions of the text file to indicate some processing that is to be applied to that section of text. For example, including the element

```
<H1>Rick and Stu's Home Page</H1>
```

in our code instructs the browser to display the included text ("Rick and Stu's Home Page") as a type 1 header.

Elements are indicated by bracketed *tags*, such as `<H1>` and `</H1>`. The `<H1>` is a *start tag*, because it marks the start of a blocked region of text, and the slash in `</H1>` tells us that it is an *end tag*. Elements that use start and end tags to mark text are called *container* elements. Other elements, like `<BR>`, which introduces a line break into a displayed page, do not mark blocks of text and so do not require end tags. These kinds of elements are referred to as *empty* elements.

Elements may also include *attributes*, which specify additional information to the browser about how it is to process a particular element. The element

```
<A HREF = "http://www.pws.com/aeonline.html">AE Home</A>
```

applies a container tag of type anchor (`<A> . . . </A>`) to the text "AE Home." Anchor tags are used, among other things, to indicate that text is to serve as a hyperlink to another page. Our element specifies that a click on the text "AE Home" is to take us somewhere by means of the HREF attribute that is included in the anchor's start tag. The *value* of the HREF attribute is the quoted string, which specifies the URL of the page to link to. As mentioned before, empty elements have no contents, no enclosed text, and do not require end tags. Figure 4.1 summarizes this terminology.

You should also be aware of a couple of grammatical issues that apply to elements. Tag names and attribute names are *case insensitive*. That is, browsers

[1] HTML is an evolving language that has undergone substantial change in recent years. While we won't conform to a particular version or standard, all of the features and commands that we refer to in this module are implemented by most modern browsers.

FIGURE 4.1
The parts of an HTML element

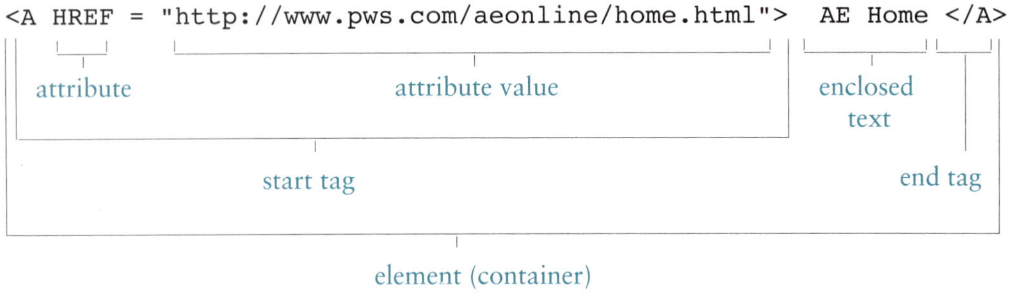

regard <A> and <a> as designating the same element. Attribute values, since they are most often quoted strings, are case sensitive. As a matter of style, and in the interest of helping to make our HTML code more readable for humans, we adopt the convention of using strictly uppercase characters when writing tags and attributes.

Speaking of making code easier to read, HTML provides us with a special notation so that we can include *comments* in our code. The comment

```
<!-- any text can go in here -->
```

can be filled in with any characters whatsoever, because everything between <!-- and --> is ignored by the browser, and has no effect on the displayed page. Comments are typically inserted to provide human readers (including the author of the code) with descriptions or reminders of anything idiosyncratic about the code—such as what it is intended to do, who wrote it, or any nonstandard features that are used that might cause browsers problems. As the HTML code we write gets increasingly complex, comments become increasingly useful to describe in English its organization and details.

As our code gets more complex it is also likely that you'll make the mistake of overlapping elements, like this:

```
<A HREF="http://..."> <H1> Module Quiz </A> </H1>
```

It is permissible, and often useful, to have elements within other elements, as in the following example:

```
<A HREF="http://..."> <H1> Module Quiz </H1> </A>
```

It is never, permissible, however, to overlap elements.

◆ A browser will generally ignore any tags that it can't recognize. If your displayed page looks weird, check that you used the tags correctly.

Depending on your browser, one of three things can happen when we ask it to display an element that is somehow ill formed. The browser might completely ignore the entire element, text included, and simply continue its processing with the next element. The browser might provide you with an error message indicating the element with which it had trouble. Or the browser might ignore the tags and attributes involved and simply display any enclosed text without applying any formatting. This latter approach is the one recommended in the HTML specification for when a tag or attribute is mislabeled or misspelled.

Page Structure

We will devote the next section to describing a variety of HTML elements that control the details of how a page gets displayed. Before doing so, we need to introduce the three elements that dictate the overall structure of any HTML file. Every HTML document[2] has the following basic structure:

```
<HTML>
        <HEAD>
        . . .
        </HEAD>
        <BODY>
        . . .
        </BODY>
</HTML>
```

The HTML element surrounds the entire page description and identifies it to the browser as an HTML document. Nested (completely) inside the HTML element are, in order, the HEAD element and the BODY element. Note that we indented the tags to make the structure more obvious. Indentation like this is only for our convenience—the browser will ignore any indentation, returns, and tabs, treating them as single blank spaces.

◆ The structure of an HTML document is determined solely by the tags, and not by any returns or tabs we type.

You will see in our descriptions of all subsequent elements that we identify them as being either head or body tags, meaning that they can appear in only that section of the document. The HEAD element contains relatively few elements, which provide the browser with meta-information about the document, such as its title and its relationship to other documents. The BODY element contains all of the text to be displayed and elements that control the text's display.

For example, look at the HTML code in Figure 4.2 and its displayed form in Figure 4.3. There isn't much there beyond some simple text broken into two paragraphs (which we'll explain in detail in the next section).

The TITLE element is required to be in the head of every HTML document. It encloses text that will not appear on the page itself, but will typically appear in the title bar of the page's window and will be used by WWW search engines to index the document. The TITLE element should describe the document in a way that will be meaningful regardless of the context in which the page is viewed, and should not contain any other tags.

Notice the attributes that we have added to the start tag of our BODY element. The BGCOLOR attribute lets you specify a background color for the entire page. Its value (white) is one of HTML's predefined colors that can be referred to by name. There are sixteen color names you can expect any graphical browser to recognize: aqua, black, blue, fuchsia, gray, green, lime, maroon, navy, olive, purple, red, silver, teal, white, and yellow. In addition, there is a large collection of color names—like burlywood, thistle, and moccasin—that are recognized by some, but not all, browsers.

[2] Well, *almost* every HTML document has this structure. We'll see at the end of the next section that pages composed using frames vary from this structure ever so slightly.

FIGURE 4.2
A sample HTML document

```
<!-- This example illustrates the structure of an ordinary HTML document. -->
<HTML>

<HEAD>
 <TITLE>Origins of the Internet</TITLE>
</HEAD>

<BODY BGCOLOR = “white” TEXT = “darkblue”>
      <P>The history of the Internet begins at the height of the cold war in the 1960s.
      People at the Rand Corporation, America’s foremost military think tank,
      were trying to figure out an important strategic problem: How could US
      authorities talk to each other in the aftermath of a nuclear attack?</P>

      <P>Communication networks of the day were chained point-to-point, with each
      place on the network dependent on the link before it. If one point in the
      network was blown up, the whole network would become useless.</P>

      <!-- The rest of the text would go here -->
</BODY>

</HTML>
```

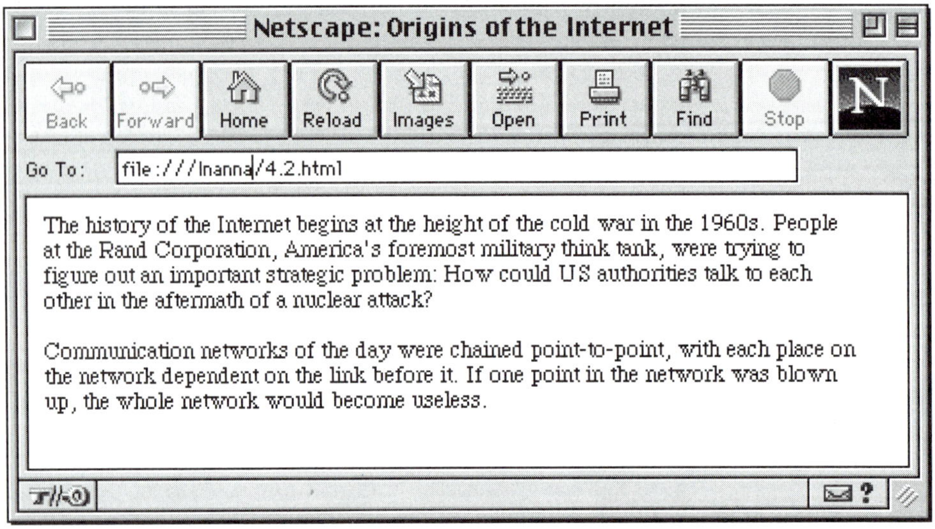

FIGURE 4.3
The Figure 4.2 document displayed by a browser

Colors in HTML

If you want to use a color that's not one of the basic sixteen, it's better not to use a name, but rather to specify the desired color by a different scheme, the *hexadecimal triplet*. Hexadecimal triplets are formed from three numbers representing, respectively, the amount of red, green, and blue to be mixed to form the resultant color. In a hexadecimal triplet, each of these three values is represented as a two-digit hexadecimal (base 16) number with values in the range of 0 to 255. We'll talk more about hexadecimal notation in Module 6, but all you need to know for now is that such numbers are represented by the digits 0 to 9 and by the characters A, B, C, D, E, and F (where A stands for 10, B for 11, and so on up to F for 15). The smallest two-digit hexadecimal number is thus 00 (corresponding to decimal value 0) and the largest is FF (corresponding to 15 groups of 16, plus 15 groups of 1, for a total value of 255).

This notation sounds more forbidding than it really is. Here's how we count from 0 to 255 in hexadecimal:

00, 01, 02, 03, 04, 05, 06, 07, 08, 09, 0A, 0B, 0C, 0D, 0E, 0F,

10, . . . , 1F, 20, . . . , 2F, 30, . . . , 3F,

(40 to 8F omitted)

90, . . . , 9F, A0, . . . , AF, B0, . . . , BF,

(C0 to DF omitted)

F0, . . , FF

In color terminology, then, 00 is none of a color, 10 is a little, 80 is a medium amount, A0 is high intensity, F0 is even higher, and FF is maximum. Black, then, is #000000 and white is #FFFFFF. To take another example, fuchsia, with color code #FF00FF, is a mixture of bright red (FF), no green (00), and bright blue (FF); violet, with code #800080, is a darker version of fuchsia, with only 80 of red and blue. You can see, then, that the color #400040 would be a violet that's almost black. This gets a bit tricky when you have a color in mind and want to find its hexadecimal triplet. Fortunately, there are some Web sites that have *color pickers*—applications that let you choose a color and generate the corresponding code.

◆ Be aware that what you see on your Web page isn't necessarily what someone using a different browser or monitor will see. Chocolate on your screen may be olive drab for someone else.

You can also specify color values, either by name or by hex triplet, for other body attributes as follows:

`TEXT = "color"`	Specifies a color for all document text (darkblue in our example).
`LINK = "color"`	Specifies a color for the text of hypertext links.
`VLINK = "color"`	Specifies a color for the text of all links that have been visited.
`ALINK = "color"`	Specifies a color for the text of all links that are actively processing.

While we didn't choose to do so in our first sample page, you can also specify a pattern (as opposed to a color) to be used to cover your page's background. The `BACKGROUND` attribute used within the `BODY` start tag takes as its value a URL that identifies a file containing a graphical image. The image is then used to tile the background of the page.

LAB 4.1

www/intro.html

Every Web page that you have viewed through your browser is described as an HTML document. In fact, most browsers allow you to see the HTML source code that was written to describe the page. While the type of information displayed and its format vary dramatically across pages, the basic structure of the HTML documents that define them is quite standard. In this set of exercises, you'll review some HTML and view firsthand this common structure.

1. Use your browser to look over the HTML code for

   a) This page
   b) Rick & Stu's Home Page
   c) Any Web page that you find interesting

   Then, print out the HTML code for each page. (*Note:* Depending on your browser, you may have to copy the HTML code and paste it into your favorite word processor in order to print it.)

2. Mark each of the printouts to identify

   a) The head and body of the document
   b) The tags and the sections of the document that correspond to particular parts of the displayed page (for example, "here's the 4.1 header," and "here's the code for displaying the picture of Rick")

3. Now, open your favorite word processor and type in the following:

```
<HTML>
<HEAD>
<TITLE>Home Sweet Home</TITLE>
</HEAD>
        Home is where the HTML is!
</BODY>
</HTML>
```

4. Save the document as a text file (and *not*, for example, as a Word document, or in any other formatted style). Name the file whatever you like, but make sure to use the extension .html (for Mac, Unix, and Windows 95/NT machines) or .htm (for Windows 3.1 machines), so that your browser will know it's an HTML document.

5. Open your browser again and use it to view your fledgling home page. This can be accomplished in Netscape, for example, by selecting Open File in Browser... from the File menu.

6. Repeat steps 4 and 5, changing your HTML code each time to incorporate some of the simpler HTML elements you found in the sample pages you reviewed earlier. Try, for example, to set the background to some color or image other than plain white. Then experiment with different colors for displaying the text.

This and all subsequent exercises may take some fiddling. You may type something incorrectly, or may leave out a necessary tag. From now on, when we ask you to "add something to your page," we mean that you should add code to your HTML file, save the file, open the file in your browser, verify that the page looks the way you want it, and, if it doesn't, just start over.

Review Questions

1. Define the HTML terms *element, tag,* and *attribute.*
2. What are the three major elements that are required in every HTML document?
3. What element is required in the `HEAD` element?
4. What colors are represented by the hex triplets #808080, #00FF80, and #800000?

4.4 ESSENTIAL HTML

If HTML is the language in which we express the design of our building, our goal in this section is to get you to the point where you can read and understand a set of blueprints. Practically speaking, we want to help you to develop your HTML vocabulary. As opposed to presenting you with a single long list of HTML elements and their descriptions, we will divide the elements into three categories and discuss them one group at a time. These groups are not "official" in any sense. They just represent our attempt to organize some of the more useful HTML elements into task-oriented subgroups, like an architect would for plumbing, electrical, foundation, and heating and cooling subcontractors. In order, we will describe groups of elements that relate to text processing and formatting, hyperlinks, and multimedia effects (images and sounds). We'll start with the most basic group of elements, those related to the displaying of text.

Text Formatting

Unless you specify differently, text in an HTML document will be poured into the window by the browser in a default, plain, style. There will be times, though, when you want more control over the look of your page. HTML provides a number of tags that allow you to change how text looks and how it is displayed in the browser window. In Figure 4.4 we show some of the formatting tags in a sample HTML document; you can see their effects on the displayed Web page in Figure 4.5.

FIGURE 4.4
HTML text formatting elements

```
HTML>

<HEAD>
 <TITLE>Text Formatting</TITLE>
</HEAD>

<BODY BGCOLOR = "white">
       <H1>Doing it Your Way</H1>
       <H2>Emphasis</H2>
       <P>We can modify text by making it <I>italic,</I> <B>bold,</B> or
       <U>underlined.</U> We can also <EM>emphasize</EM> text or
       <STRONG>strongly</STRONG> emphasize it. We can even <B>use these <I>in
       combination</I></B> if we want.</P>
       <H2><FONT COLOR = "Red">Paragraphs</FONT></H2>
       <P ALIGN = CENTER>We can declare a paragraph to be center-aligned,
       like this.</P>
       <P ALIGN = RIGHT>If we wish, we can align it to the right margin, as
       we do here. If we don't specify alignment, the text will be aligned to
       the left.</P>
       <BR>
       <BR>
       <P>Browsers will generally put a single blank line between paragraphs. We
       can insert extra spacing of our own, if we wish, using the BR tag.</P>

       <HR WIDTH = 50% ALIGN = CENTER> <!-- NOTE: BR doesn't have a close tag. -->

       <P>We can also place horizontal rules between text elements, using
       the HR tag.
</BODY>

</HTML>
```

The heading elements (H1 to H6) allow for a variety of header sizes and styles to be used within a page. Remember that these are guidelines, and that they may vary from browser to browser. The visual importance of these tags depends on the number after the H. As you can see in Figure 4.5, an H1 header ("Doing it Your Way," in the example) is used for major heads: It's big, bold, and set off from the rest of the document by several blank lines. Going down to an H2 head ("Emphasis" and "Paragraphs," in Figure 4.5) gives a smaller, but still emphatic header. Head elements H3 through H6 give headers that are progressively smaller, as you'd expect. The decision of exactly how headers will appear is left to the designers of individual browsers, but you can count on an H1 head to be at least as emphatic as an H2 head, and so on down to an H6 header, which should be only slightly more emphatic than plain text.

The B, I, and U elements are called *physical* style elements because they specify more or less exactly how the enclosed text is to be displayed (as bold, italic, or underlined, respectively). They can be used individually, or in combination, as demonstrated in the following examples.

FIGURE 4.5 *Displaying formatted text*

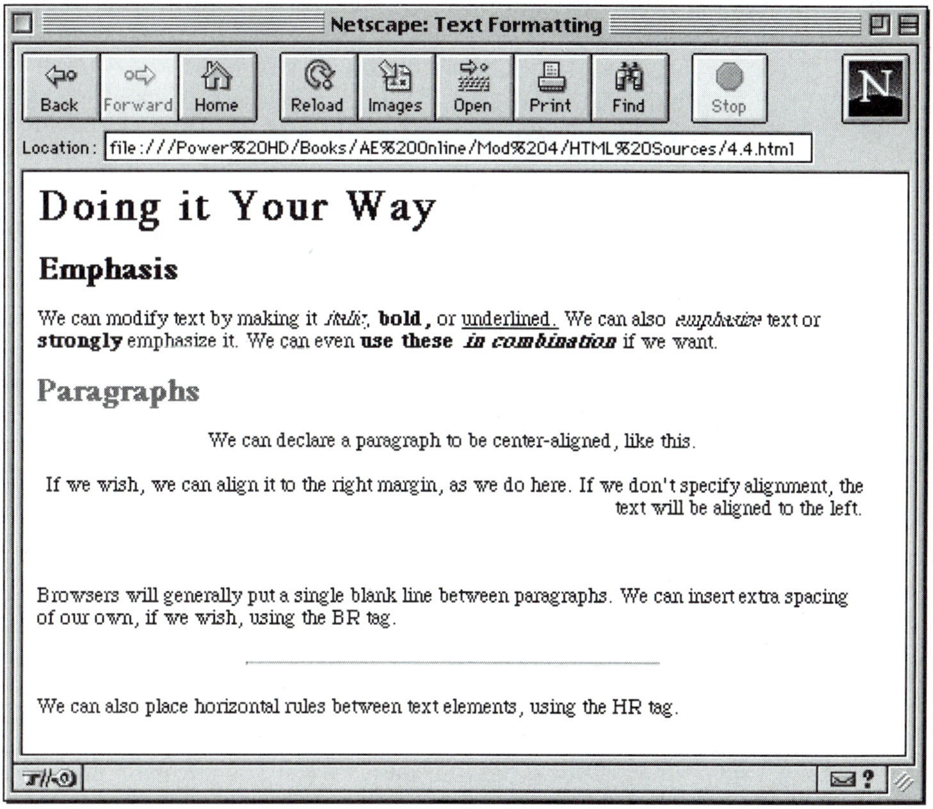

- <B>This text would be displayed in boldface</B>
- This <I>word</I> would be italicized
- <U>This phrase</U> would be underlined
- These tags can be used <B><I>in combination</I></B> by nesting them

Since some machines still do not support specific typefaces, HTML includes the *logical* style elements, EM and STRONG. These leave it to the browser to determine how best to emphasize or strongly emphasize enclosed text. Emphasized text in an EM element is typically rendered as italic, and strong text is most often rendered in bold. HTML guidelines used to recommend the use of these logical styles over the physical ones, in the interest of having your page displayed reasonably on any machine. This advice is less important nowadays, since most computers have no trouble displaying italicized or bold text.

The P tag is used to set off text as a paragraph. In most browsers, text within a P element will be set off from the text above with a blank line. The P element has an ALIGN attribute, which you can set to LEFT, CENTER, or RIGHT to change the justification of the enclosed text. The BR tag can also be used to separate text by introducing a blank line. As we mention in Figure 4.4, the BR is an empty element, meaning that it doesn't have an end tag.

◆ BR and HR don't have end tags.

Both the HR (for "horizontal rule") and the FONT elements derive most of their power from their attributes. In specifying a horizontal rule, we can provide values for its ALIGN (LEFT, CENTER, or RIGHT), SIZE (a number indicating its thickness in pixels), and WIDTH (a percentage to indicate how long the rule should be relative to the width of the page as currently displayed) attributes. Fonts are specified in terms of the attributes SIZE (which can be an absolute size in pixels, or a relative increase or decrease from the current font), COLOR, and FACE (a list of fonts in order of preference). Since FONT is a container element, FONT information applies only to the enclosed text. These elements and attributes are illustrated in the following code.

- <HR> A thin line the full width of the page.
- <HR WIDTH = 66%> A thin line, roughly two-thirds the width of the page.
- <HR SIZE = 5 ALIGN=CENTER WIDTH=33%> A thick line, in the middle third of the page.
- <FONT SIZE = -3> This text would appear in the default face, but much smaller. </FONT>
- <FONT FACE = "Times Roman, New York" COLOR = "#CCCCCC" SIZE = +1> This text should appear in one of the typefaces listed, in a light gray color, and slightly larger than the default. </FONT>

There are several other formatting elements that we won't cover in detail here. They can be useful in special situations, but we'll just list them here and encourage you to try them out on your own. Table 4.1 summarizes the text-related HTML elements.

- CODE Displays the enclosed text in computer code form, usually in a fixed-width font, like this.
- BLOCKQUOTE Displays the enclosed text as a quote, usually indented on the left and right.
- PRE Displays the text exactly as it appears in the HTML document, with the same spacing. This overrides the usual browser behavior of treating repeated spaces, tabs, and returns as a single space.
- SUB, SUP Displays the enclosed text as a subscript or superscript, respectively.

Hyperlinks

The most important feature of Web pages is the ability to link text or images to another location, either in the same page or on a different page. This is accomplished by using the HTML *anchor* tag. The A element is a container element that designates its enclosed text as a source or destination (or both) of a link. Some non-whitespace text should be enclosed (optionally, for a link destination), and at least one of the following attributes must be provided:

NAME = "#someName" Names the anchor so that it can serve as the destination of a link.

LAB 4.2

Text Processing

Let's now turn to developing content for your home page. Since most HTML documents consist primarily of text (hyper and otherwise), we'll start by describing how text gets presented and formatted.

In all of the remaining lab exercises for this module we'll be using Rick & Stu's Home Page as a model for illustrating a variety of HTML features. Each exercise set will focus on just a few of the features of the page.

To help you see just those features we're interested in, we present you with two windows: one for viewing an HTML file describing a mini-version of our home page, and the other to see what the code looks like when it is interpreted by your browser. You'll notice that many of the HTML tags are colored and underlined in the code window. This indicates that they can be clicked on (in these demonstrations only), to view the corresponding part of the browsed page.

1. In this case, our mini-page is primarily text. Look, now, at the text portion of our home page, and scroll through the highlighted HTML code to see which tags produce which portions of the text. In particular, find the tags that produce the following items.

   a) The header for Rick's bio
   b) The silver-colored "Silver Fox"
   c) The italicized quote at the end of Stu's bio
   d) The underlined title of the text for this course
   e) The bold-faced, italicized question posed when describing *The Analytical Engine*
   f) The font used to display the programming.java header
   g) The bold-faced word "fun," used in the description of our curriculum
   h) The horizontal rule near the very bottom of the page

2. Now, return to your home-page-in-the-making (from Lab 4.1), and add some text to describe yourself and your interests. You are, of course, free to write whatever you wish (remembering that others, probably including your instructor for this course, will be reading what you write). For the sake of these exercises, though, be sure to include the following stylistic elements.

   a) Three or more paragraphs
   b) Text that is underlined
   c) Text in bold face
   d) Some italicized text
   e) At least two different fonts
   f) At least two different headers, at different levels
   g) At least two horizontal rules
   h) A favorite quote

TABLE 4.1 *Summary of text-related HTML elements*

Element	Function
<B>...</B>	Displays enclosed text in boldface
<I>...</I>	Displays enclosed text in italics
<U>...</U>	Underlines enclosed text
<EM>...</EM>	Enclosed text is emphasized
<STRONG>...</STRONG>	Enclosed text is given strong emphasis
<CODE>...</CODE>	Enclosed text is displayed as computer code
<DFN>...</DFN>	Enclosed text is displayed as a definition
<PRE>...</PRE>	Displays enclosed text exactly as pre-fomatted in HTML code
<BLOCKQUOTE>... </ BLOCKQUOTE >	Displays enclosed text as a quotation
<H1>...</H1>	Enclosed text is displayed as a type 1 (most prominent) header
<H2>...</H2>	Enclosed text is displayed as a type 2 header
<H3>...</H3>	Enclosed text is displayed as a type 3 header
<H4>...</H4>	Enclosed text is displayed as a type 4 header
<H5>...</H5>	Enclosed text is displayed as a type 5 header
<H6>...</H6>	Enclosed text is displayed as a type 6 (least prominent) header
<CENTER>...</CENTER>	Centers the enclosed text
_{...}	Enclosed text is displayed as a subscript
^{...}	Enclosed text is displayed as a superscript
 	Inserts a line break
<P>	Inserts a paragraph break
<HR>	Inserts a horizontal rule
<FONT>...</FONT>	Displays enclosed text in the font specified by the attributes

`HREF = "destination"` Renders the anchor as the source of a link, and provides the destination for it. The destination can be an anchor name on the current page, the URL of another page, or an anchor name on another page.

Figure 4.6 illustrates the use of the `A` element and its attributes.

- `<A NAME = "#here">This text can serve as the destination of a link, either from this page, or another.</A>`
- `<A HREF = "http://www.pws.com/aeonline/Rick&Stu.html">Clicking on this text would send you to the page at the indicated URL.</A>`
- `<A HREF = "here">Clicking on this text would send you to the anchor on this page with NAME equal to "#here"</A>`

FIGURE 4.6
Using the anchor tag for links and destinations

To http://www.jones.com/explain.html

```
...
<H1>Moving Around</H1>
<P> You can use the A tag with HREF attribute to move
   to <A HREF = "#in">  another place</A>  in the same
   document or to
   <A HREF = "http://www.jones.com/explain.html">
    some other</A>  HTML document entirely.
</P>
<BR>
<P><I>Much text deleted here. . . .</I></P>
<BR>
<A NAME = "#in"></A>
<!-- NOTE: No contained text needed -->
<H2>Internal Links</H2>
<P>You can use the A tag with NAME attribute to
      specify the destination of a link, too.
</P>
...
```

FIGURE 4.7
How links appear in a browser window

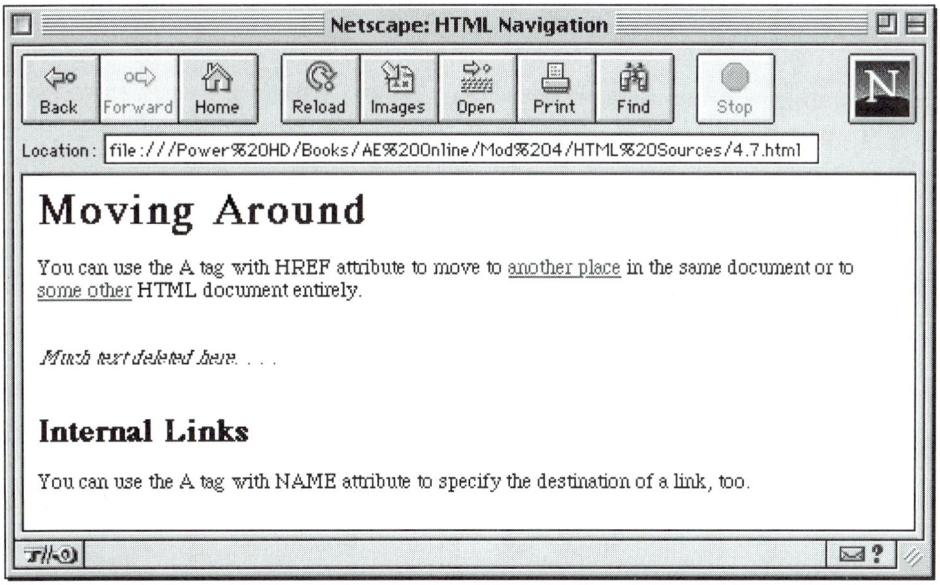

- `<A HREF="http://www.pws.com/aeonline/Rick&Stu.html#Books">Clicking on this text would send you to the anchor on Rick and Stu's page with NAME equal to "#Books"</A>`
- `NAME ="Home" HREF="http://www.pws.com/aeonline/Rick&Stu.html#Books"> This text would serve as both a link source and destination.</A>`

Figure 4.7 shows how the Figure 4.6 document would look when displayed. Clicking on the highlighted words "another place" would cause the browser display to place the destination at the top of the screen. This is useful for a long HTML document—you could place a collection of internal links at the start to serve as an active table of contents. Doing so would allow the reader to go directly to a named section without having to scroll through lots of intervening text. Similarly, clicking on the words "some other" would load and display the page `explain.html` at the location specified by `http://www.jones.com`.

TABLE 4.2
Summary of hyperlink-related HTML elements

Element	Function
<A>...</A>	Identifies the enclosed text as an anchor, with the following attributes
NAME = "anchor name"	Providing a name value allows the anchor to serve as the destination of a link
HREF = "#anchor name" HREF = "URL" HREF = "URL#anchor name"	The HREF value specifies the destination for clicks on the enclosed text
TARGET = "framename""	Allows the destination of the link to be loaded into another frame or window

LAB 4.3

Getting Hyper

While HTML provides reasonable means for formatting and displaying text, most of us rely on WYSIWYG word processors for these tasks. What HTML excels in, though, and probably the real reason for its explosive growth, is its ability to make both text and images "hyper" so that clicking on them changes what you're viewing. HTML links and anchors allow you to be transported to another place in the current page, or to another page altogether, depending upon how they are defined. We'll use a slightly expanded version of our home page to illustrate how this hyper behavior is achieved.

1. We'll start by finding all of the links that are available in Rick & Stu's Home Page. This is easy to do, since they are conveniently highlighted for you in the HTML code window. We'll use a combination of playing with the page and examining its underlying code. On a separate sheet of paper, make a list of every hyper element you can detect by clicking on the displayed page. Your list need not be formal (you can just write, for example, "the Books icon" or "the Saranac.com link"), but it should be as comprehensive as you can make it. At last count, we detected 19 hyper elements (counting separate areas of images as distinct elements).

2. Now, for each hyper element listed, describe it as representing an internal link (that is, one pointing to another position on the home page) or an external link to another page, and identify its target.

3. For each element on your list, find the point in the HTML code where it is defined. Then, click on the corresponding portion of the browser page to see that it behaves as you expect.

4. You should feel ready to add some hyperlinks to your own home page. Again, you are free to add as many such elements as you wish. For the sake of developing your HTML expertise, you should include at least the following:

   a) Two links to points within the page (for example, to different headings or sections of the document)
   b) A link to any available Web resources for your school
   c) A link to this page
   d) A link to one of your favorite Web sites

■ Multimedia Effects

Your Web surfing experience would lead you to believe that images and sounds can be incorporated into pages without too much trouble. Indeed, the HTML specification dictates that `.gif` and `.xbm` files be supported, and most modern browsers also support `.jpeg` files. The `HTML` element and attributes that accomplish this are summarized below.

<IMG

`SRC` = "Some URL"	(Required) Where the image is.
`ALIGN` = `LEFT`, `RIGHT`, or `CENTER`	How to align it on the page.
`WIDTH` = *n*	Scale the image to *n* pixels wide.
`HEIGHT` = *n*	Scale the image to *n* pixels high.
`HSPACE` = *n*	Total space around the image horizontally.
`VSPACE` = *n*	Total space around the image vertically.
`ALT` = "some text"	What shows up if the image doesn't appear.
`ISMAP`>	We'll talk about this in the lab.

An image element doesn't contain anything and has no end tag.

The `IMG` element is an empty element that uses its attributes to identity an image to be inserted into the page and to describe how the image is to be presented. Images

TABLE 4.3
Summary of multimedia-related HTML elements

Element	Function
<IMG>	Places an image at this position on the page
SRC = "URL"	Specifies the source for the image
ALIGN = LEFT or RIGHT or TOP or BOTTOM or MIDDLE . . .	Specifies how the image is to be aligned with surrounding text
ALT = "text"	Specifies alternate text for non-graphical browsers
BORDER = size	Border size in pixels
HEIGHT = size	Scaled height of image in pixels
WIDTH = size	Scaled width of image in pixels
HSPACE = size	Top and bottom margins around image in pixels
VSPACE = size	Left and right margins around image in pixels
ISMAP	Indicates that the image is a clickable imagemap
<A HREF = "URL">...</A>	Use of anchor to designate link to a sound file

are identified using the required `SRC` (source) attribute, the value of which is a URL. Images don't actually live in the pages in which they appear, but are treated as implicit hyperlinks to the specified file. The image may be aligned relative to the text it appears next to by using the `ALIGN` attribute. Its size on the page can be controlled using the `WIDTH` and `HEIGHT` attributes (both of which use integer values to represent size in pixels). The `HSPACE` and `VSPACE` attributes indicate the total number of pixels of space that will surround the image. The `ISMAP` attribute, which does not take a value, is included when the image is to be part of an anchor element, where it will be used as the source for a hyperlink. Finally, the `ALT` attribute should be used to provide a text substitute for nongraphical browsers, and for use while the image is loading.

Here are a few examples of the `IMG` element and its attributes before we look at a full-blown sample page.

- `The "construction" image would appear directly below this text <BR> <IMG SRC = "construction.gif">`
- `<IMG SRC = "caution.jpg" ALIGN = LEFT> The "caution" image would appear directly to the left of this text`
- `<IMG SRC = "title.gif" WIDTH=400 HEIGHT=75 ALT="Title Bar..."> <BR> The "title" image would be scaled to 400x75 pixels, and would appear above this text. While it was loading (or as a substitute for it in nongraphical browsers) the text "Title Bar..." would appear in place of it.`
- `Below this text, the "aelogo" would appear. Clicking on it would take you to the home page for the online materials. <BR> <A HREF="http://www.pws.com/aeonline/home.html"> <IMG SRC="aelogo.gif" ISMAP> </A>`

Sounds are also implemented as hypertext links, but they are described explicitly. That is, there is no element analogous to `IMG` for sound files. To include a sound file in a page, one simply creates an anchor that serves as a link to it. The name of the sound file serves as the value of the anchor's `HREF` attribute, as illustrated in the following examples.

- `<A HREF="song.wav">` Clicking on this text would link to (and thus play) the sound at the given URL</A>
- `<A NAME="Beatles" HREF="http://www.beatles.com/yellow_sub.au">` Clicking on this text would play "Yellow Submarine." This text could also be linked to, using the name #Beatles.</A>

Our sample page illustrating the use of images and sounds is a page from a (fictitious) online music catalog. Look at the HTML source code in Figure 4.8, and how it would look when displayed by a browser (Figure 4.9). Notice how the "star" image is used repeatedly to produce the poll ratings. The image representing the CD cover is identified, resized, aligned, and spaced by the attributes of the `IMG` element. The sound clips are described by means of text serving as links to appropriate sound files.

FIGURE 4.8
Using images and sounds

```
 <HTML>
       <HEAD>
                  <TITLE>IN YOUR FACE! CD'S...Eclectic Majesty</TITLE>
       </HEAD>
<BODY BGCOLOR = "#330066" TEXT="#CCFFFF" LINK = "yellow" VLINK = ""yellow">
<IMG SRC="IYFbanner.gif"
       WIDTH = 300 HEIGHT = 100
       ALT = "IN YOUR FACE! Banner"><BR>
<HR SIZE=2>
<H1>Eclectic Majesty</H1>
<P>The band <I>Eclectic Majesty</I> is the perfect example of catchy country pop,
remixified with the saucy beats of cutting edge jungle dance. DJ Silo adds a trip-hop
flava to the work of songwriter Jud Razor, cutting each track with the styles of mel-
low Fort Smith, Arkansas hipster clubs. Add the haunting drawl of singer Maxxxine, and
you've got a sure hit in clubs from Kalamazoo to NYC.
</P>
<P>Readers poll: <IMG SRC = "Star.gif" ALIGN = CENTER>
<IMG SRC = "Star.gif" ALIGN = CENTER>
Experts poll: <IMG SRC = "Star.gif" ALIGN = CENTER>
<IMG SRC = "Star.gif" ALIGN = CENTER>
<IMG SRC = "Star.gif" ALIGN = CENTER></P>
<BR>
<P>Sound clips are in .WAV format and are about 30K. To order a CD from the
secure <B>IN YOUR FACE!</B> order page, just click on the price.
</P>
<IMG SRC = "EM1.jpg" WIDTH=150 HEIGHT = 150 ALIGN = LEFT HSPACE = 10>
<BIG><B>Lost in the Blue Barn</B></BIG><BR>
<BR>
Sound Clips:<BR>
<A HREF = "EMlost.wav">Lost in the Blue Barn</A><BR>
<A HREF = "EMhdgroove.wav">Hoedown Groooov</A><BR>
<BR>
<A HREF="www.iyf.com/order/">$16.97</A>
<IMG SRC = "cd.gif" HSPACE = 3 ALIGN = TOP><BR>
</BODY>
</HTML>
```

FIGURE 4.9 *How a browser might display the HTML in Figure 4.8*

LAB 4.4

Multimedia Effects

Hyperlinked elements change the structure of a page radically, from that of a linear, static body of text to one that more closely resembles the Web itself—a network of intricately linked information resources. Still, if we were constrained to viewing and reading text on the screen, the appeal of the Web might be limited. The fact that HTML provides us with equal facilities for including images and sounds in our pages expands both the appeal and the utility of the medium. We consider here how to incorporate these multimedia effects into our pages.

1. The first step toward including images or sounds into your pages is to obtain the files that describe them. As described in the text, this can be done in one of two

ways. You can either define the files yourself (by drawing an image using a graphics program, scanning an image and saving it as a .gif file, or recording a sound using a sound processor and saving it as an .au file), or you can download images or sounds from other sites on the Web. [Now is a good time to reread the section in Module 3 of the text that discusses intellectual property.] You saw in the Module 3 lab exercises how to accomplish downloading on your computer/browser setup.

If you haven't done so already, go now and collect at least two images and one sound file that you would like to incorporate into your home page. Store them on the same disk/folder/directory as your home page.

5. Let's review, again, how we used images and sounds in Rick & Stu's Home Page. The images are easy to detect just by looking at the displayed page. The lone sound is a bit less obvious, but it's in there. Look at the HTML code to identify where and how each of these is described.

6. Using our home page as a guide, add your image and sound files to your home page. Place them in the document at positions that are consistent with nearby text (or add text that relates to the images and sounds, if you wish).

7. Make one of your images clickable, like the "Back to Top" icon that is scattered throughout our home page.

Review Questions

1. The element `B` modifies the text it contains from plain text to boldface. List five other HTML elements that modify the displayed form of the text they enclose.

2. In an HTML document, how would you cause the word "Wow" in a sentence to appear as blue, bold, italic, and larger than the rest of the words in the sentence?

3. Which of the elements `B`, `FONT`, `BR`, `HR`, `IMG`, and `A` do not have end tags?

4. Explain the differences between the `A` element attributes `HREF` and `NAME`.

5. List the attributes of the `IMG` element. Of these, which, if any, are required?

4.5 INFORMATION STRUCTURES

It is often useful to present information on Web pages in formats other than simple, linear text and images. Many pages you have seen (and will see in this section) contain lists of items and two-dimensional tables of data. In early versions of HTML, these kinds of structured data were implemented using the `PRE` element, and required the designer to format the data by hand within the HTML code. Necessity being the mother of invention, elements were added to HTML to facilitate the descriptions of a variety of list forms and tables. The most common of these are illustrated in Figure 4.10, where we have the HTML for three lists and what the lists look like when displayed, all shown within a table with four rows and two columns.

Lists

The two kinds of lists shown in Figure 4.10 (there are others, as well) are the `OL` (ordered list) and `UL` (unordered list). Each is a container element that is somewhat different from any we have seen so far. Most of the container elements we have examined enclose text, and may have other elements nested properly within. List elements do not directly enclose text, but must enclose list items (`LI` elements), which, in turn, contain text, images, or other elements (like sublists). Since `LI` elements always occur in the context of some list element, they do not require end tags. A list item is terminated either by the appearance of another `LI` start tag or by the end tag for the enclosing list.

The various list elements differ in how they display their list items. Ordered lists usually appear with their list items numbered. The default starting number for ordered list items is 1, unless the `START` attribute is used to designate a different starting value or the `TYPE` attribute is used to set the index type to "`a`", "`A`", "`I`", "`i`", or "`1`." Unordered lists precede their list items with bullets, the precise form of which can also be specified using the `TYPE` attribute (values can be `DISC`, `CIRCLE`, or `SQUARE`). One of the interesting features of lists is that they can be used in

FIGURE 4.10
A screen snapshot of three lists in a table

The HTML	The Result
<OL> <LI>This is an <I>ordered list</I> <LI>With two list items. </OL>	1. This is an *ordered list* 2. With two list items.
<UL> <LI>This is an <I>unordered list</I> <LI>With two list items. </UL>	• This is an *unordered list* • With two list items.
<OL> <LI>This is an ordered list</I> <LI>Containing... <OL TYPE = "a"> <LI>Another ordered list, <LI>Here </OL> </OL>	1. This is an ordered list 2. Containing... a. Another ordered list, b. Here

combination. That is, a list item may be another list, with or without additional text, as we did in the last row of the table in Figure 4.10.

Here's a summary of the list elements:

```
<OL
  TYPE = "A", "a", "I", "i", or "1"   Type of label for items.
  START = n>                          Starting value for labels.
  An ordered list can only contain LI elements.
</OL>

<UL
  TYPE = "DISC", "CIRCLE",
    or "SQUARE">                      Type of label for items.
  An unordered list can only contain LI elements.
</UL>

<LI
  TYPE = "DISC", "CIRCLE",
    or "SQUARE"                       (In UL) Type of label for this and
                                        later items.
  TYPE = "A", "a", "I", "i", or "1"   (In OL) Type of label for this and
                                        later items.
  VALUE = n>                          (In OL) Label value.
  A list item can contain text, lists, images, tables, and links.
  A list item doesn't require an end tag.
```

Tables

Tables are a natural extension of lists to two dimensions, and are described using a notation similar to that used for lists. Like lists, tables do not enclose text directly, but are defined in terms of nested items that contain the table's text. The differences are that, first, there is only one kind of table, a rectangular area of rows and columns designated by the `TABLE` element, and, second, instead of list items, tables are described in terms of rows (using `TR` elements), which in turn contain individual data items (defined by `TD` or `TH` elements). The `TD` and `TH` elements are the ones that actually contain the table's data. The difference between `TD` and `TH` elements is that the latter treat their enclosed text as header data and so automatically center them within their cells and display them in bold. For example, this is the way we laid out the table in Figure 4.10:

```
<TABLE BORDER = 5>
<!-- The first row, containing the two headers -->
<TR>
<TH>The HTML</TH>
<TH>The Result</TH>
</TR>
<!-- The second row, showing the ordered list -->
<TR>
<TD>
```

```
<!-- Some text, formatted with PRE -->
</TD>
<TD>
<!-- The ordered list code -->
</TD>
</TR>
<!-- The two remaining rows look like the one above -->
</TABLE>
```

The numbers of rows and columns (data elements) in a table are indicated by the number of TR and TD or TH elements, respectively, that are contained in the TABLE element. Other properties of the table are specified using the attributes that apply to these three elements. The TABLE element, for example, can be described using the attributes BORDER (with an integer value indicating the border width in pixels around each data cell), ALIGN (whether to place the table to the LEFT, RIGHT, or CENTER of the page), and WIDTH (the width of the overall table, either in pixels or as a percentage of the current page width).

◆ **Useful tip: You can do very sophisticated page layout using an invisible table, by setting** BORDER = 0.

Table rows can be described by specifying the following attributes for the TR element: ALIGN (justifies text in this row to the LEFT, RIGHT, or CENTER within data cells) and VALIGN (to align text in the row to the TOP, MIDDLE, or BOTTOM).

The elements that actually enclose the table's text, TD and TH, allow for the specification of the attributes ALIGN and VALIGN (as for the TR element), as well as ROWSPAN and COLSPAN. The last two attributes allow individual table data items to span more than one row or column. The value provided for each of these attributes is an integer indicating the number of rows or columns, respectively. To see some of these attributes in action, this HTML

```
<TABLE BORDER = 5 CELLPADDING = 5>
      <TR>
      <TD COLSPAN = 2 ALIGN = CENTER>First</TD>
      </TR>
      <TR>
      <TD ALIGN = CENTER>Second</TD>
      <TD ROWSPAN = 2 ALIGN = CENTER>Third</TD>
      </TR>
      <TR>
      <TD ALIGN = CENTER>Fourth</TD>
      </TR>
</TABLE>
```

produces this table

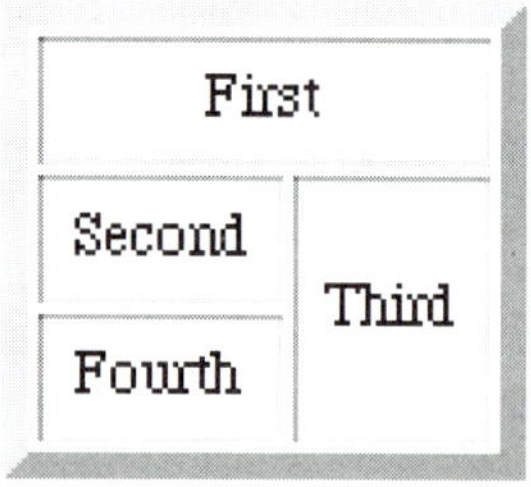

It's easy to get tripped up by the COLSPAN and ROWSPAN attributes. Keep in mind that a browser will lay out a table by rows and by columns within each row, as we've indicated by the numbering of the cells in the table above. If you have trouble getting things to look right, don't forget that you are allowed to put tables within cells of another table—sometimes that works better than using cells that span several rows or columns.

The table-related tags are listed below.

<TABLE	
BORDER = *n*	Width of the table border.
CELLSPACING = *n*	Space between cells.
CELLPADDING = *n*	Blank space within cells.
WIDTH = *n* or *n*%>	Width of the table in pixels or as a portion of the page.
A table can contain only TR elements.	
</TABLE>	

<TR	
ALIGN = "LEFT", "RIGHT", or "CENTER"	Alignment of contents of data in cells.
VALIGN = "TOP", "BOTTOM", or "MIDDLE">	Vertical alignment in cells.
A table row can contain only TD or TH elements.	
</TR>	

<TH	
ALIGN = "LEFT", "RIGHT", or "CENTER"	Alignment of contents in this cell.
VALIGN = "TOP", "BOTTOM", or "MIDDLE"	Vertical alignment in this cell.
COLSPAN = *n*	Width, in columns, of this cell.
ROWSPAN = *n*>	Height, in rows, of this cell.
A table header can contain text, images, links, lists, and tables.	
</TH>	

<TD	
ALIGN = "LEFT", "RIGHT", or "CENTER"	Alignment of contents in this cell.
VALIGN = "TOP", "BOTTOM", or "MIDDLE"	Vertical alignment in this cell.
COLSPAN = *n*	Width, in columns, of this cell.
ROWSPAN = *n*>	Height, in rows, of this cell.
A table data cell can contain text, images, links, lists, and tables.	
</TD>	

TABLE 4.4
Summary of list and table-related HTML elements

Element	Funtion
<OL>...</OL>	Creates an ordered list of list items
<UL>...</UL>	Creates an unordered list of list items
<DIR>...</DIR>	Creates a directory-style list of list items
<LI>	Defines a list item to be included in any list type
<TABLE>... </TABLE>	Creates a two-dimensional table composed of rows and data elements
<TR>...</TR>	Encloses a row in a table
<TD>	Defines a data item to be included in a table row
<TH>	Defines a data item to be included in a table row, but presents it as a bold, centered header in the corresponding cell

LAB 4.5

Structured Information

Even with text, images, sounds, and hyperlinked elements, our home page is still just a linear set of elements, at least from a display standpoint. That is, the words, links, and images are constrained to follow one another in order—indeed, in the same order in which they're described in the HTML code—on our page. It is often useful to organize information in other, nonlinear ways, such as in hierarchical lists and two-dimensional tables of data.

In the course of your surfing, and in the course of using these lab materials, you have already seen many examples of lists and tables, which means, of course, that these types of structured information can be described in HTML. In fact, it's pretty easy to do so once you familiarize yourself with the appropriate HTML elements, and that's what we'll do in this lab.

1. Look first at the HTML code to find the unordered list near the end of Rick & Stu's Home Page describing sites of interest. It is, in effect, a list of lines, each with some accompanying text. Find the section of the HTML source code that describes the list, and review it now. Click on the code to see how the list is displayed by your browser.

2. Add a similar list of links—this one pointing to your favorites places on the Web—to your home page.

3. Add another unordered list to your home page. This one can contain text items describing your hobbies, your favorite musical groups, or your favorite places to visit.

4. Add an ordered list near the top of your home page to serve as a table of contents (even though it's not formally a table!) for your page. That is, let this be a list of links to the subsections of your page, as you may have seen on many Web pages.

5. Find evidence of a table that we've developed, both on Rick & Stu's Home Page and in the HTML code. Review the code carefully so that you see the effects of each tag and attribute. After doing so, you should be able to answer the following questions.

a) How many rows are in our table of courses?
b) How many cells are in each row of that table?
c) With what text are the columns (or the cells) of the course table labeled?
d) How many tables are there in the page?

6. Define a table that shows your current course and extracurricular schedule for a typical week, and add it to your home page wherever you see fit. It is a good idea to sketch the table out on a piece of paper. This will give you an idea of how to organize your HTML code.

■ Frames

We saved the newest HTML topic for last, as frames are not yet considered standard HTML. They are supported by most modern browsers, however—including yours, if you've been using the Æ Online lab materials. Frames represent a powerful addition to the HTML elements because they afford us two related luxuries. First, they allow us to think about a single page as being composed of multiple independent, but related, subpages, if you will. A frame is really nothing more than an HTML page that is displayed in its own area within another page. Second, frames allow us to use a given page in a variety of frame settings. That is, a page containing, say, a corporate logo can serve as the contents of any number of other frames, so the HTML code that describes it need not be replicated.

From a design standpoint, these features combine to give us tremendous flexibility. Not only can we design more complex pages (because multiple frames can be used on a single page), but we can write the code for each frame involved in a frameset, test it separately, and use it as often as we wish.

Let's look first at our sample page for this section, illustrated in Figure 4.11. Note that the page is divided into two sections. Across the top of the page is a logo for an imaginary pizza parlor; across the bottom is an automated order form. None of this looks too unusual. You can probably even imagine writing the HTML code that produced the image, tables, and the like.

The surprise comes when you look at Figure 4.12. The HTML for this page is all of nine lines long! How can such an interesting page be implemented in only nine lines of code? If you look closely at the code, you can get a hint of how this is possible. Clearly, this is a different kind of HTML document than any we have seen so far. It doesn't even have a `BODY` element: Its body has been replaced by a `FRAMESET` element, which, in turn, contains two `FRAME` elements that correspond to the two sections of our page. Each of those frames is a separate page that is defined in the traditional fashion. Those pages compose the frameset that constitutes the page we are viewing.

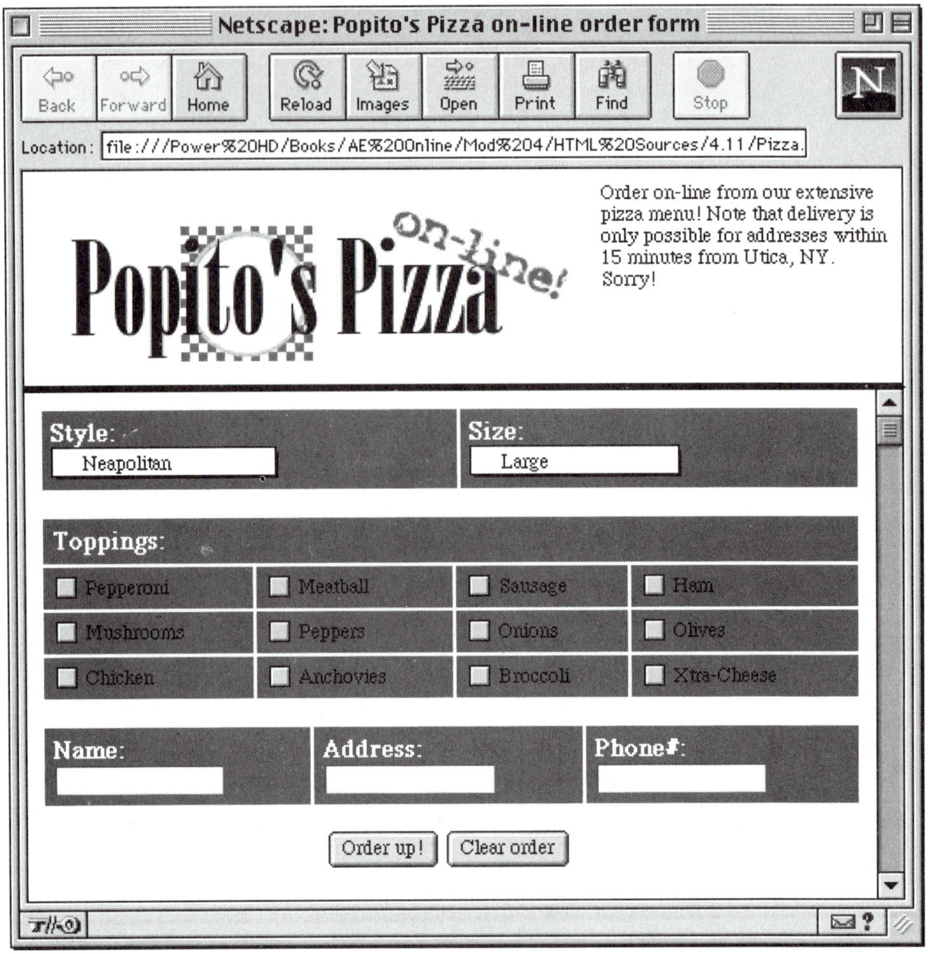

FIGURE 4.11
A page with two frames

FIGURE 4.12
The HTML for Figure 4.11

```
<HTML>
        <HEAD>
        <TITLE>Popito's Pizza on-line order form</TITLE>
        </HEAD>
        <FRAMESET ROWS="125,*" BORDER = 2 BORDERCOLOR = "black">
        <FRAME SRC="Pizza1.html" SCROLLING = NO NORESIZE>
        <FRAME SRC="Pizza2.html">
        </FRAMESET>
</HTML>
```

It is interesting that we need not concern ourselves here with how we implemented the individual pages that are serving as our frames.[3] We can simply refer to

[3] This is also fortunate, since we haven't yet showed you how to describe interactive forms, such as Popito's order form. Not to worry—you'll see this in Module 5.

the pages that we want to appear as part of our frameset, and use the frame-related tags and attributes to organize them on our page. These tags and attributes are summarized in Table 4.5.

The key element is obviously the `FRAMESET`. As we've seen, it replaces the `BODY` element in our code and controls the `FRAME` elements that create the viewed page. Attributes are used to control the number and size of the rows (`ROWS`) and columns (`COLS`) in the frameset. In our pizza order form, the `ROWS` attribute is assigned the value `"125,*"`. This indicates that there are two rows (one for each item in the comma-separated list), that the first row should be 125 pixels tall, and that the second should be allocated all remaining space on the page (that's what the asterisk means). Values for the sizes can also be provided as percentages. In any case, the values provided for each row must total to the full size of the frameset

TABLE 4.5
Summary of frame elements

`<FRAMESET`	
`ROWS` = *n*, *n*, . . . or *n*%, *n*%, . . .	Height of the frames in pixels or as a portion of the page (can use * for filling).
`COLS` = *n*, *n*, . . . or *n*%, *n*%, . . .	Width of the frames in pixels or as a portion of the page (can use * for filling).
`BORDER` = *n*	Space, in pixels, between frames.
`BORDERCOLOR` = "color"	Color of the border between frames.
`FRAMEBORDER` = `"yes"` or `"no"` `>`	Display a border between frames?
The `FRAMESET` element replaces the `BODY` element of a page. A frameset can contain only `FRAME` and `FRAMESET` elements, along with at most one `NOFRAMES` element.	
`</FRAMESET>`	
`<FRAME`	
`SRC` = "Some URL"	(Required) URL of the HTML document that will appear in this frame.
`MARGINWIDTH` = *n*	Blank pixels to be used to left and right of this frame's contents.
`MARGINHEIGHT` = *n*	Blank pixels to be used to top and bottom of this frame's contents.
`SCROLLING` = `"yes,"` `"no,"` or `"auto"`	Allow scrolling in this frame?
`NORESIZE`	Don't allow manual resizing of this frame.
`BORDERCOLOR` = "color"	Color of the border between frames.
`FRAMEBORDER` = `"yes"` or `"no"` `>`	Display a border between frames?
A frame element has no end tag and no contents.	
`<NOFRAMES>`	
A `NOFRAMES` element can contain any HTML that can be used in a `BODY` element. This element is ignored by a frames-capable browser.	
`</NOFRAMES>`	

(whether in pixels, or to 100%). A frameset with two rows and two columns (and thus capable of holding four separate frames) evenly dividing the page into quarters might be described in part as follows:

```
<FRAMESET ROWS="50%,50%" COLS="50%,50%" . . .
```

The other interesting `FRAMESET` attributes allow us to specify whether frames within the frameset will have borders (`FRAMEBORDER`), the width of the borders in pixels (`WIDTH`), and the color of any border (`BORDERCOLOR`).

The frame elements themselves specify the contents of each part of the frameset, with the key attribute being `SRC`, the source of the page. As you would expect, the value for this attribute is the URL of the page to be displayed in the frame. Individual frames are often assigned names (with the `NAME` attribute) so that they can be targeted by links in other documents. Not only are the individual frames in a frameset distinct pages, but they can also be controlled (scrolled and resized) independently of other frames. The `SCROLLING` attribute is used to specify whether or not a frame should be given scroll bars. The default value for this attribute is `AUTO`, which leaves it to the browser to determine this based on the relative sizes of the frameset, the frame, and the page. Another default feature of frames is that they can be resized by dragging their borders. To disable this feature, we can specify the attribute `NORESIZE`, which does not take a value.

As we mentioned, some browsers don't support frames. For the convenience of users of such browsers, you should include a `NOFRAMES` element in your `FRAMESET`. The `NOFRAMES` element can contain any HTML that's allowed in a `BODY` element and will appear if the page is accessed by a browser that's not frame-capable. Often, this element will contain an explanation of what the user is missing and will have a link to a nonframed version of the same page.

Table 4.5 lists the important features of the frame-related elements.

LAB 4.6

You've Been Framed

In the text we describe frames as a powerful new addition to the HTML language. Frames allow you to manage portions of a page as if they were separate pages (which, as you will see, they are!), altering the contents of one section while leaving another the same. Frames also afford tremendous flexibility in defining new pages, because we can use previously defined and debugged pages as our building blocks. We'll use this lab to show you an example of a page composed of frames, and then have you apply the technique to your home page.

1. Look through Rick & Stu's Home Page, both as displayed by your browser and in its HTML code form, for evidence of frames: You won't find any. If frames are so

powerful and so cool, why haven't we incorporated them into our home page? The answer is that we didn't have to! In all of the recent lab exercises for this module you've been viewing framed pages. Frames are what allowed us to display and manage the pop-up windows (showing HTML code and a version of our home page) that are common to these pages.

You can get a better appreciation for how these pages have been defined by viewing the source code for the pop-up page that opened in its own window when this page was loaded. Its body is a frameset that, in turn, identifies and places two frames within it. Most modern browsers allow you to look at the HTML code for the individual frames used to compose a page as well.

Use whatever information is available to you from your browser to see if you can come up with answers to these questions about this page:

a) How many framesets are used in defining the pop-up page?
b) How many frames are contained in each frameset?
c) What are the names of all of the pages used to compose that page?

2. We did, in fact, prepare a framed version of Rick & Stu's Home Page for your viewing pleasure. Check it out now, and you'll see that we took the main navigation image (which we had originally called "network") and placed it in a separate file from the rest of the original page. We then described the new page as a frameset composed of our two HTML files.

3. Produce a framed version of your home page now. Put the table of contents (or whatever you use to control navigation from the top of your page) in a frame along the left edge of the page. Use the rest of the page to display the contents of individual sections of your home page.

Review Exercises

1. How would you write the HTML for an outline like the one below?

    I. First topic
      A. Subtopic
      B. Another subtopic
        1. A sub-subtopic
        2. And another
    II. Second topic
      A. First part
      B. Second part

2. Why doesn't the `LI` element have an end tag?
3. What elements can be contained in a `TABLE` element?
4. How is a `FRAME` element like an `IMG` element?
5. What are the similarities between `FRAME`s and `TABLE`s?

4.6 DOING IT RIGHT

The Winchester House, in San Jose, California, is a classic example of bad design. It contains somewhere around 160 rooms, closets that open into other rooms, hallways that are dead-ends, stairwells that lead to nowhere, and a door that opens to a ten-foot drop into a kitchen sink below. While the house met the design criteria of its owner, Sarah Winchester,[4] it violates almost every architectural design principle imaginable. Clearly, in the design process, it's not enough to know how to put the parts together; we must be able to put the parts together to produce an elegant and functional whole.

We have already mentioned some of the general desiderata of a good computer system: It should be transparent, forgiving, visually oriented, and user-configurable. If you put yourself in the position of a frequent user of computers (which you may become after going through this text), it would probably not be too difficult to come up with a wish list of other features.

For instance, an application should be *fully functional* for its intended purpose. This book, for instance, was produced in a contemporary page layout program with the ability to include graphics along with text. This means that we didn't have to estimate the amount of space the pictures would take, leave blank spaces, and cut and glue the graphics in later.

A good application should also be *seamless*. In an ideal publishing application, we should not have to switch between a word processor and a graphics program to produce a manuscript for a textbook such as this. At the very least, we should be able to take a document from one application and import it into another application, and we should expect that at least some of the standard commands function in an analogous way across applications. Further, as we mentioned before, we should be able to start a new application and run it at the novice level without having to master an intimidating manual of unfamiliar commands.

These are just two of the guidelines that were first published by Apple computer to help software developers ensure that their products would be familiar to experienced Macintosh users and compatible with those of other manufacturers. To give you a feel for the full scope of these guidelines, we have excerpted below some portions of "The Macintosh User Interface Guide" from *Inside Macintosh*, volume 1 (New York: Addison-Wesley, 1985, quoted with permission). While intended for Mac developers, these guidelines are good advice in any environment.

> The user should feel in control of the computer, not the other way around. This is achieved in applications that embody three qualities: responsiveness, permissiveness, and consistency.
>
> Responsiveness means that the user's actions tend to have direct results. The user should be able to accomplish what needs to be done spontane-

[4] The house was built on the advice of a medium, to keep Mrs. Winchester from being tormented by the ghosts of people who had been killed by Winchester rifles made by her husband's company. It's open to the public and is well worth a visit.

ously and intuitively, rather than having to think: "Let's see; to do C, first I have to do A and B and then. . .". For example, with pull-down menus, the user can choose the desired command directly and instantaneously.

Permissiveness means that the application tends to allow the user to do anything reasonable. The user, not the system, decides what to do next. Also, error messages tend to come up infrequently. If the user is constantly subjected to a barrage of error messages, something is wrong somewhere.

The third and most important principle is consistency. Since Macintosh users usually divide their time among several applications, they would be confused and irritated if they had to learn a completely new interface for each application.

A fundamental object in Macintosh software is the icon, a small graphic object that's usually symbolic of an operation or of a larger entity such as a document.

Icons can contribute greatly to the clarity and attractiveness of an application. . . . Whenever an explanation or label is needed, consider using an icon, instead of text.

To choose a command, the user positions the pointer over the menu title and presses the mouse button. . . . Nothing actually happens until the user chooses the command; the user can look at any of the menus without making a commitment to do anything.

The most frequently used commands should be at the top of a menu; research shows that the easiest item for the user to choose is the second from the top. The most dangerous commands should be at the bottom of the menu, preferably isolated from the frequently used commands.

Some characters that can be typed along with the Command key are reserved for special purposes, but there are different degrees of stringency. Since almost every application has an Edit and a File menu, the keyboard equivalents of those menus are strongly reserved, and should never be used for any other purpose:

Character	Command
C	Copy (Edit menu)
Q	Quit (File menu)
V	Paste (Edit menu)
X	Cut (Edit menu
Z	Undo (Edit menu)

Note: The keyboard equivalent for the Quit command is useful in case there's a mouse malfunction, so the user will still be able to leave the application in an orderly way (with the opportunity to save any changes to documents that haven't yet been saved).

> One of the strongest ways in which modern computer applications can take advantage of the consistency of the user interface is by using standard menus. The operations controlled by these menus occur so frequently that it saves considerable time for users if they always match exactly. Three of these menus, the Apple, File, and Edit menus, appear in almost every application.
>
> Every user of every application is liable to do something that the application won't understand or can't cope with in a normal manner. Alerts [like the "Do you really want to erase your hard disk" box we illustrated earlier] give applications a way to respond to errors not only in a consistent manner, but in stages according to the severity of the error, the user's level of expertise, and the particular history of the error.
>
> The preferred (safest) button to use in the current situation is boldly outlined. This is the alert's default button; its effect occurs if the user presses Return or Enter.
>
> It's important to phrase messages in alert boxes so that users aren't left guessing the real meaning. Avoid computer jargon.
>
> Under no circumstances should an alert message refer the user to external documentation for further clarification. It should provide an adequate description of the information needed by the user to take appropriate action.

If much of this seems to be common sense applied to computer systems, that's because it is. The most important thing about user interface guidelines such as these is that they exist at all. Such guidelines not only let system designers know what users expect across applications, but also relieve the designers of the burden of designing the interface from the ground up for every application.

Programs and operating systems that conform to modern GUI guidelines have been around only since the mid-1980s, and there is certainly more to be learned. Despite recent trends toward informal standards for software, computer hardware as it relates to user interface is still in a volatile state. As technologies are developed, incorporated into products, and evaluated by the constantly growing population of computer operators, the successful ones will influence our interpretation of what constitutes an effective interface.

Imagine, for example, using your voice, instead of a keyboard, as the primary input device to your computer. This could at once render guidelines about shortcut keys meaningless, and necessitate a whole new set of guidelines devoted to speech etiquette and volume control. Things happen quickly in computer science and, as a result, we have yet to reach anything like the degree of standardization attained in the automotive industry.

We will close this module by presenting some user interface guidelines that we have adopted to help us in designing our Web pages (including those for the lab modules). As you would expect, they can all be summarized by saying "be nice to your audience." That said, here are some hints about how to be nice, in the time-honored form of a Top 10 list.

Rick & Stu's Top 10 Page Design Tips

10 Use standard HTML.
There are many browser-specific features that you use at your—and your audience's—peril. A page that looks great on your browser and machine could be a real mess for someone else. Review the HTML standards carefully to see which tags and attributes are supported by all browsers, and stick to those.

9 Use restraint with colors and backgrounds.
It's easy to go overboard with both colors and backgrounds, but remember the following: (1) Color is most effective when used as an accent, (2) your page should still be legible to viewers with black-and-white monitors, and (3) some colors of text (e.g., black) are virtually impossible to read on some backgrounds (e.g., psychedelic rainbow).

8 Avoid big stuff.
High-resolution graphics, sounds, and movies all require lots of bits, and all of those bits have to be shipped over the Net to your visitors. If a page takes too long to download, people will leave your site before they've seen anything. Also, there are still a bewildering number of different sound and video formats out there, many of which require a browser to have just the right helper application in order to play them. Since you can't be confident that your audience will be able to see or hear these things anyhow, leave them out.

7 Make navigation easy.
Provide plenty of clearly identified navigation tools, particularly if your site contains multiple pages. Do everything you can to ensure that visitors to your pages have a clear mental map of the organization of your site, know where they are within that organization at all times, and can move to, from, and within the site easily.

6 Don't blink.
Talk about irritating . . .

5 Make reading easy on the eyes.
This may not seem like a big deal to you, but the older you get, the more important it becomes (trust us!). Wide lines of text are hard to read and follow—that's why books aren't three-feet wide. Limit your text lines to about 400 pixels in width and you won't overwhelm your readers.

4 Do you kiss your mother with that mouth?
Remember two important aspects of this medium when adding content to your pages: (1) you cannot, by and large, control who has access to your pages, and (2) you don't have many nuancing clues at your disposal to let your audience know that you're only kidding. So, don't be an offensive ****head. While we're on the subject of giving offense, we note that libel laws still apply in cyberspace.

3 K.I.S.S.
Good design isn't something you learn overnight. Start developing your own sense of style by looking at other pages and asking yourself "What is it that makes this page so good?" or "Why does this page make me want to hurl?" Keep your overall design simple and consistent, and let it evolve gradually.

2 Eddit!
For sum reason, many peeple is intensely irritated by speling and grammatical error. Poor sentance structure, too. Edit your pages before you make them available to the browsing public. You won't regret it.

1 Verify your pages.
Speaking of editing, there are a growing number of services that will review your pages for compliance with standard HTML and will check them for spelling, and even grammar, errors. Check out the online resources we provide in the Module 4 lab, and use them.

LAB 4.7

Design Considerations

We mention in the text that Web page development is as much an art as a science, and that notions of style play a large part in what constitutes a "good" page. Review the tips and guidelines that we provided in the text to help you in evaluating your home page.

1. Evaluate your home page now in light of the design criteria provided in the text. If you feel your home page can be improved, do so now.

2. Trade home pages with one of your classmates so that you can review one another's work. Comment on both the browser and HTML versions, and then trade back. Make whatever changes to your page you think are appropriate in light of the comments you receive.

3. Finally, verify your page by submitting it to a verifier program.

Review Questions

1. Define the following terms in the context of an application user interface: *seamless, transparent, forgiving*.

2. For the terms in question 1, explain how they are or aren't part of the interface of the browser you've been using to do the lab exercises.

3. In what ways are keystroke combinations useful substitutes for menu choices?

4. Invent a different-looking scrollbar and discuss the advantages and disadvantages of your invention over the scrollbar you're accustomed to using.

4.7 EXERCISES

1. List three ways that advances in computer hardware—that is, the machines themselves—have influenced the evolution of the computer user interface.

2. List five features that have become standard parts of the automobile user interface.

3. In describing various computer applications in Modules 2 and 3, we used the term *microworld* to describe the interface presented to users. Do WWW pages project microworlds to their visitors? If so, what real-world setting do they model? If not, why not?

4. What features of HTML contribute to its general utility?

5. In what ways is HTML like a programming language?

6. What does it mean to say that a Web page, just like a spreadsheet document, is user-configurable?

7. Defend or disagree with the HTML specification recommendation that incorrect tags or attributes be ignored and that their enclosed text be presented as unformatted.

8. We mentioned that HTML is an evolving language. Use any resources available (including the WWW) to find three new features that are being planned for subsequent versions of HTML.

9. What is the difference between logical style elements and physical style elements in HTML? Why do you think HTML provides both types?

10. Pick any page from our online materials and evaluate it in terms of Rick & Stu's Top 10 Page Design Tips. Do we violate any of our own guidelines?

11. In what ways do you think computers of the future will be easier to use?

12. Crank up your browser and search for the worst Web page you can find, in terms of user interface. Critique its failings in terms of the guidelines we've presented.

MODULE 5

Cordon Bleu Computer Science

5.1 INTRODUCTION

HTML gives us the ability to lay out Web pages in almost any way our imaginations dictate. In fact, just about the only limitation to the pages we can design with what we've seen so far is that presenting information is all they can do. To be sure, we can click on our pages to navigate within them and around the WWW, but what happens when we want to design pages that are capable of even more interaction? What if we want our pages to process information as well as they present it?

The kinds of processing that could be described in the earliest versions of HTML were limited to implementing hypertext links. Subsequent versions of the language included elements that allowed one to design interactive forms, which in turn could include a variety of now-standard GUI widgets (like buttons, text fields, and selection lists). Forms represented a major advance in interactivity on two counts. Not only could pages now include the kinds of widgets to which users were accustomed for providing input, but forms also allowed this input, which went well beyond just specifying URL links, to be submitted to a Web server for processing. Still, forms left all of the processing to the Web server on which the original copy of the page resided. Unless the Web page designer had permission to write programs on the server machine, he or she was out of luck.

The current generation of browsers has been designed to remedy this situation, by allowing HTML documents to include their own *scripts*—lists of instructions for manipulating the data presented on the page in a variety of ways. That is to say, HTML documents can now contain programs as well as data. Such programs, written in a language called JavaScript,[1] are understood by modern Web browsers just

[1] You may have also heard about the language *Java*. Although somewhat related to JavaScript, Java is a different creature entirely. In your authors' opinion, it is unfortunate that the two languages have such closely similar names.

as other HTML elements are, and are executed on the client machine, as opposed to a server. As a result, page designers can now become, with some coaching and a little practice, Web programmers. Our goal in this module is to provide you with both the coaching and the opportunity to develop and practice your programming skills.

MODULE OBJECTIVES

In this module, we will

- Show you how to use HTML forms and image maps to enhance the interactivity of Web pages.
- Discuss the basic structure of a JavaScript program and the ways in which one can be embedded within an HTML document.
- Present the types of information that can be described in JavaScript and the statements that are used to manipulate information.
- Review the control statements that JavaScript provides for affecting the order of execution of statements.
- Describe how to use some of JavaScript's built-in objects, and how to write functions of our own.

The Algorithm Machine

JavaScript is the language used to write HTML scripts. Scripts describe the actions associated with the components of a Web page. In the pages to come, we will teach you the fundamentals of JavaScript programming. Along the way, we will discuss the similarities between JavaScript and other programming languages, pointing out JavaScript's comparative strengths and weaknesses. Finally, we will discuss some programming principles. Programming a computer is similar in many ways to any other large cognitive task, such as writing an essay. We will see that the precepts of efficient programming are nothing more than commonsense rules applied to the task of designing a collection of instructions to the computer.

Metaphor: The Electronic Kitchen

In Modules 2 and 3 we explored the worlds of computer applications. Using those programs to conduct the associated lab exercises was similar to being a guest at a dinner party—the sequence of courses and their contents had been chosen for you, and all you had to do was sample them. In Module 4, when you designed Web pages of your own, you were the host of the dinner party, choosing the courses for the meal from a menu so they would blend together in a pleasing evening's experience.

In this module we will take you into the kitchen and show you how to combine the raw ingredients to produce each dish. Just as in a cooking school, we will begin by discussing the ingredients themselves, then instruct you in the fundamentals of combining these ingredients—the computer equivalent of a basic white sauce—and finally discuss how to blend all the individual components into a pleasing and functional whole. At the end, you will have more than a cookbook knowledge of programming and will be on your way to creating your own recipes with taste and elegance. Although we won't be able to transform you into a master of the electronic kitchen in a single module, we hope that these first steps will be enjoyable and enlightening, providing the flavor of the programming process itself.

Æ Online

With the HTML we have seen so far, we are constrained to designing pages that look good, but have limited functionality. We can control in great detail where and how components will appear on the page, but we cannot specify how these components are to behave, beyond creating simple hyperlinks. To attain a greater level of control over our pages we must expand our HTML repertoire in two related directions. First, we must learn how to incorporate HTML form elements and imagemaps into our pages. You will see in this text module that these are nothing more than collections of the kinds of widgets that we use to provide input to and control the actions of most modern programs. Then, we must learn to write the JavaScript statements and functions that implement the desired behavior of our page's widgets.

The labs for this module concentrate on the second of these tasks, providing a hands-on introduction to the JavaScript language. In these labs we focus on the scripts of an adventure game, in which you are charged with the task of collecting the necessary items that will get you into a concert. You will use the program to see how it performs, read and develop an understanding of its code, revise it to see the implications of changes, and, finally, extend it so that it accomplishes altogether new behaviors. In doing so, we'll scratch the surface of JavaScript. As was the case in Module 4 wherein we introduced HTML, we can't expect to provide you with a full description of either JavaScript or computer programming in a single module. Rather, our goal is to expose you to some of the algorithms and one of the programming languages that underlie the behavior of Web pages. Our hope is that you will, at last, be able to see through the inner workings of these pages—that they will become clear boxes.

LAB 5.1

Get Smashed . . . Bananas

This set of exercises is intended merely to familiarize you with the JavaScript game that is the basis for the rest of the Module 5 lab exercises. The game is an adventure in which you are provided with tickets to a virtual concert. Your job is to accumulate the necessary items (like money, transportation, clothes, munchies, etc.) and to get yourself there. You do so by clicking on the items you want to acquire and the activities you want to perform, and keeping track of your inventory of goods.

The game operates in two modes. When in Look mode, clicking on the images presented doesn't actually perform any actions. Instead, messages appear on the screen informing you about whatever you clicked on. Clicking on the images in Action mode moves you through the game, taking you places and allowing you to acquire goods and make purchases.

1. Start the program now by loading the appropriate page from Module 5 into your browser. Play the game by clicking anywhere on the image presented. Investigate the game thoroughly by clicking on everything in both Look and Action modes. Try to make it all the way to the concert.

2. Reload this page now in your browser, so that you can start the game from the beginning. Run through the program now with an eye toward answering the following questions about how it is organized. Write your answers on a separate sheet of paper.

   a) What must you take with you to go shopping from the first screen?
   b) What happens if you try to get cash from the ATM when you already have ATM cash in your inventory?
   c) What happens when you try to go to the convenience store?
   d) Are there any items that you cannot buy at the clothing store?
   e) What happens if you try to check out with the cashier at the store when you don't have any money?
   f) What happens to the ATM cash in your inventory when you check out with the cashier at the clothing store?
   g) What happens when you select the leather jacket at the clothing store twice?
   h) What inventory items do you absolutely need in order to get to the concert?
   i) What happens when you get to the concert and you click on the entrance (in Action mode)?

3. Now we'll examine the JavaScript code that implements our game. You can do so in at least two ways. First, you can select View|Document Source (or something similar) while viewing the game page from your browser. Do so now and look over the HTML file, with its embedded JavaScript scripts.

4. Since all of your lab activity from this point on will involve editing this HTML file, and since you can't edit the document source on our server or on the CD, choose File|Save As... from the menu and save this file on your hard drive as "My Game.html." This file can be opened by any word processor or HTML editor that you like. You can then edit the file, per our instructions in subsequent labs, and run your version of the game by opening the file in your browser (using the File|Open File in Browser command). The game also requires some images that we asked you to download, unzip, and save back in the lab exercises for Module 3. If you have not already done so, download them now. Then unzip them, and put them in the same directory/folder as the file MyGame.html.

5. Review the code more carefully now. In particular, add comments (comments are lines within the `<SCRIPT>` tag that begin with //) to your version of the code to indicate which lines of JavaScript explain each of your answers in Excercise 2, above. That is, add a comment that says "`// this explains answer 2a`" at the point in the script that explains what items you need in order to go shopping from the first screen. Do the same for questions 2b through 2i.

5.2 SETTING THE TABLE: IMAGEMAPS AND FORMS

The first step we will take toward making our pages more responsive to our processing demands is to incorporate into them the HTML elements that are made to interact with scripts. We describe in the following sections two such elements, imagemaps and forms. While we can describe forms and imagemaps strictly in interface terms—that is, solely in terms of the effects they have on the appearance of a page—their full benefits are realized once we couple them with JavaScript programs. In effect, we're setting the table so that we'll be ready for what is the main course of this module—JavaScript.

■ Imagemaps

One way to enhance the interactivity of your pages is to include clickable *imagemaps*—images that not only allow you to click on them to initiate some action, but also vary their actions based on where in the image you click. You've seen an example of this in one of our earlier sample pages. Remember Rick & Stu's Home Page from Module 4, and the networklike image that appeared near the top of the page (Figure 5.1)? Clicking on different parts of the image linked you to different places in the page. Here is the code that accomplished this behavior. It includes three HTML features we haven't discussed before.

```
<IMG SRC = "network.gif" BORDER = 0 USEMAP = "#Network">
...
<MAP NAME = "Network">
    <AREA SHAPE = RECT COORDS = "0,0,72,52" HREF = "#Rick">
    <AREA SHAPE = RECT COORDS = "249,136,308,188" HREF = "#Stu">
    <AREA SHAPE = RECT COORDS = "96,87,189,138" HREF = "#Books">
    <AREA SHAPE = RECT COORDS = "175,26,284,79" HREF = "#Classes">
    <AREA SHAPE = RECT COORDS = "25,158,107,210" HREF = "#Links">
</MAP>
```

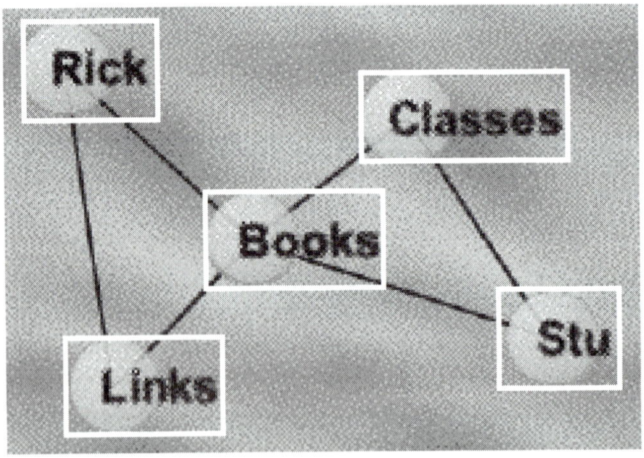

FIGURE 5.1
An imagemap, with clickable regions revealed

The first new feature is the USEMAP attribute in the IMG element. By specifying this attribute for an image we accomplish two things. We notify the browser that we intend to use the image being described as a clickable imagemap, and we identify the MAP elements, the second new feature, to be used to respond to clicks on the image. The MAP element is where we describe the coordinate system to be imposed on the image, and the links to be generated by clicks on different coordinates. The third new feature, the AREA element, describes this information for the map.

As you can no doubt discern from this example, the MAP element is a container element that encloses any number of AREA elements. The MAP element should be named (using its NAME attribute) so that it can be referenced as the USEMAP value for some image. AREA elements are empty elements (and thus require no end tags) that are described in terms of four attributes. The SHAPE value (which can be RECT, CIRCLE, or POLYGON) describes the geometry of each region of the map. The coordinates defining each area are specified as the value for the COORDS attribute, the only required attribute. The COORDS value is a string describing a region of the image in terms of two points, which in turn are specified as *x,y* coordinate pairs. The string provides the values for the left, top, right, and bottom bounds, respectively, of the rectangle, where (0,0) corresponds to the top-left corner of the image. The HREF attribute is what you would expect, the URL or anchor to be linked to by a click on this area. If no hyperlink is to be generated for a particular area, the NOHREF attribute can be specified.

◆ We'll discuss only rectangular shapes here.

Forms

The FORM element expands our HTML repertoire so that our pages can contain collections of widgets—buttons, checkboxes, radio buttons, selection lists, text fields, and the like—that are useful for communicating with the user. We'll see in subsequent sections how we make this communication two-way, so that we can not only solicit input from users of our pages but also process their input in meaningful ways. For now, though, we'll concentrate on defining these interface elements and displaying them.

You have already seen examples of forms, whether you've realized it or not. Any pages that you may have come across in your surfing that contain standard GUI widgets were most likely implemented using forms. If these pages responded to your input (beyond processing hyperlinks), they most certainly were. In fact, one of the sample pages we discussed in Module 4 used a form. You may remember one of the pages we used to demonstrate frames, the one describing Popito's Pizza Parlor. You may also remember that that page was defined as a frameset containing two frames (one displaying Popito's logo, and the other the pizza order form), and that we told you not to worry about how the order form had been defined. We can describe that page for you in full detail once we understand how HTML forms are defined.

The elements and attributes that support the description of forms are summarized in Table 5.1, starting with the most important one, the FORM element. FORM elements (there can be more than one) appear in the body of an HTML document and enclose all the other elements that are to appear as part of the form. These other elements can include standard HTML elements such as text, formatting commands, anchors, lists, and tables (but not other forms). In addition, there are three new element types that can only appear in the context of a form: the INPUT, SELECT, and TEXTAREA elements.

TABLE 5.1
Form-related HTML elements and attributes

<FORM>...</FORM>

Can contain:
Any standard HTML elements (but *not* another FORM), INPUT, SELECT, TEXTAREA.
Attributes:

NAME = "*name*"	Names the form so that its elements are accessible to scripts
ACTION = "*URL*"	The URL of the program that will process the form when it is submitted

<INPUT>

An empty element used to designate some type of input mechanism
Can contain:
Nothing.
Attributes:

TYPE = "text"	A single-line text field
"image"	An image or part of the form
"checkbox"	A clickable field, either selected or not selected
"radio"	A clickable field that can be part of a group, so that only one can be selected at a time
"button"	A clickable button
"submit"	A clickable button designated to send form data to the server (we won't discuss this in detail)
"reset"	A clickable button designated to reset all form elements to their default values
SRC = "*URL*"	URL of an inline image
NAME = "*name*"	Names this form element
VALUE = "*string*"	Default for text elements; submitted value for checkboxes, radios, and buttons
CHECKED	Indicates radio buttons or checkboxes that have been selected
SIZE = *num*	The number of characters allowed in a text field

<SELECT>...</SELECT>

Encloses a selection list composed of OPTION elements
Can contain:
OPTION elements
Attributes:

NAME = "*name*"	The name for the selection list
SIZE = *num*	The number of options to be displayed at one time
MULTIPLE	Allows more than one option to be selected

<TEXTAREA>...</TEXTAREA>

A multiple-line text field with default contents equal to the enclosed text
Can contain:
Text
Attributes:

NAME = "*name*"	The name of the text area
ROWS = *num*	The number of lines to be displayed
COLS = *num*	The number of characters per line to be displayed

The `INPUT` element is used to describe some kind of a GUI widget within a form. Its `TYPE` attribute specifies which type of widget we are describing. Permissible values for the `TYPE` attribute include "text" (to identify a single-line text field), "image" (an image as part of the form), "checkbox" (a clickable entry that is either selected or not selected), "radio" (a radio-style button that can be part of a group of same, so that only one of the group is selected at a time), "submit" (a clickable button with the predefined action of sending the form's data—the names and values of all of its enclosed elements—to a server program for processing), and "reset" (another predefined button, which sets the values of the form's elements to their initial values).

The `NAME` attribute will prove to be very useful for scripting purposes for any type of `INPUT` element. Other attributes have different meanings depending on the type of the element. For example, the `SRC` attribute provides the URL for an `INPUT` element of type "image." The `CHECKED` attribute sets the status of a checkbox or a radio button. The `SIZE` attribute defines the number of characters that will be visibly displayed in a text field. The `VALUE` attribute can be used to provide default values for text fields, checkboxes, and radio buttons. Here's an example of setting up a form that uses some of the `INPUT` widgets. Figure 5.2 shows what they look like in one browser.[2]

FIGURE 5.2
Some `INPUT` widgets, as displayed by a browser

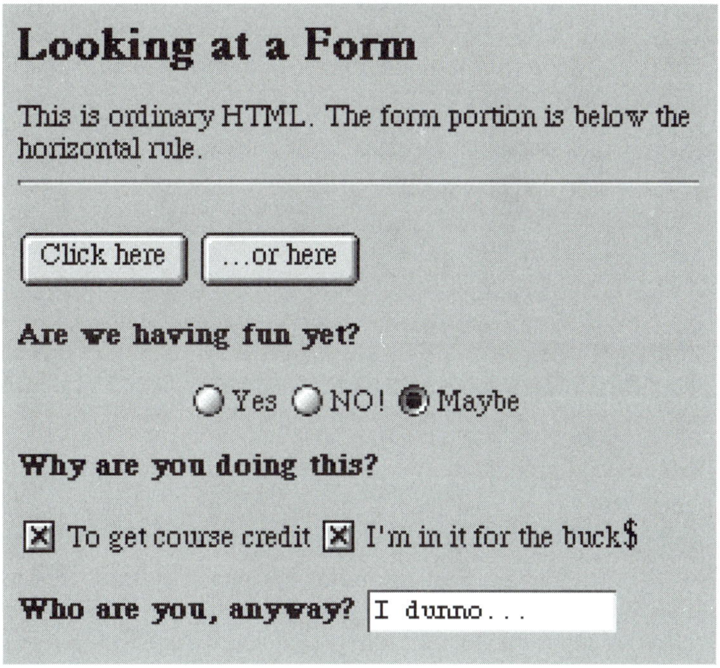

[2] The look of the widgets will vary somewhat, depending on the browser and the underlying system.

```
<HTML>
<HEAD>
   <TITLE>Form Widgets</TITLE>
</HEAD>

<BODY>
   <H2>Looking at a Form</H2>
   This is ordinary HTML. The form portion is below the
   horizontal rule.
   <HR>
   <FORM NAME = "colors">
      <INPUT    TYPE = "button"
                VALUE = "Click here">
      <INPUT    TYPE = "button"
                VALUE = "...or here">
      <P><B>Are we having fun yet?</B></P>
      <CENTER>
      <INPUT    TYPE = "radio"
                NAME = "fun"
                VALUE = "yes">Yes
      <INPUT    TYPE = "radio"
                NAME = "fun"
                VALUE = "no">NO!
      <INPUT    TYPE = "radio"
                NAME = "fun"
                VALUE = "maybe" CHECKED>Maybe
      </CENTER>
      <P><B>Why are you doing this?</B></P>
      <INPUT    TYPE = "checkbox"
                NAME = "credit" CHECKED>To get course credit
      <INPUT    TYPE = "checkbox"
                NAME = "bucks" CHECKED>I'm in it for the
                        buck<BIG>$</BIG>
      <BR><BR>
      <P><B>Who are you, anyway?</B>
      <INPUT    TYPE = "text"
                NAME = "name"
                VALUE = "I dunno..."
                SIZE = 15>
   </FORM>
</BODY>
</HTML>
```

By assigning all of the radio buttons the same value ("fun") for their NAME attribute, we tell the browser to treat them as a single unit so that only one can be selected at a time. In addition, notice that we used a number of ordinary HTML elements, such as CENTER, P, B, BR, BIG, and ordinary text in the FORM element, as well as the INPUT elements that can appear only in the context of a FORM.

Whereas the INPUT element encompasses a wide variety of GUI widgets, two other widgets are described by their own form elements. A pull-down selection list has its own list-style element, the SELECT element. SELECT is a list in the HTML sense in that it encloses a series of items that define the constituents of the list. The constituents of a selection list are identified by the OPTION tag (which, like most list items, does not require an end tag). So, the general format of a selection list will be

```
<SELECT NAME = "name of this list">
   <OPTION> selection 1 text
   <OPTION> selection 2 text
   ...
   <OPTION> selection N text
</SELECT>
```

The OPTION elements enclose the text of the selection list entries. In addition to a NAME attribute, the SELECT element can have attributes SIZE (the value of which defines the number of list options that will be visible at one time) and MULTIPLE (which takes no value, but when it is included designates that more than one option may be selected from the list at one time). OPTION elements can have attributes SELECTED (with no value, to indicate that a particular option should be selected by default) and VALUE (the value of which, effectively, names the option element).

In Figure 5.3 we have two SELECT elements, as they would appear in a FORM. To the right of the HTML we show what they might look like when displayed by a browser, with the second shown both in its default state and as pulled down by the user. Notice that setting SIZE to a number other than 1 changes the displayed element from a pull-down menu to a selectable list.

The TEXTAREA element is the third and last form-only element. It is a container element used to describe multiple-line text fields (Figure 5.4). It encloses the (optional) text that will appear as the default text in the field, and can take three attributes: NAME (so that we can access the contents of the field), ROWS (the number of lines of text to be displayed at once), and COLS (the number of characters per line to be displayed). The browser will determine if and in which directions text areas are scrollable based on the values of these attributes and the enclosed text.

FIGURE 5.3
Two SELECT objects

```
<SELECT SIZE = 4
        NAME = "Choices"
        MULTIPLE>
   <OPTION> First option
   <OPTION SELECTED> Another
   <OPTION> The last option
</SELECT>
```

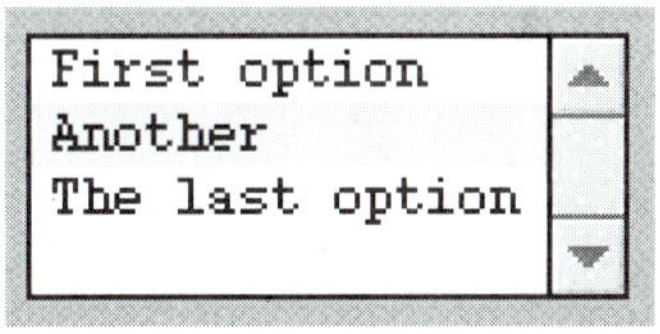


```
<SELECT SIZE = 1
        NAME = "Choices">
   <OPTION> First option
   <OPTION> Another
   <OPTION> The last option
</SELECT>
```

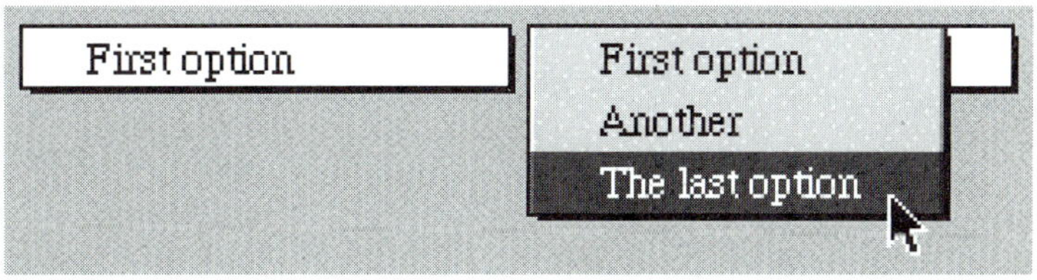

FIGURE 5.4
A TEXTAREA, *code and display*

```
<TEXTAREA NAME = "display"
          ROWS = 5
          COLS = 15>
Plain text can go in
here, but <B>no</B>
HTML formatting.
</TEXTAREA>
```

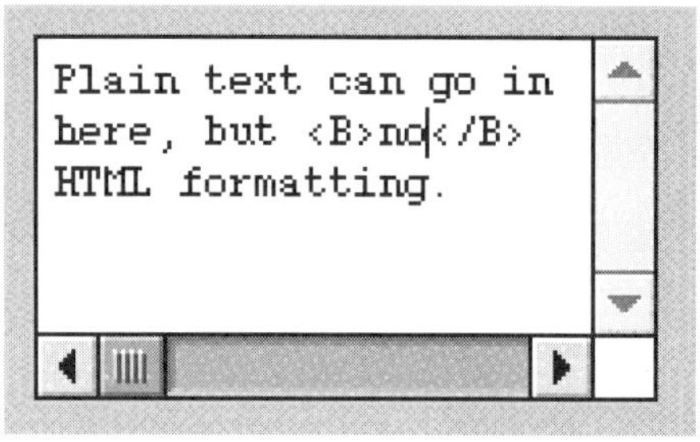

FIGURE 5.5
Part of an online pizza order form

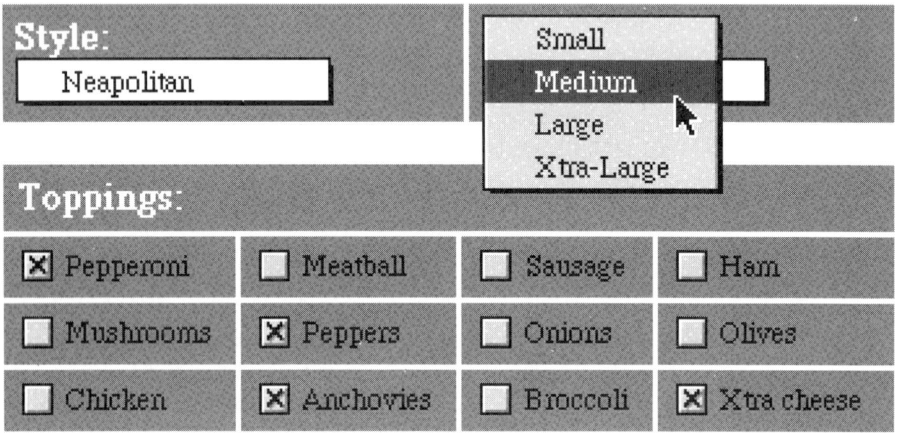

As we said before, many of these form-related elements are illustrated in the page that defines the order form part of our Popito's Pizza frameset. Figure 5.5 shows what part of the page looks like in a browser. This is a realistic example because it not only illustrates a few different form elements (like selection lists and checkboxes), but it also shows how to use other elements (like text, format elements, and tables) to lay out a form's elements in a way that is attractive and helpful to the user.

Below, we list the part of the code that generates the display in Figure 5.5. Take particular note of how we used tables to place the form elements in a pair of rectangular arrangements.

```
<HTML>
<HEAD>
   <TITLE>Popito's Pizza on-line order form</TITLE>

<!-- Lots of JavaScript not shown here -->

</HEAD>

<BODY BGCOLOR = "white" TEXT = "black">
   <FORM NAME = "Order">
      <TABLE    WIDTH = 100%
                BORDER = 0
                CELLPADDING = 5>
<TR>
```

```
<TD BGCOLOR = "gray">
   <FONT COLOR = "white"><BIG><B>Style:</B></BIG></FONT><BR>
   <SELECT NAME = "Type">
      <OPTION VALUE = "Neapolitan" SELECTED>Neapolitan
      <OPTION VALUE = "Sicilian">Sicilian
      <OPTION VALUE = "Deep-Dish">Deep-Dish
      <OPTION VALUE = "Tomato Pie">Tomato Pie
      <OPTION VALUE = "Stuffed Crust">Stuffed Crust
   </SELECT></TD>
<TD BGCOLOR = "gray">
   <FONT COLOR = "white"><BIG><B>Size:</B></BIG></FONT><BR>
   <SELECT NAME = "Size">
      <OPTION VALUE = "Small">Small
      <OPTION VALUE = "Medium">Medium
      <OPTION VALUE = "Large" SELECTED> Large
      <OPTION VALUE = "Xtra Large">Xtra-Large
   </SELECT></TD>
</TR>
</TABLE>
<BR>
   <TABLE      WIDTH = 100%
               BORDER = 0
               CELLPADDING = 5
               BGCOLOR = "gray">
   <TR>
   <TD COLSPAN = 4>
     <FONT COLOR = "white"><BIG><B>Toppings:</B></BIG></FONT>
   </TD>
   </TR>
   <TR>
   <TD><INPUT  TYPE = "checkbox"
               NAME = "Pepperoni">Pepperoni</TD>
   <TD><INPUT  TYPE = "checkbox"
               NAME ="Meatball">Meatball</TD>
   <TD><INPUT  TYPE = "checkbox"
               NAME ="Sausage">Sausage</TD>
   <TD><INPUT  TYPE = "checkbox"
               NAME ="Ham">Ham</TD>
   </TR>
<!-- Two table rows omitted here, to save space -->

   </TABLE>
   <BR>
<!-- Quite a bit more code omitted here -->
   </FORM>
</BODY>
</HTML>
```

The first table has one row and two data items. Each data item contains some simple text and a selection list. Each list is designated by a SELECT element, and is assigned a name ("Type" and "Size"). Note how in each case the SELECT element contains a series of OPTION elements that, in turn, define the entries in the list.

Note, too, how the text marked by the `OPTION`[3] is what appears in the list when it is displayed. The `VALUE` attribute assigned to each option is effectively a name, which we'll use to refer to the list item when we write scripts.

The second table in our sample form contains, in addition to a simple text label spanning all four columns, three rows of four checkboxes each. The checkboxes are defined as `INPUT` elements with `TYPE` attribute set to "checkbox". As was the case with our selection list options in the first table, the text enclosed by the table data (`TD`) element is what appears next to each checkbox. Checkboxes by themselves do not have text labels. The `VALUE` attribute for the checkbox specifies both the name for referencing the checkbox and the value that will be associated with it if it is checked (selected) when the form is submitted to a server for processing. We were careful to completely enclose each checkbox description (remember, the `INPUT` element is an empty one) within a `TD` element.

As you will see in lab, we make extensive use of both forms and image maps in the page that serves as the basis for all of the Module 5 lab activities. Figure 5.6 shows that page as presented by a browser, and the use of a form is evident from the radio buttons ("Action" and "Look"), the textarea (labeled "Inventory"), and the text field ("Status"). The image that occupies most of the page is defined with a `USEMAP` attribute that refers to an imagemap that breaks the 320-by-240 pixel image into 768 10-by-10 rectangular regions. The `MAP` element and all of its enclosed `AREA` tags do

FIGURE 5.6
The main screen of the adventure game

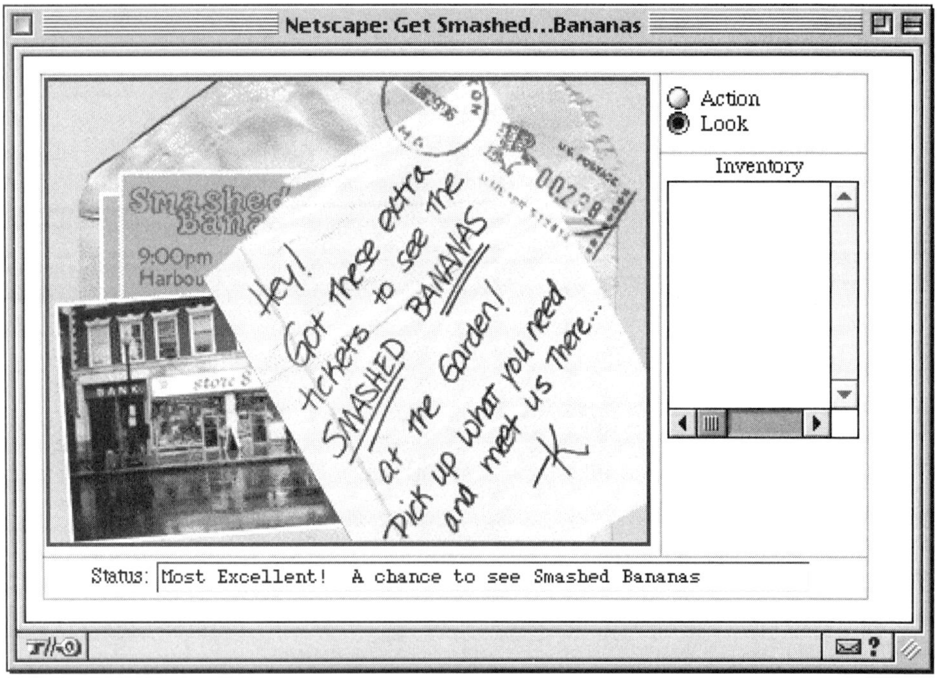

[3] Even though there is no end tag specified, the `OPTION` element is in fact a container, in the same sense that the `LI` element is.

not appear directly in the HTML code. Rather, we have (in the interest of keeping the HTML file shorter) written JavaScript programs to produce the imagemap dynamically, while the page is being loaded. We have also written a set of JavaScript programs to interpret where clicks on different regions of different images are to link to (since the image being displayed changes as you progress through the game). In order to understand how all of this interaction takes place, we'd better turn our attention to the real topic of this module, programming with JavaScript.

Review Questions

1. Define the following attributes and elements, and show how they're used in an imagemap: `USEMAP`, `MAP`, `AREA`.
2. What are the width and height of the rectangle described by the attribute/value pair COORDS = "30, 40, 100, 150"?
3. Can HTML formatting and layout elements be used in a `FORM` element? Can a `FORM` appear within another `FORM`?
4. In what way does a `SELECT` element resemble an `UL` element? In what ways do they differ?
5. What are the seven types of `INPUT` elements?

5.3 RECIPES: THE STRUCTURE OF JAVASCRIPT PROGRAMS

Having looked at the HTML code for our concert game in lab, you may have been struck by the length of the HTML document. This code is much longer than that of any of the pages we've discussed so far. That's because the file contains a good deal of JavaScript code that we have not included in previous examples. Indeed, most of the file is JavaScript code, with only a page or two devoted to the more conventional HTML elements that lay out its interface. When you think about it, this corresponds quite realistically with the game itself. The interface is pretty straightforward; the way the page responds to and interacts with the user is what makes it interesting. Where, then, does one start in attempting to understand this morass of code?

The key, initially at least, is to understand the basic notation used in writing the code. In order to follow the recipe presented in Figure 5.7 a cook must understand, as most of us do, how recipes are described. Ingredients tend to be listed first, but can be folded into the recipe steps (as in "add 1 cup of sugar"); "c." stands for cup; "tsp." stands for teaspoon; the ingredients are not to be carried out; the steps are to be carried out, in the order listed; a similarly organized recipe must exist for Rick & Stu's Flaky Pie Crust; "dribble" in this context does not mean drool—all of this information is implicit in every recipe. Let's see if we can explain the comparable information for a JavaScript program.

■ The Core Example

We'll start by taking a look at a complete example of JavaScript in action. This page, illustrated in Figure 5.8, appears much simpler than the code that's necessary to bring it to life. Clicking on the Change button will change the background color's

FIGURE 5.7
Rick & Stu's Deep Dish Apple Pie

Ingredients

1-1/2 c. quartered apples, peeled and cored
1/2 c. honey
1-1/2 tsp. lemon juice
1/4 c. unbleached white flour
1-1/2 tsp. cinnamon
1-1/2 tbsp. butter

Place apples in bowl.
Toss with flour and cinnamon until covered.
Follow recipe for Rick & Stu's Flaky Pie Crust.
Place bottom portion of crust into 2-inch deep baking dish (either 8-inch round or 6-inch × 10-inch rectangle).
Arrange apple mixture in baking dish.
Blend honey and lemon juice in a cup.
Dribble cup contents over apple mixture.
Dot with butter.
Cover apple mixture with top portion of crust.
Bake at 425 degrees for 45 minutes, or until top is golden brown.

FIGURE 5.8
A color-changing page

red, green, and blue components. When the background color changes, the hex values of the components are displayed in the three small text fields at the bottom.

Below, we provide the code that produces the page you see. There's quite a lot here that may seem incomprehensible at first—that's to be expected, since we haven't described any of JavaScript's features yet. We present this example because it illustrates not only the structure common to most JavaScript-based applications, but also because its details cover most of the programming we'll mention in this and subsequent sections. We'll come back to this example a number of times, gradually bringing order to this apparent chaos, until we've covered enough of JavaScript for you to be able to sit down and write something comparable from scratch, with no more than the usual amount of cursing and hair-pulling that even the most seasoned programmers experience.

```
<HTML>
<HEAD>
   <TITLE>Most of JavaScript</TITLE>
   <!-- This page contains most of the JavaScript features we'll -->
   <!-- discuss in Module 5. Not only does it serve as a good -->
   <!-- example of what's to come, but it's also amusing to use. -->

   <SCRIPT LANGUAGE = "JavaScript">
   <!-- Hide this code from JavaScript-ignorant browsers

      /* These integers represent the RGB components
         of the background color. */
      red = parseInt(document.bgColor.substring(1, 3), 16);
      green = parseInt(document.bgColor.substring(3, 5), 16);
      blue = parseInt(document.bgColor.substring(5, 7), 16);

      function hexChar(n) {
      // Return the hex equivalent of a number between 0 and 15.
         if (n == 10)
           return "A";
         else if (n == 11)
           return "B";
         else if (n == 12)
           return "C";
         else if (n == 13)
           return "D";
         else if (n == 14)
           return "E";
         else if (n == 15)
           return "F";
         else
           return "" + n;
      }

      function toHex(n, d) {
      /* Return the hex equivalent of n as a string
         of length d, truncating or padding with zeros
         as necessary. */
         var s = "";
         for (var i = 0; i < d; i++) {
           s = hexChar(n % 16) + s;
           n = Math.floor(n / 16);
           }
           return s;
      }

      function report() {
      // Show the color components in the three fields of
```

```
        // the "colors" form.
           document.colors.redHex.value = toHex(red, 2);
           document.colors.greenHex.value = toHex(green, 2);
           document.colors.blueHex.value = toHex(blue, 2);
        }

        function changeColors() {
        // Modify the components of the background color.
           red += 3;
           green += 5;
           blue += 7;

           document.bgColor =
              toHex(red, 2) +
              toHex(green, 2)+
              toHex(blue, 2);
           report();
        }
        // end hiding -->
     </SCRIPT>

  </HEAD>
  <BODY ONLOAD = "report()">
     <H1>Colorful JavaScript</H1>
     We start with the usual background you see every time you
     crank up your browser. Click the "Change" button and watch
     what happens to the background color.
     <HR>
     <FORM NAME = "colors">
        <CENTER>
        <INPUT    TYPE = "button"
                  VALUE = "Change"
                  ONCLICK = "changeColors()">
        <H4>Background Color Components (hex)</H4>
        <FONT COLOR = "red">red</FONT>:
        <INPUT    TYPE = "text"
                  NAME = "redHex"
                  SIZE = 3> 
        <FONT COLOR = "green">green</FONT>:
        <INPUT    TYPE = "text"
                  NAME = "greenHex"
                  SIZE = 3> 
        <FONT COLOR = "blue">blue</FONT>:
        <INPUT    TYPE = "text"
                  NAME = "blueHex"
                  SIZE = 3>
        </CENTER>
        </FORM>

  </BODY>
  </HTML>
```

Scripts

◆ When a browser is inside a SCRIPT element, it interprets the contents using different rules – it's in programming mode rather than HTML mode.

The first thing to know about a JavaScript program is that it is an extension of HTML; that is, it is written directly into an HTML document and so is defined by an HTML element. The SCRIPT element is a relatively recent addition to HTML, with the express purpose of designating programming language statements that are to be interpreted by the browser. SCRIPT is a container element (the begin and end tags enclose the statements) with a LANGUAGE attribute, the value of which identifies the programming language in which the statements are written. Every SCRIPT element we see in this module will have the basic form shown below:

```
<SCRIPT LANGUAGE = "JavaScript">
    JavaScript statements go here
</SCRIPT>
```

The second thing to know about a JavaScript program is that it may be composed of many SCRIPT elements. In fact, SCRIPT elements can appear in both the head and the body of a page. SCRIPT elements, like all other HTML elements, are processed in the order in which they appear in the document. Statements in the document head are processed before any in the body, and those nearer the beginning of the body are processed before those toward the end. Most of the time, though, we'll put the vast majority of our JavaScript in a single SCRIPT container in the HEAD portion of a document, as we did in our colors example:

```
<HTML>
<HEAD>
    <TITLE>Some title goes here</TITLE>
    <SCRIPT LANGUAGE = "JavaScript">
    <!-- Hide this code from JavaScript-ignorant browsers

    Here's where the JavaScript goes

    // end hiding -->
    </SCRIPT>
</HEAD>
<BODY>

    Ordinary HTML, perhaps with one or more forms. You already know
    almost everything that appears here.

</BODY>
</HTML>
```

Comments

◆ We might also use the NOSCRIPT container to provide a link to alternate pages that can be read by browsers that don't recognize scripts.

Take a look at the portion of our core example we excerpted above. Notice the HTML comment symbols immediately following the script's start tag and immediately preceding the script's end tag. This is an easy way to safeguard your page from a browser that is not JavaScript-savvy (as some older browsers are not). We don't have to hide the SCRIPT start and end tags—browsers will simply ignore any tags they don't recognize—but we do have to hide the JavaScript that's contained in the tags; otherwise, the browser would treat it as ordinary text and display it, much to the dismay of the reader. What we do, then is "comment it out" by enclosing it within the HTML comment tags `<!--` and `-->`.

◆ The JavaScript comments `//` and `/*...*/` have no meaning in HTML, so use them only within the confines of a `SCRIPT` element.

Speaking of comments, JavaScript provides two comment forms for use within `SCRIPT` elements. Whenever the symbols `//` appear together, the remaining text on that line is treated as a comment—that is, it is ignored by the browser. We also used JavaScript's multiple-line comment indicator, which begins with the string `/*` and ends, any number of lines later, with the string `*/`. This notation allows us to include more lengthy comments in our JavaScript code. As we write increasingly complex `script` elements, we'll find comments increasingly useful as a means for explaining the parts of our programs, both to our readers and ourselves, as you can see here:

```
/* These integers represent the RGB components of the
   background color. */
red = parseInt(document.bgColor.substring(1, 3), 16);

...

function hexChar(n) {
// Return the hex equivalent of a number between 0 and 15.
   if (n == 10)
      return "A";
   else if (n == 11)
      return "B";

   ...

}
```

Statements and Functions

◆ Variable: A named container for information.

As useful as they are to people, from a browser's perspective comments are the least interesting things we can put into a script. The fundamental action unit of a script is the *statement,* some JavaScript code that says, "do this." The snippet above, for example, begins with three statements that set the values of *variables* `red`, `green`, and `blue` to some initial values. These variables are just user-defined names for containers of information, in this case the amounts of red, green, and blue in the background color. The first statement, for instance, just says "set the value of `red` to the amount described in the first two characters of the background color descriptor." Such statements are like the steps in a recipe—they are descriptions of actions that are to be performed in the order they appear.

The next script element, though, is a different kind of beast. It begins with the word `function`, provides a name for this function ("hexChar"), and specifies a *parameter list* of incoming information (a number, n, in this case), and a *body* for the function. The body of the function is a collection of JavaScript statements enclosed in curly braces, `{...}` and separated by semicolons. We'll explain functions and their constituent parts in full detail in subsequent sections. For now, the key notion to understand is that functions, unlike any other kind of JavaScript statement, are not executed when they are encountered by the browser, but rather are held in waiting until they are invoked by name. Function definitions are identified and described at the beginning,

◆ Function invocation is sort of like summoning a demon in fantasy literature.

and are called into action in the recipe's steps. In this case, we define the function `hexChar` in the head of the page and *invoke* it—call it into action—a few lines later, by using its name. It is not until the function is invoked that the statements in its body get executed by the browser. In recipe terms, invoking a function is like saying "Follow the procedure for Rick & Stu's Flaky Pie Crust [which is defined elsewhere]."

The example script contains four functions we wrote ourselves, along with invocations of functions (such as `parseInt`, `floor`, and `substring`) that are built into the language. In the sections to come, we'll list some of the most useful predefined functions (and their cousins, known as *methods*), and we'll tell you how to write functions of your own.

Events

Here's the skeleton of the single `SCRIPT` on our example page. The first three statements are executed as soon as they're loaded by the browser. That's easy enough to understand, but most of the work is apparently being done by the four user-defined functions:

- The function `changeColors` calls `report`.
- Both `report` and `changeColors` call `toHex`.
- `toHex` calls `hexChar`.

But how does this chain of function calls start? Where is `changeColor` called in the first place?

```
red = parseInt(document.bgColor.substring(1, 3), 16);
green = parseInt(document.bgColor.substring(3, 5), 16);
blue = parseInt(document.bgColor.substring(5, 7), 16);

function hexChar(n) {
...
}

function toHex(n, d) {
...
   s = hexChar(n % 16) + s;
...
}

function report() {
...
   document.colors.redHex.value = toHex(red, 2);
...
}
function changeColors() {
// Modify the components of the background color.
...
   document.bgColor =
     toHex(red, 2) +
     toHex(green, 2) +
     toHex(blue, 2);
   report();
   }
```

Well, where would you expect it to be called? The comment says that `changeColors` modifies the background color, so why not look at the button Change? If you look down in the form in the body, you discover two function calls, tucked away in the body HTML:

```
<BODY ONLOAD = "report()">
   ...
   <HR>
   <FORM NAME = "colors">
      <CENTER>
      <INPUT    TYPE = "button"
                VALUE = "Change"
                ONCLICK = "changeColors()">
      ...
      </CENTER>
   </FORM>

</BODY>
```

This page makes use of special HTML attributes that can be associated with form elements and links to execute JavaScript statements and invoke JavaScript functions. Look at the start tag for our sample page's body. It includes the attribute `ONLOAD`, which is assigned a value that is a JavaScript statement. This instructs the browser to begin executing the function `report`. Similarly, the attribute/value pair `ONCLICK` = "`changeColors()`" tells the browser to execute the `changeColors` function whenever the button Change is clicked.

These new attributes, `ONLOAD` and `ONCLICK`, are but two examples of JavaScript *event handlers,* which are attributes that apply to form elements and links. Their values are JavaScript statements (a single statement, a function call, or any list of statements and function calls, separated by semicolons) that are executed by the browser when an event occurs that is appropriate to the element in question. The nine events in the JavaScript sense include things such as a page being loaded, a mouse click on a button, text being typed into a field, the mouse passing over a link, and a checkbox being selected.

Fortunately for us, the browser constantly monitors the events that occur while a page is being displayed, and so we don't have to instruct it to do so. In particular, the browser monitors the page for the following events:

Event	Occurs When
`blur`	Input focus is removed (often by clicking elsewhere)
`change`	Value of a text field, text area, or `select` element is changed
`click`	A form element or link is clicked
`focus`	A form element is active for input
`load`	The page is loaded into the browser
`mouseOver`	The mouse passes over a link or an anchor
`select`	A form element's input field is selected
`submit`	A form is submitted
`unload`	The page is unloaded (another page is loaded or the browser quits)

While we don't have to do anything to get the browser to report interface events as they occur, we do have to instruct it if we want our page to respond to any of these events, and that is the role of the event handler attributes. So, for example, if you want to catch a click event in a particular element, you provide an `ONCLICK` attribute for the element. Similarly, you can associate `ONLOAD`, `ONFOCUS`, `ONBLUR`, `ONMOUSEOVER`, `ONSELECT`, `ONCHANGE`, `ONSUBMIT`, and `ONUNLOAD` attributes with various form elements and links.

From this brief description of them you can tell that only certain event handlers can be associated with certain form elements and links. It does not make sense, for example, to think of a `SELECT` event in the context of a submit button, or a `LOAD` event in terms of a text area. The following table specifies which event handlers apply to which interface elements.

Event	Applies To
`blur`	Text fields, text areas, select lists
`change`	Text fields, text areas, select lists
`click`	Buttons, links, resets, submits, checkboxes
`focus`	Text fields, text areas, select lists
`load`	Windows (page bodies) only
`mouseOver`	Links
`select`	Text fields, text areas
`submit`	Submit buttons, forms
`unload`	Windows (page bodies) only

Our second example, shown in browsed form in Figure 5.9, uses a few of these event handlers to accomplish its deliberately irritating behavior. An `ONLOAD` attribute is associated, as we have seen, with the body of our page, and an `ONCLICK` handler allows our page to respond to clicks on the page's only button. Any attempt at changing the text in the page's text field will invoke a response from the field's `ONCHANGE` handler (which, in turn, calls our JavaScript function `changeBack`). And, if the mouse moves over (without clicking) the phone image that serves as an anchor, another message appears on the screen. Again, the details of the JavaScript statements used as values for these event handlers don't matter for now. Notice, though, that we have specified individual statements (for the `ONLOAD` and `ONCLICK` handlers), a function call (for the `ONCHANGE` handler), and a pair of statements (for `ONMOUSEOVER`) as attribute values.

```
<HTML>
<HEAD>
    <TITLE>No Escape!!!</TITLE>

    <SCRIPT LANGUAGE = "JavaScript">
    <!--
        function changeBack() {
```

```
            status = "No way!!";
            document.events.textField.value = "type here..."
         }

         function dontGoThere() {
            alert("Don't even think about trying to escape...")
         }
      // -->
      </SCRIPT>
   </HEAD>

   <BODY>
      <H2>Don't Bother Me!</H2>
      <CENTER>
      <FORM NAME = "events">
         <INPUT
                  TYPE = "button"
                  VALUE = "As if..."
                  ONCLICK = "confirm('Forget it!')">
         <BR>
         <BR>
         <INPUT
      TYPE = "text"
                  NAME = "textField"
                  VALUE = "type here..."
                  ONCHANGE = "changeBack()">
      </FORM>

         <BR>
         <A HREF = ""
         ONMOUSEOVER = "alert('Sorry, out of order.'); return true">
         <IMG     SRC = "phone.gif"
                  HSPACE = 3
                  ALIGN = MIDDLE
                  BORDER = 0>
      </A>
      Try calling someone...

      <BR> <BR>
      Click <A HREF = "JavaScript:dontGoThere()">here</A> to escape...
      </CENTER>
   </BODY>
   </HTML>
```

There is one final way to invoke JavaScript commands in response to interface events, and it involves anchors that serve as links. As we have seen, anchors that serve as a link source use their `HREF` attribute to specify the URL of the destination for any clicks on that anchor. What if we want a click on an anchor to invoke a JavaScript command, like a function call?

One approach might be to include an `ONCLICK` attribute in the anchor's tag (`ONCLICK`s can be used with links), and to write the desired function call as its value. The problem, when you think about it, is that we have then described two different things we want done in response to a click on the anchor—one wants to

FIGURE 5.9 *Our user-hostile program*

link to some other location or page, the other to invoke a JavaScript function. This can cause brain damage (or, at least, irrational behavior) in many browsers. A better fix is to use the JavaScript command directly as the value for the anchor's `HREF` attribute. This avoids the ambiguity and produces the desired behavior. We have illustrated this technique in the anchor element near the bottom of our sample page that appears within the text "Click here to escape...".

■ Objects

The last part of JavaScript illustrated by our example appears in the statements

```
red = parseInt(document.bgColor.substring(1, 3), 16)

n = Math.floor(n / 16)

document.colors.redHex.value = toHex(red, 2)
```

The common feature of all these statements is that they refer to *objects,* such as `document` and `Math`. We'll discuss the most important predefined objects in detail later, but the important thing to know now is that any object contains data, known as *properties,* and functions, called *methods,* for acting on its data. Although we won't go into too much detail about how to do it, it's also possible for a JavaScript programmer to define his or her own objects.

◆ Object: A programming construct that may contain data and operators to manipulate its data.

The `document` object, for example, refers to the current page. A `document` object has a property (`bgColor`, in this example) describing what its background color is (in the form of a hex triple string like "`#C0C0C0`"). When we say `document.bgColor.substring(1, 3)`, we are thus referring to the `substring` method, acting on the `bgColor` string that's part of the current `document`. Similarly, `Math.floor(n / 16)` invokes the `floor` method of the `Math` object (which we'll explore later), and `document.colors.redHex.value` is the `VALUE` string that's part of the `redHex` text field that's contained in the `colors` form of the current `document` object.

Review Questions

1. Use your understanding of how an HTML document is interpreted by a browser to answer a question we didn't cover in this section: Can a `SCRIPT` element appear within another `SCRIPT` element?
2. How are comments indicated within a `SCRIPT`?
3. What is the primary difference between the way a browser executes JavaScript statements and the way it executes a functions?
4. In the event handler `ONCLICK = "some string"`, what can appear within *some string*?
5. Name and describe the types of JavaScript events.
6. What is an object? Give an example.

5.4 INGREDIENTS: VALUES, NAMES, AND TYPES

Prior to performing the actions described in either a program or a recipe, one needs to know the ingredients to be used. In most recipes (and, in fact, in many programming languages), the ingredients are listed explicitly and in detail at the head of a recipe. The actions make references to and use these ingredients. At various points in the cooking process, ingredients are stored in containers and combined with other ingredients in intermediate containers, which can then be referred to collectively in subsequent steps. You can even wash out containers and reuse them to collect different ingredients.

The basic ingredients of a program are the pieces of information it processes. Information can be simple, like numbers, or character strings (or, even more abstractly, names of buttons or values of text fields). Like the contents of a kitchen pantry, simple information can be saved in containers (called *variables*), combined with other ingredients, and moved from container to container as dictated by the program.

■ Simple Information

There are three basic types of information in JavaScript: numbers, strings of characters, and the logical type, consisting of the values `true` and `false`. Before we describe how these types of information can be manipulated, we need to spend a moment discussing how the three types may be written in a program.

◆ Although we won't discuss it, there's actually a fourth type, consisting of the single value `null`.

Numbers in JavaScript come in two flavors: whole numbers, known as *integers*, such as 13; and real numbers, such as 0.3. The rules for numeric *literals*, specific number values written in a program, are fairly simple (see box). For example, `0`, `–13`, and `556556` are legal integer literals, but 3,778 isn't (because of the comma). The literal `034` represents what we'd call 28 (since it's $3 \times 8 + 4$) and the hex literal `0x34` has the decimal value 52 ($= 3 \times 16 + 4$). The numbers `22.3`, `–13.0`, `.0008878`, `2.3e2`, and `–4E–1` are all legal real literals. The exponent part of a real literal indicates multiplication by the specified power of 10, so `2.3e2` is the same as `230.0` ($= 2.3 \times 10^2$). This is a handy way to save typing when writing very large or very small reals, since `0.0000000057` represents the same value as `5.7e–9`.

◆ The integer following the `e` tells you how many places left or right to shift the decimal point.

Syntax: Numeric Literals Integer literals must take the following form:

- They begin with an optional + or – sign.
- The sign is followed by a collection of one or more digits (0 . . . 9).
- A decimal integer's leftmost digit cannot be zero. A leading 0 indicates that the number is written in base 8 (or *octal*) and a leading 0x indicates that the number is to be interpreted as a hexadecimal number.

Real literals must take the following form:

- They begin with an optional + or – sign.
- The sign is followed by a collection of zero or more digits.
- There must be a decimal point.
- The decimal point is followed by a collection of zero or more digits.
- The literal may end, optionally, with an *exponent* of the form e*integer* or E*integer*.
- A real literal must have at least one digit and either a decimal point or an exponent (or both).

Strings are lists of zero or more characters, as you've seen. String literals in JavaScript are enclosed by matching single or double quotes, like this:

```
"Godzilla"
'Godzilla'
""
"This is a fairly long string, with non-letters like ·3:\° ]*$"
```

Note, first, that the start and end quotes must be the same kind. It is also quite legal to have an *empty* string, containing no characters at all. If you need to include special characters in a string, JavaScript provides special *escape sequences*, including the following:

◆ Why do we need special codes for quotes?

`\n`	The *newline* character, to move down a line
`\r`	The *return* character, to move to the left of a line
`\t`	The *tab* character, to advance to the next tab stop
`\'`	Single quote
`\"`	Double quote

◆ Boolean is named after the nineteenth-century logician George Boole.

Finally, there are only two *Boolean* literals, `true` and `false`. As you'll see in Section 5.6, this type is often used in statements that control the flow of execution through a program.

An important difference between JavaScript and many other programming languages is that JavaScript makes little distinction between types of information. Languages like Pascal and C++, in contrast, consider integers and reals as separate types and permit only limited mixing of objects of different types (in arithmetic expressions, for example). JavaScript is a *loosely typed* language, which simply means that it is less strict about how we may use and combine information of different types. So, as you will soon see, when we tell a JavaScript program to add a real number to an integer number, it does so without question. Actually, what it does—without us telling us—is convert the integer to its corresponding real (so 3 converts to 3.0) and then adds the two real values (we'll see why this is necessary in Module 7). It performs similar behind-the-back conversions when we ask it to concatenate an integer to a character string, converting the integer from its internal numeric form to a string of characters.

Variables

An important feature of JavaScript and other high-level programming languages is that, in addition to representing information explicitly as literals, information can also be represented symbolically, by a named variable. If, for instance, we want to add a collection of numbers, we might decide to keep the running sum in a variable named `totalSoFar`.

Syntax: Variable Names

- A variable name must begin with a letter or the underscore (_) character.
- This first character may be followed by any combination of zero or more letters, digits, and underscores.
- A variable name cannot be the same as any of JavaScript's *reserved words*—that is, words such as `function` and `alert` that have special meaning in JavaScript.

`C3PO`, `line_count`, and `convertToDecimal` are legal JavaScript variable names, but `line count`, and `2decimal` are not (see box). Finally, variable names are *case sensitive*, so JavaScript regards `MYSUM`, `MySum`, and `mysum` as three distinct variables.

◆ This case sensitivity is a common source of programming errors.

JavaScript's loose notion of type also has implications for variables. In other, more strongly typed languages, one must associate each variable used in a program with a particular type of information prior to its use. Once a variable is declared to be, for example, of type integer, it can be used only to represent integers. One cannot, in such cases, use the same variable at various points in the program to represent a real, string, or Boolean value. In JavaScript, the rules are less strict. The same variable that at one point holds the integer 79 can later be used to represent a string like "this value has changed", and can be used in different contexts depending on the type of its current value.

If you're going to use a variable in a JavaScript program, you must *declare* it first so that the browser can add its name to an internal list of recognized names. Declaring variables in JavaScript can be accomplished in one of two ways, depending on the intended *scope* of the variable. A variable's scope is that portion of the JavaScript program in which it can be used. Variables with *global* scope can be used in any of the page's `SCRIPT` elements. Variables with *local* scope are declared and used within a single function, and have meaning only within the innermost pair of braces containing them. Our core example program uses both local and global variables:

```
/*1*/
   blue = parseInt(...);
   // blue is a global variable
/*2*/
   function toHex(n, d) {
/*3*/  ...
      var s = "";
        // s is a local variable
      for (var i = 1; i <= d; i++) {
        // so is d
        s = hexChar(n % 16) + s;
/*4*/...
   }
/*5*/
```

In the example above, the global variable `blue` could be used in expressions at locations 2, 3, 4 and 5, but not at location 1, since it hadn't yet been declared there. The local variables `s` and `i` could be used in location 4, but not in locations 1, 2, 5 (which are outside the scope of the braces containing them), or 3 (which is within the scope, but before the declarations).

When a variable is declared, it doesn't start with any reliable value—you have to provide it with a starting value. This is done by using a declaration of the form

```
variableName = initialValue
```

The *initialValue* part can be a literal (as with `s = ""`) or an expression that produces a value (like `blue = parseInt(...)`). Although global variables may be declared in a `SCRIPT` element anywhere on the page, the intended nature of global variables (that they be accessible from any script or event handler) makes it good programming practice to declare all such variables in your page's head. That way, you know they'll be created and initialized before they are used in any JavaScript code.

◆ You can place `var` before a global declaration if you want, but you *must* use `var` in a local declaration.

Local variables are temporary in the sense that they are declared and used only within the body of a function. We declare local variables by using the keyword `var` at the start of the declaration, as we did with `s` and `i` above. Local variables can be declared at any point in a pair of braces. They must, however, be declared before they are used. Remember that a local variable that is declared and used in one function will not be recognized by the browser if it appears in another function. The browser will regard local variables in different functions as distinct variables (possibly with distinct values), even if they have the same name. In addition, if a local variable has the same name as a global variable, the local variable "hides" the global one within its local scope, meaning that the browser will resolve the name confusion in favor of the local variable.

■ Objects

◆ The object hierarchy is determined by which objects are contained in which others.

Variables are not the only kind of names to which we can refer within our scripts. All of the HTML form elements are globally accessible to us as well, and their names and values can be used in our processing. We refer to form elements and their properties using JavaScript's dotted *`object.property`* notation, which, in turn, is based on JavaScript's *object hierarchy*, part of which is illustrated in Figure 5.10.

FIGURE 5.10
Part of the JavaScript object hierarchy

```
window
 |  ...
 |- history     Documents that have been in this window
 └- document    Current document
     |  ...
     |- image   Images in this document
     |- link    Links in this document
     └- form
         |  ...
         |- button
         |- checkbox
         |- radio
         |- select
         |- text
         └- textArea
```

The object hierarchy indicates that every window viewed from within the browser has properties that provide information about its history and its document. Similarly, every document has properties that include its forms, links, and images. Every form object, in turn, has individual form elements as properties, and these, as we have seen, have attributes (simple properties) of their own. So, to refer to, say, the contents of a text field from within JavaScript, we would use the general notation

document.*formName*.*textFieldName*.value

where the *formName* and *textFieldName* parts of the expression would be replaced with the names (as specified by the `NAME` attribute) of the particular form and text field being referenced.[4] Remember, too, that these names are identifiers that are being referred to from within JavaScript, and so they are case sensitive. The `document` and `value` parts of the expression would be used as is, since there is only one document within a given window to which we could refer, and only one value attribute for the chosen text field. To refer to any other of the text field's attributes, likes its name, we would simply replace `value` with `name`. The periods used to join the objects and properties into a single name indicate the hierarchical organization. In our core example, the term

```
document.colors.redHex.value
```

refers to the `value` property (a string) of the `redHex` text field in the `colors` form in this document.

◆ **You access objects and properties in the hierarchy by working from left to right, from the largest collection to the smallest.**

Let's look at another sample page, this one displayed in Figure 5.11, that illustrates many of these concepts. The page is entitled "JavaScript Flashcards" because it performs very simple arithmetic calculations and displays the results in flashcard form. If you enter a numeric value (either integers or real numbers) into the two text fields and click on one of the operation buttons, you'll see the results of that calculation displayed in the page's text area. We will return to this example shortly to

[4] Now you see why the `NAME` attribute of forms and form elements is so useful.

FIGURE 5.11
The Flashcards program

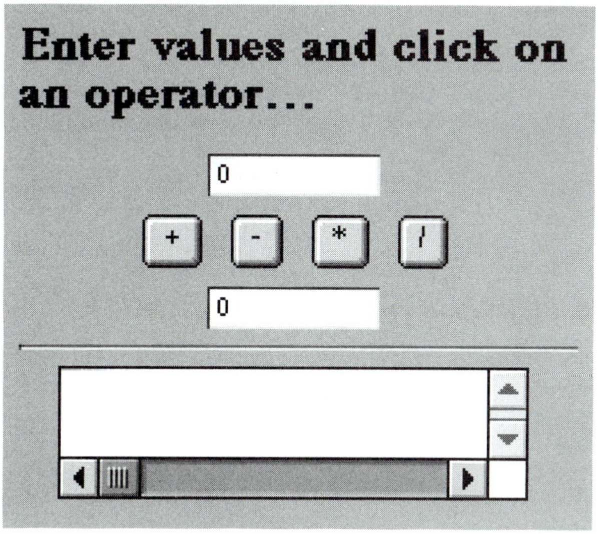

explain how the calculation actually gets performed. For now, we'll concentrate on the page's use of variables and names.

```
<HTML>
<HEAD>
   <TITLE>JavaScript Flashcards</TITLE>

   <SCRIPT language = "javaScript">
   <!--
      currentOperator = "+";
      currentOperatorName = " plus ";

      function calculate() {
         var result = eval(document.Flasher.firstNumber.value+
                           currentOperator +
                           document.Flasher.secondNumber.value);
         document.Flasher.answer.value =
                           document.Flasher.firstNumber.value +
                           currentOperatorName +
                           document.Flasher.secondNumber.value +
                           "equals:\ r\ n\ t" +
                           result;
      }
      // -->
   </SCRIPT>
</HEAD>

<BODY>
   <H2> Enter values and click on an operator...</H2>
   <FORM NAME = "Flasher">
      <INPUT TYPE = "text" NAME = "firstNumber" VALUE = "0"
             SIZE = 10>
```

```
<TABLE>
<TR>
<TD> <INPUT TYPE = "button" NAME = " plus " VALUE = "+"
            ONCLICK = "currentOperator = this.value;
                       currentOperatorName = this.name;
                       calculate()">
<TD> <INPUT TYPE = "button" NAME = " minus " VALUE = "-"
            ONCLICK = "currentOperator = this.value;
                       currentOperatorName = this.name;
                       calculate()">
<TD> <INPUT TYPE = "button" NAME = " times " VALUE = "*"
            ONCLICK = "currentOperator=this.value;
                       currentOperatorName = this.name;
                       calculate()">
<TD> <INPUT TYPE = "button" NAME = " divided by " VALUE = "/"
            ONCLICK = "currentOperator = this.value;
                       currentOperatorName = this.name;
                       calculate()">
</TR>
</TABLE>

<INPUT TYPE = "text" NAME = "secondNumber" VALUE = "0" SIZE = 10
       ONCHANGE = "calculate()">
<HR WIDTH = "33%" ALIGN = LEFT>
<TEXTAREA NAME = "answer"
          ROWS = 2
          COLS = 25>
</TEXTAREA>
</FORM>
</BODY>
</HTML>
```

Look first at the body of the page. We have a form (named "Flasher") containing two text fields (named "firstNumber" and "secondNumber"), a table that itself contains four buttons ("plus," "minus," "times," and "divided by"), and a text area, named "answer." The body contains no script elements, but rather executes JavaScript statements and invokes JavaScript functions (which we have defined in the page's head) by means of event handlers. This is the first time you've seen an event handler with anything but a function call in it: recall that we can include as many JavaScript statements as we like in an event handler, enclosing them all in quotes and separating them with semicolons. Before looking in detail at these, we'd better check out the HEAD element.

We use the head element to declare the function `calculate`, which we invoke from the body, and two global variables named `currentOperator` and `currentOperatorName`. Each variable is initialized to contain a string value. Because these are declared globally—that is, in the head element and not within the body of a function—they can be referenced from any JavaScript command on the page. In particular, they are used (their values are changed by the assignment operator) in the `ONCLICK` handler for each of the four operator buttons, and in the body of the function `calculate` (where they are combined with other strings to form longer character strings).

This is in direct contrast to variable `result`, which is local to function `calculate`. Variable `result` is declared and initialized at the start of the function, and is used later in it as well. Any attempt, though, to refer to variable `result` from outside of the function's body would cause the browser to report an error.

Function `calculate` shows numerous examples of how to refer to the page's form elements from JavaScript. To refer to the value of text field `firstNumber`, we use the (somewhat lengthy) name `document.Flasher.firstNumber.value`. To refer to the context of text area answer, we use `document.Flasher.answer.value`.

We need not resort to such lengthy names when the JavaScript code that refers to a form element is part of the form element itself. For example, the `ONCLICK` handler for the `plus` operator button refers to `value` and `name` directly. Because these references occur within the defining element of this button, they are understood by the browser to refer to the `VALUE` and `NAME` attributes of button `plus`. Similarly, when we use `name` and `value` in the code for the event handlers for the other three buttons, they refer to the corresponding attributes for those buttons.

It is also worth noting that one of the string literals to which we refer in function `calculate` (`"equals: \r \n \t"`) illustrates the use of the special escape characters we mentioned earlier to insert, in this case, a carriage return, a line feed, and a tab character in the text area we use to display the program's output.

Although we didn't make use of it in this example, JavaScript provides a notational shorthand that can save us some typing when spelling out these long form-element names. If a section of JavaScript code (no matter whether it resides in a `Script` element or in an event handler) makes extensive use of, say, a particular form, we enclose that section of code in a `with` statement. A `with` statement takes the following general form:

```
with (document.formName) {
    any statements
}
```

Enclosing a group of statements in this way notifies the browser that we intend to refer to the named form from those statements, and allows us to omit the "document.*formName*" prefix from any part of the form. Function `calculate` from our example could be rewritten somewhat more concisely as follows, with no effect on its behavior:

```
function calculate () {
    with (document.Flasher) {
        var result = eval(firstNumber.value + currentOperator +
                          secondNumber.value);
            answer.value = firstNumber.value + currentOperatorName +
                          secondNumber.value + "equals:\ r\ n\ t" + result;
    } // end of the with statement
} // end of the function
```

Review Questions

1. Why do we need the escape sequence `\"`? Why can't we put a quote within a string literal?
2. Which of the following are legal numeric literals?

```
-0    8,900    $445.80    3e3    07A
0.00909E-90    TWO
```

3. Which of the following are legal variable names?

```
mySum    2more    number3    with
this_is_the_answer    floor
```

4. What do we mean by the *scope* of a variable?
5. What is the difference between an object and a property?
6. In the Flashcards example, what would be wrong with referring to `document.answer.value`?

5.5 INFORMATION PROCESSING: TOSS, BLEND, DRIBBLE

Implicit in every recipe is the assumption that the cook has a standard repertoire of actions that can be carried out. Each action operates on one or more ingredients, so, for example, "blend honey and lemon juice" instructs the cook to perform the "blend" operation on the two operands "honey" and "lemon juice," with the assumption that the resulting mixture will then be used elsewhere. JavaScript provides a collection of operators that can be used to manipulate values, along with a collection of rules that govern how these operators may be combined into more complicated expressions.

■ Operators and Expressions

First, we have a collection of arithmetic operators that act on one or more numbers. These include the ones you'd expect, along with some others that are likely to be less familiar.

Operator	Result
`op1 + op2`	Sum of the operands
`op1 – op2`	Difference of the operands
`op1 * op2`	Product of the operands
`op1 / op2`	Quotient of the operands (real result)
`op1 % op2`	modulus: The remainder of `op1` divided by `op2` (both operands must be integers)
`–op`	Negate the operand
`op++`	Increase operand by 1 (operand must be a variable)
`op--`	Decrease operand by 1 (operand must be a variable)

All of these operations produce a result that can then be used as an operand of another operator, allowing us to build arbitrarily complicated expressions, like `3 + 4 * 5`. Notice that there's an ambiguity here: should the result be 35, which we'd get if we added first and then multiplied, or should we multiply first and then add, giving the result 23? JavaScript solves this problem in the same way we do, by assigning *precedences* to the operations and evaluating expressions by doing high-precedence operations before low-precedence ones. This is reflected in the table above, where we've collected the eight operators into three precedence levels, with the lowest at the top and the highest at the bottom of the table. We can override the standard order of operations by using parentheses, since parentheses have the highest possible precedence. Thus, `3 + 4 * 5` evaluates to 23; if we wanted to force the addition to be done first, we'd write `(3 + 4) * 5`. JavaScript has fourteen levels of precedence, all told, and it's a bit tricky to keep all of them in mind. Fortunately, you don't have to:

> If there's the slightest doubt about the precendences in a complicated expression, parenthesize it to force the order of evaluation you want.

The most useful operator that applies to string data is the *concatenation* operator (also designated by the + symbol). Like the arithmetic +, it appears between the two strings that it operates on, and produces as its result a new string formed by combining string versions of its operands (converting numbers to their equivalent strings if necessary). So,

`"abc" + "def"` produces `"abcdef"`
`"123" + 456` produces `"123456"` (the number `456` is converted to a string)

However, if the first operand is a number, the + operator is assumed to be addition, so

`123 + "456"` produces `579` (the `"456"` is converted to a number)

JavaScript also can operate on the Boolean values `true` and `false`, using a number of operators that will be of considerable use to us in the next section. The comparison operators == (equality), <, >, <=, >=, and != (not equals) all return `true` or `false` to indicate the result of comparing the value to their left with the value on their right. Be careful to write the two-symbol combinations without intervening spaces, and be careful with order: <= is a meaningful operator, while =< is not (though it makes a nice "frowny face" for e-mail).

Operator	Result
`op1 < op2`	`true` when `op1` is less than `op2`
`op1 <= op2`	`true` when `op1` is less than or equal to `op2`
`op1 > op2`	`true` when `op1` is greater than `op2`
`op1 >= op2`	`true` when `op1` is greater than or equal to `op2`
`op1 == op2`	true when `op1` and `op2` have the same value
`op1 != op2`	15

As with the arithmetic operators, these can be combined to produce Boolean expressions of any complexity, using parentheses as needed to clarify expressions with more than one operator. These comparison operators have lower precedence than any of the arithmetic operators, so

```
index + 1 <= pivot
```

would be evaluated as

```
(index + 1) <= pivot
```

There are also operators that allow us to combine Boolean operands, often as the result of earlier comparisons:

Operator	Result
`op1 || op2`	OR: `true` when either `op1` or `op2` (or both) is `true`
`op1 && op2`	AND: `true` only when `op1` and `op2` are both `true`
`!op1`	NOT: `true` when `op1` is `false`, and vice versa

Here are some examples of expressions using Boolean operators and comparisons:

```
x == y
(x + 1) < 7
y >= 0
(0 < myData) && (myData < 100)
(thisVal != 0) && !((x == 1) || (x == -1))
```

◆ For our purposes here, the left operand of an assignment *must* be a variable.

◆ Be careful not to confuse the comparison operator (`==`) with the assignment operator (`=`).

One set of operators, the *assignment* operators, is essential to even the simplest programs because they allow us to combine variables or objects with operators and expressions to actually change values in our program. The simplest assignment operator, denoted by the equal sign (=), evaluates the expression on its right and places the resulting value into the variable to its left. All of the following, including the final three that come from our last sample page, are potentially legal uses of the assignment operator:

```
x = 5
tempString = "  "
boolValue = (0 < y) && (y < 10)
currentOperator = "+"
currentOperator = value
currentOperatorName = name
```

Each of these expressions returns as its value the value of the right side. The first expression thus evaluates to 5, and the last to the value of `name`. This implies that expressions such as

```
x = (y = 0.0)
```

are legal shortcuts for performing multiple assignments (since the subexpression `(y = 0.0)` not only assigns `0.0` to `y`, but also returns as its value `0.0`, which can then be assigned to `x`). Speaking of shortcuts, JavaScript provides us with a few operators that combine assignment and arithmetic. The expression `x += y` is shorthand for `x = x + y`; that is, it adds `x` and `y` and sets `x` to the result (and also returns that value). In other words, `x += y` increases `x` by the amount `y`. In similar fashion, we can decrement `x` by `y` (`x -= y`), multiply `x` by `y` (`x *= y`) and divide `x` by `y` (`x /= y`).

Conversion Functions

In addition to its numerous operators, JavaScript comes complete with a number of predefined functions that perform a variety of useful tasks. These are functions that we don't need to define in the head of our page. We can simply invoke them from within any JavaScript code, as long as we know how to do so. That means we need to know a function's *signature* (its name, the number and types of its parameters, and the kind of value, if any, that it returns). Since this section has been devoted to the basic information types we can use, let's look at the signatures and descriptions of a few of the built-in functions that convert information from one type to another.

Conversion functions such as these are very useful in JavaScript because of the language's relationship to HTML forms. The value of any form element is, from a JavaScript perspective, string data. So, if we want to write a program that interprets form data numerically (for example, to represent the number of CDs you want to order from an online catalog), we must be able to convert these strings to numbers. Three functions that help us in this regard are described in the boxes. The first two are useful for turning strings into specific numeric types. The third takes a string and determines its numeric value.

```
parseInt(string, integer) returns integer
```

This function takes a string and an integer as parameters, and returns the integer value that the string represents in the provided base. So,

`parseInt("123", 10)`	returns the integer 123
`parseInt("123", 8)`	returns the integer 83 (since 123 in base 8 is 83)
`parseInt("123", 16)`	returns the integer 275 (123 base 16 is decimal 275)
`parseInt("101010", 2)`	returns the integer 42 (101010 base 2 is decimal 42)
`parseInt("ABC", 10)`	returns "NaN," standing for "Not a Number"

```
parseFloat(string) returns real
```

This function attempts to interpret its string parameter as a real number, and returns the resulting numeric value. So,

`parseFloat("123.456")`	returns the real 123.456
`parseFloat("123.ABC")`	returns "NaN"

```
eval(string) returns numeric
```

The string parameter to the `eval` function can represent any JavaScript expression, statement, or sequence of statements. In any case, `eval` interprets the string as if it were ordinary JavaScript statements, returning the value of the expression or executing the statements. This is particularly useful for evaluating a string that represents a numerical expression. So, if the variable `index` contained the value 2,

`eval("6 * index + 1")` would return the value 13

The `eval` function combined with the concatenation operator are the keys to the operation of our flashcard page, which we can now explain fully. When either of its text fields are changed, function `calculate` is called. The function `calculate` uses `eval` to evaluate a string, that it composes by concatenating three smaller strings: the value of the first text field, the current operator, and the value of the second text field. The result of the evaluation is saved (as local variable `result`) and then is used to compose a new string, which ultimately gets assigned as the value of the page's text area.

This all works correctly because the current operator gets its string value when any of the operator buttons is clicked. Each operator button assigns its `VALUE` attribute to global variable `currentOperator` in its `ONCLICK` event handler. It also assigns its `NAME` attribute to global variable `currentOperatorName` so that it can be used to compose the text area string.

Statements and Punctuation

The basic unit of action in JavaScript is the *statement*. Just as a single step in a recipe, a statement says "perform this action." So far, you've seen four kinds of statements:

- *Comments,* which don't accomplish anything, but are still considered to be statements.
- *Declarations,* such as `var i = 0` or `function` definitions.
- *Expression statements,* consisting of a single expression, either complicated, like `document.colors.redHex.value = toHex(red, 2)`or simpler, like `i++` or `report()`.
- The `with` statement.

There are a few more we haven't covered in detail, like the `return` statement, some that we haven't mentioned yet, like the `if ... else` statement, and a few, like `continue` and `break`, that we won't cover at all.

You've also seen what are called *compound statements* in other languages, that is, collections of statements enclosed within braces. In spite of the fact that compound statements can be used anywhere a single statement can, they're not considered to be statements in JavaScript. So far, the most common use of compound statements has been in the statement body of function definitions, like this:

```
function foo(){
    statements go here
}
```

Although it seems implicit in the template above, we don't have complete freedom about what can go within the braces. First, we can't put a function definition within the braces—the language's rules of syntax simply don't allow it. That's not much of a problem, unless you've had previous exposure to languages like Pascal, where you can define a function within another. There is, however, an important rule we need to keep in mind, both in function definitions and in multistatement action handlers, such as

```
ONCLICK = "currentOperator = this.value;
           currentOperatorName = this.name;
           calculate()"
```

Note the semicolons here—each statement is separated by a semicolon from the statement that follows. The semicolon punctuator is absolutely necessary here, since it's the way that the browser knows where one statement stops and another begins. The same rule holds within function bodies—although your browser may be clever enough to deduce the end of a statement and the beginning of another, you can't count on it.

> Statements within an action handler and within the body of a function definition must be separated by semicolons.

When you're declaring global variables, the JavaScript language standard says that semicolons aren't necessary as long as the declarations occur on separate lines, but it's good practice to use them nevertheless. It won't cause any harm to end every statement with a semicolon, and it's better to get in the habit of correct punctuation than to run the risk of leaving out a semicolon where it's needed.

While we're on the subject of punctuation, we should mention that JavaScript, like HTML, is a *free-format* language, which means that you can use spaces, tabs, and carriage returns as freely as you wish to make your programs easy to read. Of course, you can't put *whitespace* (as those characters are called) in the middle of operators (like <=), reserved words (like `function` or `with`), or names of variables or objects (like `document`), but you can otherwise use whitespace to your heart's content. If you look over our example programs, you'll find that we make heavy use of indentation to make the logical structure of a program more obvious. While the following code is perfectly legal JavaScript,

```
function changeBack(){ status = "No way!!";document.events.textField.value
= "type here..."} function dontGoThere(){
alert("Don't even think about trying to escape...")}
```

you'll probably agree that it's quite a bit more difficult to read than

```
function changeBack(){
    status = "No way!!";
    document.events.textField.value = "type here..."
}

function dontGoThere(){
    alert("Don't even think about trying to escape...")
}
```

> Use spaces, tabs, and returns. The browser won't pay any attention to whitespace, but it makes programs much easier to read.

LAB 5.2

HTML and JavaScript

This set of exercises concentrates on the relationships between HTML and JavaScript. JavaScript statements and functions often depend critically on the HTML document in which they are embedded. Names that are used in JavaScript commands are determined by the names given to HTML components on the page. JavaScript functions can be invoked from event handlers that are described in HTML descriptions of `FORM`s, input areas, and the like. The common theme in the exercises below is How do I write and invoke JavaScript statements and functions from within an HTML document?

1. Each of the following exercises asks you to make a simple editing change to your version of the concert game. For each exercise, make the proposed edit(s) to the original version of the game. Then try loading the page into your browser. If there is no noticeable change in the game's behavior, just write down "no change" for that exercise. If there is a change in behavior (for example, an error message appearing on the screen), write down the error message that appeared or the observed difference. In any case, try to explain what happened in your own words.

   a) Move the statement from the beginning of function `initScreen` that reads

   ```
   bankImg.src = "images/bank.gif"
   ```

   to follow the line near the start of the first `<SCRIPT>` that reads:

   ```
   currentMode = "Look"
   ```

   b) Move the statement from the `<SCRIPT>` between the document head and body that reads

   ```
   initMap()
   ```

   to come immediately before the `</SCRIPT>` that concludes the first (large) script in the document head.

   c) Remove the word `checked` from the line that reads

   ```
   <INPUT type = "radio" name = "lookMode"
   onClick = "setMode(Look')" checked>
   ```

   d) Remove the phrase `onLoad = "initScreen()"` from the `<BODY>` start tag.

   e) Remove the phrase `onClick = "setMode(Action')"` from the `<INPUT>` tag for radio button `actionMode`.

   f) Change the HTML line that reads

   ```
   <FORM NAME = "rightForm". . .
   ```

   to read

   ```
   <FORM NAME = "badForm". . .
   ```

g) Change the HTML line that begins

```
<img name = "mainImage". . .
```

to begin as follows (leave the rest of the line unchanged)

```
<img name = "anotherImage". . .
```

h) Change the HTML line that begins

```
<textarea name = "inventoryList". . .
```

to begin as follows (leave the rest of the line unchanged):

```
<textarea name = "inventory". . .
```

i) Change the line in function `setMode` that reads

```
document.rightForm.lookMode.checked = true
```

to read

```
document.rightForm.look.checked = true
```

j) Change the line in function `setStatus` that reads

```
document.statusForm.statusList.value = st
```

to read

```
document.statusList.value = st
```

k) Change the line in function `clearInventory` that reads

```
document.rightForm.inventoryList.value = ""
```

to read

```
document.statusList.value = st
```

l) Change the line in function `clearInventory` that reads

```
document.rightForm.inventoryList.value = ""
```

to read

```
rightForm.inventoryList.value = ""
```

2. Our program already makes extensive use of JavaScript's `alert` statement. Insert another `alert` statement into your copy of the game that identifies the game as yours. Place the statement so that it is executed before the game actually begins (that is, before any images or frames are displayed).

3. Now let's try to add an HTML component of our own and get it to do some useful processing. As you define and play increasingly complex versions of your concert game, you may find yourself stuck at a particular location, or you may want to undo a recent click. In such cases, it would be helpful to have a button that you could click to simply start the game over. You could of course, just click on your browser's Reload button, but there's a much quicker way. We've defined a JavaScript function (called `initScreen`) that basically resets everything back to the start of the game without having to reload the entire page. Add a button to your copy of the game page (put it wherever and name it whatever you like) that calls function `initScreen` whenever it is clicked.

Review Questions

1. Evaluate the following expressions. You may assume that `angle` contains 17.9, `limit` contains 3 and `result` contains true.

   a) `limit + 4 * angle`
   b) `limit++`
   c) `angle /= limit`
   d) `result && ((angle < 30) || (limit != 3))`
   e) `result == !result`

2. One of these expressions will correctly test that input is greater than 0 and less than 10. The other isn't even syntactically correct. State which is which and explain.

```
0 < input < 100
(0 < input) && (input < 100)
```

3. With the exception of one set, the two-operand operators all group from the left, meaning that operators with the same precedence are evaluated from left to right.

   a) What's the value of `5 - 4 - 3`?
   b) The assignment operators are the only two-operand operators that group from the right. Why are they different?
   c) If we have `x = 1` and `y = 3` at the start, what values do they have after evaluation of the expression `x += y += 2`?

4. What are the values of the following expressions?

   d) `parseInt ("C0", 16) / 5`
   e) `eval ("3" + "+" + "4")`

5.6 UNTIL GOLDEN BROWN: CONTROL STRUCTURES

Does it matter in our recipe if one dots the apple mixture with butter before arranging the apples in the baking dish? What if you dribble the cup contents over the apple mixture before blending the honey and lemon in the cup? Of course the linear order of the operations is important; that's why we write them down that way! Similarly, we write commands within each part of a script in the order in which we want them carried out. This type of implicit control works well in both contexts because it reflects how cooks and computers assume they are to carry out instructions—linearly. When there is a need to perform operations in nonlinear ways, we must resort to explicit transfers of control.

This is the role of the phrases "until covered," "for 40 minutes," and "until golden brown" in our recipe. They are not operations themselves. Nor are they ingredients. Rather, they indicate that the operations to which they refer are being conditionally qualified. The scripts we will see in this section contain comparable phrases (like "if . . . then," "for," and "while"), which control the logical flow of commands in a script.

■ Selection

Consider, for example, the page displayed in Figure 5.12. Our goal in writing it was to provide an automated version of something you might see in a college bookstore. You click in the checkboxes to indicate in which courses you are enrolled, then click the Display Order button to see the list of the books you need to purchase for those courses. Clicking on Verify Order gives you a chance to confirm that your order is correct. If you indicate that it is, the order would (in theory) be printed or otherwise transmitted to the cashier. If you indicate that your order is somehow incorrect, the

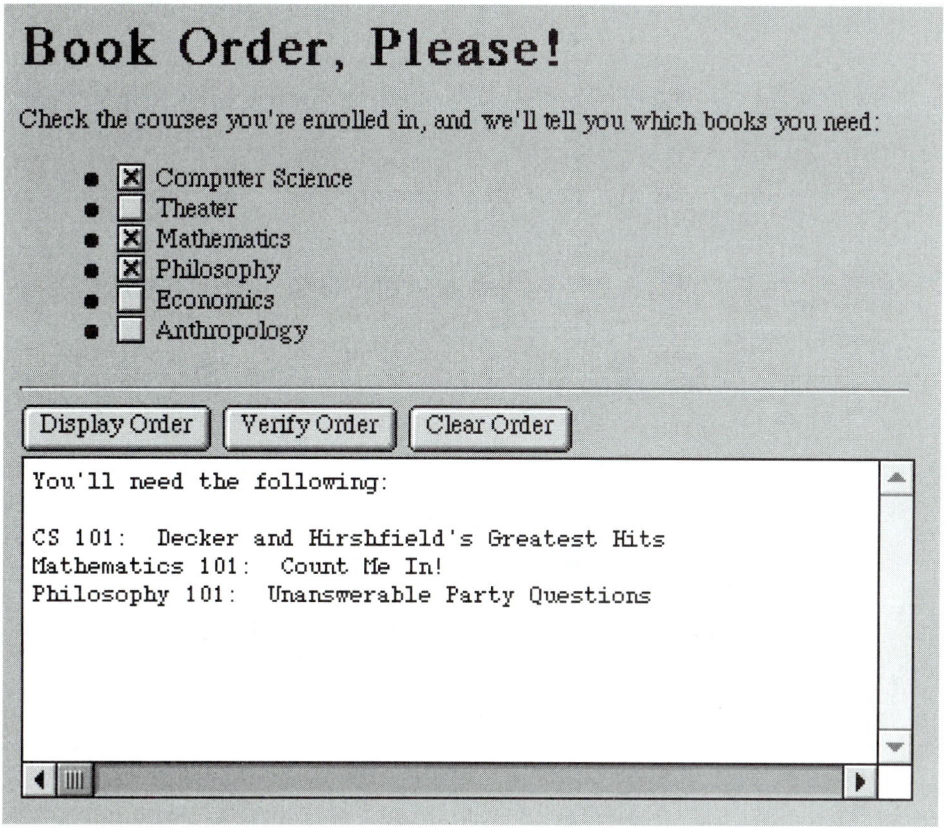

FIGURE 5.12
Online order form

form is reset automatically. If at any point you realize that you made a mistake in ordering, you can click the Clear Order button to reset the order form immediately.

How might we implement such behavior with the JavaScript we have seen so far? We will undoubtedly want to build a string to represent the list of books, concatenating book names to it based on the checked boxes, and we can probably use a reset button to clear the form. We could write `ONCLICK` event handlers to detect when any of our checkboxes are clicked. Unfortunately, the actions they detect include whenever the box is clicked—that is, whether it is turned on or turned off. We could write a Boolean expression to represent the checked state of each checkbox (using the general form `document.formName.checkBoxName.checked`), but how can we alter the actions of our program based on these values? The answer, of course, is by taking advantage of one of JavaScript's control structures.

The `if` statement, wherein a Boolean expression is evaluated and different statements are executed based on the value of the expression, comes in two flavors:

```
(1) if (Boolean expression)
        then-clause
(2) if (Boolean expression)
        then-clause
    else
        else-clause
```

The *then-* and *else-clauses* in this notation can be one or more JavaScript statements. If more than one statement is to be used, they much be enclosed in braces, { and }. In the first form, the Boolean expression is evaluated according to the rules described previously. If the result of that evaluation is `true`, the statement or statements in the then-clause are executed in order, after which execution continues with the statement following the then-clause. If the Boolean expression is `false`, however, the then-clause is not performed, and control passes directly to the statement following the then-clause.

In the second version of the `if` statement, the one with the `else` clause, the Boolean expression is evaluated as before. If the expression evaluates to `true`, the then-clause is executed. If it evaluates to `false`, the else-clause is executed instead. In either case, control then passes to the statement following the else-clause.

```
<HTML>
<HEAD>
   <TITLE>Automated Book Order</TITLE>

   <SCRIPT LANGUAGE = "JavaScript">
   <!--
   function writeBookOrder () {
      var books = "You'll need the following:\ r\ n";
      if (document.bookList.CS.checked)
         books +=
         "\ r\ nCS 101: Decker and Hirshfield's Greatest Hits";
      if (document.bookList.Theater.checked)
         books += "\ r\ nTheater 101: Acting Out";
      if (document.bookList.Math.checked)
         books += "\ r\ nMathematics 101: Count Me In!";
      if (document.bookList.Philo.checked)
         books +=
         "\ r\ nPhilosophy 101: Unanswerable Party Questions";
      if (document.bookList.Eco.checked)
         books += "\ r\ nEconomics 101: For the Love of Money";
      if (document.bookList.Anthro.checked)
         books += "\ r\ nAnthropology 101: Can You Dig It?";

      document.bookList.finalOrder.value = books;
      }

   function verifyBookOrder () {
      var youAreSure = confirm("Is your order correct?");
      if (youAreSure)
         document.bookList.finalOrder.value =
         "Order confirmed . . ."
      else
         document.bookList.resetter.click();
   }
   // -->
   </SCRIPT>
</HEAD>
```

```
<BODY>
   <FORM NAME="bookList">
   <H1>Book Order, Please!</H1>
   <P>Check the courses you're enrolled in, and we'll tell you
   which books you need:</P>
   <MENU>
      <LI><INPUT TYPE = "checkbox"
                 NAME = "CS"
                 CHECKED>Computer Science
      <LI><INPUT TYPE = "checkbox"
                 NAME = "Theater">Theater
      <LI><INPUT TYPE = "checkbox"
                 NAME = "Math">Mathematics
      <LI><INPUT TYPE = "checkbox"
                 NAME = "Philo">Philosophy
      <LI><INPUT TYPE = "checkbox"
                 NAME = "Eco">Economics
      <LI><INPUT TYPE = "checkbox"
                 NAME = "Anthro">Anthropology
   </MENU>
      <HR>
      <INPUT TYPE = "button"
             VALUE = "Display Order"
             ONCLICK = "writeBookOrder()">
      <INPUT TYPE = "button"
             VALUE = "Verify Order"
             ONCLICK = "verifyBookOrder()">
      <INPUT TYPE = "reset"
             NAME = "resetter"
             VALUE = "Clear Order">
      <TEXTAREA NAME = "finalOrder"
                ROWS = 10
                COLS = 60>*** WELCOME ***</TEXTAREA>
   </FORM>
</BODY>
</HTML>
```

We see numerous examples of `if` statements in the JavaScript code for our latest sample page. Function `writeBookOrder` is invoked when button `Display Order` is clicked. This function builds our string of book titles as follows: It declares and initializes a local variable, `books`, to hold our string. For each of the checkboxes on the form, it uses an `if` statement to evaluate the checked status of the box. If the box is checked, a string holding the appropriate book title (along with carriage return and line feed characters) is concatenated to our `book` string. If a particular box is not checked, no action is taken for that box. The final value of the `book` string is then displayed in the text area near the bottom of the form.

The `verifyBookOrder` function in our book order page uses an `if-else` statement to control the processing involved in verifying the order. It also illustrates two JavaScript features we haven't discussed yet, and so warrants closer examination.

JavaScript has three built-in functions that can be used to communicate with the user (see boxes). Each presents a dialog box on the screen as a means for soliciting a response. The look of the dialog and the returned response differ for each function (see Figure 5.13).

```
alert(messageString)
```

This function displays `messageString` in a dialog box with an OK button. The user must hit OK for processing to continue. No response is recorded.

```
confirm(messageString) returns Boolean
```

This function displays `messageString` in a dialog box with buttons labeled OK and Cancel (or Yes and No). If the user clicks OK (or Yes), the function returns `true`; if the user clicks Cancel or No, the function returns `false`.

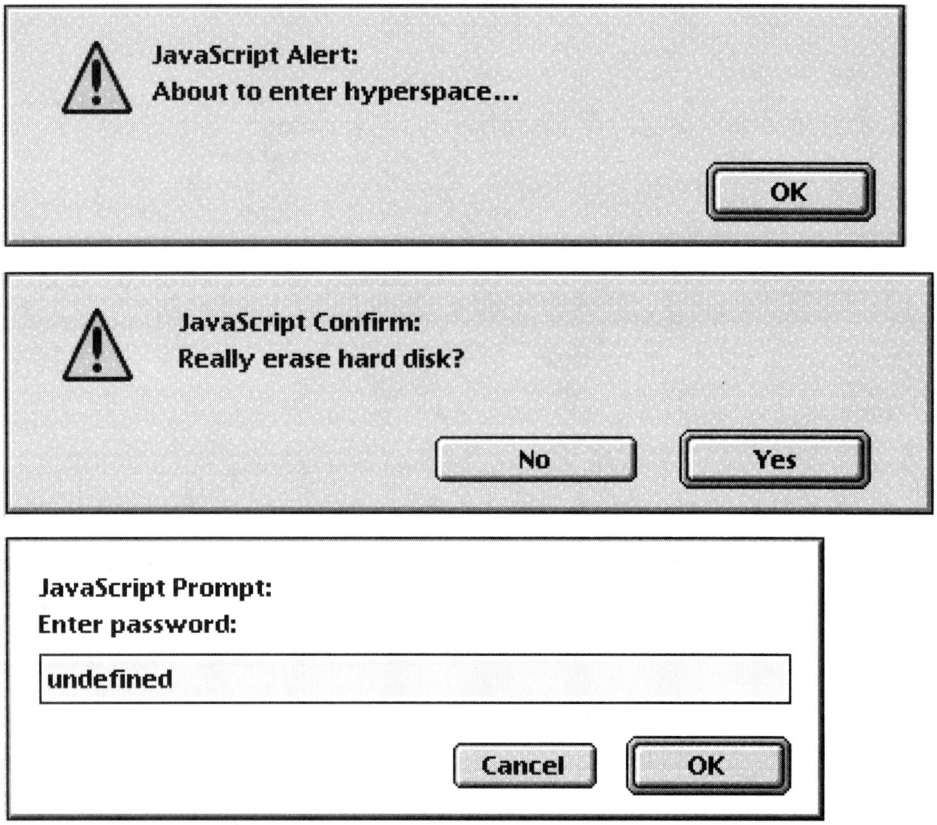

FIGURE 5.13
`alert`, `confirm`, and `prompt` dialogs

```
prompt(messageString) returns string
```

This function displays `messageString` in a dialog box with a text field for user input, and OK and Cancel buttons. If the user clicks OK, the returned value is that of the string in the text field; if the user clicks Cancel, the returned value is `null`.

These functions are particularly interesting for three reasons. First, they make it easy for us to display and control dialog boxes as a means for communicating with users of our pages. Second, by providing us with three variations on this interface theme, JavaScript lets us fine-tune our program's response to the users' actions. The `alert` function simply forces the user to acknowledge a message. The `confirm` function gives the user a Boolean choice, and records for us the choice made. The `prompt` function gives the user the opportunity to enter a string, which is recorded so that our program can process it. All three of these functions exercise temporary control over the processing of our pages. That is, they interrupt whatever was happening on our page and wait for—or, more accurately, force[5]—the user to respond to the dialog box presented. In a sense they represent mini control structures of their own.

In our example, we use the `confirm` function to return a Boolean value indicating whether or not the proposed selection of courses was correct. If the user clicks OK, `confirm` returns a value of `true`; if the user clicks Cancel, the function returns `false` as its value. In either case, the returned value is assigned to local variable `youAreSure`, which is then used to control our `if...else` statement. We could have written `if (youAreSure == true)`... to the same effect, but that is slightly redundant. If the order is confirmed, a "thank you" message is displayed in the page's text area. If the user clicked Cancel in response to the `confirm` dialog box, the function uses JavaScript 's `click` function to simulate a click on the page's reset button (named "resetter") to reset the form to its original state.

Iteration

In our core example program, one task that must be performed is converting a color component to hexadecimal form so it can be displayed in one of the three text fields. Converting a number to base 16 is really quite simple: All you have to do is repeatedly divide by 16, recording the remainders as hex digits in a string, from right to left. For example, suppose we had the component value 196. To convert that to hex we'd take the following steps:

```
// startup
   set n to 196
   set the string s to the empty string, ""
```

[5] That is what we mean when we describe a dialog box as being *modal*. Once the dialog appears, the user is in what might be called dialog mode and can't do anything else until the dialog is dismissed.

```
// step 1
   divide n by 16, giving quotient 12 and remainder 4
   append the hex value of the remainder, "4," to the string: "4"
   set n to the quotient, 12
// step 2
   divide n by 16, giving quotient 0 and remainder 12
   append the hex value of the remainder, "C", to the string: "C4"
```

The code to do this is simple; we call our function `hexChar` to do the conversion to a hex "digit" and we use the `Math` class's `floor` function to get the quotient of `n / 16`:

```
// startup
n = 196;
s = ""
// step 1
s = hexChar(n % 16) + s; // s = "4" now
n = Math.floor(n / 16);   // n = 12 now
// step 2
s = hexChar(n % 16) + s; // s = "C" + "4" = "C4"
n = Math.floor(n / 16);   // n = 0
```

The problem here is that this code gives us only two hex digits. What if we had a different program that needed more digits? What we need is a way to repeatedly execute the two assignment statements, without having to write them over and over again. JavaScript provides us with just such an iterative control statement, called the `for` statement. In general, the `for` statement takes the following form:

```
for (initial-expression; condition; increment-expression)
    statement(s)
```

The *initial-expression* typically assigns an initial value to a variable that will serve as a counter for the loop. The *condition* is a Boolean expression describing under what condition (usually involving the control variable) the loop should continue. The *increment-expression* describes the change to be made to the control variable after each pass through the loop. A pass through the loop is one execution of the enclosed statement(s). As was the case with the `if` statement, the controlled *statement(s)* can be one or more JavaScript statements, enclosed if necessary in curly braces.

More specifically, here is what happens when the browser processes a `for` statement:

1. The *initial-expression* is evaluated.
2. The condition is evaluated.
   a) If the condition evaluates to `true`, the controlled statement(s) are executed and then control passes to step 3.
   b) If the condition evaluates to `false`, control passes out of the loop, to whatever follows.
3. The *increment-expression* is executed and control returns to step 2.

The simplest, and most common, use of the `for` loop iterates the loop statement(s) some number, say *n*, times, and can be written generally as follows:

```
for (var i = 0; i < n; i++)
    statement(s)
```

We call these *counter loops*. Here are a few simple examples.

```
//compute n factorial (1 * 2 * ... * n)
var result = 1
for (var index = 1; index <= n; index++)
    result *= index;

function toHex(n, d) {
// from the core example program
   var s = "";
   for (var i = 0; i < d; i++) {
        s = hexChar(n % 16) + s;
        n = Math.floor(n / 16);
   }
   return s;
}
```

JavaScript provides us with another iterative control structure that is useful for controlling loops that are Boolean in nature, as opposed to numeric. We use the `while` statement to indicate that we want a group of statements executed as long as some Boolean condition is true. The general form of the `while` statement is as follows:

```
while (loop-condition)
      statement(s)
```

The *loop-condition* is a Boolean expression, and *statement(s)* is, as usual, any group of JavaScript statements, enclosed in braces, if necessary.

The first step in interpreting a `while` statement is to evaluate the loop condition. If it evaluates to `true`, the loop statement(s) are executed. The loop condition is then evaluated again, and the process continues. From this description, it is clear that the `while` statement is a kissing cousin to the `for` statement. Both control iterative sequences, and both involve evaluating a Boolean condition as the means for determining when to stop the iteration. In fact, one can simulate a `for` loop with a `while` loop. These two code segments would produce the same result.

```
for (var i = 0; i < max; i++)    var i = 0;
  statement(s)                   while (i < max) {
                                    statements(s);
                                    i++;
                                 }
```

The critical distinction, though, is that it is easy to make sure a `for` statement terminates. All one must do is use the control variable in each of the controlling expressions (the initial, test, and increment expressions) in a logically consistent way. The browser then takes care of adjusting the control variable as part of interpreting the `for` statement. In the case of a `while` statement, it is the programmer's responsibility to include the equivalent of the increment-expression within the body of the loop. Otherwise, the potential exists for an infinite loop, such as,

```
var x = 0;
while (x < n)
   n++;
```

or, worse yet,

```
while (true)
   alert("GET ME OUTTA HERE!");
```

The page displayed in Figure 5.14 illustrates the control statements we have touched on in this section. It shows a simple ATM-like interface that allows you to make deposits to, withdrawals from, and inquiries concerning a virtual account. It allows you to do so only after you have entered a legal Personal ID Number (PIN, of which there is only one, "7777"). The code for the figure is as follows.

```
<HTML>
<HEAD>
   <TITLE>Bank on it...</TITLE>

   <SCRIPT LANGUAGE = "JavaScript">
   <!-- hide
      var balance = 0.0;
```

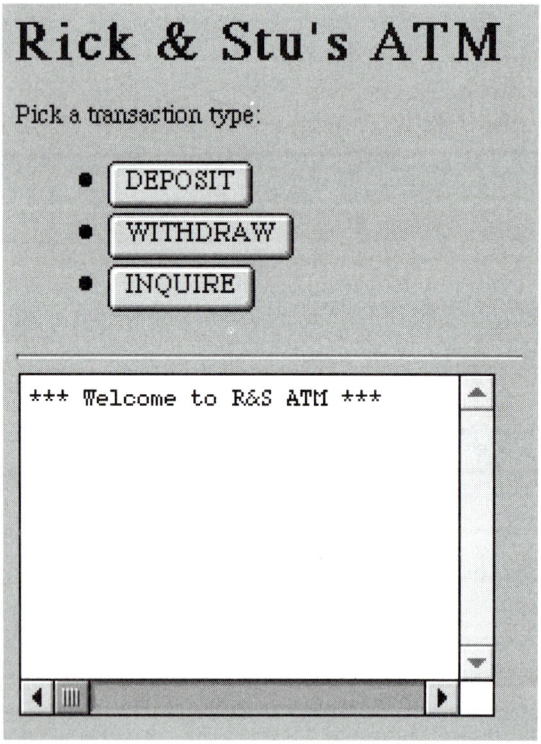

FIGURE 5.14
The ATM program

```
function newLn() {
// We need this, since different browsers require different
// ways to drop down to the next line of output.
   if (navigator.appVersion.lastIndexOf('Win') != -1)
      return "\r\n"
   else
      return "\n"
}

function getPIN () {
   document.ATM.display.value = "*** Welcome to R&S ATM ***" +
                                newLn();
   var thisPIN = prompt("Please enter your PIN:", "");
   // Catch bad PINs--only allow three tries.
   var count = 1;
   while ((thisPIN != "7777") && (count < 3)) {
         thisPIN = prompt("Please enter your PIN:", "");
         count++;
   }
   if (count == 3) {
      document.ATM.display.value = "3 Strikes and you're out!";
      window.close();
   }
}

function doDeposit () {
   var depositAmt = prompt("Enter deposit (without '$'):", "");
   // Make sure the user has entered a deposit amount.
   if ((depositAmt != null) && (depositAmt !="")) {
      balance += parseFloat(depositAmt);
      with (document.ATM.display) {
         value += newLn() + "Amount deposited: $" + depositAmt;
         value += newLn() + "Current balance: $" +
            balance + newLn();
      }
   }
}

function doWithdrawal () {
   var withdrawAmt = prompt("Enter withdrawal
      (without '$'):", "");

   // Make sure the user has entered a withdrawal amount,
   if ((withdrawAmt != null) && (withdrawAmt !="")) {
      // and make sure there's enough money to cover it.
      if (withdrawAmt > balance) {
         with (document.ATM.display) {
            value += newLn() +
            "***ILLEGAL TRANSACTION***" + newLn();
         }
      }
```

```
                else {
                    balance -= parseFloat(withdrawAmt);
                    with (document.ATM.display) {
                        value += newLn() + "Amount withdrawn: $" +
                        withdrawAmt;
                        value += newLn() + "Current balance: $" +
                        balance + newLn();
                    }
                }
            }
        }

        function doInquire () {
            with (document.ATM.display) {
                value += newLn() + "*** Current balance: $" + balance;
            }
        }
        // end hiding -->
    </SCRIPT>
</HEAD>

<BODY ONLOAD = "getPIN()">
    <FORM NAME = "ATM">
        <H1>Rick & Stu's ATM</H1>
        <P>Pick a transaction type:</P>
        <MENU>
            <LI><INPUT TYPE = "button"
                       VALUE = "DEPOSIT"
                       ONCLICK = "doDeposit()">
            <LI><INPUT TYPE = "button"
                       VALUE = "WITHDRAW"
                       ONCLICK = "doWithdrawal()">
            <LI><INPUT TYPE = "button"
                       VALUE = "INQUIRE"
                       ONCLICK = "doInquire()">
            </MENU>
            <HR>
            <TEXTAREA  NAME = "display"
                       ROWS = 10
                       COLS = 30>*** Welcome to R&S ATM ***
            </TEXTAREA>
        </FORM>
</BODY>
</HTML>
```

You can see that the `getPin` function is invoked from the body's `ONLOAD` handler, and is controlled by a `while` loop. The `while` loop, in turn, is controlled by a compound Boolean expression that will continue iterating as long as the correct PIN has not been entered and the user has had fewer than three attempts to enter the legal PIN. In effect, we are using a `while` loop to check a condition and control a counter. The loop can thus terminate by violating either of the conditions. If it terminates by virtue of the `count` reaching 3, we know that the PIN was never correctly entered. The `if` statement at the end of function `getPIN` detects this and responds by issuing a message and closing the page's window.

Notice, too, that whereas function `doDeposit` readily accepts and processes any input value, function `doWithdrawal` is more careful. It embeds its processing in an `if-else` statement that first checks to see if there is enough of a balance to permit the requested withdrawal.

Finally, notice how the program manages user input. In the case of the PIN, it is solicited using the `prompt` function, which returns a string as its value (whatever string was entered by the user). So, variable `thisPin` contains a string value that can be compared directly to the string literal "7777". In `doDeposit` and `doWithdrawal`, `prompt` is again used to return string values, but since these values are to be used for arithmetic, they are run through the `parseFloat` function, which performs the required conversions.

LAB 5.3

Game On!

In this set of exercises we begin programming in earnest, asking you to add some basic statements and data items of your own to the existing code. All of these exercises are to be conducted on *your* copy of the concert game. In each case, make changes to your file to accomplish the proposed change in the game, and then test your changes by loading your file into your browser and running it.

You should attempt the excercises one at a time (that is, make changes to address one exercise, and work on that until it has been solved), and in the prescribed order (since we've ordered them to reflect their relative difficulty). Feel free to copy and paste sections of code to make your work easier.

1. Create a global variable called "playerName" and initialize it to be an empty string ("").

2. Add a statement that prompts the user of the program for his or her name and saves the name in variable `playerName`. Place this statement so that it gets executed immediately after the screen is initialized, but before the game (and the clicking) begins.

3. Now modify some of the messages that are displayed in alert boxes and in the document's status window so that they use the player's name.

4. You have undoubtedly noticed that whenever the image (or your location in the game) changes, you are put back into Look mode. Change the program so that this is not the case. That is, you should change from Look to Action mode, and vice versa, only when you click on the appropriate radio button.

5. At present there is a relatively short list of items that you need in order to proceed to the concert. Change this so that you must also have sneakers in your inventory to make it all the way to the concert. Notice that we have provided you with a function that will tell you when sneakers have been "clickedOn" when visiting the clothing store.

6. Speaking of the clothing store, notice how the cashier insists that you have ATM cash before allowing you to leave the store, even when you haven't selected anything to purchase. Change function `processBeat` so that you are checked for money only if you have actually purchased something at the store. [*Hint*: A function named `inventoryContains` is already defined in the program, which can be used to tell you whether or not the inventory contains a particular item.]

Review Questions

1. There's a potential ambiguity with the `if` statement.

a) Show that there are two possible interpretations for this statement:

```
if (x == 1)
if (y == 0)
statement1 // done when x == 1 and y == 0
else
statement2 // when is this done?
```

b) JavaScript resolves this ambiguity by the rule that an `else` clause should always be matched with the nearest unmatched `if`. With this in mind, under what circumstance would *statement2* be executed in the code above?

c) Indent the code above to reflect the correct interpretation of `if ... else`.

2. What is the difference in the action of the following two segments? Describe the final values of `s` in each segment for each of the (`x`, `y`) pairs (1, 0), (1, 1), (0, 0), and (0, 1).

```
s = "";
if (x == 1)
  s += "One"
if (y == 0)
  s += "Two"
```

```
s = "";
if (x == 1)
  s += "One"
else if (y == 0)
  s += "Two"
```

3. Any or all of the three parts of the head of a `for` loop may be omitted, though we commonly use all three. Describe the possible trouble that the statements below might cause.

a) `for (i < 8; i++)`
b) `for (var i = 0; i++)`
c) `for (var i = 0; i < 8)`
d) `for ()`

4. Write a statement that will set the variable sum (already initialized to 0) to the sum of the first n odd integers. For example, if n is 3, the sum is 1 + 3 + 5 = 9.

5. What types of information, if any, are returned by each of the functions `alert`, `confirm`, and `prompt`?

5.7 FLAKY PIE CRUST: FUNCTIONS, REVISITED

We've been using functions in our sample pages throughout this module. To this point we have described them only informally as a way to group statements together, give the group a name, and cause the group to be executed by invoking the function name. When viewed in this way, a function is like the recipe for a pie crust that we can refer to from any pie recipe without having to duplicate any of the instructions. As useful as that is, JavaScript functions are even more powerful than we have let on. They can, with a few minor tweaks, be written so that they operate on different data every time we invoke them (for example, one time using graham crackers and another time using walnuts). They can also notify us about the results of their processing (in effect, delivering the crust to us ready to be loaded with the filling of our choice).

◆ Parameters: Information provided to a function when it is called.

The first of these advanced behaviors is made possible by the use of *parameters*. When we use the `alert` function, for example, we don't simply write `alert`. We provide it with a string parameter (in parentheses, following the function name), which gets displayed as part of the resulting dialog box. The value provided to `alert` can be different (and usually is) every time we call it. As long as we provide it with the right type of information (a string in this case), `alert` will do its thing. Similarly, we must provide string values to functions `parseFloat`, `confirm`, and `eval`.

Function `parseInt` is interesting because it requires two parameters—a string and an integer. While `parseInt` can be called with any string and any integer values, they must both be provided, and must be provided in the correct order (the string as the first parameter, the integer as the second). In general, parameters can be variables, literal values, the values of form elements, or any expression at all that evaluates to a value of the appropriate type.

When we write functions of our own, we have the added responsibility of deciding how our functions will be invoked. We choose a name for the function and we determine how many, what type, and the order of the parameters it will require. All of this, as we have seen, is dictated by how we write the function's definition, which takes the following general form:

```
function functionName(parameter1, parameter2,...) {
   statement(s) // generally using the parameters
}
```

◆ Techspeak: A *formal parameter* is the name used in the function definition; an *actual parameter* is the value supplied to the formal parameter when the function is called.

A function definition begins with the keyword `function`, which is followed by the function name and its parameter list. The *parameter list* (which may be empty, but still must be written as "()") is a comma-separated list of names enclosed in parentheses. These names serve as the placeholders for the values that are provided when the function is invoked. That is, they are used to hold the information that varies every time we invoke the function. We write our functions using the parameter names within the statements, and we presume that the values provided for our parameters will suit their intended purpose. Although we don't know the details of how JavaScript's `parseInt` function is defined, we can feel certain that its definition looks something like this:

```
function parseInt(thisString, thisBase) {
        ...
}
```

More formally, you can think of function parameters as local variables that get initialized with the corresponding parameter values when the function is invoked. "Corresponding" in this sense means corresponding positionally—that is, the first parameter in the invocation is assigned as a value to the first parameter, the second parameter is assigned to the second parameter, and so on. The function then carries out its business in terms of these local variables, like this:

<table>
<tr><th>The Code</th><th>What Actually Happens</th></tr>
<tr><td><pre>function increase(value){
    value += 3;
}

...
var x = 15;
increase(x);</pre></td><td><pre>function increase(value){
    var local_value = value;
    local_value += 3;
// copy is now 18
}
...
var x = 15;
increase (x);
// x is still 15</pre></td></tr>
</table>

This interpretation of parameter passing implies that JavaScript functions cannot modify the values of their parameters. They can, and often do, modify the values of their parameters, but because these are local variables that just happen to get their initial values from the function's parameters, those parameters (even when they are variable names) are unaffected by any modifications. Functions can, as we have already seen, affect the values of global variables and form elements that are referenced directly in their statements.

> Any changes to function parameters are purely local, and can't be seen outside the function. However, functions can change the values of global variables and objects.

Our core example uses four programmer-defined functions (along with the built-in function `parseInt` and the method `Math.floor`). Both `report` and `changeColors` take no parameters, and `changeColors` calls `report` by invoking it by name in a statement of its own:

```
function report() { // Note--no parameters coming in
   document.colors.redHex.value = toHex(red, 2);
```

```
    document.colors.greenHex.value = toHex(green, 2);
    document.colors.blueHex.value = toHex(blue, 2);
}

function changeColors() {
    red += 3;
    green += 5;
    blue += 7;

    document.bgColor =     toHex(red, 2) +
                           toHex(green, 2) +
                           toHex(blue, 2);

    report();
}
```

Note that although these two functions don't require any information when they're called, they both access and modify global information: `report` modifies the values of the three text fields; `changeColors` increases the three global variables `red`, `green`, and `blue`, and also sets the `bgColor` property of the `document` object.

The other two functions, `hexChar` and `toHex`, are different from `report` and `changeColors` in two important ways. First, they both accept parameters when they are called and, second, they both *return* a value to the location where they're called. The function `hexChar`, for example, takes in a number, `n`, and returns the hexadecimal character equivalent:

```
    function hexChar(n) {
    if (n == 10)          return "A";
    else if (n == 11)     return "B";
    else if (n == 12)     return "C";
    else if (n == 13)     return "D";
    else if (n == 14)     return "E";
    else if (n == 15)     return "F";
    else                  return "" + n;
}
```

`toHex` takes in two parameters, the number, `n`, to be converted to a hex string and the length, `d`, of the result. Notice the way it calls `hexChar`: Since `hexChar` returns a string, the call appears in an expression, exactly as if it were a string (since, after all, that's what it returns). Notice that we do the same thing with the call to the `Math` object's method `floor`:

```
function toHex(n, d) {
    var s = "";
    for (var i = 0; i < d; i++) {
        s = hexChar(n % 16) + s;
        n = Math.floor(n / 16);
    }
    return s;
}
```

A `return` statement can be placed anywhere without a function's body. Its general form is

```
return expression
```

When it is executed, its effects are to immediately terminate the processing of the function it is in, and to transmit the value of the provided expression back to the point of the function's invocation. The returned expression can be of any simple type. For example, the following function returns the maximum value of its two parameters:

```
function maxValue(x1, x2) {
   if (x1 > x2)
      return x1
   else
      return x2
}
```

Functions that return values must be invoked in a manner that is consistent with the type of the returned value. That is, we invoke functions that return values not as separate statements, but rather as expressions that serve as parts of another statement. So, when we invoke function `maxValue` we do so as if we were referring to a numeric value—because we effectively are. We can think of its invocation as being replaced by the returned value. It, thus, makes perfect sense to invoke `maxValue` as follows:

```
var bigNum += maxValue(num1, num2)
```

> A function that doesn't return a value is called in its own statement, by giving its name and any necessary parameters. A function that does return a value is generally called as part of an expression and such a call may be made wherever a variable of the appropriate type could appear.

Neither `toHex` nor `hexChar` are invoked from an event handler—they can be thought of as helper functions, written primarily for the purpose of simplifying and clarifying the code in the rest of the program. One could almost directly replace the six calls in `report` and `changeColors` with the body of `toHex`, and accomplish the same processing. This, however, would result in a much larger, much more confusing, and much more repetitious body of code, which, as we'll discuss in the final section of this module, is something we want to avoid.

> Avoiding repetition of code is a good reason to define helper functions. We can *encapsulate* the group of operations that are to be performed more than once as a function, and invoke it whenever we need it.

LAB 5.4

Functions at the Junction

In this set of exercises we continue our efforts to expand our concert game by making changes to the JavaScript code at the function level. Each of the following exercises asks you to define and invoke a function of your own. As before, you should make changes to *your* version of the code to accomplish the proposed changes, and then test your changes by loading your file into your browser and testing it.

1. There are two different places in the original program where we use the following statement to clear the inventory list:

```
document.rightForm.inventoryList.value = ""
```

Write a function named `clearInventory` to accomplish this processing. Then, replace the occurrences of the statement with calls to your new function.

2. There are five different places in our original program where the following lines of code are repeated exactly:

```
SetMode ("Look")
SetImage (mapImg)
document.statusForm..statusList.value = "Gettin' ready for the
show..."
```

Write a function named `returnToMap` that encapsulates these statements. Then, replace each group of the three statements with a call to function `returnToMap`.

3. Throughout the JavaScript code, status window text is displayed below the current image using statements like the one below:

```
document.statusForm.statusList.value = "whatever string is to
be displayed"
```

Write a function named `setStatus` that accomplishes this operation, and replace all of the statements like the one above with calls to `setStatus`, as follows:

```
setStatus ("whatever string is to be displayed")
```

Use function `setImage` as a model.

4. Write three functions named `clickedOnHair`, `clickedOnHat`, and `clickedOnNail`, which will return `true` or `false` to indicate whether or not you have clicked on the respective articles while at the clothing store. Use your browser's status bar to help you determine the appropriate coordinate range for each article within the clothing store image. Add these functions to the script tag that contains all of the other `clickedOn...` functions.

5. In the course of playing the game you have probably noticed that an individual item (say, the jacket at the clothing store) can get added to your inventory many times. In fact, if you click on an item repeatedly when in Action mode, that article will be added to your inventory once for each click. Modify function `addToInventory` so that it precludes this behavior. That is, if an article already appears in the inventory list when it is clicked on, an alert should be displayed indicating that the item has already been purchased and it should not be added to the inventory again.

6. Now, change function `processBeat` so that it uses your new `clickedOn...` functions (from Exercise 4) to recognize clicks on the hair, hat, and nail polish. When any of these is clicked, whether in Look or Action mode, an alert box should be displayed indicating that service is currently unavailable.

Review Questions

1. Define *function signature, parameter, parameter list,* and *return statement.*

2. Suppose we have two functions, defined as follows:

```
function inOrder(x, y){
  if (x <= y)
    return true
  else
    return false
}

function writeMany(s, n){
    for (var i = 0; i < n; i++)
    document.write(s)
}
```

Which of the following statements are legal? For those that aren't, explain why.

a) `if (inOrder(4, 2))`
`ok = true;`
b) `x = 3 + inOrder(x, 1);`
c) `inOrder(2, 3 / 4.7);`
d) `writeMany("Hello!");`
e) `writeMany(inOrder(2, 6), 5);`
f) `x += writeMany(2, 2);`

3. In Question 2, what do the two functions do?

4. Write a function `sumPowers` that takes a positive integer `n` as its parameter and returns the sum of the first `n` powers of 2. For example, if we called `sumPowers(4)`, the function would return 15 (= 1 + 2 + 4 + 8).

5. Although a function cannot be defined inside another function, it's perfectly legal for a function to call itself in its definition. What does the following function do, when called with parameters such as 0, 1, 2, 3, 4, 4.5, and "Hello"?

```
function mystery(n){
  if (n <= 1)
    return 1
  else
    return n * mystery(n - 1)
}
```

◆ A function that calls itself is known as *recursive.*

5.8 PREPARED FOODS: JAVASCRIPT OBJECTS

Even the best cooks rely to a certain degree on ingredients and foods that have been prepared for them and sit ready to be used in their pantries and spice shelves. JavaScript provides an analogous pantry of predefined objects that programmers can use to enhance their pages. In fact, we have made extensive use of many built-in objects already. The "functions" we described back in Section 5.4 (such as `alert`, `confirm`, `eval`, `parseInt`, `parseFloat`, `prompt`, and `write`) are, to be more precise, *methods* of objects that we can refer to directly from within our scripts. The `prompt` method, for example, is part of the `window` object that is created when our program is loaded by the browser. When we set a page's background color from a script (as in `bgColor="#C0C0C0"`) we are referring to a property (`bgColor`) that is part of the `document` object describing the current page. We've been even more upfront when we refer to any form element from within a script, where we explicitly use the built-in objects `document`, `form`, and `textarea` (for example, in `document.colors.redHex.value`).

In fact, aside from the variables, literal values, programmer-defined functions, and keywords that identify JavaScript statements, most of the rest of any JavaScript program is a reference to a built-in object. Objects come complete and ready to use. They include properties that define the object and functions that manipulate it,[6] all of which can be accessed using the dot notation we have grown accustomed to when referring to form elements (which are objects!). So, to refer to any of an object's properties we use

```
objectName.propertyName
```

and to invoke one of its methods we write

```
objectName.methodName(parameters...).
```

Taking advantage of these objects is mostly a matter of knowing that they exist. Once we tell you what the objects in programs are (there are 23 different kinds) and describe for you some of their properties and methods (there are hundreds), you can begin to incorporate them into your scripts. Clearly, we can't tell you about all of them in the space of this module, but we'll do our best to point out the most useful ones. For the sake of discussion, we'll divide the objects into two groups: those that are part of our program by virtue of their being an HTML component of the page (we'll refer to these as *implicit objects*); and those that are created explicitly by the programmer for representing and manipulating information within scripts (the *explicit objects*).

■ Implicit Objects

We'll start with the implicit objects because you've already had a good deal of experience using them. Every time, for example, that we use the notation

```
document.formName.elementName.value
```

[6] The functions associated with built-in object are usually referred to as *methods,* to distinguish them from programmer-defined functions.

we are accessing our page's `document` object, one of its forms (which is a property of the `document` object, and is itself an object), one of the form's elements (again, a property of the `form`, and an object in its own right), and the `value` property of that element. If this sounds familiar to you, it is because it reflects exactly the object hierarchy we described for you back in Section 5.2 when we talked about names in JavaScript. We can now be a bit more precise, and describe long names like this in terms of objects and properties. In fact, every form element is an object with its own properties and methods. Some of JavaScript's implicit built-in objects and some of their more useful properties and methods are displayed in Table 5.2.

TABLE 5.2
JavaScript built-in objects (implicit)

OBJECT: `button`	
Property of:	`form`
Properties:	
`name`	Corresponds to the `NAME` attribute
`value`	Corresponds to the `VALUE` attribute
Methods:	
`click`	Simulates a click on the button

OBJECT: `checkbox`	
Property of:	`form`
Properties:	
`checked`	Simulates checking a checkbox
`defaultChecked`	Corresponds to the `CHECKED` attribute
`name`	Corresponds to the `NAME` attribute
`value`	Corresponds to the `VALUE` attribute
Methods:	
`click`	Simulates a click on the checkbox

OBJECT: `document`	
Property of:	`window`
Properties:	
`alinkColor`	Corresponds to the `ALINK` attribute
`anchors`	An array of all the anchors in a document
`bgColor`	Corresponds to the `BGCOLOR` attribute
`fgColor`	Corresponds to the `TEXT` attribute
`forms`	An array reflecting all the forms in a document
`lastModified`	The date a document was last modified
`linkColor`	Corresponds to the `LINK` attribute
`links`	An array reflecting all the links in a document
`location`	The complete URL of a document
`referrer`	The URL of the calling document
`title`	The contents of the <TITLE> tag
`vlinkColor`	Corresponds to the `VLINK` attribute

OBJECT: `document` *(continued)*

Methods:

`clear`	Clears the document
`close`	Closes the document
`open`	Opens the document
`write`	Writes a string to the document
`writeln`	Writes a string, followed by an new-line indicator, to the document

OBJECT: `form`

Property of: `document`

Properties:

`action`	Corresponds to the `ACTION` attribute
`elements`	An array reflecting all the elements in a form
`encoding`	Corresponds to the `ENCTYPE` attribute
`length`	The number of elements in a form
`method`	Corresponds to the `METHOD` attribute
`target`	Corresponds to the `TARGET` attribute

The following objects are also properties of the `form` object when they are part of the form: `button`, `checkbox`, `hidden`, `password`, `radio`, `reset`, `select`, `submit`, `text`, `textarea`

Methods:

`submit`	Submit form data to the server

OBJECT: `radio`

Property of: `form`

Properties:

`checked`	The checked status of a radio button
`defaultChecked`	Corresponds to the `CHECKED` attribute
`length`	The number of radio buttons in a `radio` object
`name`	Corresponds to the `NAME` attribute
`value`	Corresponds to the `VALUE` attribute

Methods:

`click`	Simulates a click on the radio button

OBJECT: `reset`

Property of: `form`

Properties:

`name`	Corresponds to the `NAME` attribute
`value`	Corresponds to the `VALUE` attribute

Methods:

`click`	Triggers a click on the reset button

TABLE 5.2 *(continued)*

OBJECT: `select`	
Property of:	`form`
Properties:	
`length`	The number of options in a `select` object
`name`	Corresponds to the `NAME` attribute
`options`	An array of the `<OPTION>` tags
`selectedIndex`	The index of the selected option (or the first selected option, if multiple options are selected)
Methods:	
`blur`	Triggers a blur event on the select list
`focus`	Triggers a focus event on the select list

OBJECT: `submit`	
Property of:	`form`
Properties:	
`name`	Corresponds to the `NAME` attribute
`value`	Corresponds to the `VALUE` attribute
Methods:	
`click`	Triggers a click on the submit button

OBJECT: `text`	
Property of:	`form`
Properties:	
`defaultValue`	Corresponds to the `VALUE` attribute
`name`	Corresponds to the `NAME` attribute
`value`	The current contents of the text field
Methods:	
`blur`	Triggers a blur event on the text field
`focus`	Triggers a focus event on the text field
`select`	Triggers a select event on the text field

OBJECT: `textarea`	
Property of:	`form`
Properties:	
`defaultValue`	Corresponds to the `VALUE` attribute
`name`	Corresponds to the `NAME` attribute
`value`	The current contents of the text area
Methods:	
`blur`	Triggers a blur event on the text area
`focus`	Triggers a focus event on the text area
`select`	Triggers a select event on the text area

OBJECT: `window` *(continued)*	
Property of:	None
Properties:	
`defaultStatus`	The default message displayed in the window's status bar
`frames`	An array reflecting all the frames in a window
`length`	The number of frames in a parent window
`name`	The `windowName` parameter
`parent`	Refers to a window containing a frameset
`self`	Refers to the current window
`status`	Specifies message in the window's status bar
`top`	Refers to the topmost window
`window`	Refers to the current window
The following objects are also properties of the `window` object, when they are part of a window: `document`, `frame`, `location`	
Methods:	
`alert`	Displays an alert dialog box
`close`	Closes the window
`confirm`	Displays a confirm dialog box
`open`	Opens the window
`prompt`	Displays a prompt dialog box

Most of the properties and methods described in Table 5.2 should make sense to you. Obviously you have used many of them already, and you can probably imagine how to use many of the other ones as well. Before we show you some new sample pages, however, there are a couple of entries in the table that warrant additional explanation. Notice, for example, how every `document` object has a property named "`forms`", and that `forms` is described as an array. An array is just an indexed collection of values. The values in a particular array can be of any type—but they all must be the same type. That is, you can have an array of numbers, or an array of strings, or, in the case of the `forms` property, an array of forms. The `forms` array is defined for us as the browser interprets our page, making one entry in the `forms` array for each form in the page.

Once the page is loaded, our JavaScript code can refer to the forms by their names (as we have always done in our examples) or by using *array notation*. Array notation allows us to access the individual values in an array, no matter what their type, using numbered subscripts. For example, to refer to the first form in a forms array, we could write `document.forms[0]`. For reasons that reflect history and how programming languages are translated, subscript values for an implicit array range from 0 to the number of values in the array minus one. Every JavaScript array also has a `length` property, which indicates how many values it contains.

Combining arrays with `for` statements gives us an effective—and notationally efficient—way to apply similar processing to each value in an array. We can write loops like the following to, say, do something to every form in a document:

```
for (var i = 0; i < document.form.length; i++)
      // process document.form[i]
```

Notice how we use the control variable from the `for` statement (`i`) as the subscript to our forms array in the body of the loop. The value of `i` (which is automatically controlled by the `for` statement) changes with each iteration, thereby causing each pass through to refer to a different form. Remember that since an array is a collection of values of some type, an individual element of the array is a value of that type and can be used anywhere it makes sense to refer to a value of that type. So, one can use the expression

◆ You can also use the particular form's name inside the square brackets, rather than an index number.

```
document.forms[0].length
```

to refer to the number of elements in the first form of a document, and

```
document.forms[0].name
```

to refer to the name of that form.

A number of similar arrays are created for us implicitly as parts of other built-in objects. Each contains values of a particular kind, each allows reference to its values using integer subscripts starting with 0, and each can be used in conjunction with `for` statements to process its values in order. Some of these are described in Table 5.3.

Explicit Objects

There are several objects that are not directly related to any of the HTML elements in our page. In fact, these objects are not properties of any built-in object. As such, they are not created for us by the browser as it loads our page. Instead, these are "programmer" objects in the sense that we decide we want to use them within our JavaScript code, and we must take explicit steps to use them. There is good reason to use them because they allow us to represent and manipulate some very useful information. And, as has been the case so often in this module, you have seen numerous examples of them before we got around to explaining them. We summarize three important explicit objects in Table 5.4, and then illustrate their use.

The properties of the `Math` object are just numeric constants that can be used directly in your code. The methods, as you can probably tell, calculate and return the results of a variety of standard mathematical functions. To make use of the `Math` object's properties or its methods, we simply refer to them as

TABLE 5.3 *Some of JavaScript's implicit arrays*

Array Name	Property of	Description
`anchors`	`document`	All anchors in a document
`elements`	`form`	Form elements, in the order in which they appear in the page
`forms`	`document`	Array of forms, in the order in which they appear in the page
`frames`	`window`	Frames in the window
`links`	`document`	All links in a document
`options`	`select`	Options in a given selection list
`radio`	`form`	Radio buttons with common name in a form

TABLE 5.4
Some JavaScript explicit built-in objects

OBJECT: `Date`

Property of:	None
Properties:	None
Methods:	
`getDate`	Return the date of this `Date` object
`getDay`	Return the day of this `Date` object
`getHours`	Return the hours of this `Date` object
`getMinutes`	Return the minutes of this `Date` object
`getMonth`	Return the month of this `Date` object
`getSeconds`	Return the seconds of this `Date` object
`getTime`	Return the time of this `Date` object
`getYear`	Return the year of this `Date` object
`setDate`	Establish the value of this `Date` object
`setHours`	Establish the hours of this `Date` object
`setMinutes`	Establish the minutes of this `Date` object
`setMonth`	Establish the month of this `Date` object
`setSeconds`	Establish the seconds of this `Date` object
`setTime`	Establish the time of this `Date` object
`setYear`	Establish the year of this `Date` object
`toGMTString`	Convert time to Greenwich Mean Time (GMT)
`toLocaleString`	Convert to local time

OBJECT: `Math`

Property of: None

Properties: (sundry mathematical constants)

`E, LN2, LN10, LOG2E, LOG10E, PI, SQRT1_2, SQRT2`

Methods: (mostly self-explanatory)

`abs, acos, asin, atan, ceil, cos, exp, floor, log, max, min, pow, random, round, sin, sqrt, tan`

OBJECT: `String`

Property of:	None
Properties:	
`length`	The length of the string
Methods:	
`big`	Displays string in big style
`bold`	Displays string in bold style
`charAt`	Returns the character at the given position in the string (beginning at zero)
`fixed`	Displays string in fixed style
`fontcolor`	Sets the font color
`fontsize`	Sets the font size
`indexOf`	Returns the position of the first occurrence of the parameter in the string
`italics`	Displays string in italic style

TABLE 5.4 *(continued)*

OBJECT: `String` *(continued)*	
Methods:	
`lastIndexOf`	Returns the position of the last occurrence of the parameter in the string
`small`	Displays string in small style
`strike`	Displays string in strike style
`sub`	Displays string in subscript style
`substring`	Returns a substring of the string beginning at one position, for a given length
`sup`	Displays string in superscript style
`toLowerCase`	Returns string value as lowercase
`toUpperCase`	Returns string value as uppercase

`Math.propertyName` or `Math.methodName(parameters...)`, as we did in our core example when we called

```
Math.floor(n / 16)
```

to find the largest whole number less than or equal to n / 16, giving us the quotient that results from division of `n` by 16.

Using the `Date` object is a bit trickier because, even though it is a built-in object, the values returned by its methods change constantly. Thus, to obtain a `Date` object we must use the `new` operator to create and initialize one, as in

```
var today = new Date();
```

This would create a `Date` object that contains all of the up-to-the-second information as of when it is executed. If we want a `Date` object that describes a particular date, you can provide parameters to the `Date` *constructor* method (that's what the function Date() is called, since it constructs and returns a new `Date` object), as follows:

```
var firstDayofCentury = new Date(2000, 0, 1)
```

It is worth noting that the `new` operator has other interesting uses, beyond creating `Date` objects. It can be used to create new objects of other types as well, including arrays. We described earlier the implicit arrays that are created for us based on the HTML elements in our pages. We can create our own programmer arrays as well that are useful objects within our code. To do so, we use the `new` operator, but this time specify that we want a new array, as follows:

```
powersOfTwo = new Array(128, 64, 32, 16, 8, 4, 2, 1)
```

Variable `powersOfTwo` now represents an array of eight integer values. As with any array, its values are accessible using zero-based subscripts (so, `powers-OfTwo[0]` is 128, and `powersOfTwo[7]` is 1).

To use `String` objects we need not resort to anything more than referring to them in our JavaScript code. Every time we write a string literal or refer to a value of type string (as, say, the `value` property of some `form` element), we are dealing with a `String` object, and have access to all of its attendant properties (there's only one—`length`) and methods (there are plenty of these). We refer to them using our standard notation, as in the following.

```
var myString = "Oh yes, I have a plethora!"
myString.length              //returns 26
myString.charAt(4)           //returns "y"
myString.substring(17,25)    //returns "plethora", characters at
                               positions 17
                             //up to, but not including 25
myString.toUpperCase()       //returns "OH YES, I HAVE A PLETH-
                               ORA!"
```

LAB 5.5

Objects of Attention

In this set of exercises, we'll spice up our code by making use of some of JavaScript's built-in objects and properties. As in the earlier labs, treat these as independent exercises that should be attempted and tested one at a time.

1. It is often helpful in situations in which you are working on a program over an extended period of time to have an indicator that tells you which version of the program you are working on. Use JavaScript's `Date` class to display the current date and time somewhere on your game page.

2. Let's make use of JavaScript's facility with colors to make our program a bit more colorful. Change function `setMode` so that every time the game's mode is changed (between Action and Look), the background color of the document changes. That is, pick a color to correspond to Action mode, and another color to represent Look mode, and set the document's background color to reflect the current mode. Note that you'll have to remove the default color assigned in the original HTML description.

3. While our original program did not make explicit use of JavaScript arrays, any JavaScript program that works with HTML forms uses an array implicitly. In fact, the forms array is a property of every document, and it contains an entry for each form in the document. Forms are ordered in the array by their appearance in the document, and are referred to beginning with subscript zero. This means that in our concert game, `document.forms[0]` is another way to refer to form `rightForm`, and `document.forms[1]` is another name for form `statusForm`. Replace some occurrences of `rightForm` and `statusForm` with their forms array counterparts, and verify that your code works as the original did.

4. Review the description in the text of JavaScript's `String` class so that we can use it to make our program a bit more realistic. In particular, notice that while you need ATM cash in your inventory to purchase anything (like the jacket) at the clothing store, money is not deducted from your inventory when you do make a purchase. Write a function named `SpendATMCash` that removes ATM Cash from the inventory list (if it indeed is in the list to begin with). Then, change function `processBeat` so that it removes ATM Cash from your inventory whenever you check out at the cashier.

Dynamic Code

Almost every object, property, and method that we have used in our sample pages is somehow related to the `document` object. As we saw above, among its properties are three arrays that combine to describe the document at a high level. The methods of a `document` object are particularly interesting as well, since they allow pages to be defined dynamically. That is to say, we can write JavaScript code that creates HTML code for us as a page that is being viewed and interacted with. Indeed the HTML code that is produced can reflect how the user is interacting with the page, displaying suitable messages along the way. The resulting code is then used to create and view a new document.

This kind of dynamic programming, if you will, is accomplished primarily by the `document` object's `write` and `writeln` methods. Both take as parameters a list of expressions, each of which is either a JavaScript expression or the property of an existing object, and return no values. How they operate depends on whether they are invoked in the process of loading the page or after the page is loaded. The former typically happens when `write` or `writeln` are called from within script elements, either as free statements or as parts or programmer-invoked functions. The latter occurs when these methods are invoked from event handlers, either directly or indirectly through functions.

When `write` and `writeln` are invoked in the process of interpreting and loading a page, they write the values of their expressions—anything that can legally appear in an HTML file, including text, tags, and elements—to the current page (the one being loaded). Thus, their parameters become part of the displayed page. A useful example would be, say, a script that determines the current date and displays it on the current page. This date (and time), of course, changes daily, so we can't just hard-code it into our HTML. Instead, we could use the statement `document.write(today)` to place the value on our page as it was being loaded, as we illustrate in Figure 5.15.

We put the date and time on the page by putting a `SCRIPT` element in the body of our page, like this:

```
<BODY>
<!-- Some HTML deleted here -->
    <SCRIPT>
    <!--
    today = new Date();
    document.write("<HR><B>Today is </B>", today, "<HR>");
    // -->
    </SCRIPT>
<!-- Some more HTML deleted here -->
</BODY>
```

When the browser reached the script, after the introductory HTML and before the `FORM` element, it executed the JavaScript statements to make a new date and `write` it and its surrounding code, just as if the <HR> and text were part of the document.

Even more interesting is the situation wherein `write` and `writeln` are invoked from event handlers after a page is loaded. In this case the HTML code that `write` and `writeln` compose (which is identical save for the line break

FIGURE 5.15
Programming a page

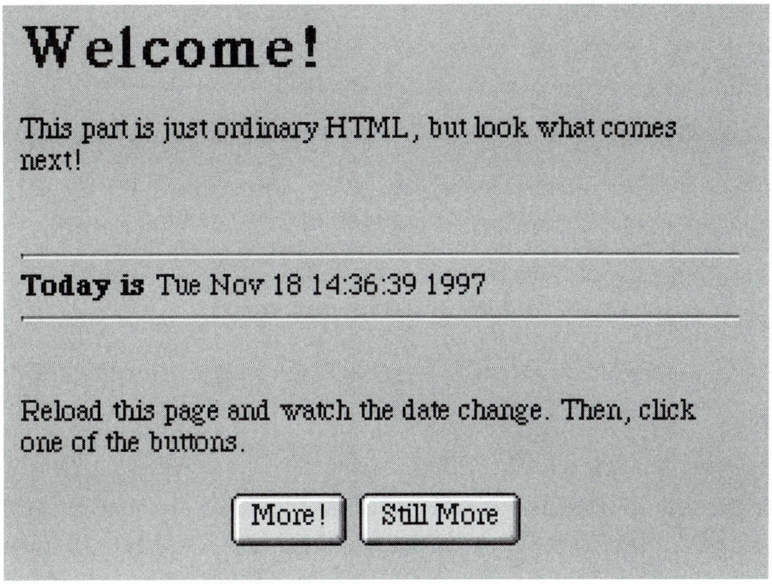

automatically appended to the end by method `writeln`—it stands for "write line") is loaded into a new document in the current window, which can reflect the user's interaction with the page. This effectively allows your code to create a brand-new document to be displayed as the result of its processing. Remember, too, that the values provided as parameters to `write` and `writeln` can contain string versions of HTML elements, so our dynamically created pages can even be formatted.

```
<HTML>
<HEAD>
    <SCRIPT LANGUAGE = "JavaScript">
    <!--
    function doWriting(n){
    // Write a message on a new document in the same window.
    // Note the HTML tags we used to format the output.
       if (n == 1)
          document.write("<H3>You clicked the \ "More!\ " button</H3>")
       else
          document.write("<H3>You clicked the \ "Still More\ " button</H3>")
    }
    // -->
    </SCRIPT>
</HEAD>

<BODY>
    <H1>Welcome!</H1>
    This part is just ordinary HTML, but look what comes next!
    <BR><BR><BR>
    <SCRIPT>
```

```
        <!--
        today = new Date();
        document.write("<HR><B>Today is </B>", today, "<HR>");
        // -->
    </SCRIPT>
    <BR><BR>
    Reload this page and watch the date change. Then, click
    one of the buttons.
    <FORM NAME = "dynamo">
        <CENTER>
        <INPUT    TYPE = "button"

    VALUE = "More!"

    ONCLICK = "doWriting(1)">
        <INPUT
    TYPE = "button"

    VALUE = "Still More"
    ONCLICK = "doWriting(2)">
        </CENTER>
    </FORM>
</BODY>
</HTML>
```

LAB 5.6

Dynamic Code

This final set of exercises concentrates on the definition and use of the image map that allows us to recognize and respond to all of the clicking that goes on during the game. When function `initMap` is called at the very start of the game, it extends the HTML code to define a complete imagemap (including all of the area coordinate tags with their respective calls to our main branching function, `mapGoto`). We'll start by looking at function `initMap` in detail, and then we'll use it to fill in all of the missing pieces of our game.

1. On a separate sheet of paper, trace the operation of function `initMap`. That is, write down the HTML code that is the output of this function. We'll start you out with the first couple of lines. You fill in enough of the rest to see the pattern.

```
<MAP NAME = "ImageMap">
<AREA SHAPE = RECT
    COORDS = "0, 0, 10, 10"
    HREF = "JavaScript:mapGoto(0,0)">
```

2. While the size of our main image is fixed at 320 × 240 by its HTML description, the resolution of our imagemap (which currently reports clicks on 10 × 10 squares) can be refined as we see fit to give us slightly more precision in recognizing mouse clicks. Fix function `initMap` now so that it correctly produces the HTML code necessary to track clicks within 5 × 5 squares on our images. If you do this correctly, you will not have to change any of the `clickOn...` functions—they will just work more precisely.

3. Now, let's take advantage of our imagemap to expand our program so that it can respond to clicks on previously unrecognized parts of images. In particular, write `clickedOn...` functions to recognize clicks on the following image parts.

a) The postmark on the envelope image
b) Each article on the convenience store ("store8") image, including the soda, mints, candy bar, bagel, map, licorice, and the cashier
c) The car and the man in the car image
d) The poster on the concert image

4. Now that your program can recognize clicks on any part of any image in the game, it's up to you to make up the rest of the game. Include as many features as time permits. Here are some suggestions. Feel free to make up your own, as well.

a) Allow the user to purchase (and add to the inventory) any article in the clothing store.
b) Allow the user to purchase (and add to the inventory) any article in the convenience store (except the cashier, of course).
c) Allow the user to purchase a poster (and add it to the inventory) when arriving at the concert.
d) Make it so that clicking on the man in the car image (in Action mode) adds "Dad's cash" to your inventory, and clicking on the car adds "car keys" to your inventory.
e) Allow the user to purchase items in any store as long as the inventory contains either ATM cash or Dad's cash.
f) Add items that must be secured in order to get to the concert (for example, the map and the car keys).
g) Fix it so that certain items (like gum and candy) are not allowed in the concert, and that bringing them to the concert forces the player to start over.
h) Fix it so that if soda has already been purchased when the user attempts to purchase the jacket at the clothing store, an alert is produced indicating that soda was spilled on the jacket, and the player must start over.

Review Questions

1. Almost every implicit object has a `name` property. Which two don't? Why?

2. Why do you need to use `new` to create a `Date` object, but not to create a `Math` object?

3. How would you make a text field *toggle*, so that its contents would change from "Hello" to "Goodbye" each time the user clicked the mouse in the field? (This, by the way, won't work to change the label of a button—only text fields and text areas update their values.)

4. In our core example, explain in detail what the following statements do.

```
red =   parseInt(document.bgColor.
        substring(1, 3), 16);
green = parseInt(document.
        bgColor.substring(3, 5), 16);
blue =  parseInt(document.
        bgColor.substring(5, 7), 16);
```

5.9 EXERCISES

1. Define the following terms:
   a) Form element
   b) Event handler
   c) Helper function
   d) Implicit object

2. If you were designing a programming language that distinguished between real and integer types, how would you define the type of value returned by mixed expressions such as 3 + 4.76, 2.667*3, or 2/3?

3. JavaScript deals with the open and close HTML comment markers, <!-- and -->, in different ways, in that it recognizes one as a comment marker but not the other. Look at any of our sample programs and tell which comment is ignored and which requires special treatment.

4. What does it mean to describe JavaScript as a "loosely typed" language?

5. What are the values of the following JavaScript expressions?
   a) `10 / 5 * 2 + 4`
   b) `Math.abs(4.2 - 7)`
   c) `true && (5 <= 4)`
   d) `(!(x == x) || (1 >= 2))`

6. What is JavaScript's object hierarchy, and how does it affect how we write JavaScript programs?

7. Why are functions `parseInt`, `parseFloat`, and `eval` particularly useful in a language like JavaScript?

8. Suppose that a form, `data`, has two text fields, named `field1` and `field2`. Write a function that swaps the contents of `field1` and `field2`.

9. Why do JavaScript control statements require the use of curly braces when their bodies consist of more than one statement?

10. For what possible values of *x* and *y* are statements A and B executed in the following two structures?

a) if (x == 3) {

```
if (y == 4)
statement A   Done when:
else
statement B   Done when:
}
```

b) if (x == 3) {

```
if (y == 4) {
statement A   Done when:
}
else
statement B   Done when:
}
```

11. Are either of the structures in Exercise 10 equivalent to the following?

```
if ((x == 3) && (y == 4))
  statement A
else
  statement B
```

12. What does the following `for` statement do? Describe its output.

```
for (var b = n; b > 0; b--)
document.writeln(b);
```

13. Rewrite our sample Flashcard page so that it does not use function `eval`. Rather it should use

an `if ... else` statement to determine which operator to apply in its calculation, and perform the corresponding operation using an assignment expression.

14. Write the following function so that it doesn't use the word `else`. [*Hint:* Consider the `return` statement.]

```
function comment(){
  if (document.info.amountField.value
      < 1e6)
  document.info.commentArea.value =
      "That\ 's a normal amount"
  else
  document.info.commentArea.value =
      "That\ 's BIG!"
}
```

15. Use the `with` statement to simplify the function in Exercise 14.

16. This statement is exactly equivalent to what other statement? [*Hint:* Look at the review questions at the end of Section 5.6.]

```
for (x >= 0)
   statement
```

17. Rewrite function `writeBookOrder` of our book order sample page so that it uses a `for` loop and the page's `elements` array to check the status of all of the checkboxes.

18. Suppose that the form `textStuff` contains nothing but a collection of text fields. Write a function `smallest` that returns the smallest value in any of the fields. You may assume that the fields will all contain numbers.

19. Any executable statement can be used in the body of a loop, including another loop. For the loops below, indicate how many times the *statement* is executed.

a)
```
for (var i = 0; i < 5; i++)
for (var j = 0; j < 5; j++)
   statement
```

b)
```
for (var i = 0; i < 5; i++)
for (var j = 0; j < i; j++)
   statement
```

20. The `status` property of a `window` object contains the string that appears in the status bar at the bottom of the browser window. It's not hard to fill the status bar with all sorts of text, merely by assigning some string to `window.status`. Explain why doing so can be very annoying to people who are reading your page.

MODULE 6

Program Translation

6.1 INTRODUCTION

Countess Lovelace, in describing the principles of the Analytical Engine, said, "The Analytical Engine has no pretensions whatever to originate anything. It can do whatever we know how to order it to perform." Substitute *computer* for *Analytical Engine,* and her statement is as true today as it was nearly a century and a half ago. You have seen that a computer is a general-purpose information processor, and that in order to use the speed and power of the computer, we must provide a program—a list of instructions—for the computer to execute. In this module, we ask What is a program, and how is it that a computer can execute its instructions?

MODULE OBJECTIVES

In this module, we will move from the lowest hardware-level programming to the translation of high-level languages, such as JavaScript. We will

- Introduce the binary representation of information used by modern computers.
- Discuss machine language, the language that is used to instruct a computer's hardware at the level of binary representation.
- Introduce several contemporary high-level languages, concentrating on how they make the programming process more efficient.
- Take a necessarily brief look at the problems involved in translating high-level languages into a form that a computer can execute.

The Binary Machine

A modern computer can run programs written in JavaScript, Pascal, Logo, APL, LISP, Prolog, COBOL, and many others of the scores of programming languages available today. It appears that the computer is multilingual, but that's a fiction. In fact, every computer ever built "understands" one and only one language—the

◆ **Machine language: The only language a computer's hardware can use.**

machine language it is wired to use. The machine language of a Sun workstation is different from that of an IBM PC, and neither is the same as the machine language of a DEC Alpha. How is it, then, that in spite of this Tower of Babel of different machine languages, all three computers can execute the same FORTRAN program? The answer is based on our ability to write a program that allows the computer to translate a program written in a language such as FORTRAN into the computer's own machine language.

■ Metaphor: The Rosetta Stone

At first glance, a program—particularly one in a language other than JavaScript—might seem like so much hieroglyphics. Consider the two texts shown in Figure 6.1, one written in Egyptian hieroglyphics and the other written in the APL programming language. (The APL sample comes from Terrence W. Pratt, *Programming Languages* [Englewood Cliffs, NJ: Prentice-Hall, 1984].) The hieroglyphic sample concerns a tax reduction in the time of Ptolemy V; the APL produces a list of prime numbers. If both seem confusing to you, you're in good company. You would have at least a chance of deciphering the hieroglyphic passage, given some help, but a computer would be completely lost. With the APL passage, both you and the computer are on equal grounds: Both of you would have to rely on outside help to make any sense of the program.

To understand the nature of the help that you and the computer need, we go back in time two hundred years. The eighteenth century was a time of increased interest in the artifacts of ancient Egypt. French explorations of Egypt unearthed countless artifacts of the time of the pharaohs, leading to adaptations of Egyptian style in architecture and interior design and to heightened scholarly activities in the period. Unfortunately, hieroglyphics, the language of scribes of ancient Egypt, resisted any attempts of translation until the discovery in 1799 of the Rosetta stone. This basalt slab contained a royal proclamation, written in hieroglyphics, demotic (a cursive version of hieroglyphics), and Greek, and provided the first steps toward a translation of the formerly impenetrable pictorial language (see Figure 6.2).

This notion of translation is central to this module. A modern programming language is designed with two audiences in mind: the programmers who use the language to write programs for a computer, and the computer itself, which must execute the instructions in the language. Neither audience can use the programming language without some help; both must be taught to translate the language into

FIGURE 6.1
Egyptian hieroglyphics and APL

```
)CLEAR
∇RES ← PRIMES N; T
RES ← 2, T ← 3
→0 × ι N < ρ RES
T ← T + 2
→3 × ι ∨/0 = RES | T
RES ← RES, T
→2
∇
```

FIGURE 6.2
The Rosetta stone (© Corbis-Bettman)

what for each is a usable form. In this module, you will see what a programming language is, and what sort of outside help a computer requires to execute a program written in a programming language.

Æ ONLINE

How can a computer, which is capable of executing only programs written in binary machine language, run a program in a high-level language, such as JavaScript? The lab exercises for this module will demonstrate for you how a translator can convert code written by human programmers into machine-executable commands.

You'll begin by exploring the internal representations that computers use for numbers, characters, and other types of data. Having done that, you'll explore the process used to translate statements in a high-level language into statements in the low-level language of a hypothetical computer (which you'll build, more or less, in Module 7).

6.2 WHAT THE COMPUTER DOES

Here's a sample of a machine language program, written for a hypothetical computer:

```
0000010010000000
0000000010000001
0000010110000000
0000111100000000
```

Even if we told you that this program was designed to add the contents of memory locations 128 and 129, place the sum in memory location 128, overwriting whatever was originally stored there, and then halt, you would probably still find these instructions about as understandable as the hieroglyphic text in Figure 6.1. In this section we will pick apart the machine language for an imaginary computer, and discover how to write programs in this language.

■ Binary Representation

Part of the difficulty of understanding the program just shown stems from the fact that these instructions are represented using just zeros and ones. We mentioned earlier that the nature of the machine language of a computer is a direct result of the way the computer was designed. You will see in the next module that a design feature common to all modern computers is that they represent all their information in *binary notation,* that is, as strings of zeros and ones. You will see that the decision to represent information in binary form is not made for capricious reasons or to confuse the layperson. Rather, it is a reflection of the fact that *at the fundamental hardware level, a modern computer can distinguish between only two values,* which we label 0 and 1 solely for our convenience.

◆ Modern computers must express all information in terms of 0 and 1.

◆ BCD: A fixed-length code for digits.

If the computer can work only in terms of two values, 0 and 1, how are we to represent the information we want to store and manipulate? We are comfortable with the notion of the computer as a number cruncher, so we will begin by considering representation of numbers using this limited alphabet, {0,1} . An easy form of representation would be to use *binary-coded decimal* notation (BCD, for short), in which we invent a code for the digits 0, 1, 2, 3, 4, 5, 6, 7, 8, and 9 and use this code to represent integers. For example, we might decide to use the following code:

Digit	Code	Digit	Code
0	0000	5	0101
1	0001	6	0110
2	0010	7	0111
3	0011	8	1000
4	0100	9	1001

With this choice of representation, the number 247 would be written as three groups of four digits: 0010 (for the 2), 0100 (for the 4), and 0111 (for the 7), or 001001000111. Of course, we could have chosen any other collection of zeros and ones to represent the numbers, as long as our choice permitted a unique representation for integers.[1]

BCD representation has the advantage of being easy to read, but two disadvantages limit its use. First, it is not efficient in terms of space (in our sample code, for instance, a number that requires *n* decimal digits requires 4*n* binary digits to be represented in BCD form). Second, arithmetic on BCD numbers is complicated. For these reasons, the overwhelming majority of computers use a different form of representation of numbers, one that is somewhat more complicated to learn than BCD but quite a bit more efficient.

From our earliest years in grade school, we have been taught to represent information in *base 10 positional notation.* Positional notation means that the value represented by a digit in a number depends on where in the number that digit happens to be, and base 10 means that the value of any position is a multiple of a power of 10. The expression 247, for instance, is interpreted as the sum $(2 \times 100) + (4 \times 10) + (7 \times 1)$. Notice, too, that the multipliers 100, 10, and 1 are just powers of 10, arranged in increasing size from right to left, beginning with the 0-th power. Although most people don't give it any thought, the nice thing about positional notation is that it permits unique representation of integers: Every possible integer can be represented by this scheme, and every arrangement of strings of digits corresponds to one and only one integer.

◆ Binary numbers are just like decimal numbers, except that they use implied powers of 2 and the "digits" 0 and 1.

There is nothing special about using 10 as our base—we use ten digits only because that's the way things have been done for several thousand years (perhaps having something to do with the fact that most of us have ten fingers). Since the computer could be regarded as having only two fingers, it is appropriate to use *base 2 positional notation,* also known as *binary notation,* instead. Let's see how that would work. The first few powers of 2 are 1, 2, 4 ($= 2 \times 2$, or 2^2), 8 ($= 2 \times 2 \times 2$, or 2^3), 16, 32, 64, 128, 256, 512, 1024, 2048, 4096, and 8192, where we form the sequence by beginning with 1 and multiplying each term by 2 to find the next one. Using only the digits 0 and 1 as multipliers of these powers of 2, we find, perhaps by trial and error, that the decimal number 247 would be represented in this scheme as

```
247 = (1 × 128) + (1 × 64) + (1 × 32) + (1 × 16) + (0 × 8)
         + (1 × 4) + (1 × 2) + (1 × 1)
```

or 11110111, as a binary number. Notice that this representation requires only 8 bits (binary digits), whereas the BCD encoding takes 12.

◆ To convert from binary to decimal, add powers of 2.

To convert from binary representation to decimal is easy: Below the binary digits we write the powers of 2 in increasing order from right to left. For each position, multiply the digit by its corresponding power of 2. Finally, add the terms together.

Example 1 To convert the binary number 10111 to decimal, we write

```
the binary string:        1 0 1 1 1
over the powers of 2:    16 8 4 2 1 = 16 + 4 + 2 + 1 = 23
```

[1] We could not have used, for instance, 1 → 1, 2 → 11, 3 → 111, and so on, since then the code 111 could be interpreted as any of the numbers 111, 12, 21, or 3.

Conversion in the opposite direction, from decimal to binary, is a trifle more complicated, but not much more once we realize that the last digit in the binary representation of n is just the remainder we get when we divide n by 2, and the next digit is obtained by repeating the division on the quotient of the first division. In other words, we can convert a decimal number to binary by repeatedly dividing by 2 and keeping track of the quotients and remainders.

◆ **To convert from decimal to binary, repeatedly divide by 2 and write out the remainders.**

Example 2 To convert the decimal number 23 to binary, we do the following divisions, recording the quotients and the remainders:

1. 23 divided by 2 has a quotient of 11 and a remainder of 1. We remember the remainder and use the quotient in the next step.
2. 11 divided by 2 has a quotient of 5 and a remainder of 1, which we also save.
3. 5 divided by 2 has a quotient of 2 and a remainder of 1.
4. 2 divided by 2 has a quotient of 1 and a remainder of 0.
5. 1 divided by 2 has a quotient of 0 and a remainder of 1. We have a zero quotient, so we stop the process.
6. The sequence of remainders we obtained, when read from right to left, is the binary representation of 23, namely 10111.

In more compact notation, our example might take the following form:

```
     0        1
2  )1         0
2  )2         1
2  )5         1
2  )11        1
2  )23
```

Then the binary equivalent of 23 is found by reading the column of remainders from top to bottom—10111. We stop the process when we have a zero quotient, since any subsequent divisions by 2 will simply append zeros to the front of our binary answer, and it is clear that 00010111 and 10111 represent the same number.

Binary notation is somewhat cumbersome—the decimal number 12,092 takes fourteen digits to write in binary: 10111100111100. We can get a more compact representation, while still keeping the binary information in an easily accessible form, by considering the binary digits in chunks of four, starting from the right, and then assigning a code to each chunk of four. A four-bit number can take sixteen values, so we'll code the chunks from 0 to 9 and A to F. The chunks 0000 to 1010 will be coded by their decimal value (so 0111 would be represented by the code 7) and the chunks 1010, 1011, 1100, 1101, 1110, and 1111 will be represented by A, B, C, D, E, and F, respectively.

Here's how this coding works for our example number:

1. Start with a binary number, like 10111100111100.
2. Break it into four-bit chunks (called *nybbles* in the jargon), padding with zeros on the far left, if necessary: 0010 1111 0011 1100.
3. Finish by replacing each chunk with its code: 2F3C.

Look familiar? It should—it's just the *hexadecimal* representation we discussed when we talked about HTML color codes in Module 4. Another way to think of hex notation (as it's called) is that we're just representing a number in base 16, using the "digits" 0 . . . 9, A . . . F and the place values 1, 16, 256 (= 16^2), 4096 (=16^3), and so on. In the example above (bearing in mind that F represents 15 and C represents 12), we see that the number 2F3C represents (2 × 4096) + (15 × 256) + (3 × 16) + 12, which you can verify is what we would write as 12,092, just as expected.

◆ Computers don't work in hexadecimal, but it saves a lot of writing for people.

Now that we can represent any nonnegative integer[2] as a binary number, we can expand this scheme to represent other information in the computer—we simply find a suitable coding for the information to be stored in integers and represent the integers as binary numbers. For example, to represent strings of characters, we first decide on a suitable integer code for each character. This coding varies from machine to machine, but many computers represent characters by what is known as ASCII code, where ASCII (pronounced "ask-ee") stands for American Standard Code for Information Interchange. Table 6.1 lists some characters and their ASCII codes.

◆ ASCII: Integer codes for characters.

To read the table, note that the code for a character is the sum of the digits in its row and column labels. For instance, the character A is in the row labeled 60 and the column labeled 5, so the ASCII code for A is 65. ASCII codes less than 32 are

TABLE 6.1
ASCII codes

Last Digit

First digits	0	1	2	3	4	5	6	7	8	9
30			space	!	"	#	$	%	&	'
40	(	)	*	+	,	-	.	/	0	1
50	2	3	4	5	6	7	8	9	:	;
60	<	=	>	?	@	A	B	C	D	E
70	F	G	H	I	J	K	L	M	N	O
80	P	Q	R	S	T	U	V	W	X	Y
90	Z	[	\	]	^	_	`	a	b	c
100	d	e	f	g	h	i	j	k	l	m
110	n	o	p	q	r	s	t	u	v	w
120	x	y	z	{	|	}	~			

[2] In the exercises, we explore some of the ways we might represent negative integers and real numbers, such as 3.1415926535.

reserved for nonprinting characters, such as return and tab. In addition, some systems use an extended version of ASCII, in which codes between 128 and 255 are used for special characters such as •, ¶, and £.

Using this representation of characters, we might decide to represent a string of characters by a number representing the length of the character string, followed by the codes for the characters. For example, the string "CAB" could be represented by the code for 3 (the number of characters in "CAB"), followed by the codes for 67, 65, 66 (for the three letters). In the computer, then, this information would take the form 00000011 01000011 01000001 01000010; we've included spaces between groups of eight bits only to make it easier to read.

Of course, we're not limited to numbers, characters, and strings. We could encode pictures, sounds, and any other form of information we need—all we have to do is decide on a suitable format for representing such information using just zeros and ones.

Encoding Instructions

Since modern computers represent information in binary, it is not hard now to see what form their instructions must take. Just as we decided to represent characters by a more or less arbitrary binary code, we can also represent instructions by deciding on a binary code for each instruction. In a hypothetical computer, we might decide that each instruction will be represented by an eight-bit *operation code,* followed by eight more bits that provide details about what the instruction will do, as shown in Figure 6.3.

◆ Instructions are represented in binary, too.

To explain one possible use for the eight extra bits of information, consider that our hypothetical computer will include some memory—that is, storage locations for binary information. You can think of a location in memory as a cell into which you can place a character or number. Each of these memory cells is referenced by an address (location number), and these addresses will range from 0 to 255 in our computer. Since each number from 0 to 255 can be expressed in eight or fewer binary digits, we could use that part of the instruction code to refer to any location in memory—to store or retrieve the contents of that cell, for example.

We will also endow our computer with an *accumulator,* a special location used for storing intermediate results of computations. An accumulator is just the computer version of a scratchpad. If, for instance, we need to add 3 + 4 + 5, we might add 3 and 4, save the sum temporarily (in our mental accumulator), and then add 5 to the sum we saved. Our computer, then, takes the form illustrated in Figure 6.4. For this computer, the operations and their codes might include the following:

Code	Information	Action
00000100	X	Load accumulator with the contents of memory location X.
00000101	X	Store accumulator value into memory location X.
00001111	X	Halt execution.
00000000	X	Add contents of memory location X to accumulator.

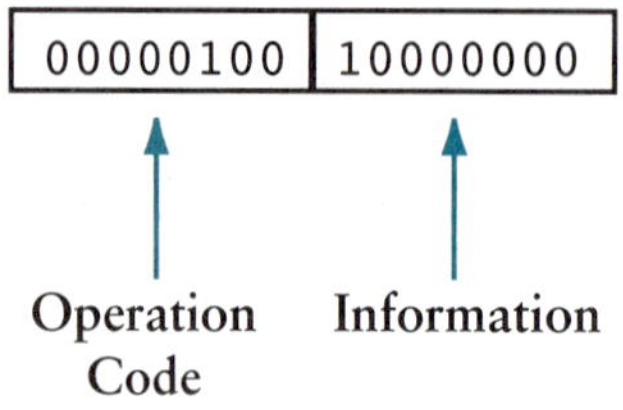

FIGURE 6.3
Coding an instruction

FIGURE 6.4
A hypothetical computer

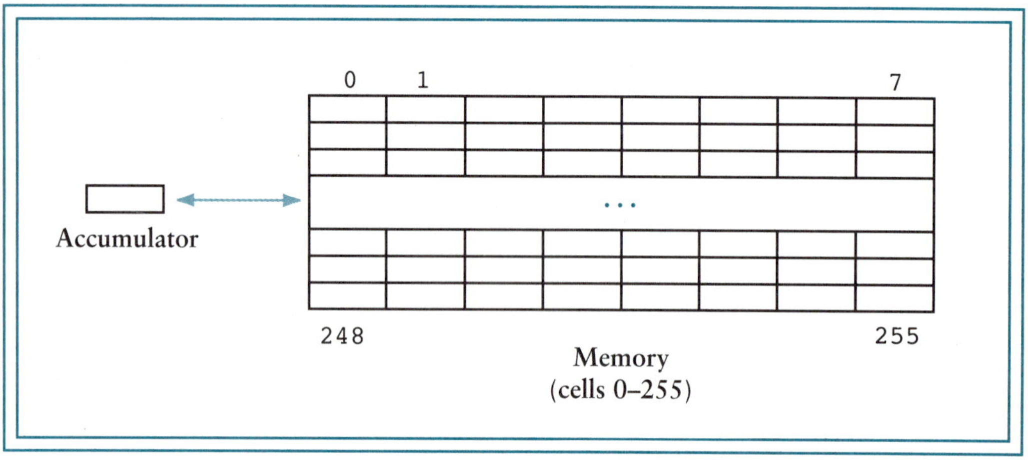

We can now read the program that appeared at the beginning of this section. We'll insert spaces to make it easier to read (although the computer has no need for them), and number the instructions for our reference:

```
[1] 00000100 10000000
[2] 00000000 10000001
[3] 00000101 10000000
[4] 00001111 00000000
```

Instruction 1 begins with 00000100, the code for "load accumulator," and continues with the binary number 10000000, equivalent to 128 in decimal. This instruction, then, tells the computer to make a copy of whatever is in memory cell 128 and place that value into the accumulator. Instruction 2 begins with 00000000, the code for "add to accumulator," and continues with the binary representation for 129, so the computer will add a copy of whatever is in cell 129 to the accumulator. Instruction 3, with code 00000101 and auxiliary information 10000000, is a command to copy the value in the accumulator into memory cell 128. Instruction 4 tells the computer to halt. A trace of the action of this machine language program is given in Figure 6.5, in which we assume that memory location 128 originally contains the representation for the number 6 and location 129 originally contains the representation for 9.

There's probably little need for us to point out what would become very obvious if you tried to write a program of even moderate length in this language—pro-

FIGURE 6.5
Tracing the action of a program

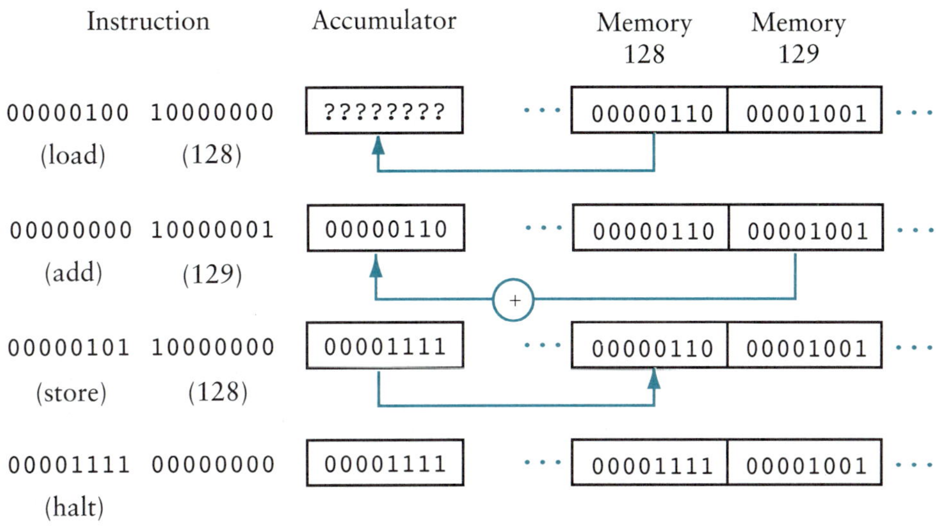

gramming in machine language is *hard*. As you'll see in the next module, the machine has no difficulty executing programs in machine language. After all, it was built from components designed to run programs in that language, and, in fact, machine language programs are all that it can execute. Machine languages were the only computer languages available to early programmers. Now that you have had some programming experience, you might be able to imagine how difficult it was for those hardy souls to write programs at all, much less debug the programs in the all too likely event that they didn't run perfectly the first time. Even when a machine language program was finally running more or less reliably, imagine the challenge of revising it at a later date. Suppose you were given someone else's program, a mountain of code in zeros and ones, and the boss said, "Smith's been transferred to our Seattle office; I want you to take over his accounts receivable program and fix it so that the quarterly report lists accounts by states, and alphabetically within states."

It didn't take early programmers long to see the shortcomings of machine language. Five or ten minutes is a good guess. It also didn't take them very long to arrive at a way to make their lives easier. It is likely that every programmer of those days kept a pad of paper at hand with something like this written on it:

(x ↔ cell 12, y ↔ cell 13)
Load x
Add y
Store x
Halt

From there, it's a short step to the realization that one could write a program (in machine language, of course) that would translate these mnemonics to machine language, so that whenever the new program saw the characters "Add," it would produce output "0000." Thus was born the first program translator, the *assembler.* An assembler is a program that takes as its input a source code written in an

◆ Assembly language consists of word codes (easy for people) for machine language codes (necessary for computers).

assembly language, like the language of mnemonic names just shown, and produces the corresponding machine language program, or object code, by translating each line of assembly language into the corresponding machine language (see Figure 6.6).

> *Source code* is what goes into a program translator; *object code* is what comes out.

◆ A continuing theme in the history of computers is the steady movement away from the dictates of the machine.

The invention of the assembler was the first step away from the tyranny of the machine and toward the realization that programs are written for people as well as for the machine. People must write, maintain, and modify programs, and programmers' time is expensive. Anything that makes programming more efficient not only makes the programmer's life easier, but also saves his or her employer money. Assemblers are still around today, despite the fact that higher-level languages such as JavaScript are easier to use. Still, if you need direct, precise control of the computer's functions—for example, if your program must fit into a prescribed amount of memory, or if there is a piece of your program that absolutely must run as efficiently as possible—there is no better method than assembly language.

■ The PIPPIN Assembler

For reasons we'll make clear in the next module, we call our assembler PIPPIN. PIPPIN has fourteen instructions, listed in the following User's Guide. For convenience, we assume that each PIPPIN program consists of a collection of statements, consecutively numbered from 1. In the User's Guide, we adopt the following conventions:

1. All variables refer to eight-bit binary numbers.
2. Unless the program instructs differently, by using a *jump* (JMP or JMZ), execution begins with statement 1 and thereafter proceeds through the instructions in order.
3. Variables can represent a number or an address. In PIPPIN, a number is indicated by a leading pound sign. If the sign is omitted, the number *n* is assumed to represent the contents of memory location *n*. For example, the instruction `LOD #128` places the *number* 128 into the accumulator, while `LOD 128` loads the *contents of memory cell* 128 into the accumulator.
4. We use the letter A (or ACC) to refer to the accumulator.

◆ These are known as *addressing modes*—an operand like 128 is called *direct mode* and #128 is known as *immediate mode.*

FIGURE 6.6
Programming in assembly language

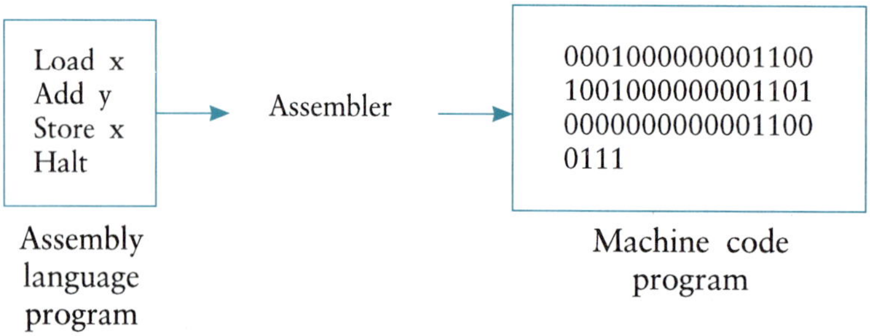

5. An arrow refers to the operation of copying information from one location (that to the left of the arrow) to another (to the right of the arrow). For example, the notation X → A transfers a copy of X's data (or the number X) to the accumulator.

PIPPIN's fourteen instructions can be divided into three groups: data flow, control, and arithmetic-logic.

The PIPPIN User's Guide

Data Flow	
`LOD X (or #X)`	X → A, place X into accumulator.
`STO Y`	A → Y, store contents of the accumulator in location Y.

Control	
`JMP Y`	Go to instruction number Y.
`JMZ Y`	If A = 0, go to instruction number Y; otherwise go to next instruction.
`NOP`	No operation; do nothing but go to next instruction.
`HLT`	Halt execution; don't do anything more.

Arithmetic-logic	
`ADD X (or #X)`	A + X → A, add X to contents of accumulator.
`SUB X (or #X)`	A − X → A, subtract X from contents of accumulator.
`MUL X (or #X)`	A * X → A, multiply accumulator by X.
`DIV X (or #X)`	A / X → A, divide accumulator by X.
`AND X (or #X)`	A AND X → A. If contents of A and location X are both ≠ 0, put 1 into accumulator; otherwise, put 0 into accumulator.
`NOT`	NOT A → A. If A contains 0, set A to 1; otherwise, set A to 0.
`CPZ X`	(Compare zero) If X = 0, set A to 1; otherwise, set A to 0.
`CPL X`	(Compare less) If X < 0, set A to 1; otherwise, set A to 0.

In the following examples, a semicolon signals a *comment*. Anything from (and including) the semicolon to the end of the line is ignored by PIPPIN, and in fact will not be part of the PIPPIN input when you are writing PIPPIN programs in the lab exercises of this module. In addition, when we need to make it clear that we are using the contents of address X, we'll indicate it in our commentary by using the form [X].

Example 1 This program uses two numbers, stored in cells 129 and 130, which we refer to in the comments as X and Y. The program instructions themselves are stored in memory locations 1 through 10. If `[X] < 2 * [Y]`, then cell 131, called `ANS`, is set to 0; otherwise, `ANS` is set to 1.

```
;double the contents of Y (which is cell 130 here)
[1]    LOD 130    ;load [Y] into ACC
[2]    MUL #2     ;ACC now contains twice Y's value
[3]    STO 130    ;store new value back in Y
                  ;store [X] - twice original [Y] value in cell Y
                  ;(X is in cell 129)
[4]    LOD 129    ;load [X] into ACC
[5]    SUB 130    ;now ACC has what we'd call [X] - 2[Y]
[6]    STO 130    ;which we store in cell Y
                  ;set answer to 0 if [X] < 2[Y];
                  ;otherwise, set answer to 1
[7]    CPL 130    ;if X - 2Y < 0, put 1 into ACC, else put 0
[8]    NOT        ;invert value in ACC (swap 0 ↔ 1)
[9]    STO 131    ;store the result in ANS (cell 131)
[10]   HLT        ;quit
...
[129]  ;storage for X
[130]  ;storage for Y
[131]  ;storage for ANS
```

You might find it easier to understand the PIPPIN version if you keep the analogous JavaScript version in mind (the line numbers, obviously, are included only for your convenience and aren't part of JavaScript syntax).

```
[1]    acc = y;    // We're using "acc" to represent the accumulator.
[2]    acc *= 2;
[3]    y = acc;
[4]    acc = x;
[5]    acc -= y;
[6]    y = acc;
[7]    if (y < 0)
         acc = 1;
       else
         acc = 0;
[8]    acc = 1 - acc;
[9]    ans = acc;
```

Notice that while we could simulate the PIPPIN program with JavaScript (which is exactly what we will do with the PIPPIN assembler in the lab), the JavaScript simulation is much wordier than it needs to be. We could have achieved exactly the same result with a single control structure:

```
if (x < 2 * y)
  ans = 0;
else
  ans = 1;
```

Example 2 The following program computes the sum 1 + 2 + . . . + *limit*, for some positive integer *limit*. This program contains an example of a loop in which the index, stored in cell `INDEX`, successively takes on the values 1, 2, . . . , which are added into a running sum, stored in cell `SUM`. The loop terminates when the value in `INDEX` is equal to the value stored in `LIMIT`.

```
;initialize index (cell 128) to 1
[1]     LOD #1     ;set ACC to 1
[2]     STO 128    ;and load that into cell INDEX
                   ;initialize running sum (cell 129) to 0
[3]     LOD #0
[4]     STO 129    ;start of loop
                   ;if index < limit (cell 130), jump out of loop
[5]     LOD 128    ;load index into ACC
[6]     SUB 130    ;ACC now has index - limit
[7]     SUB #1     ;and now has index - limit –1
[8]     JMZ 16     ;if that's zero (so index = limit + 1), exit
                   ;add index to running sum
[9]     LOD 129    ;load running sum into ACC
[10]    ADD 128    ;ACC has index + running sum
[11]    STO 129    ;which we store back in running sum
[12]    LOD #1     ;increase index by 1
[13]    ADD 128    ;ACC now has index + 1
[14]    STO 128    ;which we place back into index
[15]    JMP 5      ;jump to start of loop, line 5
[16]    HLT        ;out of the loop from JMZ step, done
...
[128]   ;INDEX
[129]   ;SUM
[130]   ;LIMIT
```

There's more to this example than might appear at first. Although much of the simplicity of this approach is obscured by the fact that it's written in PIPPIN, the underlying idea is very tidy: We loop with `INDEX` varying from 1 to `LIMIT`, and in each iteration of the loop we add the current value of `INDEX` to the running `SUM`. In JavaScript terms, we are doing this:

```
var sum = 0;
for (var index = 1; index <= limit; index++)
       sum += index;
```

While this algorithm is simple enough, we can do better. Notice that the time it takes to compute the sum depends on how large `LIMIT` is: If `LIMIT` is 10, we must run through the loop 10 times, and if `LIMIT` is 1000, we make 1000 iterations of the loop, which might take a considerable amount of time. A good programmer, though, has studied enough mathematics and theory of algorithms to realize that this sum is special. It happens that for any positive integer $n > 1$,

$1 + 2 + 3 + \ldots + n = n(n + 1)/2$ (See footnote)[3]

[3] You could prove this if you looked at, say, $1 + 2 + \ldots + 9 + 10$. Add the numbers in pairs, in a different order: $1 + 10 = 11$, $2 + 9 = 11$, $3 + 8 = 11$, and so on. There are five pairs, each of which is equal to 11, so the sum is $5 \times 11 = 55$. Now replace 10 everywhere by n and you have a proof.

With this in mind, all we would have to do is compute *limit* * (*limit* + 1)/2, which takes a single statement (in JavaScript, at least), no matter how large *limit* is.

It is worth noting in passing that there are two common features of assemblers that we left out of PIPPIN:

1. *Symbolic references* to variables—that is, the option to give names to location in memory, through the use of the `EQ` assembler directive. The statements `TOTAL EQ 12, ADD TOTAL` would together be equivalent to `ADD 12`. The `EQ` statements are not translated into machine code; rather they provide information for use by the assembler.
2. *Statement labels*, so that if statement 38 was `HLT`, we could label it as `DONE: HLT` and have another statement `JMP DONE`, which would, when encountered, transfer control directly to the statement with label `DONE`, which in this case would be equivalent to `JMP 38`.

These enhancements make assembly language programming simpler by increasing the readability of the programs. Consider, for instance, the program in Example 2. With symbolic references and statement labels, the program would take the following form:

```
        INDEX EQ 128
        SUM EQ 129
        LIMIT EQ 130
        LOD #1
        STO INDEX
        LOD #0
        STO SUM
LOOP:   LOD INDEX
        SUB LIMIT
        SUB #1
        JMZ END
        LOD SUM
        ADD INDEX
        STO SUM
        LOD #1
        ADD INDEX
        STO INDEX
        JMP LOOP
END:    HLT
```

We think you would agree that this form is considerably easier to read, even without comments. Symbolic references and statement labels are actually just two aspects of the same thing, if you recall that a program is stored in memory just as its data are. Another benefit of symbolic variable references and statement labels is that we are not forced to place a program in a specified location in memory. A more sophisticated assembler would make these references available to the *loader* program, which could then place the assembler program and its data in an available location in memory. This is particularly important when your program must compete with others for space in a computer's memory.

LAB 6.1

Representations

These lab exercises rely on two complementary programs, both of which are translators in the sense that each accepts as input a program written in one language and produces as its output a version of the input program in another language. One translator demonstrates the two basic steps involved in translating a program from a high-level language like JavaScript into a lower-level assembly language, like the PIPPIN language described in our text. The other translates a program from its assembly language form into a machine-readable and machine-executable binary form. Taken together, these programs form a modern-day Rosetta stone.

We start with the CPU Simulator. This program does much more than just translate a program written in PIPPIN assembly language into its binary form. It actually shows how the resulting binary program is executed by the machine. At this point, though, we're concerned only with how information—numbers, names, and operations that appear in PIPPIN—can be represented in binary. (We'll concentrate on the simulator's ability to execute programs in the next module.)

To do this we need concern ourselves only with the right and bottom portions of the program window. Along the right-hand side are memory locations (stored in our machine's "RAM"). The top group of those locations (labeled 0–14, in increments of two) is intended to hold instructions to be executed by our virtual computer. The buttons along the bottom of the window can be used to control the machine as it does the execution. For now, the only buttons we will use are the two labeled Symbolic and Binary. These allow us to view the instructions we enter into the memory locations in either their symbolic form (that is, as we entered them, using PIPPIN codes, variable names, and numbers) or in their binary equivalents.

1. Enter the following list of symbolic PIPPIN instructions into memory locations 0, 2, 4, and 6, respectively, of our CPU simulator.

```
LOD   #2
ADD   Y
MUL   X
STO   W
```

2. Click on the Binary button to see the binary representation of memory.

3. Toggle back and forth between Symbolic and Binary modes, until you can see the correspondence between the two representations of the same information. Then answer the following questions.

   a) At what address is the `MUL X` instruction stored? How is that address represented in binary?
   b) What is the binary operation code that corresponds to the symbolic instruction `LDI`?

c) How is the number 2 represented in binary?
d) At what address is variable `Y` stored, and how is that address represented in binary?
e) Answer question d, this time for variable `X`.
f) Answer question d, this time for variable `W`.
g) What are the binary operation codes corresponding to the symbolic PIPPIN instructions `ADD`? `MUL`? `STO`?

4. Let's reverse the process now to test your understanding. See if you can determine the symbolic PIPPIN program that corresponds to the following sequence of binary codes as they would appear in the first 8 locations (16 addresses) of RAM.

```
00010100 00000101
00000000 10000000
00000001 10000011
00000011 10000001
00000101 10000010
00001110 00000000
00001110 00000000
00001110 00000000
```

Review Questions

1. Count from 0 to 20 in binary.
2. Convert 704 to binary, and check your answer by converting it to decimal.
3. What string of characters does 1001111 1001011 0100001 represent?
4. What is an assembler? Why use one?
5. Write PIPPIN programs to perform the following tasks:
   a) Triple the value presently in the accumulator.
   b) Move the contents of cell 12 to cell 13.

6.3 WHAT PEOPLE DO

Among their other activities, people solve problems. For our purposes, that means that people write computer programs to help them solve problems. Writing programs in machine language is tedious, error prone, and time-consuming, so much so that hardly anyone writes programs in machine language anymore. Writing programs in assembly language is less tedious and error prone, but is still time-consuming. Assembly language programs seem to be more verbose than they need to be, though: It is far more natural for us to think in terms of statements such as

```
c = a + b;
```

rather than the assembler equivalent

```
LOD A
ADD B
STO C
```

Clearly, a higher-level language—that is, a more expressive, natural one—would be closer to the terms we typically use for solving problems.

Beyond the Assembler

Verbosity is one reason why assembly language is time-consuming. Some studies indicate that the total number of lines of debugged code a professional programmer can produce in a day is more or less independent of the language in which the programs are written. That means that if we could program in a language that used only one-fifth as many statements as assembly language (or, equivalently, machine language) to do the same task, it would be reasonable to expect that we could finish our programming task five times faster in the less verbose language.

◆ It's better to work smart than work hard—especially if you're a programmer.

We have already mentioned another reason why we would like to avoid having to write all our programs in assembly language: It's hard for most of us to think in assembler terms. A few decades ago, some linguists had the idea (largely discredited today) that one's native language dictates to a certain degree the way one thinks. A similar property does hold for computer languages, however. If we could design a programming language (without worrying for the moment about how to get a computer to understand programs in this language), it would certainly make good sense to design our language so that it makes writing, reading, and maintaining programs easier. In short, our goal should be to make the programming process as productive and efficient as possible.

One way of facilitating the programming process would be to sacrifice control over some aspects of the programming process, leaving them to the discretion of the computer, in return for the freedom to solve problems in higher-level terms. In particular, we could design our language so that much of the detail work was handled by the computer. After all, it is almost always easier to perform a large task if you are confident that the detail work is being handled for you—this is why you rarely see corporation presidents working on the production line or out in the field handling sales. Corporation presidents should concern themselves with corporate strategy and leave it to their subordinates to make sure that the doors are bolted on correctly and the bills get paid on time. This is an excellent strategy for programming, especially since detail work, done tirelessly and without flaw, is what the computer does best. What we want, then, is an "intelligent" programming language, one that handles the details of where to store information, when to move it, and so on, allowing us to concentrate on the big picture.

◆ Again, we're moving away from being dictated to by the machine.

It's all very nice to make a wish list of features that a programming language should have, but such designing is purely an academic exercise unless we can figure out how to get a computer to execute programs in a language that it is not wired to recognize. The answer, of course, is simple: we need to construct our own Rosetta stone. We want a program to do what an assembler does, only better, and in a more sophisticated fashion.

For every modern computer language, there is a program that takes a source code file in the high-level language and produces as its output object code in machine language, which the computer can then run. These translators come in two flavors, depending on whether they translate and run the source code one line at a time, or translate the entire source code at once and then turn it over to the machine to run. The first type of translator, which translates a line of source code into one or more lines of object code and then instructs the computer to perform those instructions until another line has to be translated, is called an *interpreter.* Interpreters have the advantages that they are fairly easy to write, and when the source code program produces an error, the interpreter can easily point to the line of source code that caused the error. The major disadvantage of interpreters is that they are slow when running programs. A source code line inside a loop that is repeated 1000 times will be translated each of the 1000 times it's encountered, which could make a significant dent in execution time. BASIC, LISP, and JavaScript are commonly implemented by interpreters.

If speed is of the essence, a better but more complicated solution is to use a *compiler,* which translates the source code once and for all, producing a complete machine language program. However, when the machine language program fails, it is much more difficult (though not impossible) to show the programmer where in the source code the error resides. This disadvantage is offset by the increase in speed. In fact, since compilation and execution are separated, the time of translation has no direct effect on execution speed. After a correct program has been completely translated, you never have to translate it again. Pascal, C, and FORTRAN are languages that are generally compiled.

◆ An interpreter says "Beat the eggs, beat the eggs, beat the eggs, . . ." as many times as it takes. A compiler says "Beat the eggs until they form soft peaks."

In theory, then, our job is simple. We can design a language of our own, by

1. Specifying precisely the form that statements in the language will take, and what each statement will do.
2. Writing an interpreter or compiler that takes programs in our language and produces object code programs in the machine's language.

That means that once we've written the translator, the user of our language does not need to be concerned with the details of the machine. A particular FORTRAN program should run identically on a Sun workstation or an IBM PC or a DEC Alpha or any other computer, as long as there is a FORTRAN-to-machine-language translator program for that machine. As far as the programmer is concerned, the FORTRAN program is written for a *virtual machine,* wired to run FORTRAN, which has nothing to do with the real machine being used. In other words, the fact that the FORTRAN program is being translated to run on a specific machine is of no concern to the programmer—he or she can pretend to be working on a machine that understands FORTRAN. We'll return to this idea in later modules.

◆ To make the PC run FORTRAN programs, therefore, all we need to do is buy a program that translates FORTRAN to the PC's machine language.

Designing a Language

Machine language is dictated by the circuits inside the computer, as we'll see in Module 7. We as language designers don't have any control over that, in general. However, we can make our programming language take any form we want, subject only to the restriction that we can build a translator for it (which is why

English isn't a programming language—we don't yet know how to write a program to translate all of English into any machine language). Most programming languages are designed to make the programmer's job easier, but exactly what this means has almost as many interpretations as there are languages. To take just a few examples, FORTRAN was designed for scientific and engineering programs; COBOL is tailored for business users; Pascal, BASIC, and Logo are teaching languages; Ada is a single standard for U.S. Department of Defense contractors; and JavaScript provides a simple, flexible data management environment within an HTML document.

Scores of programming languages are available today, all with relative strengths and shortcomings. A programmer can do things in Pascal that require complicated workarounds in FORTRAN; a simple JavaScript program would require a large and complicated Pascal program to duplicate its look and action; and a JavaScript program would take an annoyingly long time to do some of the things that a FORTRAN program can do in seconds. In spite of the plethora of languages, a simple taxonomy serves to classify most languages into four major groups: imperative, functional, declarative, and object-oriented.

In *imperative* languages the fundamental unit of abstraction is a procedure. That is, a program is composed of a group of procedures under the control of one main procedure. Each procedure is a group of statements describing in recipelike fashion the steps for accomplishing some portion of the program's processing. Consistent with this perspective, imperative languages tend to provide features that support the detailed description of algorithms—for example, if-then-else statements and while- and do-loops. FORTRAN, Pascal, and Ada are examples of imperative languages. Here is part of a program in Pascal that adds the odd numbers in a list of numbers:

```
type    TermIndex = 1 .. 100;
        TermArray = array [TermIndex] of integer;
var     myTerms : TermArray;
procedure SumOdds(n : TermIndex; terms : TermArray;
        var sum : integer);
        var i : TermIndex;
begin
        sum := 0;
        for i := 1 to n do
        if Odd(terms[i]) then
        sum := sum + terms[i]
end;
```

From another perspective, a program can be viewed as an object that, given input parameters, computes and returns a particular value—like a mathematical function. *Functional* languages, such as LISP, afford programmers with language support for defining functions. Functions can be defined in terms of other functions (including themselves), which ultimately can be described as simple computations. There is no explicit notion in functional languages of a "main" program. Rather, there is one function to be evaluated for specific inputs that, in turn, can reference any number of other functions in the process of performing the calculations. Following is the LISP program to sum odd numbers. (This, and the Pascal version, are adapted from Lawrence G. Tesler, "Programming Languages," *Scientific American*, vol. 251, no. 3, September 1984, pp. 70–74.)

```
(DEFUN SUMODDS
       (LAMBDA (TERMS)
       (COND
       ((NULL TERMS) 0)
       ((ODD (CAR TERMS)) ((PLUS (CAR TERMS)
                (SUMODDS (CDR TERMS))))
       (T SUMODDS (CDR TERMS))))))
```

For many applications (including much of what is commonly referred to as *data processing* or standard business applications, as well as knowledge-intensive tasks such as medical diagnosis systems and airline reservation systems), program complexity is not a function of complex calculations or algorithms, but one of the volume and complexity of the information being processed by the program. COBOL and Prolog are examples of *declarative* languages, in which the emphasis is on describing the information being processed by a program, as opposed to the processing algorithms themselves. Such languages offer only modest support for describing algorithms, but allow programmers to be very expressive about the type and format of the input and output data. The program to sum the odd numbers in Prolog would take the following form:

```
sumodds([], 0).
sumodds([H|T],N) :- sumodds(H,N1), sumodds(T,N2), sum(N1,N2,N), !.
sumodds(X,N) :- mod(x 2 1), eq(X, N), !.
sumodds(X, 0).
```

Object-oriented languages such as C++, Object Pascal, and Smalltalk can be seen as hybrids that combine many of the features of the other three language classes. When the processing to be accomplished by a program is organized in terms of "objects" of the programming domain—buttons, choices, and checkboxes, for example—we first describe the organization of these objects and their interrelationships in detail, as we would in a declarative language. We can then associate imperative algorithms (such as scripts) with each of the program objects. Finally, we allow scripts and their corresponding objects to communicate by passing "messages" along communication lines that reflect their organization (the object hierarchy) or by explicitly invoking one another as functional objects. As with functional languages, there is no formal notion of a main program in object-oriented languages. Which part of a program (or which script) is executed first depends on the input to which the program is responding, and then on which part of the program is designated to respond to that input. Finally, here is the program to sum the odd numbers in Smalltalk:

```
sumOdds
        |total|
        total ← 0.
        self do: [ :each | each \ \ 2 = 0 ifTrue: [total ← each + total]].
↑ total
```

Designing a computer language, in any of these categories, requires that we make decisions about several major features. First, we must decide exactly what information the language is capable of manipulating. PIPPIN is a very simple language in this respect—the only type of data available to it is integers, and only a small subset of the integers, at that. When designing a programming language, though, one typically keeps the needs of the user uppermost in mind, and so includes in the language the ability to handle the kind of data the user will commonly require. Such data almost always include integers and real numbers, such as –65.092615; and frequently include *Boolean* data, which can be either *true* or *false;* and characters, such as A, $, ?, b, and so on.

Along with these simple types of data, we might wish to include *structured types,* consisting of logically grouped collections of simple data types. Some languages include strings of characters (such as "MOON," "this is a string," and "FOOBAR456"), each consisting of a collection of characters arranged in order. A generalization of strings is the *array,* which, like a string, is a collection of data of a single type, each element of which can be accessed by specifying its position in the group. Figure 6.7 shows two examples of arrays.

Another common structured data type is the *record,* consisting of a named collection of data, not necessarily all of the same type. A record named "employee," for instance, might have fields called "name," consisting of a string; "age," which is an integer; and "payrate," a real number. For an example of a record, see Figure 6.8.

Data are not much use unless we can manipulate them, so the next decision we need to make is what operations our language will permit on its data types. Most languages have some sort of assignment statement to set one variable equal in value to another. To include assignment in any language, we must specify the form such statements will take (Pascal uses :=; JavaScript, C, and C++ use =; and other languages use ←, to name just a few). Not only do we have to specify the *syntax* of the

FIGURE 6.7
Two arrays

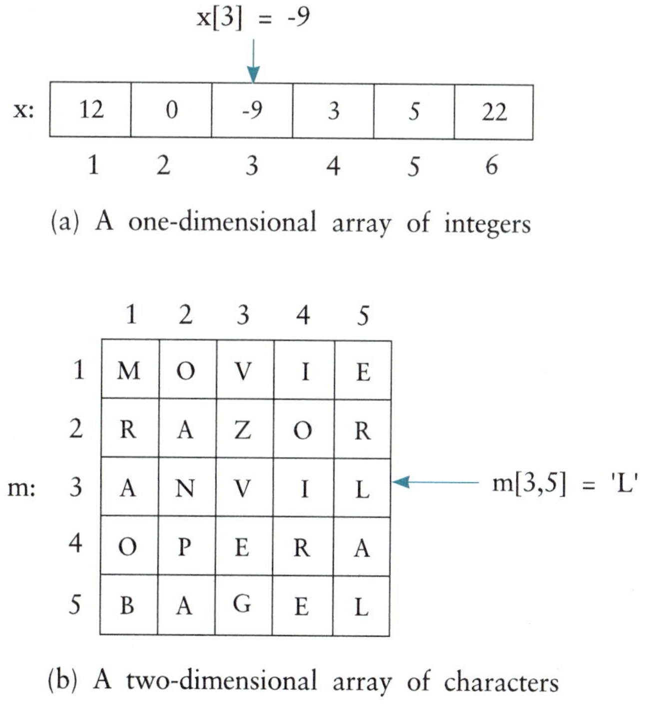

FIGURE 6.8
A record with three fields

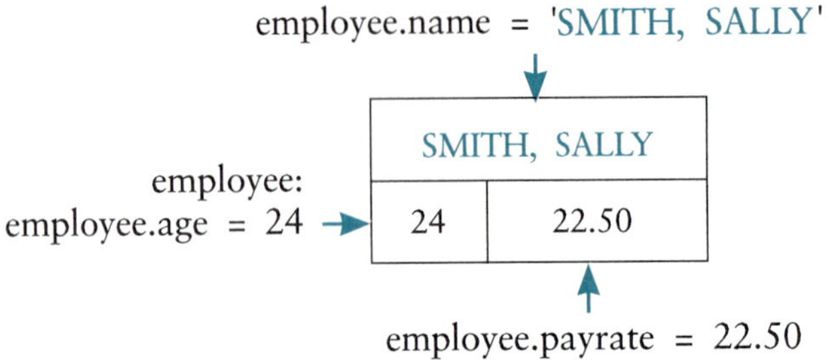

assignment statement—that is, the form in which it must be written—but we also have to specify its *semantics,* which is to say, precisely how it will work. Do we want to allow values of different types to be assigned to each other and let the compiler sort out what it means to assign the string "abc" to the variable *total,* which previously held an integer? This adds flexibility, but at the cost of making programs more difficult to understand and debug. At this stage we also have to decide on the set of arithmetic operations we will include, as well as how they will work. For instance, if our language supports integers and reals as distinct types, what type will we decide that the sum of an integer and a real number should be?

As if life weren't complicated enough, we also have to decide what *control structures* we will include in our language. If our language is imperative, with a program consisting of a sequence of statements to be executed in order, we'll need a way to alter the order of execution within the program, using constructs such as if statements and repeat loops. If our language is object-oriented, we need to be able to pass messages from one object to another. Unrestricted transfer of control, such as BASIC's `GOTO` statement or the PIPPIN `JMP` statement, enables the programmer to move freely from one statement to another, but at the price of producing code that can sometimes be exceedingly difficult to read and understand.

At a higher level of control, we might want to include unit-level transfers of control to subroutines, which are in effect mini-programs (like command and function handlers) that can be called on by a main program. This makes a program easier to understand, since it hides the details of the action of a subunit from the reader, thereby making the action of the program easier to understand. The program

```
GetALetter(theLetter);
ConvertToASCII(theLetter, ASCIIValue);
y = ConvertToBinary(ASCIIValue, binaryValue);
```

is relatively easy to understand, but might not be so easy if the 30 or more statements that made up the details of the subroutines `GetALetter`, `ConvertToASCII`, and `ConvertToBinary` were listed directly in the main program in place of the calls to the subroutines. The price we have to pay for including subroutines, though, is greater complexity of our language, both syntactic and semantic.

As you can see, designing a programming language is anything but trivial. We haven't even mentioned the options available for handling input and output, or how our language will react to errors such as division by zero or an accidental call to a nonexistent function. Language design is now, and likely will remain, more of an art than a science. As we have seen, "good" languages—languages that are flexible, powerful, general, easy to read and use, and simple to modify—can take many forms, depending on one's emphasis. This is one of the reasons why there are so many different programming languages today. Eventually, we might be able to program a computer in a language close to English, using an intelligent compiler or interpreter that converts our fuzzy, possibly ambiguous specifications to a logically correct, precise machine language program. Although that day may seem to be in the distant future, look at the difference between JavaScript and any machine language. We've come a long way already, and computer science is still in its infancy. It is unlikely, however, that programming languages will eventually all be like English or any other natural language: Programmers will always be willing to pay the price of learning a precise and unambiguous language if they can thereby avoid having to answer a multitude of "Exactly what do you mean by this?" questions.

6.4 IMPLEMENTING A LANGUAGE

Once we have designed a language, how do we accomplish its translation? By now, you should know the answer—We write a program to do the translation for us. The assembler had a simple task: It translated assembly language into machine language on a one-statement-for-one-statement basis. With just a little more experience, you could write a PIPPIN assembler. Translation is appreciably more complicated when you design a more sophisticated language, however. As you might expect, the more a language does for you, the harder it is to write its translator.

Generally, the action of any translating program can be divided into three phases:

1. *Scanning,* in which the source code—really nothing but a long string of characters—is broken down into *tokens,* the smallest chunks of characters that are meaningful in our language, for instance, words, names, numbers, and special symbols such as +. Scanning is the machine equivalent of what we do when we read a sentence and take note of the words it contains.
2. *Parsing,* in which the string of tokens is transformed into a syntactic structure, which represents the logical sense of the program. In human terms, this step is similar to recognizing the subject, verb, and object of a sentence.
3. *Code generation,* in which the syntactic structure that was constructed during the parsing phase is used to produce the output code, just as we might paraphrase a sentence so that a six-year-old could understand it.

■ Scanning

The scanning process is usually straightforward, if the language was carefully designed. JavaScript variable names, for instance, can be any collection of contiguous characters, subject to the restrictions that (1) they do not duplicate the words reserved for JavaScript, such as `var` and `if`; (2) they begin with a letter and thereafter contain only letters, digits, or the underscore character; and (3) they are the largest consecutive collection of characters that meet the first two conditions. These rules for variables are not arbitrary, but rather exist to make scanning easy. To see this, consider the statement `mySum = a + b`. This statement contains five tokens: `mySum`, `=`, `a`, `+`, and `b`. Remember, a token is the smallest meaningful unit of information, which is why `myS` or `=a` wouldn't be considered tokens for this statement. To recognize that `mySum` is a token, the scanner uses the rules that a JavaScript variable or reserved word begins with a letter and ends at a blank, and that no other kind of token begins with a letter. The scanner identifies these tokens using a process that looks (in highly simplified form) something like this:

```
repeat until the end of the line has been reached
skip over blanks in the source string
if a letter is seen then
        save it and all following characters, up to a blank or
          end of line
else if a digit or minus sign or plus sign is seen then
        save it and all following characters, up to a blank or
          end of line
else if a special symbol (like =) is seen then
        save that symbol
else
        something wrong happened--send an error message
send what has been saved to token storage
```

Of course, the scanner, or *lexical analyzer,* for JavaScript is considerably more complicated than our previous example, but in principle it is just the same.

◆ The lexical analyzer reads characters and returns tokens.

After receiving the tokens, the next part of the scanner replaces them by some convenient internal code, so that it no longer has to deal with strings of characters. In our previous example, the tokens in `mySum = a + b` might be stored as the sequence of codes 229, 36, 230, 30, 231.

Parsing

Once the scanner is finished with its work, the parser takes over, trying to make sense of the string of tokens. This is the most difficult part of the translator to design. What usually happens in a compiler or interpreter is that the list of tokens is converted to a parse tree in memory via a complicated algorithm. To give you an idea of how a data structure could store meaning, consider the parse tree in Figure 6.9, which stores the "sense" of the algebraic expression $x * (2 + y)$.

This parse tree represents the sense of the algebraic expression in that we could reconstruct the expression (or evaluate it) from the parse tree. To understand a parse tree, we adopt the convention that each box with an operator in it operates on the results of evaluating the left and right subexpressions below it.[4] We can't evaluate the expression until we first add 2 and y (that is, we evaluate from the bottom up), but having done that, we could then multiply x by the result to complete the expression.

[4] We should alert you that the parser in the lab exercises draws its parse trees in the opposite orientation, from bottom down to the top. You'll see when you use the parser that this unusual representation is easier to watch in action.

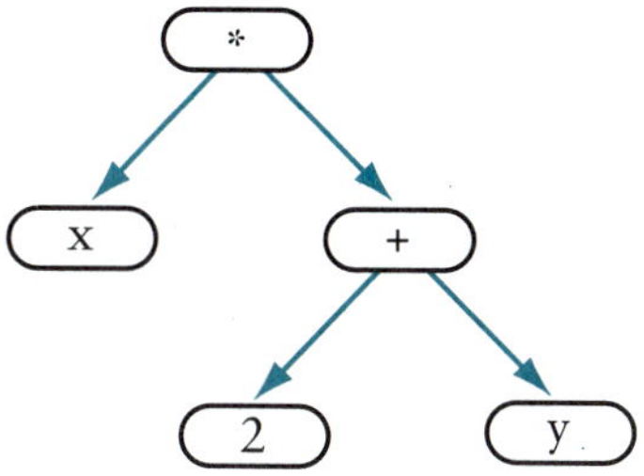

FIGURE 6.9
A parse tree for `x * (2 + y)`

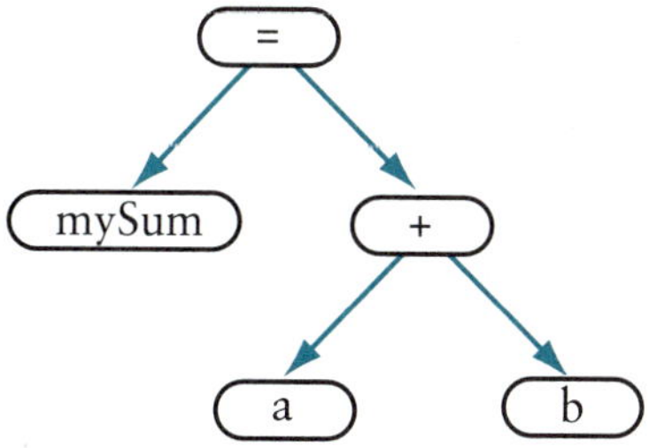

FIGURE 6.10
A parse tree for `mySum = a + b`

◆ **Think of parse trees as sentence diagrams.**

In a similar way, we could represent the sense of `mySum = a + b` by the parse tree of Figure 6.10. In English, the parse tree says, "Add `a` and `b` first (since they're at the lowest level) and then put the result into `mySum`." How the parser converts tokens into parse trees is not for us to discover at this stage; suffice it to say that this is a very complicated process that, like scanning, can be facilitated by careful design of the language.

LAB 6.2

Parsing Out

The previous exercise showed you how simple symbolic information can be represented in binary form. Still it is not at all clear how a statement in a high-level language like JavaScript gets translated into PIPPIN-like form. The program below, named Rosetta, is capable of this type of translation. Rosetta can perform both parsing and code generation on a very specific kind of statement: one in the form of an equation, much like an assignment operation in JavaScript. In our case, though, the statement can refer only to the variables W, X, Y, and Z, and to the operators +, –, * (for multiplication), and /. The equal sign (=) is used to designate assignment, and parentheses may be used to group expressions. So, the statement

```
W = X * (Z + Y)
```

is a legal one for our program.

1. Enter this above statement into the equation window near the top of the program window. Then, click the Set Equation button to indicate that you are done typing.

2. Click on the Parsing button.

3. Click on the Play button (the right-facing arrow) to have the program produce the parse tree for our statement.

4. Click the Reset button to reset the parser.

5. Now, click on the Step button to watch the parsing process in more detail. After the first click, the parser recognizes the Z and Y as tokens, and sees that they are to be combined by an addition operator. Each token is considered to be an expression (E), and expressions can be combined by operators to form more complex expressions. That's what the notation along the right side of the program window is describing.

6. Click the Step button three more times, watching as each part of our complicated statement gets described as a series of operations on its token expressions. The notation "S --> E = E" indicates that our statement was ultimately recognized as an assignment statement between two expressions.

7. Enter the following statement into the equation window, and repeat the above steps to watch it get parsed:

```
X = (3*Y) + (2/W)
```

8. Now, let's try to parse a few expressions by hand. For each of the statements below, draw its parse tree on a sheet of paper. Then, use Rosetta to see if your tree is correct.

a) `Y = 5 - Z + X`
b) `Y = 5 - (Z + X)`
c) `Y = 5 - ((Z + X)/2)`

9. Let's reverse the process, and see if you can match parse trees with their corresponding statements. For each of the parse trees below, write the statement that it represents. Use Rosetta to confirm your answers.

a)

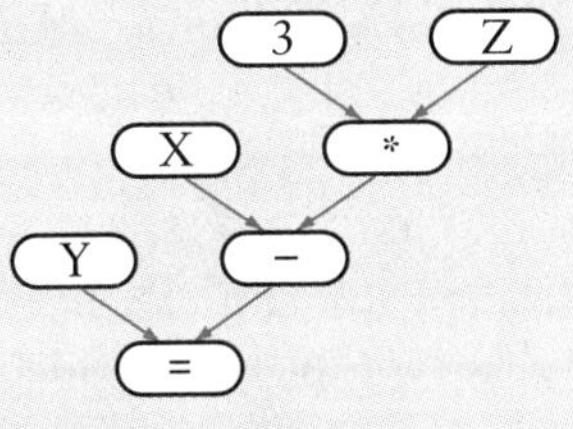

b)

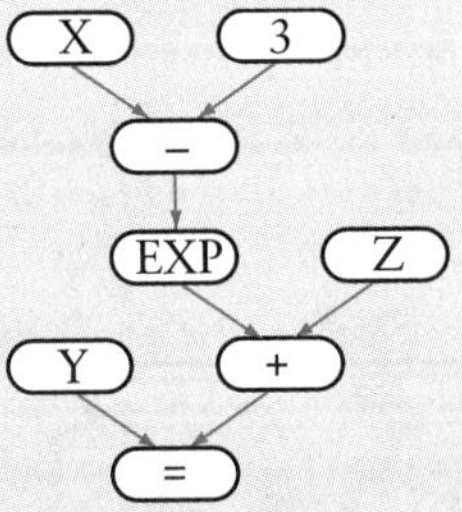

c)

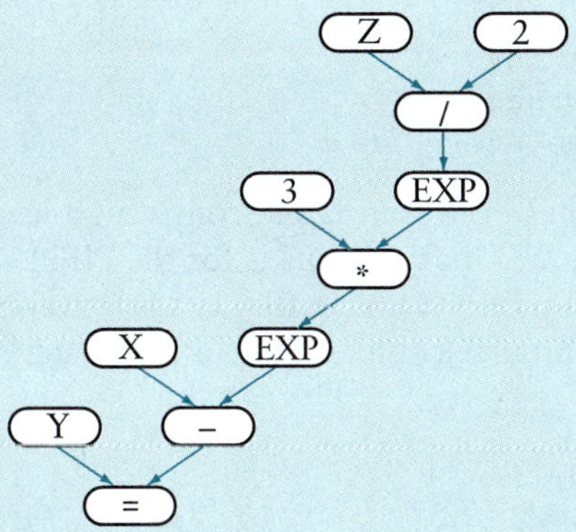

Code Generation

◆ We do parsing easily, but have trouble translating into another language. For computers it's just the opposite.

Finally, to complete the translation process, these parse trees are used to generate code. Code generation is accomplished by tracking through the syntax tree in a systematic manner, using the information stored in the boxes to help us. Assume that we are generating PIPPIN code from the syntax tree of Figure 6.10. The code generator would act roughly as follows:

1. Using the table of symbols produced during the scanning phase, recognize that `a`, `b`, and `mySum` are variables, so assign a location in memory for each variable.

2. The top box is "put left part into right." Such boxes always result in the generation of PIPPIN code of the following form: `STO LEFT_SIDE`, where it is assumed that the right part has been evaluated and the result has been placed in the accumulator, and that `LEFT_SIDE` is the location in memory of the variable on the left. We look up the token for `mySum` and find it has been assigned memory cell, let's say, 6, so we'll eventually generate

```
STO 6
```

We will defer placing the `STO` instruction into our machine language listing until we have completed evaluating the left side of the parse tree.

3. The right side is an addition operation. For such boxes we generate `ADD RIGHT_SIDE`, where we assume that the result of evaluating the left part is in the accumulator. At this level in the tree, `RIGHT_SIDE` corresponds to `b`, which we have assigned memory cell 5. We will list the instruction

```
ADD 5
```

as soon as we have evaluated the left branch of our parse tree.

4. The left side at this level is the token for `a`. The variable `a` has been assigned cell 4, so we generate `LOD 4`, to place `a` in the accumulator.

5. We back our way out of these pending calculations, listing the instructions produced along the way (comments included only for benefit of the reader):

```
LOD 4   ;place a into ACC
ADD 5   ;ACC now has a + b
STO 6   ;which we store in c
```

6. One statement has been translated from a high-level language into PIPPIN assembly language. All that remains is for the PIPPIN code to be translated to machine language, which we have seen is a relatively straightforward process. Then, at last, a computer could execute our instruction.

LAB 6.3

Generating Code

The code-generating part of our translator program starts with the parse tree for a statement and uses it to produce a list of PIPPIN instructions that correspond to the original statement. Let's use Rosetta now to demonstrate code generation.

1. Start as we did in the previous lab, by entering and setting the equation `W = X * (2 + Y)` into Rosetta's equation window.

2. Now click on Code Generation in the control panel at the bottom of the program window. Notice that the parse tree is generated immediately, since that is the starting point for code generation.

3. Click the Play button to watch Rosetta produce PIPPIN instructions as it works its way through the parse tree. Examine the PIPPIN code along the right side of the program window to convince yourself that it corresponds to the original statement.

4. Hit the Reset button, and then Step through the code generation to see which PIPPIN statements correspond to which branches of the parse tree.

5. Repeat steps 1 through 4 to generate code for the following equation:

```
X = (3 * Y) + (2 / W)
```

6. For each of the following statements, determine—without using Rosetta!—the PIPPIN code that would be generated for it. Then use Rosetta to verify your answers.

a) `Y = Z * 3 - X`
b) `X = (Y + 5) /2`
c) `Z = (W * W) + (X * X)`

7. For each of the PIPPIN code segments below, find a statement that corresponds to it. Use Rosetta to confirm your suspicions.

a)
```
LOD Z
DIV #2
STO X
```
b)
```
LOD Z
DIV #2
MUL Y
STO X
```
c)
```
LOD #2
MUL Y
STO T1
LOD Z
DIV T1
STO X
```

Generations

We've covered a lot of ground in this module. It may seem confusing now, but that's because this is the barest introduction to a very large and complicated subject, and, like it or not, some things are difficult by their very nature. Just bear in mind that the fundamental ideas are simple, however complex the details may be.

◆ We characterize generations of languages by how far they are from what the machine does and how close they are to what people do (our continuing theme again).

We have traced the subject of program translation in roughly historical order. In the passage from *first-generation languages* for the machine, through *second-generation languages* with the development of the assembler, and *third-generation languages* such as Pascal, FORTRAN, and C, we have seen an increasing independence of the programmer from the machine. A FORTRAN or C programmer doesn't even need to know what kind of machine his or her program is running on, as long as there's a compiler available for the language/machine combination. We have also seen an increasing independence from the machine in the sense that more and more of the details are handled invisibly to the programmer. A *fourth-generation language* such as JavaScript includes many software *agents* that further extend the power of the language. For example, making a checkbox display on the screen and behave as it should when it is clicked could take dozens of lines of code in older languages. In a JavaScript program, though, the checkbox agent takes over and does the task for you.

We expect that future generations of languages will carry this process even further as software agents are designed to be increasingly clever. It's not unreasonable to expect a "smart" sorting agent, for example, that first looks at the data to be sorted and then chooses the appropriate algorithm for the data—perhaps a simple memory-hogging routine to sort short lists of data, and a complex but more memory-efficient one for long lists of data.

LAB 6.4

Symbols and Bits

We asked you in the previous lab to confirm to your own satisfaction that the PIPPIN code produced by the Rosetta program did in fact correspond to—or simulated the effects of—the original equation. This is tough to do by hand, but there's a better way. We can use our CPU simulator, PIPPIN, to actually run the program, and then observe the effects of the program on the simulator's memory.

Clearly, we anticipated that these two programs, our translator and our simulator, would be related. It is no accident that Rosetta produces as its output PIPPIN instruction codes, which can then serve as input to the simulator. Neither is it an accident that the Rosetta program has a button in its control panel that saves the resultant PIPPIN code and loads it directly into the simulator's memory. (The button is named SAVE FOR CP SIMULATION. *Note:* This will work only if your browser allows saving from applets).

1. Enter and set our standard equation, `W = X * (2 + Y)`, into the Rosetta program, set it to perform Code Generation, and hit the Play button.

2. Now, click on SAVE FOR CP SIMULATION, and look at the simulator. Notice how the PIPPIN code is automatically loaded into memory.

3. Make sure that the simulator is operating in Symbolic mode.

4. Notice, too, how the memory locations associated with variables `W`, `X`, and `Y` are uninitialized. In order for our statement to accomplish anything that we would notice (besides, say, setting `W` to zero, which it already is!), we should set the locations corresponding to `X` and `Y` to reasonable values, so that we can see if the code actually works. Click on the memory cell for variable `X`, and set it (by typing into it) to 4. Similarly, set `Y`'s memory cell to contain 5.

5. If all goes well, when you click the Play button on the simulator, it should (after some pretty serious work) leave the value `28` (the result of evaluating `4 * (5 + 2))` in the location `W`. Click Play now to watch this occur.

6. Click Reset to clear the simulator, and reset the value of memory location `W` to zero (resetting the simulator does not clear the memory cells for our variables).

7. Repeat steps 1 through 6 for our more advanced equation:

```
X = (3 * Y) + (2/W)
```

In this case, when you set the values of variables (as in step 4, above), set `Y` to 14 and `W` to 1. This should produce a value of 43 for variable `X` when the code is played by the simulator.

8. Finally, write and test a PIPPIN program that calculates the average of the values in memory locations `X`, `Y`, and `Z`, and stores the result in `W`.

Review Questions

1. What are the advantages and disadvantages of high-level languages over assembly languages?
2. What is the difference between an interpreter and a compiler?
3. Define the following language types: procedural, functional, declarative, and object-oriented.
4. What do we mean by syntax and semantics? Explain, using English as an example.
5. Draw the parse trees for the following expressions:
   a) (3 * x) + (2 * (y - 4))
   b) 1 + 2 * (3 + 4)

6.5 EXERCISES

1. Convert the following binary numbers to decimal:
   a) 11111
   b) 101101
   c) 1100011
2. Convert the following decimal numbers to binary:
   a) 47
   b) 358
   c) 1023
3. Convert the following hex numbers to decimal:
   a) CAB
   b) B00
4. Convert the following decimal numbers to hex:
   a) 64,206
   b) 16,383
5. Find a rule that describes which numbers have binary representations consisting solely of ones.
6. If *b* is a binary number, what number is represented by *b*0—that is, what number do you get when you place a zero at the end of a binary number? What happens if you place two zeros at the end? Generalize your answer.
7. One way to represent fractions in binary (which, by the way, is not the way they are represented in most computers) is to mimic the way we represent decimal fractions: Each binary digit represents a power of 1/2, so, for instance, the binary fraction 0.1011 would represent

   $$1 \times (1/2) + 0 \times (1/4) + 1 \times (1/8) + 1 \times (1/16) = 11/16$$

   To convert a decimal fraction to this binary form, we could perform the following steps:

   a) Take the original fraction, f, and repeat steps b through d until you have as many digits as you want.
   b) Double f.
   c) Write down the integer part (which will be 1 or 0).
   d) Replace f with its fractional part.
      i) 11/16 has decimal representation 0.6875. Show that this algorithm, applied to 0.6875, yields the binary fraction 0.101100000. . . .
      ii) Show that this algorithm represents 3/10 as the infinite repeating binary fraction 0.0100110011001. . . .
8. How might we represent negative integers in a computer? Either come up with a scheme of your own or research the techniques that are in use today.
9. Write your name in ASCII, as we did in the text with the string "CAB."
10. Write PIPPIN programs to perform the following tasks:
    a) Swap the contents of cells 12 and 13.
    b) If [X] < [Y] for two cells X and Y, then place 1 in the accumulator; otherwise, place 0 in the accumulator.

11. Write a PIPPIN program that will replace the contents of cell X with half its original value, ignoring any remainders, so the values 8 and 9 would both be replaced by 4.

12. Suppose a vending machine has a small computer embedded in it. The computer is programmable, so that the service person only needs to reprogram the computer to modify its actions. Design a programming language for the vending machine's computer, paying attention to the data types and statements you will include. Assume that the vending machine has space for items of different kinds and prices, and that it can make change and detect counterfeit coins. In your language, write the program that would set the price of item 3 to 65 cents.

13. Some LISP compilers are written in LISP rather than in machine language. How is this possible? (*Hint:* The process may require more than one step. Think about attacking the problem in stages.)

14. JavaScript terminates statements with a semicolon. Is this for ease of scanning or parsing? What would happen if we eliminated semicolons from JavaScript?

15. Draw the parse trees for the following algebraic expressions:

   a) (x + (4 + y)) * (x + y)
   b) 1 + (2 * (1 + (2 * (1 + x))))
   c) x * y + z (There are two different ways to parse this expression. Which is correct under the usual rules of algebra?)

16. Describe the steps the code-generating process might take in translating the following statements:

   a) x += 1
   b) if (x == 2)x = 0

17. Look over the Pascal, LISP, Prolog, and Smalltalk versions of the program `SumOdds`. Which one seems easiest to understand? What syntactic features of the less comprehensible ones make them hard to read?

ADDITIONAL READINGS

BYTE Magazine. Issue on object-oriented programming. 11, no. 8 (Aug. 1986).

Dierker, P. F., and Voxman, W. L. *Discrete Mathematics.* San Diego: Harcourt Brace Jovanovich, 1986.

Lipschutz, S. *Essential Computer Mathematics.* Schaum's Outline Series. New York: McGraw-Hill, 1982.

Pratt, T. W. *Programming Languages: Design and Implementation,* 2nd ed. Englewood Cliffs, NJ: Prentice-Hall, 1984.

Sethi, R. *Programming Languages.* Addison-Wesley Series in Computer Science. Reading, MA: Addison-Wesley, 1989.

Tennent, R. D. *Principles of Programming Languages.* Englewood Cliffs, NJ: Prentice-Hall, 1981.

Tesler, L. G. "Programming Languages." *Scientific American* 251, no. 3 (Sept. 1984): 70–78.

Wexelblat, R. L., ed. *History of Programming Languages.* ACM Monograph Series. New York: Academic Press, 1981.

Wulf, W. A., Shaw, M., Hilfinger, P. N., and Flon, L. *Fundamental Structures of Computer Science.* Reading, MA: Addison-Wesley, 1981.

MODULE 7

Hardware

7.1 INTRODUCTION

In the text part of this module, we will see how the computer, at the lowest level, is a physical embodiment of the rules of logic. Starting with simple switches, we will build increasingly complex hardware—using switches to construct simple circuits, then using these to construct a hierarchy of more complicated circuits, and finally connecting these circuits to build a computer. By the end of this module, you will have constructed, on paper at least, a simple but fully functioning computer with nearly all of the important features of real machines.

MODULE OBJECTIVES

This module takes us to the lowest level of abstraction—the physical realization of the computer in hardware. It explains why computers understand only binary languages, and demonstrates for you how they do so. Our goal is not to turn you into a hardware engineer, but rather to demonstrate for you how computers are designed and built to perform a wide range of processing tasks.

In particular, we will

- Show how the circuits of a computer are constructed.
- Use thc Logg-O program to build and test a variety of circuits.
- Discuss the hierarchy of complexity of a computer, combining switches to make gates, combining gates to make circuits, and constructing the architectural organization of the computer by combining circuits.
- See how simple circuits, combined in complex ways, can implement a model computer.
- Explore the design of a small but complete microprocessor.

The Logic Machine

So far, we have been looking at computer science from the top down. Starting with high-level abstractions, we have seen how each level of our subject can be explained in terms of simpler levels. Applications were explained in terms of system design, systems were seen to be built from programs, and programs were translated into lower-level collections of machine language instructions. In this module, we find ourselves at the lowest level of interest to computer scientists—the hardware itself. To be sure, we don't have to stop there: Having explained how the hardware can be made to execute the statements of a program, a physicist might be interested in how the hardware itself operates. For our purposes, though, it will be enough to assume that the hardware works, without concerning ourselves with the quantum-mechanical details.

A computer is, or course, a demonstrably physical object, constructed of silicon, copper, gallium, arsenic, gold, phenolic resins, and the like. How can such an object run a program, which, after all, is really nothing but a collection of ideas? This is a simple version of a very old question: For centuries, philosophers have pondered the related problem of how brains can have thoughts. In the context of machines, it is fairly easy to imagine building a piece of equipment that can perform simple calculations—after all, the abacus can perform addition, and it is nothing but a collection of wires with beads strung on them. A computer, though, doesn't just add—it multiplies, compares, moves information, and performs a host of other basic tasks, all under the direction of a list of instructions we call a program.

Imagine a collection of units—one to add, one to multiply, one to compare numbers, and so on—that can be used to build a computer. To visualize this, think of each unit as a smallish box with sockets on its front panel, and suppose that we have a storeroom full of these boxes, along with a large collection of wires with plugs to fit into the sockets on the boxes to connect the units together. Given a computational task to perform, all we need to do is get the right boxes from the storeroom, plug them together in the right way, and set them running.

The problem with such a computer, though, is that it needs to be rebuilt for every different task. In fact, this was just the way ENIAC (and the Difference Engine, for that matter) was designed. One didn't program ENIAC; one plugged it together. John von Neumann is largely responsible for the notion of a stored-program computer (though, to be fair, Babbage had a similar idea). A machine in which the instructions are stored in memory, just as any other data, represents a considerable conceptual leap over our original model. The feasibility of the idea that a machine can be built with the potential to perform any sequence of operations is certainly not obvious at first glance. Without this capability, however, computers would be little more than novelty items. After all, it is extremely unlikely that you would want to read through a hundred pages of instructions on how to rewire your machine to switch from word processing to working on a spreadsheet.

In what follows, we will investigate just how such a general computation device can be constructed. We will see that the components are connected in such a way that the program itself controls the rewiring by signaling the hardware to switch the components on and off in the proper sequence.

Metaphor: The Switch

The metaphor for this module is the humble light switch, a box with a small lever and two wires attached. Flip the lever down and no current can flow through the wires; flip it up and current can pass. As we mentioned earlier, we won't worry about how things work inside the switch, because for our purposes, it is sufficient to assume that it does what we want. All we need to do to accomplish most of the mechanized computations we've described is remove the lever from the switch and replace it with an extra wire that can be used to control the switch. You will see that with enough of these switches, connected in the right way, we can perform any operation we want.

Æ ONLINE

The Module 6 lab demonstrated both the feasibility and the necessity of using a binary language as a means for communicating with a computer. Why, though, do computers understand only such simple languages? Because both binary numbers and a computer's hardware are essentially two-valued systems and, as such, can be used to represent and implement Boolean logic.

In this module's labs, we provide you with a program called Logg-O, for designing and experimenting with simple logical circuits. Though it is a far cry from the tools used for building modern, very large scale integrated circuits, it can be used to demonstrate the utility of logic for simulating useful instructions. Once you've had a chance to explore low-level circuit design, you'll return to the PIPPIN simulator we introduced in Lab 6 to see how all the circuit parts can be assembled to produce a simple, but fully functional, computer.

7.2 THE GATE LEVEL

In modern computers, the devices we will discuss in this section are about the size of large bacterium, far too small to be seen by the naked eye. How are these components constructed in the first place, if they're that small? The answer rests in three technologies, two of which began during Babbage's lifetime and the other about a century later.

1 The idea of *representing information by electrical signals* led to the development of the telegraph in the mid-nineteenth century. In a fashion strikingly similar to that of modern computers, information was represented as a sequence of pulses of current in a wire, so that the letter *A* was represented as a short pulse followed by a longer one, for instance.

A number of devices were developed over the following years to control this current flow, but switching devices such as relays and vacuum tubes all suffered from the disadvantages of large size, high power consumption, and slow speed. The transistor, invented in the late 1940s, overcame all three of these disadvantages.

2 In essence, a *transistor* consists of three connected pieces of silicon with small amounts of impurities added, such as phosphorus or boron, along with a wire attached to each piece. The pieces are called the *collector,* the *emitter,* and the *base.* We can ignore here the details of how a transistor

works—the important idea is that normally no current can flow between the collector and the emitter, but when an electrical signal is applied to the base a current can pass between the other two elements. In other words, a transistor is just an on/off switch with no moving parts.

The first transistor circuits were made by connecting the components with soldered wires. The size and complexity of such circuits are not limited by the size of the transistors—which, unlike relays or vacuum tubes, can be made very small indeed—but rather by the practical difficulties of soldering very small wires together in close quarters. One way around this problem is to use the last of our three contributing technologies, photography.

3 *Photography* was first successfully demonstrated at the very end of the eighteenth century, and by Babbage's time the technology was well enough developed to permit battlefield photography during the Crimean War in 1854. In essence, photography is based on the principle that some chemicals change their properties upon exposure to light. Silver nitrate, for example, when exposed to light and treated with the right chemicals, changes to metallic silver. This silver comprises the black portions of a photographic negative. It is also an excellent conductor of electricity, which brings us to our last development in circuits.

It is possible to "print" the wires of a circuit directly on a nonconducting base, using a four-step process (Figure 7.1). First, a sandwich is made by placing a layer of copper on

FIGURE 7.1
Constructing a circuit photographically

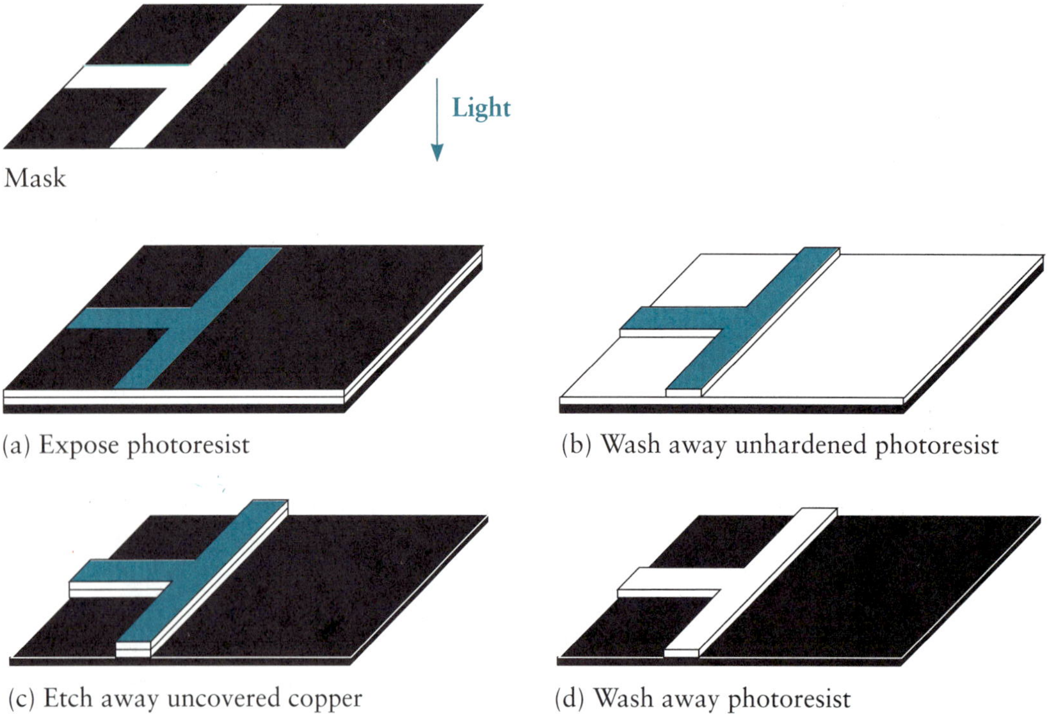

the base board and covering the copper with a chemical that reacts to light, called a *photoresist*. A photographic negative of the circuit is then made and the base-copper-photochemical sandwich is exposed to light through the negative *mask*. Where the light hits the photochemical, the chemical hardens. The next step is to wash away the unhardened photochemical, leaving only the areas exposed to light. A second chemical bath follows, etching away the uncovered copper, and finally the hardened photoresist is removed in a third bath, leaving the wires photographically printed on the base board.

With the photographically built printed circuit in hand, all that remains is to fit the components' wires into holes in the board and solder the whole assembly together. For a complicated circuit, photographic construction saved considerable manufacturing time, with the added advantage that one mask can serve as the template for building as many boards as needed.

In the 1950s, it became clear to many electrical engineers that the idea of constructing circuits photographically need not be limited to just the wires—the transistors and other components could themselves be produced by depositing the right chemicals in repeated applications of this process, thereby building an entire electronic device on a wafer of silicon. Such a device is known as an *integrated circuit*. The idea of using what is in essence the technology of the printing press to produce electronic equipment had several important consequences. The designed masks could be photographically reduced, permitting the manufacture of circuits that were far smaller than could be produced by any previous method. Additionally, the reduced masks could be duplicated, allowing dozens of identical circuits to be made at the same time on a single silicon wafer. This is particularly important because it is difficult to make large wafers of silicon, so there is a considerable saving of cost in having one wafer serve as the base for many circuits. Indeed, the decreasing size of integrated circuits—about 50 percent per year over the past three decades—is driven more by economic reasons than by a desire for small size alone.

◆ Building a transistor photographically is just like the process in Figure 7.1, but with more steps.

Building Blocks

Now that we have an idea of how the microchip in a computer is built, we can turn our attention to the design of the circuits themselves, starting with our simple switch. We can think of a switch, such as a transistor, as a box with three wires connected to it, called in, out, and control. The *control* wire controls whether current can flow from the *in* wire to the *out* wire; it replaces the lever on our light switch. (To be honest, things are actually quite a bit more complicated at this level, but the details belong in a course on electrical engineering, not here.) Our switches will come in two basic varieties: normally open and normally closed.

In a normally open switch (see Figure 7.2), current can pass from *in* to *out* only when there is a signal at the *control* wire. If we adopt the convention that a high voltage in a wire is represented by the symbol 1 and little or no voltage by 0, this switch can be viewed as a logic operator that says, "The value of *out* is 1 only when both *in* and *control* are 1; otherwise, the value of out is 0." If we interpret 1 and 0 as numbers, then, we have made a device that can be interpreted as a multiplier in the universe of numbers $\{0,1\}$.

In a normally closed switch (see Figure 7.3), current can flow from *in* to *out* unless there is a signal in the control wire. Again, we could write 1 instead of "high voltage" and 0 instead of "low or no voltage," and look at this switch as operating

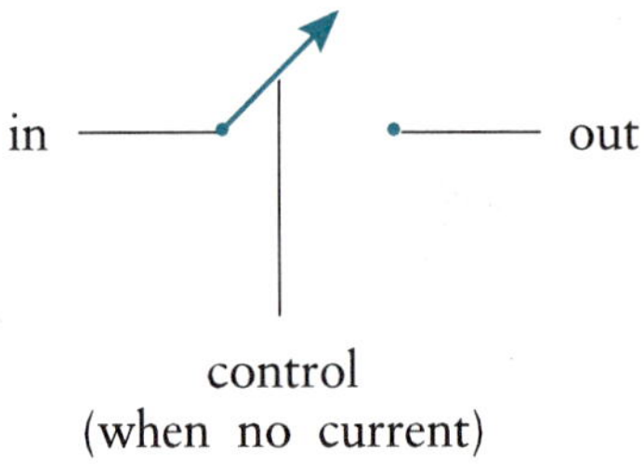

out	in: 0	in: 1
control 0	0	0
control 1	0	1

FIGURE 7.2 *A normally open switch*

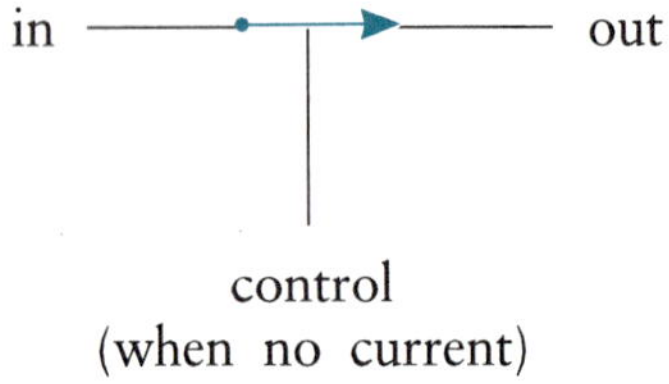

out	in: 0	in: 1
control 0	0	1
control 1	0	0

FIGURE 7.3 *A normally closed switch*

on the values of *in* and *control* to produce a value for *out*. In this case, the operation produces 1 only in the case that *control* is 0 (the switch is closed, allowing current to flow) and *in* is 1 (there is a current that can flow from *in*).

Instead of thinking of information represented by electrical current, you might find it helpful to think of information as automobiles. Then a normally closed switch would be represented as a highway junction. When there is no car on the *control* road, traffic along the main road from *in* to *out* can flow normally, but when a car comes along the *control* road and blocks the intersection, no traffic can flow from *in* to *out*.

■ Logic

The essential behavior of the normally open switch has nothing to do with electrical currents. In fact, to insist on clinging to descriptions that use the model of electricity actually obscures the basic nature of the switch, which is the same whether it controls a current of electricity, regulates the flow of water in pipes, or determines the rotation of shafts and gears. What is important is that, first, the information can be in one of two *states* (high/low voltage, water flow/no flow, or rotation/no rotation), which we can represent by 1 and 0, and, second, we can regard the switch as an operator that produces an output state depending only on the input states.

Much of the power of mathematics stems from the fact that once we have isolated the essential behavior of a system, we often find that there are other systems which, under the proper interpretation, have the same essential behavior. This means that we don't have to reinvent the wheel to prove results about the new system: The new system will obey all the rules we discovered about the system we were investigating in the first place.

◆ Logic can be viewed as a collection of rules for manipulating ones and zeros.

For example, suppose we decide to interpret 0 as *false* and 1 as *true*. Then the action of the normally open switch is the same, under this interpretation, as that of the AND operator in logic. The statement "*P* and *Q*" is true if and only if both *P* and *Q* are true. For example, "Sally is here and Joe is happy" is true if and only if both "Sally is here" and "Joe is happy" are true. The value of *out* in the normally open switch, then, is equivalent to "*in* AND *control*." Fortunately for us, a great amount of work has been done in the past three millennia to discover (or invent, depending on your philosophic point of view) the properties of logic, thereby relieving us of the chore of having to do the work again for our circuit model.

One fact that has been known for a long time, for instance, is that any logical operator can be made using only a combination of the operators AND, OR, and NOT. The AND operator you have already seen—it is true precisely in the case that its two component parts are true. OR, in contrast, is true when either or both of its components are true, and false only when both are false. NOT, of course, simply reverses the truth value of its associated statement, so "Joe is not happy" is true precisely when "Joe is happy" is false. We can express the actions of these three operators in tabular form, representing true by 1 and false by 0, and writing the AND operator as if it were multiplication, OR as if it were addition, and NOT with a prime after the expression to be negated.

Rules for Logical Operators (1 = *true*, 0 = *false*)

and			or			not	
P	Q	PQ	P	Q	$P+Q$	P	P'
1	1	1	1	1	1	1	0
1	0	0	1	0	1	0	1
0	1	0	0	1	1		
0	0	0	0	0	0		

An example should convince you that these three operators suffice to build an expression equivalent to any given logical expression. Suppose we want to produce an expression of the following form:

P	Q	Result
1	1	1
1	0	0
0	1	0
0	0	1

Of course, we could interpret *Result* as saying "*P* and *Q* are equal," but we want to show that there is an equivalent way to express this using only AND, OR, and NOT. We know how to obtain a 1 when *P* and *Q* are both 1—AND will do nicely.

Furthermore, the statement $P'Q'$ will take the value 1 only when its components, P' and Q', are 1; that is, when both P and Q are 0. We can now use or to put these statements together to produce a statement that has exactly the same values as *Result*:

P	Q	PQ	P'	Q'	P'Q'	PQ + P'Q'
1	1	1	0	0	0	1
1	0	0	0	1	0	0
0	1	0	1	0	0	0
0	0	0	1	1	1	1

◆ We can dispense with the OR operator by expressing OR as a combination of an AND and three NOTs.

In slightly more expansive notation we can say that *Result* is equivalent to (P AND Q) OR ((NOT P) AND (NOT Q)).

Notice, by the way, that the column $P'Q'$ of the previous table is exactly the negation of the OR operator $P + Q$. This means that we could dispense with OR completely, since it can be duplicated by a suitable combination of AND and three NOTs, since $P + Q = (P'Q')'$.

◆ By combining AND, OR, and NOT operations, we can build expressions to represent *any* Boolean function.

The general rule is clear: To construct an operator equivalent to any given one,

1. Look at each line in the table for which the result is 1.
2. For each of those:
   a) Find the P and Q values.
   b) Build an AND statement with the variable itself, if its value is 1, and with the negation of the variable, if its table value is 0.
3. Use ORs to connect the statements constructed in step 2.

For example, the following statement S is equivalent to $PQ + PQ' + P'Q'$.

P	Q	S	
1	1	1	*(This line is from PQ)*
1	0	1	*(This line is from PQ')*
0	1	0	
0	0	1	*(This line is from P'Q')*

◆ With n variables, there will be 2^n possible input combinations (and that many rows in the logic table).

Although we've stated the results only for two-variable statements, the same technique will work for an arbitrary number of variables—there will just be more variables in each AND statement.

So, to build any logical expression, three kinds of operators suffice (or even just two, since we also showed that we can duplicate the action of OR with an AND and three NOT operators). Why is this important? Let's return to our circuit model. The principles we just demonstrated, translated into circuit terminology, state that any circuit made of switches can be made by properly connecting three types of components, which we will call *gates*: an AND gate, an OR gate, and a NOT gate. Figure 7.4 illus-

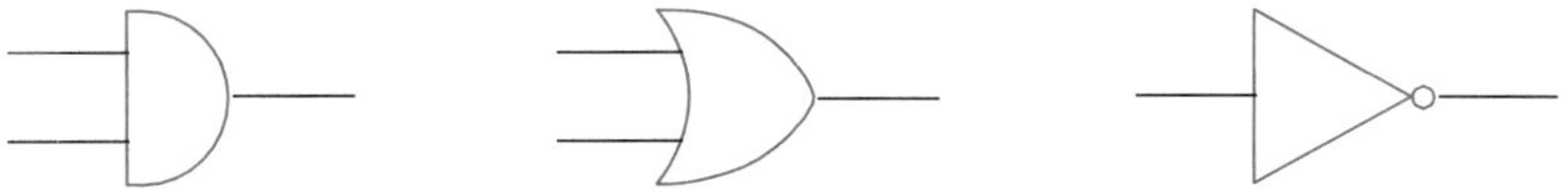

FIGURE 7.4
Three types of gates

trates the drawing conventions for these three types of gates. In each case, the input lines, representing the values on which the gates operate, are on the left, while the output line leaves from the right of the gate.

LAB 7.1

Leggo my Logg-O

The program upon which most of the exercises for this module are based, named Logg-O, provides you with an automated "breadboard," a board on which you can lay out, hook together, and test out combinations of gates. The program provides you with supplies of six different gates (AND, NAND, OR, NOR, NOT, and XOR), as well as switches (which serve as input that you can set), clocks (which serve as inputs that toggle themselves between on and off), lights (which serve as output devices to show us the net effect of a circuit), and terminals for connecting wires together.

Clicking on the "hand" tool (near the bottom of Logg-O's window) lets you drag elements from the supply bin on the left onto the breadboard. You can position gates wherever you want them, and can move them at any time using the hand tool to drag them.

Gates are connected together using the "connection" tool (shaped like a wire with terminals on each end). The terminal(s) on the left side of a gate represent its inputs; those to its right are the outputs from the gate. Clicking and dragging from one terminal to another with the connection tool places a wire between the two elements involved. These wires can be cut using the "scissors" tool.

A simple circuit can thus be constructed as follows:

1. Place switches (for now) on the board to serve as input devices.
2. Place the desired gates on the board so that they can be connected as needed.
3. Place lights on the board to serve as output devices.

Steps 1 through 3 are accomplished using the hand tool. Next, select the connect tool.

4. Connect the input switches to their input terminals on one or more of the gates (a given switch can connect to more than one terminal).
5. Connect the gates together by connecting output terminals to input terminals.
6. Connect the gate terminals that serve as circuit outputs to lights.

Once a gate has been constructed in this manner, it can be tested as follows:

1. Click on the "run" tool.
2. Set the input switches to be on or off, as desired.
3. Observe the status of the lights, as they represent the output of the circuit. A light that is turned on represents a logical value of true; lights that are off stand for logical false.

1. You are now ready to use Logg-O. Design and test circuits that demonstrate the following ("T" stands for TRUE/ON, "F" stands for FALSE/OFF).

   a) T AND F is F
   b) T AND T is T
   c) F OR T is T
   d) F OR F is F
   e) NOT T is F
   f) NOT F is T

Gates

We already have shown that AND and NOT are sufficient to produce any logical operator; all we need to complete the translation of this result to circuits is to show that we can build the gates from switches. We do this in Figure 7.5. In the NOT gate, notice that if we fix the input of a normally closed switch so that it is always 1, then if the control is 0, the 1 passes to the output line; if the control is 1, the switch flips open, breaking the circuit and sending 0 to the output line. Similarly, we can implement an AND gate, using a normally open switch in which one value is connected to the switch's input line

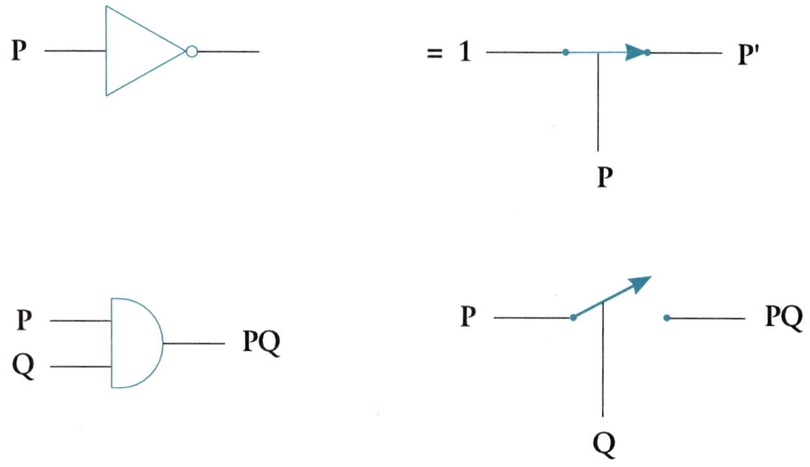

FIGURE 7.5 *Building NOT and AND gates with switches*

and the other is connected to the switch's control. In this case, the only time the output is 1 is when both the input (*P* in the figure) and the control (*Q*) are 1.

Confident that we can translate from gates to switches when the time comes to build a physical machine, we can now elevate our discussion and consider more complex collections of gates, called *circuits*.

In Figure 7.6 we illustrate a *one-bit comparator*, a circuit that sets the value of *R* to 1 if and only if *P* and *Q* have the same values. This is simply the hardware equivalent of $PQ + P'Q'$, which we just saw is equivalent to the statement "*P* and *Q* are equal." To interpret this diagram, follow the wires from *P* and *Q*: They go to the upper AND gate (producing output *PQ*), and through the two NOT gates and the lower AND gate (producing output $P'Q'$). The two outputs serve as input to the OR gate, which produces the desired result.

We mentioned before that the important property of the simple switch is its binary nature. Up to now we have been using a logic model to help us design circuits, thinking of a signal as 1 or true, and no signal as 0 or false. But another model depends on just two possible values—namely, binary arithmetic. We're used to thinking of 1 + 1 being equal to 2, but that's just because we customarily use decimal arithmetic. In binary notation, the equivalent expression would be 1 + 1 = 10, since 10 is the binary representation of 2. Binary arithmetic would certainly make a grade-school student's life easier, since all one needs to know about binary arithmetic are two simple tables.

All You Need to Know About Binary Arithmetic

+	0	1
0	0	1
1	1	10

×	0	1
0	0	0
1	0	1

◆ Arithmetic, then, is just a special case of logic.

If we think of our circuits using the binary arithmetic model, then we can design an adder that takes two digits *a* and *b* as input and returns the sum and the carry as outputs. The sum part is simple enough: The sum is 1 when $a = 1$ and $b = 0$ or when $a = 0$ and $b = 1$, and we can use our procedure to construct logic statements to construct the

FIGURE 7.6
A one-bit comparator

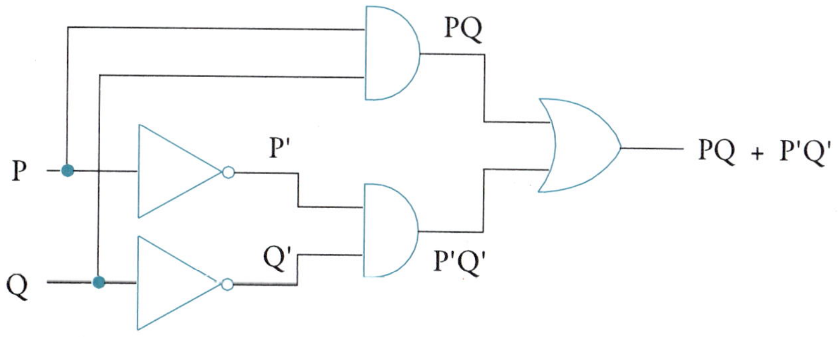

equivalent statement $ab' + a'b$. The carry part is even simpler: The carry is 1 exactly when a and b are both 1, which means we can use ab to represent the carry (notice that if we keep to our interpretation 1 = true, 0 = false, there is no difference between multiplication and the operator AND). The only difference between this circuit and those we have seen previously, aside from the fact that we are now choosing to interpret the results in terms of binary arithmetic, is that this adding circuit has two outputs. Such a circuit is called a *half adder* (HA), where the adjective *half* indicates that such a circuit has a carry *out*, but no provision for a carry *in* to the sum (see Figure 7.7).

We can modify our adding circuit slightly to allow the possibility of hooking many of these circuits together to add strings of binary digits. In that case, when adding a and b we might have to take into account a carry coming in from another part—that is, another input. To do this, we recognize that we are performing two addition operations on *three* binary digits, so we use two half adders—one to add a and b, and another to add the carry in to the resulting sum. There will be a carry out precisely when either (or both) of the half sums has a carry, which produces the full adder (FA) shown in Figure 7.8.

Even at this level, when we combine gates to produce circuits that can perform arithmetic operations, the fundamental physical units are still not visible to the naked eye. Suppose that we expanded an ordinary PC so that one of its full adders was the size of Figure 7.8. To get an idea of the scale involved, at this magnification the computer in which this circuit resides would appear to be taller than any building in the world, the chip itself would just cover a football field, and a human hair would be nearly a foot thick.

FIGURE 7.7
A one-bit half adder (HA)

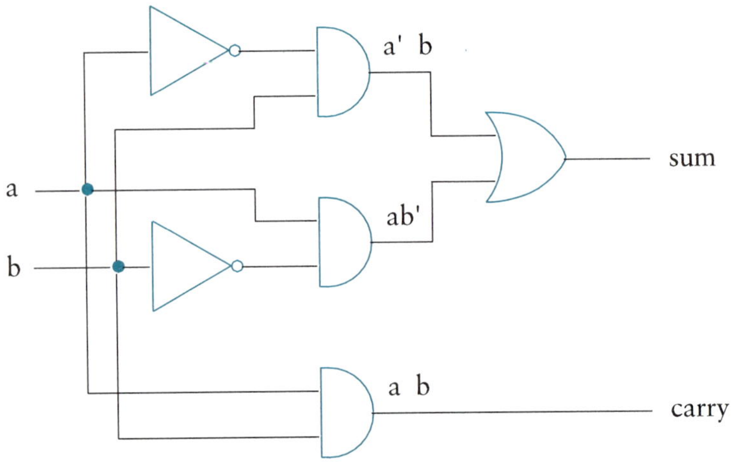

FIGURE 7.8
A one-bit full adder (FA)

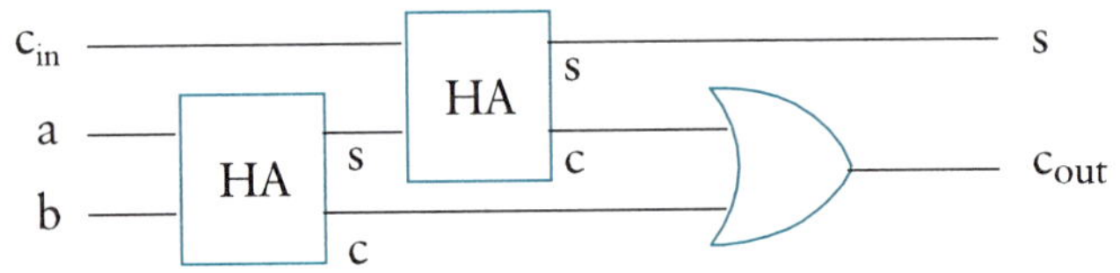

LAB 7.2

Bill's Gates

In the next few sets of lab exercises you will use Logg-O to build increasingly sophisticated, and increasingly useful, circuits. You'll start by designing some circuits to implement gates that we already have available. This way, you'll be able to verify the performance of your circuit directly.

1. Build your own version of a NOR circuit, without using the NOR gate provided by Logg-O. Your circuit should have two input switches (call them A and B) and one output light. The light should turn on when A OR B is FALSE; the light should remain off when A OR B is TRUE. That is, your NOR circuit should perform the logical negation of an OR circuit.

Here is a truth table for NOR:

A	B	(A NOR B)
OFF	OFF	ON
OFF	ON	OFF
ON	OFF	OFF
ON	ON	OFF

2. Now, place one of Logg-O's built-in NOR gates on the board, leaving your NOR circuit in place. Use the same input switches as input to this new NOR gate, and add a new lightbulb to serve as its output.

Run the circuits now. If your implementation of NOR is correct, both lights on the board should perform identically for all combinations of switch values.

3. Repeat Exercises 1 and 2, but this time build your own XOR circuit. The truth table for XOR is provided below. Note in building your circuit, that A XOR B is equivalent to (A OR B) AND (NOT (A) OR NOT (B)).

A	B	(A XOR B)
OFF	OFF	OFF
OFF	ON	ON
ON	OFF	ON
ON	ON	OFF

Test your circuit by comparing its performance (using the same switches as input) to one of Logg-O's built-in XOR gates.

4. The circuits described below are not provided directly by Logg-O. The only way to "test" these circuits is to compare their performance for all possible combinations of inputs to their truth tables.

a) Build and test a three-way AND circuit that accepts three inputs from switches (call them A, B, and C) and turns its one output light on only when all three switches are ON. Otherwise, its output light should be OFF. Use the truth table below to verify your circuit.

A	B	C	3AND
OFF	OFF	OFF	OFF
OFF	OFF	ON	OFF
OFF	ON	OFF	OFF
OFF	ON	ON	OFF
ON	OFF	OFF	OFF
ON	OFF	ON	OFF
ON	ON	OFF	OFF
ON	ON	ON	ON

b) Build and test a three-way OR circuit that accepts three inputs from switches (A, B, and C), and turns on its one output light whenever at least one of the switches is ON. Use the truth table below to verify your circuit.

A	B	C	3OR
OFF	OFF	OFF	OFF
OFF	OFF	ON	ON
OFF	ON	OFF	ON
OFF	ON	ON	ON
ON	OFF	OFF	ON
ON	OFF	ON	ON
ON	ON	OFF	ON
ON	ON	ON	ON

Review Questions

1. What were the three technologies that combined to make modern computers possible?

2. The logical operator IMPLIES is a formalization of what we mean when we say "if . . . then." In particular, *P* IMPLIES *Q* is false only in the case when *P* is true and *Q* is false. For example, "If it is sunny, then Sally is on the golf course" is a false statement only in the case that it is sunny

and Sally isn't on the golf course. Find a way to express IMPLIES using some combination of ANDs, ORs, and NOTs.

3. Create a circuit that implements the following statement: *a* AND (NOT(*a* OR NOT *b*)).

4. Show that it would be a waste of time to build the circuit in question 3, by finding the value of *a* AND (NOT(*a* OR NOT *b*)) for all four possible values of *a* and *b*.

7.3 THE ARITHMETIC LEVEL

The prospect of designing circuits that can operate on multiple binary inputs is an interesting one, especially if we want our computer to be able to handle numbers larger than 1. We do, indeed, and so we must decide how to represent larger numbers. Given the bi-state nature of our hardware, binary notation seems to be a natural choice. Again, we are in debt to von Neumann for this idea, although Atanasoff, in his earlier machines, also used binary representation. We don't have to use binary representation—some early machines used decimal representation, representing 1 by one volt, 2 by two volts, and so on. The problem with this representation, though, is that electrical signals in real circuits almost never can be fixed to exact values, and it is much easier and more reliable to worry only about high voltage versus low voltage, rather than trying to sort out ten possible voltages.

◆ An important theme in this chapter is that the efficiency of a computer comes from its doing many things at once—in parallel, that is.

If we are to represent the number 37 by its binary equivalent 100101, though, we still have to work out the details of this representation. One way would be to mimic the telegraph and have the digits arranged in time, so that 37 would be represented as a sequence of six pulses: high, low, low, high, low, high. This *serial* representation has the obvious disadvantage that it takes time, and, as is often the case, time is of critical importance to us. It behooves us to trade an increase in complexity for a decrease in time and use a *parallel* representation for our numbers. In a parallel representation, we decide ahead of time how many digits our computer will use for numbers and assign a wire for each binary digit, as indicated in Figure 7.9. In this example, a number *a* is represented by six parallel wires, a_0 (representing the least significant or rightmost digit) to a_5 (representing the most significant or leftmost digit).

Since we are going to represent information in parallel, we will operate on this information as a unit, rather than a bit at a time, thereby complicating our circuits. For example, suppose we wish to design an adder in a machine that represents information

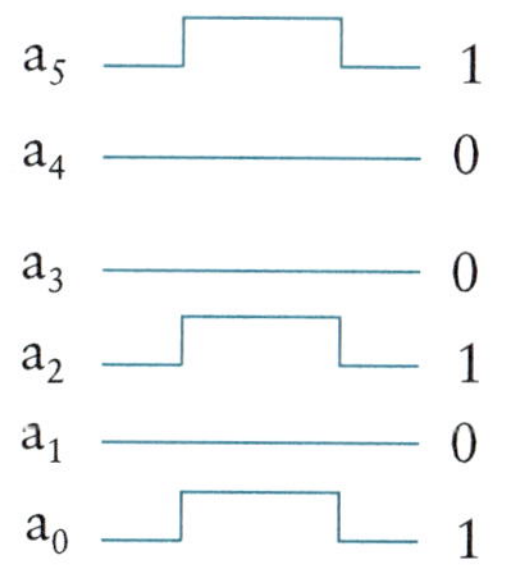

FIGURE 7.9 *Parallel representation of 37*

with four parallel lines. The input to the adder would be four lines, a_3 to a_0, for one number and four lines, b_3 to b_0, for the other, and the output would be another four lines, s_3 to s_0, for the sum. We can build such a *four-bit adder* with four one-bit adders by linking the carry out of digit i to the carry in of digit $i + 1$, as shown in Figure 7.10.

In the four-bit adder, the carry in line of the low-order adder (at the top of the figure) is always set to 0, reflecting that the least significant part of the sum has no incoming carry. The carry out line of the high-order adder signals an *overflow*, indicating that the sum is larger than can be expressed in four binary digits. This line might be used to turn on a light or other signal indicating that something went awry with an arithmetic calculation, for instance.

Using these simple principles, we can do more than just add. Binary multiplication looks just like decimal multiplication. For example, to multiply 12 (= 1100) by 7 (= 0111) we perform the following steps:

```
    0111   binary 7
   ×1100   binary 12
   -----
    0000
   0000
  0111
 0111
 -------
 1010100   add four partial products = 84
```

Implementing multiplication by circuits is a trifle more complicated than implementing addition, but the essential idea is to be able to shift a number to the left by one position. For example, the four-bit number 0111, representing 7, would be shifted to the number 1110, representing 14, accomplishing a multiplication by 2. General binary multiplication can be accomplished by a collection of adds and shifts.

Notice that for multiplication, the result will generally require a larger output than the size of the numbers in our machine. With four-bit arithmetic, in which the numbers are limited to those expressible in four binary digits, multiplication might require two

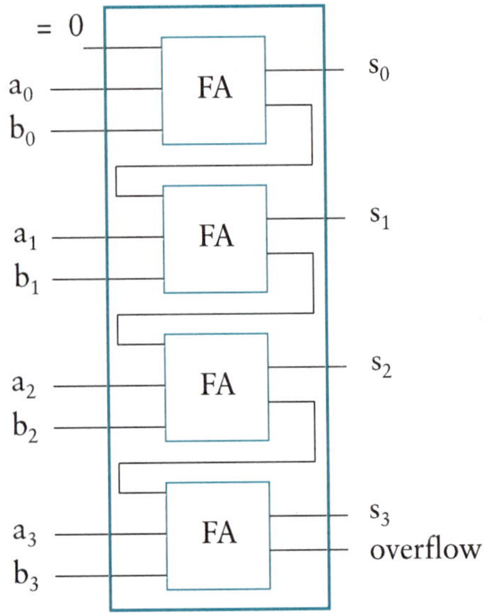

FIGURE 7.10 *Building a four-bit adder from four one-bit adders*

groups of four-bit numbers to express the result. We could deal with this in a real computer either by allowing two-group outputs, or by keeping to one group of four and signaling an overflow when the result would take more than the allowable number of bits.

LAB 7.3

Toward Arithmetic

If we are to build a computer out of Logg-O-like circuits, we had better be able to do some computing with them. The circuits described below take an (admittedly small) step toward illustrating how logical gates can be combined to simulate arithmetic.

1. Use Logg-O to build a one-bit half adder using AND, OR, and NOT gates, as described in Figure 7.7 in your text. Test it using all possible combinations of inputs.

2. Use Logg-O's Save As... button to save your circuit in a file named "halfadd.dat".

3. Add to your half adder circuit the gates and connections necessary to implement one-bit full adder, as depicted in Figure 7.8 in your text. After testing your full adder, save it as "fulladd.dat".

Control

◆ Parallelism again.

By now, it should seem reasonable that we can design circuits to perform all the operations we associate with modern computers, but we still haven't explained how to make these operations programmable—that is to say, we have avoided the question of how to make the computer a universal machine, capable of following the instructions of any program. There is a wonderfully clever trick that we use to solve this problem: A computer is designed so that every time it has to perform an operation, it performs all operations and lets the program set switches to determine which result will be used. In other words, when two numbers have to be added, the computer simultaneously adds them, subtracts them, multiplies them, compares them, ANDs them, ORs them, and so on, and lets the program tell the computer which of the babble of results it wants.

We can do this with a *multiplexor,* which is a fancy word for a multiway switch. In Figure 7.11 we illustrate a two-way multiplexor (MUX). (Note that in the figure we have adopted a shorthand convention for the NOT gate, representing it by a small circle.) In this example, we have a switch in which the *select* line determines whether to set the output line *out* to pass the value of the *a* line or the *b* line. When the *select* line is 1, the upper AND gate allows current to pass, effectively setting the output *out* to the same as the input *a*, while blocking the current through the lower AND gate. If *select* is 0, the upper AND gate blocks the flow from *a* while allowing flow from *b*, setting *out* to the value of *b*.

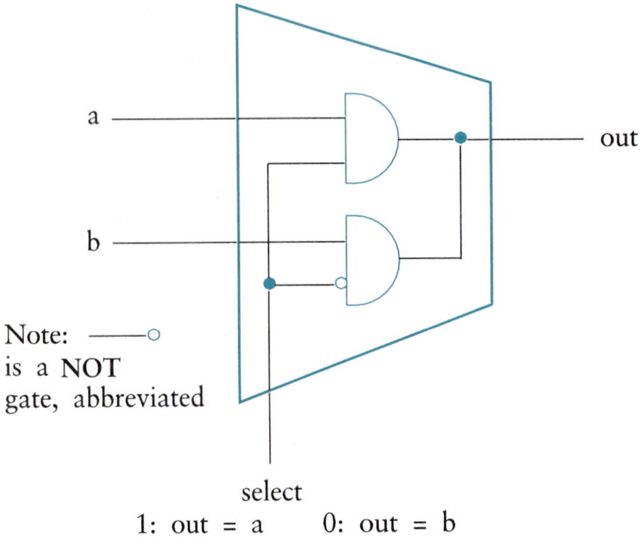

FIGURE 7.11
A two-way multiplexor (MUX)

Now we can use our multiplexors to build a multifunction operator unit. Suppose, for example, we have a computer with an adder and a multiplier. We can combine these two operators into a single circuit, a simple *arithmetic unit* that acts as follows. The unit takes the two inputs *a* and *b* and a *selection* input; if the selection input is 1, the output will be $a + b$ (the + here means addition, not logical OR); if the selection is 0, the output will be the product *ab*. We accomplish this by feeding the inputs to both the adder and the multiplier and using several two-way multiplexors, one for each output line, to control whether the output is $a + b$ or *ab* (see Figure 7.12). To make the diagram simple, we assume that we have a two-bit cir-

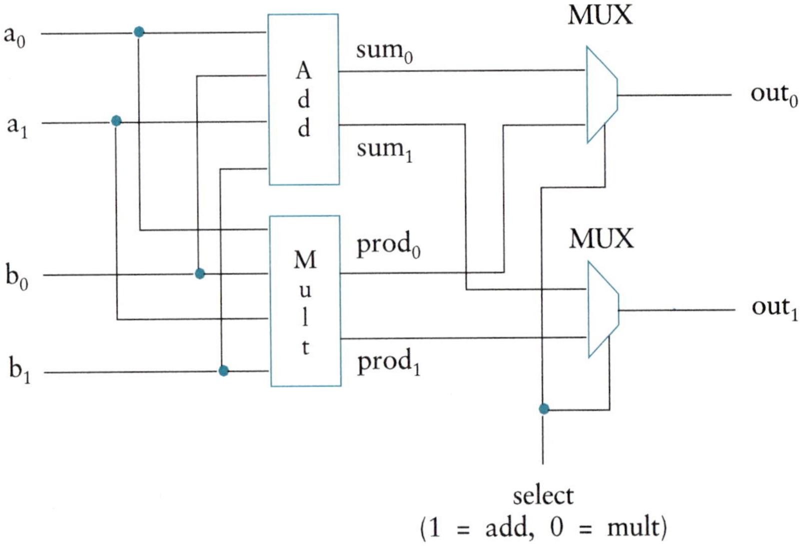

FIGURE 7.12
A two-function arithmetic unit

cuit, one that performs arithmetic on two-digit binary numbers a_1a_0 and b_1b_0 (see Figure 7.13). The principle would be the same with numbers of more digits—we'd just need more wires and more MUXs.

It would not be much harder to make a more complicated arithmetic unit, or an *arithmetic-logic unit* (ALU), by including more operations, such as subtraction, division, comparison, and the logic operations. The action would be the same as in our two-function example—all possible operations would be performed on the inputs, but a more complicated multiplexor would be required to select the desired output from the many possibilities. In the exercises at the end of this module, we provide a circuit that we ask you to verify is a four-way multiplexor.

> The ALU simultaneously performs *all possible operations* on its inputs. The result that is chosen by the select lines is the one that becomes the output.

Finally, notice that we can work the multiplexor idea in reverse and construct a *decoder* that takes a single input and a selection and, depending on the value represented by select, sends the input to one of many output lines, as illustrated by the four-line decoder in Figure 7.14. In this example, we show a circuit in which input line x_i is selected only when the select lines represent the binary number i.

Multiplexors and Decoders Are Multiway Switches

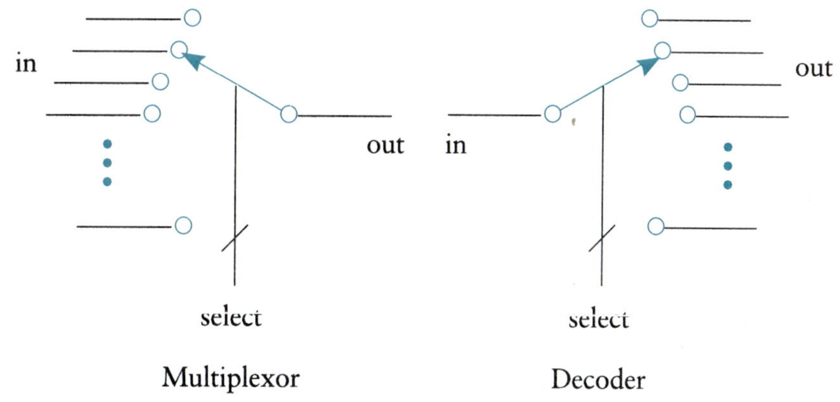

■ Storage

So far, none of the circuits we've built "remember" any of the information they have processed—when the current flow through them stops, they reset themselves to a quiescent state. To complete construction of our paper computer we must find a way to save the information it is to manipulate. We will make just such a circuit, but first we will introduce a new gate, the NAND gate. A NAND gate is built by attaching a NOT gate to the output of an AND gate (hence, its name, "N[ot]AND"), so that *P* NAND *Q* is false only when both *P* and *Q* are true.

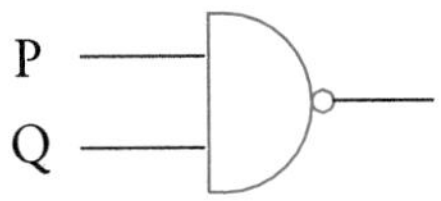

A **NAND** gate and its equivalent

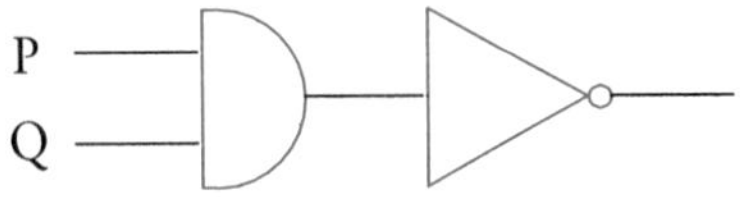

P	Q	P NAND Q
0	0	1
0	1	1
1	0	1
1	1	0

An interesting property of the **NAND** operator is that all logical operators can be constructed by a suitable combination of **NAND** alone.

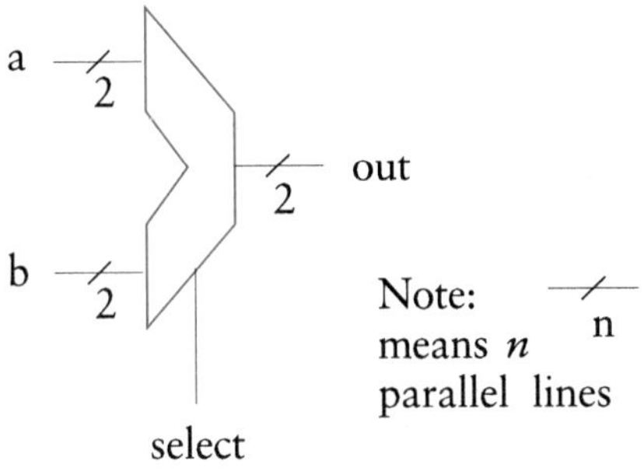

FIGURE 7.13
The circuit diagram abbreviation of the arithmetic unit in Figure 7.12

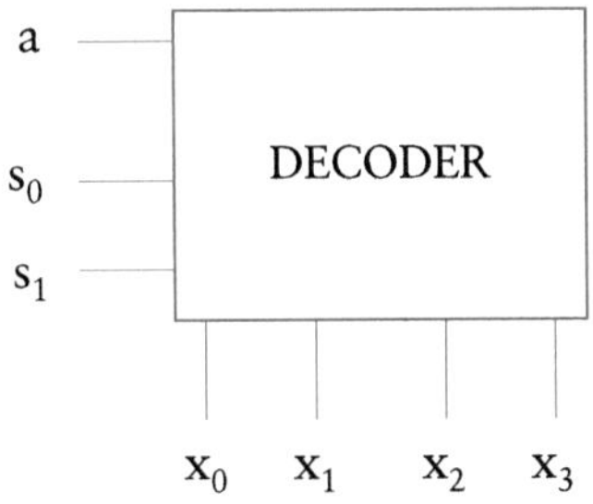

FIGURE 7.14
A four-way decoder

select values s_1	s_0	*a* value sent to
0	0	x_0
0	1	x_1
1	0	x_2
1	1	x_3

A *latch* is a circuit that can store a single 1 or 0 bit of information (Figure 7.15). It can be built from three NAND gates and a NOT gate. A latch has two input lines that serve to set and reset its stored value, along with a single output line that yields the value of the "remembered" bit.

In the table of Figure 7.15, we analyze the behavior of this latch for the four possible combinations of the input lines d and g. In the figure, x, y, and z represent the values of the output lines of the three NAND gates. When reading the table, remember that the prime represents negation, changing 0 to 1 and vice versa, and that AND is written as we would write single-digit multiplication, by the rules $00 = 0 \times 0 = 0$, $01 = 0 \times 1 = 0$, $10 = 1 \times 0 = 0$, and $11 = 1 \times 1 = 1$. A helpful consequence of the behavior of AND is that $1p = p$, and $0p = 0$, no matter what value p is. There are two main types of behavior, depending on the value of g:

1. When $g = 0$, the value of q, the circuit's lone output, is unchanged, since the new value for z is the same as the old value of q.
2. When $g = 1$, the value of z is forced to be whatever d is, regardless of the original value of q. So in this case, the value of q is eventually forced to be the same as that of d.

Aha! We have a circuit that remembers! To store a value in this circuit, we send that value in as d, set g to 1, and thus force q to have the same value as d. Thereafter, as long as g stays quiescent at 0, the value of q will stay as it was set, until we change it by sending new data in via d, along with a value of 1 for g. Figure 7.16 illustrates what happens when we force q to be 0, by setting $d = 0$ and $g = 1$. In the figure, lines with 1 are drawn to be heavier than lines with 0.

Using the latch principles, we can build a one-bit memory unit as follows. We want to be able to store and retrieve data from memory, so we will have a *data* line

FIGURE 7.15
A latch

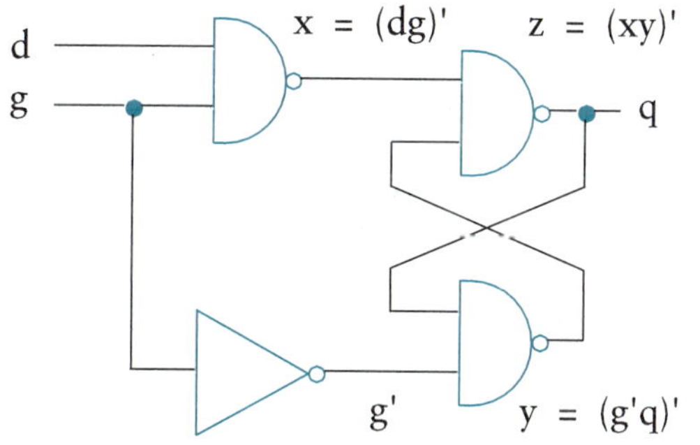

d	g	x = (dg)'	y = (g'q)'	z = (xy)'
0	0	(00)'=0'=1	(1q)'=q'	(1q')'=q
1	0	(10)'=0'=1	(1q)'=q'	(1q')'=q
0	1	(01)'=0'=1	(0q)'=0'=1	(11)'=1'=0
1	1	(11)'=1'=0	(0q)'=0'=1	(01)'=0'=1

FIGURE 7.16
Setting a latch

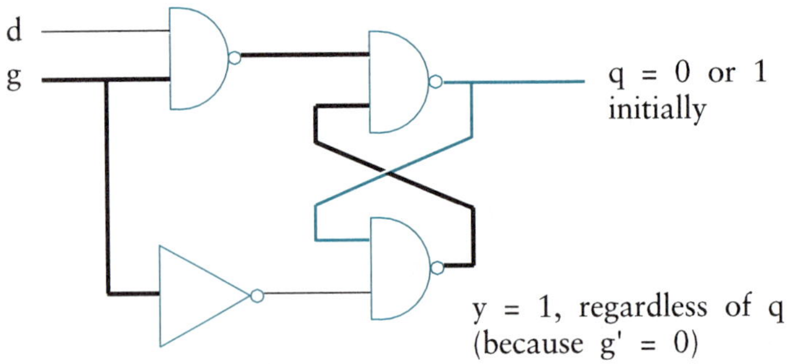

(a) Before z has had a chance to stabilize

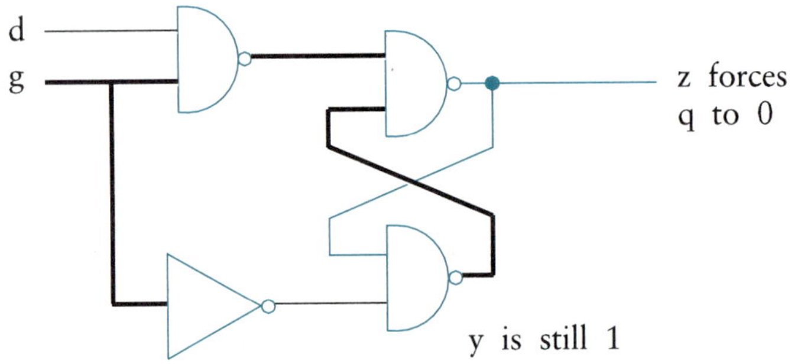

(b) After z has remained 0 long enough

that will pass information to and from memory; a *read/write* line that when set to 0 will cause data to be read from memory and appear on the data line, and when set to 1 will cause the latch to be set to the value on the data line; and a *select* line that will activate the memory, allowing reading or writing, when it is set to 1. Figure 7.17 illustrates this one-bit memory cell.

◆ We're using AND gates as traffic controllers here. We'll do more of this shortly.

Notice in Figure 7.17 that we are using the two AND gates labeled 2 and 3 as normally open switches. When *select* is 0, the two gates will not pass any information, effectively shutting off the memory. When *select* is 1, it is as if the two lower AND gates were just horizontal wires, allowing information to pass. When *select* is 1 and *read/write* is 0, no signal passes to *g*, so the value of *q* is passed through the AND gate labeled 1, then through the lower right gate and out the data line, thereby copying the memory to data. Finally, when *select* and *read/write* are 1, *g* is activated, *q* is forced to equal *data,* and the signal from *q* is blocked at the upper AND gate, thus writing to memory.

We can build larger memory circuits from smaller ones, forming a *four-bit memory* capable of reading or writing a four-bit number (Figure 7.18). Then

Our memory cell acts like this:

1. When *select* = 0, nothing happens (the cell is inactive).
2. When *select* = 1 and *read/write* = 0, a copy of the memory is sent along the *data* line (reading from the cell).
3. When *select* = 1 and *read/write* = 1, the memory cell is set to whatever *data* is (writing to the cell).

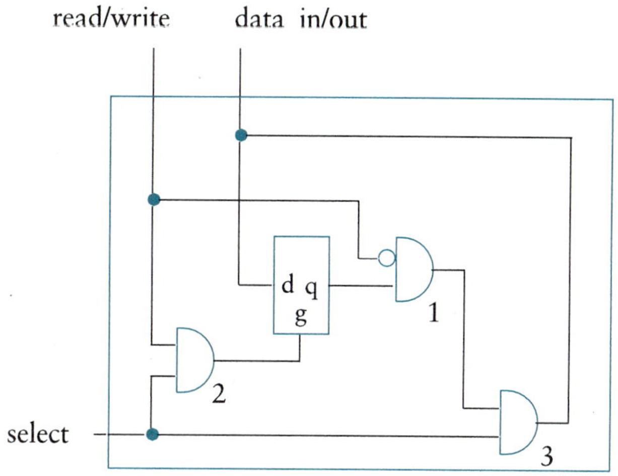

FIGURE 7.17 *A one-bit memory cell*

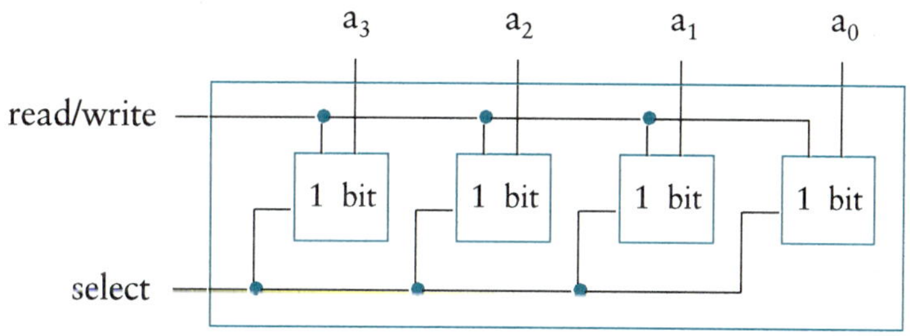

FIGURE 7.18 *A four-bit memory cell, containing a four-digit binary number*

◆ Just as we stacked one-bit circuits to build a four-bit adder in Figure 7.10, we stack one-bit memory circuits to build bigger memories.

we can use four of these four-bit memory cells and a four-way decoder to form a *4×4-bit memory,* capable of storing four different words of four bits each (Figure 7.19).

You should be able to verify that our 4×4-bit memory would require 100 AND gates and 82 NOT gates, if built from our standard components. We've skimped on the details, but the broad picture should be enough to show you how you would build a memory for a typical modern computer, in which data are represented in 32-bit groups (usually divided into four groups of eight-bit *bytes*), and memory contains several million bytes.

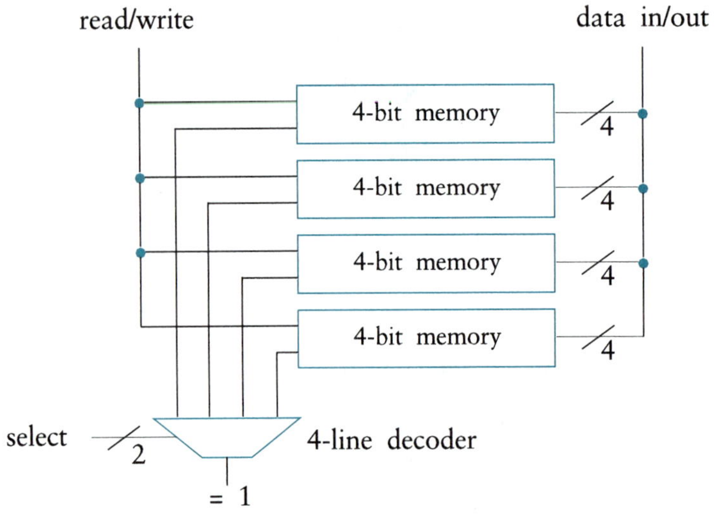

FIGURE 7.19 *A 4×4-bit memory, containing four four-bit numbers*

The important thing to remember is that our memory *does everything at once,* just as the arithmetic-logic unit does. When a request comes to read from memory location 1288, for example, the request is sent to all memory cells simultaneously, but the address decoder activates only cell 1288. All the other cells of memory remain unselected, unable to respond to the request.

LAB 7.4

Toward Memory

Arithmetic circuits alone do not make a computer. A computer needs memory—places to store and retrieve information—if it is to have data that can be operated on. And, memory must itself be describable in terms of our logical primitives. The exercises below demonstrate how a small piece of memory might be built in Logg-O.

1. Figure 7.15 in your text shows a latch circuit. Use Logg-O to build your own latch circuit. Test it to see that it performs as described in the text. Then, save your circuit as file "latch".

2. Figure 7.17 shows how a latch (the "black box" just left of the center of the diagram) can be connected to other Logg-O built-ins to produce a one-bit memory cell. Extend your latch circuit to implement this memory.

3. Once you are convinced that your memory circuit performs as it should, save it in a file named "memory".

Review Questions

1. What are the advantages of parallel representation of information in a computer? What are the disadvantages?
2. Multiply binary numbers 1011 × 1101, and check your answer by converting to decimal.
3. What is the important principle behind the working of a computer?
4. How can we use AND gates as switches?
5. What are multiplexors and decoders, and why are they important?
6. What do the *d*, *g*, and *q* lines in a latch do?

7.4 ARCHITECTURE

We are now ready to move up one more conceptual level. You can forget about gates now, just as you could forget about switches when we moved to the gate level. At this new level of organization, the pieces of a real computer are just barely visible to the naked eye. We have, in our imagination at least, a large collection of building blocks: an arithmetic-logic unit to perform the basic calculations under the direction of selection lines that tell which of the operations will be allowed to pass its output to the rest of the components, and a memory, which allows us to store not only the data, but the program instructions themselves. In this section we will use these building blocks to construct a computer.

This level is called the *architecture level* for good reason. Just as the architect of a building can concentrate on the design of a building, leaving for others the questions of how a window is constructed from glass, steel, and wood, so too can the computer architect concentrate on the larger ideas of how to fit the components together, leaving to the engineers the problem of designing the integrated circuits that will eventually realize the large ideas in physical form. At this language level, we have access to the structure of the real machine, not just the virtual machine visible to a high-level programmer.

The architecture of a computer is sometimes defined as "that which is visible to an assembly language programmer." Although JavaScript and C programmers can act most of the time as if the machine were actually wired to perform JavaScript scripts or C statements, at the architecture level there is no compiler sitting between us and the machine—all that's there is the assembler, generating machine code on a statement-for-statement basis from the assembly language source code. When we design a computer, the decisions we make are reflected directly in the form that the machine language takes.

The Microscopic Dance

A single processor executes the instructions of a program sequentially,[1] employing what is known as the *fetch-execute cycle*. At each iteration of this cycle, the next program instruction is fetched from memory, and that statement is used to determine the

[1] In recent years, *parallel* computers have been developed that execute a number of instructions simultaneously. Such parallel machines are typically constructed from a collection of sequential processors and thus represent yet another conceptual level, one higher than we're discussing here.

action of the machine. The fetch-execute cycle is implemented in an orderly fashion by endowing the computer with a sense of time.

A charming definition of time, attributed to an anonymous child, is "Time is what keeps everything from happening at once." To keep our computer from trying to do everything at once, we include a clock at the heart of the circuitry, marking off the steps of the fetch-execute cycle like an electronic metronome. At one tick, the machine fetches an instruction from its memory. At the next tick it begins to execute the instruction. At subsequent ticks the machine finishes executing the instruction, fetches the next instruction, and starts the cycle over again. This cycle continues until such time as the program signals the computer to halt, or the computer halts by itself due to a program error that makes further execution impossible. Thus, we can envision the action of the computer as an elaborate dance with thousands of performers, choreographed by the program, and conducted by the clock, at a rate of millions of steps per second.[2]

■ Design Decisions

◆ Pip: A small seed, as of an apple.

We are at last ready to build our computer. It's a standing joke among computer engineers that the first decision to accompany the birth of a new machine is what to name it and how to design the T-shirts for the project team. Since part of this text was developed with the help of products of Apple Computer, Inc. (and since our computer company is hypothetical, thereby relieving us of worry about the legal problems of trademark infringement), and since our computer will be very small, we'll name our computer Pip. Smaller than a minicomputer, smaller than a microcomputer, Pip is the world's first *nano*computer. We leak our release date to the trade press, along with some extravagant claims about Pip's performance, have a company party in celebration of our new venture, and set to work designing Pip the next day.

The first real decision we need to make is the size of the fundamental unit of data. This is generally one of the easier decisions, since it is dictated by the iron hand of economics. In our hypothetical computer the economic measure is one of complexity, rather than money, but the principles are the same. A two- or three-bit unit of data is really too small to be of any practical use, but anything like a contemporary 32-bit computer is obviously far too complex for us to build here, even in our imaginations. So, let's settle on the eight-bit *byte* as the fundamental unit of information.

With eight bits, we can express 256 different binary numbers, so our computer will be limited in the size of the numbers on which it can operate. Pip will have 256 bytes of memory, with addresses from 0 to 255 (00000000 to 11111111 in binary), so we will need eight bits to address memory. To satisfy the bean counters in the accounting department, we remark that our 256 × 8 memory (including a 256-way decoder) will cost us 12,750 AND gates and 10,455 NOT gates and will use up an area on the chip roughly twice the size of the period at the end of this sentence.

[2] With the right equipment, it is actually possible to hear or see this dance, since the circuits of a computer emit faint but detectable radio signals.

The next decision we must make is to determine the *instruction format*, that is, how the machine language instructions will be stored in memory. We could, for instance, use a *two-address* format, in which an ADD instruction, for instance, would take the form ADD X Y and would be interpreted as "add the contents of memory location Y to the contents of memory location X and store the result in location X." The problem with that format, however, is that two addresses would make an instruction too long for the limited memory that we have, since we have to store programs in memory along with the data they manipulate. Instead, we'll use a *single-address* format and rely on a hardware accumulator (the special storage unit we introduced in Module 6) to assist us in our calculations. Our accumulator is capable of holding eight bits of information, so our ADD instruction will look like ADD X and will be interpreted to mean "add the contents of byte X to the value stored in the accumulator, and store the result in the accumulator."

Since the instructions for Pip will be stored in memory, we must decide how these instructions will be stored. We can only address memory by bytes, so it will make the design easier if we store instructions in two bytes. To make life simple, we'll code the operation (that is, what the instruction does) in four bits, and leave the other four bits in the byte mostly unused. (That will give us extra bits for more operation codes if we decide to introduce Pip II later.) We will use one bit beyond the four-bit operation code, though. If the bit immediately to the left of the operation code is 0, the following *operand* byte will be interpreted as an address (direct mode), and if that bit is 1, the operand byte will be understood to mean a number, rather than an address (immediate mode). Figure 7.20 shows Pip's instruction format.

With four bits for the operation code, Pip will be limited to no more than 16 basic instructions, some of which come in two forms, depending on the value of the mode bit. As we just noted, if you want to include more instructions in a later model

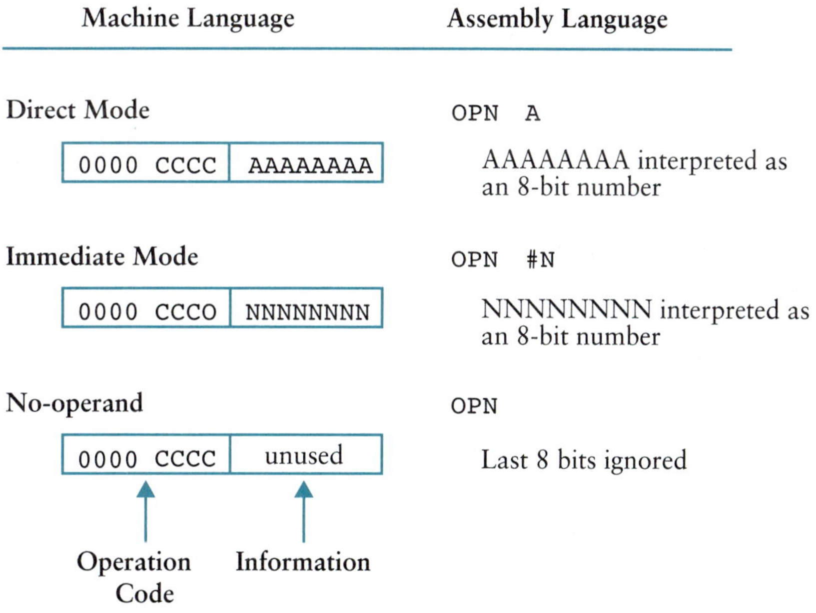

FIGURE 7.20 *Pip instruction formats*

◆ The 2048 × 8-bit memory of Pip II would be about a seventh of an inch on a side and would require about 200,000 gates.

of Pip, we have the three unused bits that we can use. Or, if we decide to stay with 16 instructions, we could employ the three unused bits to expand the addressing capabilities of Pip, so we could expand memory from 256 (=2^8) to 2048 (=2^{11}) bytes.

So, we are interested in defining a single-address language with 16 instructions, some of which can be in two modes. Now we can let you in on the secret—PIPPIN stands for "PIP Program INstruction language." To save you the trouble of looking up the PIPPIN User's Guide in Module 6, we'll reproduce it here, along with the instruction code for each of the operations. Remember, A stands for the accumulator, X stands for an address, and N stands for a number. If X is an address, [X] stands for the contents of the byte at memory location X. PC stands for the program counter (containing the address in memory of the instruction that is currently being executed).

The PIPPIN User's Guide

Data Flow		
0 0100	LOD X	[X] → A
1 0100	LOD #N	N → A
0101	STO X	A → X
0110	unused	
0110	unused	

Control		
1100	JMP X	X → PC
1101	JMZ X	if A = 0, then X → PC
1110	NOP	no operation
1111	HLT	halt execution

Arithmetic-Logic		
0 0000	ADD X	A + [X] → A
1 0000	ADD #N	A + N → A
0 0001	SUB X	A – [X] → A
1 0001	SUB #N	A – N → A
0 0010	MUL X	A * [X] → A
1 0010	MUL #N	A * N → A
0 0011	DIV X	A / [X] → A
1 0011	DIV #N	A / N → A
0 1000	AND X	A AND [X] → A
1 1000	AND #N	A AND N → A
1001	NOT	NOT A → A
1010	CPZ X	if [X] = 0, then 1 → A, else 0 → A
1011	CPL X	if [X] < 0, then 1 → A, else 0 → A

We've put the cart somewhat before the horse here for pedagogical reasons. Normally, the format of a language would be dictated by the architecture of the computer, and not the other way around. But we already have defined PIPPIN and don't want to invent another language after we have designed our machine.

We now have all we need to design Pip. We have seen the fundamental ideas behind the design of a modern computer:

1. Information is represented in binary form, using as many parallel sets of wires as we need to move this information.
2. Program instructions are stored in memory, just like any other information.
3. When the current program instruction is executed, all possible operations are executed simultaneously, and the current instruction is used to select among the choices for the result.

We have a machine language of instructions, we have discussed how the arithmetic and logic operations are implemented by circuits, and we know how we can use memory to store information and recall that information for later use. The rest of the design process is little more than working out the details.

■ Inside Pip

Although we have seen the important ideas behind the workings of a computer, we are not quite ready to actually construct a computer of our own—there is still some detail work to be done. It's time to break out the blueprints and see exactly how Pip manages to execute a program.

Pip, as illustrated in Figure 7.21, consists of six main parts:

1. The *program counter* (PC), which stores the eight-bit address of the current instruction in the memory.
2. The *instruction register* (IR), which stores the current instruction, divided into two eight-bit pieces: the *opcode* in IRH (the high-order, leftmost bits) and the *operand* in IRL (the low-order, rightmost bits).
3. The *decoder*, which takes the instruction code as input and produces several control signals as output.

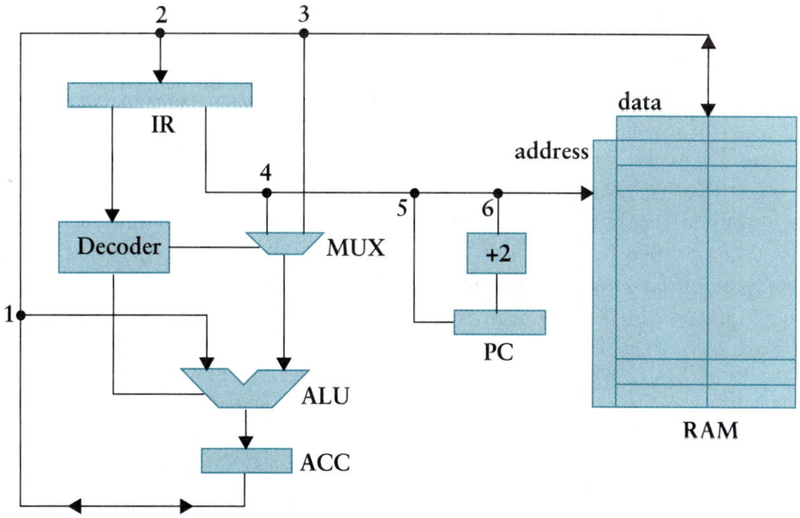

FIGURE 7.21
Pip™ Revealed

4. The *arithmetic-logic unit* (ALU), which takes, generally, two data inputs and a selection and, based on the selection from the decoder, performs one of eight operations (+, –, *, /, AND, NOT, =, <) on its data inputs.
5. The *accumulator* (ACC), used to store the results of calculations from the ALU.
6. The *random access memory* (RAM), which takes an address and a read/write signal from the decoder and reads or writes information to the specified address.

For simplicity's sake we have not drawn several lines, particularly those from the decoder and the clock. The discussion that follows, wherein we run Pip and trace its operation, will enable you to fill in the missing pieces.

The fetch part of the fetch-execute cycle is quite simple: (1) Pip sends the PC to the *address* part of RAM, thereby activating the memory location containing the instruction it wants. (2) Then Pip sends the contents of that location from *data* to IR. (3) It then increments PC by 2, so that PC will refer to the next instruction in the program.

Given an instruction code and an operand, Pip must execute the operation described by the code. The five bits of the instruction code are sent to a decoder, and the decoder activates one or more of its outgoing lines. Three of these output lines are used to select which of the eight ALU operations are selected, one of the output lines is used to select the left or right input from the MUX, and the remainder of the lines (the ones we haven't drawn in Figure 7.21) control the traffic through the intersections, indicated by the numbered black dots at the intersections of the lines.

Data Flow Suppose the instruction code is 0101, the `STO X` instruction. To store a copy of the accumulator into address X, Pip must set intersections 1, 2, and 3 to pass information from ACC to the *data* part of RAM and set intersections 4, 5, and 6 to pass information from IRL to the *address* decoder of RAM. At the same time, the decoder lines must activate ACC for reading and activate RAM for writing, so we can get the information from ACC and put it into RAM. This is what we meant when we said that the schematic of Pip's internal workings in Figure 7.21 is incomplete—the black dots connecting the groups of wires are actually collections of AND gates controlling the flow of information,[3] depending on the values of the control wires from the decoder.

Control Suppose that the instruction to be executed is 1100, the `JMP X` instruction, indicating that the next statement to be fetched will be found in memory location X. In this case, all Pip has to do is set intersections 4 and 5 to send the address from IRL to PC and activate PC for writing, so we can store the address there. Note, by the way, that we have to store a number equal to 2 less than the address we want, since the fetch operation adds 2 to the PC. We could do this subtraction in the assembler, so it wouldn't be seen by the programmer, and we could just remind the machine language programmer that the address in a jump must be 2 less than the actual destination address.

[3] The real story is a bit trickier—we can't use AND gates to control the traffic flow, but the gates that are actually used (called *tri-state buffers*) act in much the same way as AND gates.

Arithmetic-Logic Finally, if operation 0000, `ADD X`, is selected, Pip must perform a fairly complicated sequence of tasks:

1. Send the address X from IRL to the *address* part of RAM.
2. Send the selected memory value from the RAM's *data* to the multiplexor, MUX.
3. Control MUX so that the value of *data* (rather than IRL) gets sent to ALU.
4. Read the data in ACC and send it to ALU.
5. Control ALU so that addition is performed.
6. Activate ACC for writing, to receive the new value from ALU.

We're done; we have a computer (on paper, anyhow). Counting the memory, Pip requires approximately 25,000 AND and NOT gates, almost all of which comprise the memory. If we sent our design off to the integrated circuit shop for fabrication, we would find that—as with most microprocessors—the majority of the chip area is taken up by connecting wires and not by the components themselves. Even with all the wires, though, the finished computer is so small that a careless sneeze could lose it forever. Pip is well named—the complete computer would be about the size of an apple seed. It could fit comfortably in a wristwatch, and would be smaller than the battery that powered it.

The State of the Art

Just how far is Pip from a contemporary computer? Well, in purely numeric terms the answer depends on the context of the question. In terms of the sophistication of its architecture, Pip is about 30 years behind the times; in terms of complexity, it's about a hundred times simpler than the chip in a modern personal computer.

This is not a course in microelectronic technology. In an attempt to understand the ideas behind the development and practice of microprocessor design, we have taken steps that would likely distress anyone in advanced courses in engineering school. We did this deliberately and owe no apologies therefrom. As a result, though, much is missing in Pip. We list here some of the features present in modern computers and absent in Pip.

Sophisticated Addressing Because of its simple architecture, many things would be difficult to do with Pip. Even such a simple problem as setting memory addresses X to X + 10 all equal to 1 requires a complicated workaround in PIPPIN. The fault lies partly in a lack of other addressing modes. True direct-mode operations, for example, allow one to specify a memory location by its offset from the current PC, rather than its absolute location in memory. This allows a program to be moved in memory, a handy feature for sophisticated operating systems, which often relocate items in an attempt to allocate memory more efficiently.

Advanced Instruction Set Another shortcoming of Pip is its limited instruction set. While one can do most things in PIPPIN that a program should be able to do, it often takes many statements to perform what are conceptually very simple processes. In the past two decades, the number of tasks that are wired directly into hardware has increased to the point that a typical microprocessor may have a hundred varieties of operations in its instruction set, with many of these available in different modes, for a total of nearly a thousand different assembly language commands. In fact, this burgeoning instruction set has led to a reaction among some computer scientists who are now investigating *reduced instruction set computers* (RISC, for short), which use a small but powerful set of instructions in an effort not only to increase ease of use, but also to increase the speed of the computers themselves. In a related vein, a computer designer may decide to keep a complicated instruction set and still have a fairly simple processor by employing *microprogramming,* in which the instructions are translated at the hardware level into instructions for the simple processor, in effect adopting a hard-wired interpreter at a very low level.

Speed Enhancement To further increase the efficiency of our processor, we could have introduced *pipelining,* in which we fetch the next instruction at the same time that we are executing the current one. We could also add circuitry for *caching,* in which a memory access results in loading not only the desired memory value, but several of its adjacent values into a separate, very fast, small memory called the *cache* (pronounced "cash"). The advantage to caching comes from the *principle of locality,* which stems from the observation that if one memory location is needed, it is likely that its neighbors will be used shortly. There are many such interesting topics in computer architecture—as we said, we've only scratched the surface.

Ultimately, though, the shortcomings of Pip stem from its size. As long as we have the ideas at hand, little more than problems of scale separate Pip from a modern microprocessor with perhaps ten million gates and over half a mile of invisibly fine connecting wires, all packed onto a chip about an inch across.

LAB 7.5

An Architect's View

We have seen at least the seeds of how simple logical circuits can be used to describe some of the basic operations of a computer. We return now to our CPU simulator, PIPPIN, to watch the higher-level components (like memory, a MUX, a decoder, and an ALU—with its arithmetic operations) in action as they execute a program.

1. Enter the following PIPPIN program into the CPU simulator, beginning at memory location 0. You may remember that this is the PIPPIN equivalent of our example equation: W = X * (2 + Y).

```
LOD #2
ADD Y
MUL X
STO W
```

2. Set the values of memory locations X and Y to 4 and 5, respectively.

3. Run the program by clicking on the Play button.

4. Reset the program, and reset the value of memory location W back to zero.

5. Now use the Step button to execute one PIPPIN instruction at a time. Watch carefully to see how the program counter is used to retrieve an instruction from memory and how the instruction is decoded to detect which operation is to be performed. This is the fetch-execute cycle in action.

6. Reset the simulator now, and perform steps 1 through 5 again, this time using the PIPPIN code for the equation: X = (3 * Y) + (2 / W).

```
LOD #3
MUL Y
STO T1
LOD #2
DIV W
ADD T1
STO X
```

In this case, set the values of the memory locations for variables Y and W to 5 and 1, respectively.

7. On a separate sheet of paper, describe how a single instruction gets executed by our machine in terms of the components of the simulator. That is, describe the order in which components are used, and the flow of information that occurs in the processing of one instruction.

Review Questions

1. What do we mean by the *architecture* of a computer?

2. Describe the fetch-execute cycle.

3. Why did we decide to address memory in Pip by bytes, rather than by bits?

4. What decisions were involved in the choice of Pip's instruction format?

5. Describe two ways in which Pip is more primitive than modern computers.

6. What are the six major parts of Pip, and what are their functions?

7.5 EXERCISES

1. Using only NAND gates, construct circuits that are equivalent to the following.

a) NOT (x AND y)
b) x OR (NOT y)

2. Using AND, OR, and NOT gates, construct circuits with the following properties.

a) Two inputs, a and b, one output z, with z defined by the following logic table:

a	b	z
1	1	0
1	0	1
0	1	1
0	0	1

b) Three inputs, a, b, c, one output z, defined by the following logic table:

a	b	c	z
1	1	1	1
1	0	0	0
1	0	1	1
1	0	0	0
0	1	1	0
0	1	0	1
0	0	1	0
0	0	0	1

3. Construct circuits with output z equivalent to the following Boolean expressions:

a) $a(a' + b) + ab'$
b) $(a + a')b$
c) $abc + a'bc + ab'c + abc'$

4. Using logic tables, show that the following identities hold.

a) $a1 = a$
b) $a(a + b) = a$
c) $(ab)' = a' + b'$

5. Construct the logic tables for the Boolean expressions in Exercise 3.

6. Fill in the logic table that describes the action of the following circuits, and give the equivalent Boolean expressions for the output.

a)

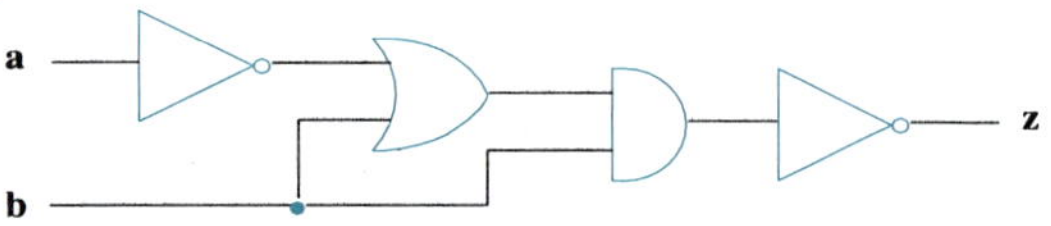

b) (Recall that the small circles represent NOT gates.)

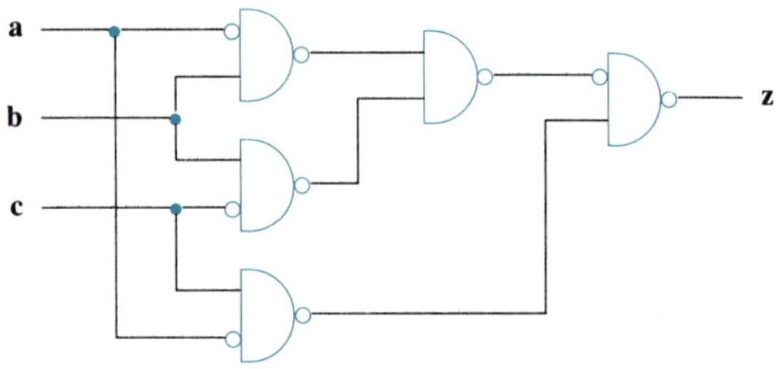

7. Find a simpler circuit equivalent to that of

a) Exercise 3b
b) Exercise 6a

8. Construct the following circuits.

a) A three-input AND gate that has output 1 if and only if all three inputs are 1.
b) A three-input OR gate that has output 1 if and only if at least one of the three inputs are 1.

3-input **AND** 3-input **OR**

9. Construct a *majority circuit,* which has three inputs and one output; the output is 1 if and only if at least two of the inputs are 1. To make your design simpler, you may use multi-input AND and OR gates, as we described in Exercise 8.

10. Verify that the following circuit is a four-way multiplexor, and describe how it works.

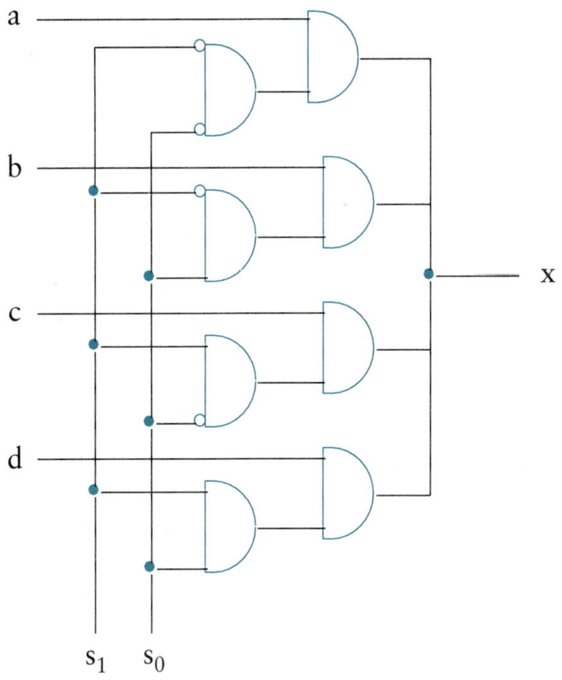

11. Using four four-way multiplexors, construct a *cyclic shifter,* which has four input lines a_3, a_2, a_1, a_0; two select lines s_1, s_0; and four output lines z_3, z_2, z_1, and z_0, defined as follows:

s_1	s_0	z_3	z_2	z_1	z_0
1	1	a_0	a_3	a_2	a_1
1	0	a_1	a_0	a_3	a_2
0	1	a_2	a_1	a_0	a_3
0	0	a_3	a_2	a_1	a_0

In other words, if s_1s_0 is the binary representation of the number n, the output will consist of the input shifted n bits to the left (or, if you prefer, $4 - n$ bits to the right).

12. Verify that the following circuit represents a four-way decoder, as described in Figure 7.14.

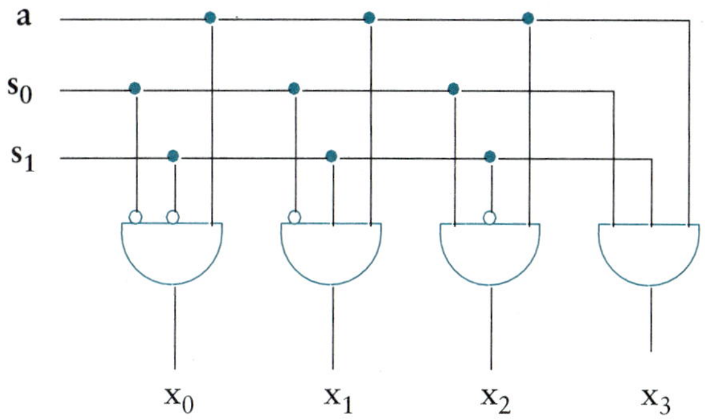

13. Show the steps Pip would make when executing the following statements:

```
LOD X
ADD #401
```

14. Show that the 4 × 4-bit memory of Figure 7.19 requires 100 AND gates and 82 NOT gates.

a) Using the conversion of Exercise 1, how many NAND gates would be required to construct the memory?

b) How many AND and NOT gates would be required to construct an 8 × 4-bit memory (with eight cells of four bits each)? There are many possible answers to this question, so be sure to describe the memory circuit precisely.

15. Recall that in a computer with a pipelined architecture, the fetch and execute steps are overlapped, so that the next instruction is fetched at the same time the present one is being executed.

a) Show how this change could make a computer run faster.

b) It is not enough to simply get the next instruction while the current one is being executed. What statement must be handled specially, and why?

c) Redesign Pip with a pipelined architecture.

ADDITIONAL READINGS

Forester, T., ed. *The Microelectronics Revolution*. Cambridge, MA: MIT Press, 1980.

Gray, N. A. B. *Introduction to Computer Systems*. Sydney: Prentice-Hall of Australia, 1987.

Johnsonbaugh, R. *Essential Discrete Mathematics*. New York: Macmillan, 1987.

Kolman, B., and Busby, R. C. *Introductory Discrete Structures with Applications*. Englewood Cliffs, NJ: Prentice-Hall, 1987.

Mano, M. M. *Computer Engineering: Hardware Design*. Englewood Cliffs, NJ: Prentice-Hall, 1988.

Newell, S. *Introduction to Microcomputing*. New York: Harper & Row, 1982.

Scientific American. Microelectronics theme issue. 237, no. 3 (Sept. 1977).

MODULE 8

Theory of Computation

8.1 INTRODUCTION

Herbert Simon has argued that the solar system can be viewed as an information processor, flawlessly computing the position of the planets by placing them exactly where they should go at each instant. The solar system, under this interpretation, differs from what we would call a computer in that it is, like the Difference Engine, a single-purpose information processor. Indeed, little of what we think of as natural science embodies the salient features of either computers or computation. Computer science is different from other sciences that it is devoted to the study of an artifact of human design. In this regard, computer science is closer to the study and practice of literature than it is, say, to physics.

There is a time-honored tradition that theoretical discussions intended for a lay audience are often presented as dialogs, and we will hold to that tradition here. We do this not merely out of a sense of historical homage, but because we believe in the importance of the way of thinking espoused by the late Ted Sturgeon: "Ask the next question." We hope that you will not be content to hear that "this is the way it is" without asking, "Why is this the way it is?" and "What are the implications, then?" We designed this module—and those that follow—with that way of thinking in mind.

MODULE OBJECTIVES

Our goal in this module is to introduce you to the Big Questions in computer science—the ones that define and delimit everything we can ever hope to do with computers. While these questions tend to be couched in highly abstract, mathematical terms, you will see that their answers have serious, down-to-earth implications for the practice of the discipline.

Toward this end, we will

- Concentrate on the view of a program as defining an abstract machine.
- Consider two ways of looking at these abstract machines: as black boxes that match input strings to outputs, and as clear boxes consisting of programs in a very simple language.

- Investigate the Turing Machine, a simple but powerful model of clear box computation.
- Provide arguments that make it reasonable to believe that any program is equivalent to a Turing Machine program.
- Show that some problems cannot be solved by Turing Machines and, hence, probably cannot be solved by any programs for any computer.

The Abstract Machine

A poem and a computer program are different, surely, but there are similarities as well. First, a poem and a program result from the author's intentional use of symbols. A poem's intent is to communicate ideas and feelings to the reader; a program's intent is to cause the computer to perform certain actions. When Carl Sandberg wrote "The fog comes/On little cat feet," he obviously didn't intend to imply that a fog bank had identifiable feet. More likely, his intent was to point out to the reader that incoming fog moves in a quiet and stealthy way similar to the way a cat walks. He may also have intended to invoke the connection between a soft, light gray cat and the soft gray nature of fog.

In the same way, a programmer who writes

```
area = height * width
```

may intend that `height` and `width` represent the values of the height and width of a rectangle, and that the resulting area be stored in the container labeled `area`. The computer doesn't "know" the programmer's intended interpretation of these variables, any more than the printed page "knows" the intended interpretation of the movement of a fog bank as catlike. If, for instance, the programmer wrote

```
area = height + width
```

the compiler or interpreter would faithfully translate the line into a series of instructions to be performed, in spite of the fact that the instructions would be incorrect under the programmer's assumptions of what the code was to do.

Poems and programs are not merely collections of symbols; they are produced within a framework of rules for symbol usage. The rules for constructing programs are more restrictive than those for poems, if for no other reason than that people can interpret symbols better than computers can. But the fact remains that rules, whether formal or informal, can be ignored only at the risk of not communicating effectively. The line "The fog creeps in two eggs over easy, coffee, no cream" is little better for its intended purpose than

```
area gets )height width &
```

Finally, we will see that an important aspect of computer science is that programs, like poems, can be *self-referential*. Just as a poem can have itself as its subject, or can talk of the nature of poetry, a program can accept other programs as input, produce other programs as output, or be written to modify itself. We saw just this behavior in Module 6, when we observed that a compiler or interpreter is nothing more than a program that takes a source code program as input and produces an object code program as its output. Indeed, a compiler could take a copy of itself as input and produce a compiled (object) version of itself as output.

In this module, we adopt the approach that *a computer scientist studies The Computer in much the same way that a student of literature studies The Poem,* and we will consider some of the tools and ways of thinking that are involved in this study. Our approach so far has been top-down, from applications to hardware, via design, programming, and program translation. Now that we've seen what programs are and how a computer can be designed to do what a program instructs it to do, we will try to go beyond computers to the nature of computation itself. We will ask what a computer is, in essence; we will ask what *computation* means; and we will see what computers can and cannot do—not just today's computers, but anything that we can imagine as a "computer." In short, the text part of this module is devoted to the big questions about computer science.

■ Metaphor: The Turing Machine

The metaphor for this module is the Turing Machine, a simple imaginary device invented by Alan Turing before there were any such things as computers. The Turing Machine consists of a tape of unlimited length, along with a device that can read symbols on the tape, write new symbols on the tape, and move to adjacent locations on the tape. We will see that this simple machine is powerful enough to embody all that we would consider as "computation," and will serve as the vehicle for our discussion of what computation is all about.

Æ ONLINE

This claim—that the Turing Machine not only is equal in power to any computer available today, but is also powerful enough to perform anything that we would consider to be computation—is strong indeed, and you have every right to be skeptical. In the lab part of this module, we will provide you with a Turing Machine of your own and encourage you to write some programs for this machine to see just how powerful it is.

It shouldn't surprise you that the lab for this module revolves around a program, named ITM, that is a Turing Machine (TM) simulator. ITM allows you to define or read in descriptions of TMs and watch them go through their paces. We will use ITM to demonstrate how these abstract machines work, how they are defined, how they "compute," and how powerful they are.

8.2 TWO WAYS OF THINKING ABOUT PROGRAMS

You said that a computer scientist studies The Computer in much the same way that a student of literature studies The Poem. What is this capitalized "Computer" you're talking about?

First of all, it certainly doesn't have anything to do with a particular technology; we've seen that already. The Analytical Engine was purely mechanical. Though it was never finished (thereby putting it in contention for the first instance of *vaporware*—promised but not delivered—in the history of computer science), the principles of its design were theoretically sound. Modern computers are electronic, but

◆ For example, there's a growing body of research on *photonic* circuits, in which information is carried by light rather than by electricity.

developments today in areas other than electronics might lead to future computers that use an entirely different technology. Just as words can be penciled on paper, graven in stone, printed on a press, or displayed on a video screen, the technology of the device that allows words to take physical form is less important than the notion of writing itself.

So the physical computer we learned about in Module 7 isn't important?

It's important, but for our purposes here we need to talk about an abstract machine that embodies the notion of computability common to all real computers. The notion of an abstract machine shouldn't require too much of a conceptual leap, since every time you write a program, you act as if you're writing a program for an abstract machine. When you write a JavaScript program, you don't need to concern yourself with the fact that your program runs on a machine with a Pentium II central processor, eight megabytes of RAM, a 2 GB hard disk, and a 1.4 M floppy, connected via Ethernet to a local area network. As far as you're concerned, your program can be written for an imaginary JavaScript computer that executes your instructions directly. Figure 8.1 contrasts the image of the imaginary, virtual computer with the real one. We can take a more general example and say, for instance, that a correctly written C program should produce the same results on any computer equipped with a functional C compiler. When we talk about processing information, it is clearly the program—rather than the computer on which the program runs—that is of interest to us.

FIGURE 8.1
Programming a virtual machine

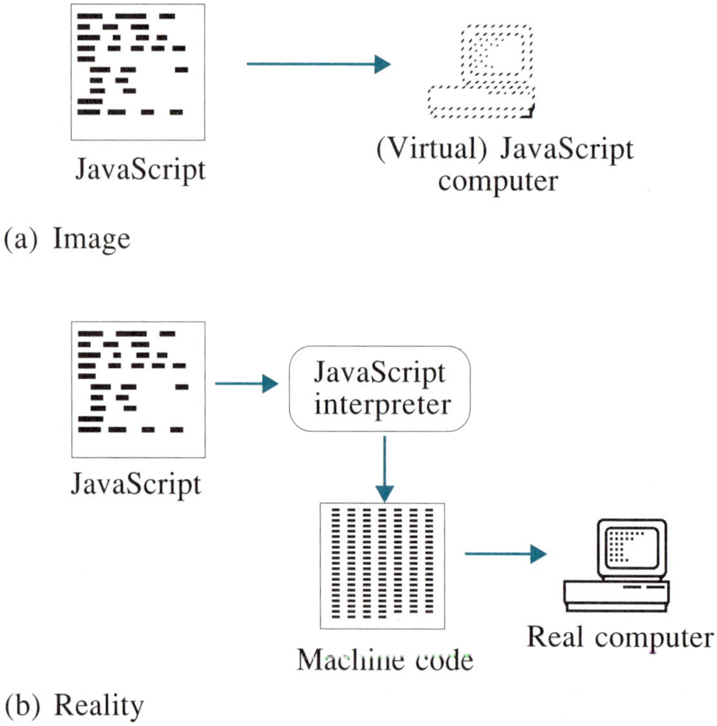

I'll accept the idea that the program is the important notion, but that just substitutes one question for another. What is a program?

There are two answers. We'll first take a black box approach. A program processes data. In essence, a program is a rule (perhaps a very complicated rule) that describes how input data are transformed to output data. For our purposes, we'll define data as equivalent to a binary string. This relieves us of having to deal with the question of meaning. The binary string 010000110100000101000010 is data with no particular meaning. We could interpret it as the string "CAB" if we think of it as the ASCII codes (in binary) for the three letters; or we could interpret it as the binary representation of the integer 4,407,618; or we could even interpret it as part of a picture, where the ones represent dark squares, and the zeros white:

The meaning of the data, if any, lies in the encoding scheme we adopt to interpret the string—but that's our problem, not the program's.

One of the reasons we adopt this approach is that we want to consider all programs, not just those that are correctly written to perform some well-defined task that humans understand. Our first definition is general enough to allow such a broad interpretation:

> A *program* is a matching from the set of all possible finite binary (input) strings to some members of the set of all finite (binary) output strings.

◆ In technical terms, a program may be regarded as a *partial function* on the set of all finite strings of zeros and ones.

In this view, we don't care at all what happens "inside" a program. All that's of interest to us is that for each binary input, a program does one of two things: (1) It eventually halts on the input string, producing no more output, in which case we say that the program matches that input with whatever output (if any) it produces, or (2) the program produces output forever, in which case we say that there is no string that the program matches to that input.

Alternatively, a given program might not run correctly with all possible inputs. Our black box definition takes care of that, too. If a program is written so that it runs correctly only on inputs of three binary digits, say, and we give it 01 as input, the program might "hang up," waiting forever for the third input. In that case, its output would just be the empty string, consisting of no zeros or ones at all. In other words, our definition not only includes all possible programs, it also includes all possible actions of these programs, both "correct" and "incorrect." (Figure 8.2 illustrates this matching process.)

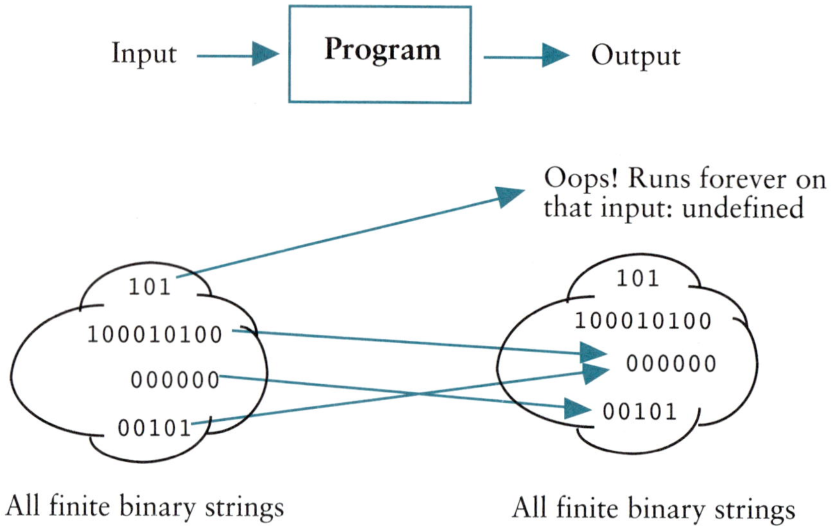

FIGURE 8.2 *Describing a program as a matching of input strings to output strings*

The Turing Machine

That's not a very satisfying answer, on two counts. First, do you mean that every *matching of inputs to outputs is a program? Second, your definition is way too abstract—sure, a program associates an output string with every input string, but shouldn't we be concerned at all about how that association is performed?*

You're right on both counts. We're not claiming that every possible input/output matching is a program. In fact, we'll show shortly that that's not the case at all: There are matchings that cannot be realized by programs. Now it's our turn to ask a question: If you're not happy with the definition of a program as a function from binary strings to binary strings, what definition of program would make you happy?

I suppose it would have to do with functionality—we need to settle on what a program can do internally.

OK. But we don't want to get hung up on details like the hardware of any particular machine or whether we're talking about a functional or object-oriented programming language.

Ah. So we need a simple model that's still sufficiently powerful to perform everything we mean when we talk about computation.

Congratulations! You've hit upon the heart of the matter. We want a simple model of computation. We could equally well look at the abstract notion of *computation* from the point of view of what we do with the computers with which we're familiar. Modern computers, though, with their registers, busses, random access memories, and the like, are just too complicated to be of any theoretical use to us.

The answer we seek lies in a 1936 paper by Alan Turing.[1] In this paper, Turing showed that what we generally mean by "computation" could be satisfied by a simple, abstract machine, such as the one diagrammed in Figure 8.3, that consisted of the following:

1. A *tape* of discrete cells and unlimited length, along with
2. A device with a finite number of *states* that could
   a) Read one symbol from the tape, and, based on that symbol and the current state,
   b) Write another symbol in place of the current symbol,
   c) Change the current state, and
   d) Move left or right on the tape.

The tape is used for recording input and output, one symbol (0, 1, or blank) per cell. Initially, the string to serve as input to our computation is recorded in the leftmost cells of the tape, and the read/write head is positioned at the leftmost tape cell.

The control device embodies the machine's program. It uses a collection of rules, its notion of "state," and the contents of the tape to determine how to process the input symbols. Each rule is a statement of the form "In state *n,* if the head is reading symbol *x,* write symbol *y,* move left or right one cell on the tape, and change the state to *m.*" One of the states is singled out as the *initial state,* the state in which the machine regards itself as being when the computation begins. Such a machine is referred to as *Turing Machine* (or TM, for short).

Sounds like a pretty simple machine. . . . You'll have to convince me that it can accomplish everything I call computation.

FIGURE 8.3
A Turing Machine

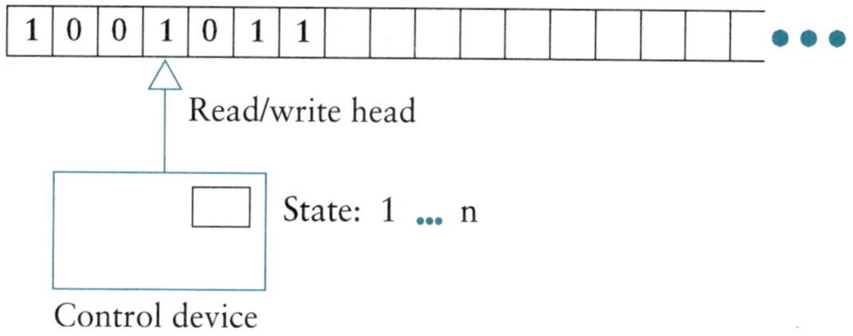

[1] The 1930s was a significant decade for theoretical computer science. Not only did Turing publish his paper on computability, but the mathematician Kurt Gödel, using a "diagonalization" argument similar to one you'll see later, demonstrated that there are theorems in arithmetic that can be stated but cannot be proved to be false or true.

OK, let's try. Here are the rules for a particular TM with five states and initial state 1 (we'll always use state 1 as the initial state):

Present State	Present Symbol	Write	Move	New State
1	0	0	Right	2
2	0	0	Right	3
2	1	1	Right	2
3	0	blank	Left	5
3	1	0	Left	4
4	0	1	Right	2

We could simplify this table by writing each row within parentheses, so the TM program would have statements (1, 0, 0, R, 2), (2, 0, 0, R, 3), (2, 1, 1, R, 2), (3, 0, b, L, 5), (3, 1, 0, L, 4), and (4, 0, 1, R, 2).

Although it is not obvious at first, this TM accomplishes integer addition, if we interpret the input in a particular way. We will decide that the input will represent the numbers to be added in *unary* notation—in other words, that n will be represented as n consecutive 1s. Suppose we agree that the integers n and m are represented on the tape, from left to right, as 0, followed by n 1s, followed by 0, then m 1s, followed by 0, so that the pair of integers (1, 2) would be represented on the tape as 010110. Then, given such an input, this TM will leave the tape with an output of 0, followed by $n + m$ 1s, followed by 0. Using our example input 010110, and writing the present state below the symbol being read, the TM's action would be as follows:

Tape	State	
0 1 0 1 1 0	1	*Start: Go right.*
0 **1** 0 1 1 0	2	*Scan past 1s.*
0 1 **0** 1 1 0	2	*End of first string; go to next.*
0 1 0 **1** 1 0	3	*Change 1 to 0; go back.*
0 1 **0** 0 1 0	4	*Copy the 1; return to second string.*
0 1 1 **0** 1 0	2	*End of first string; go to next.*
0 1 1 0 **1** 0	3	*Change 1 to 0; go back.*
0 1 1 **0** 0 0	4	*Copy the 1; return to second string.*
0 1 1 1 **0** 0	2	*End of first string; go to next.*
0 1 1 1 0 **0**	3	*Oops! No second string. Erase last 0.*
0 1 1 1 **0**	5	*Halt—no further moves possible.*

We could make the description of this sample TM easier to understand if we include comments describing the intended interpretation of every statement.

```
(1, 0, 0, R, 2)  —move right, past the first 0
(2, 0, 0, R, 3)  —we've come to the end of a string of 1s
(2, 1, 1, R, 2)  —move right past all the 1s
(3, 0, b, L, 5)  —we've moved past the last 1—done
(3, 1, 0, L, 4)  —just hit the second string of 1s; shift the 0
(4, 0, 1, R, 2)  —finish shifting the 0, and go back to state 2
```

Notice that a TM "program" need not include rules for every state/symbol combination. If a TM encounters a state/symbol combination for which no rule is defined, we imagine the machine simply halts without making any further moves, as it did in the example when it reached state 5, reading a zero.

◆ Speed of operations in a Turing machine has no meaning. Since a TM is an imaginary construct, we can imagine it performing its operations as fast as we wish.

The backing-and-filling movement of our sample machine is characteristic of TM programs. We didn't say that TM computations were efficient, but we do claim that they are effective—they work, however slowly. The lab part of this module will explore some of the other computational capacities of the TM model. A TM can do more than just add numbers: When programmed with suitable rules it can subtract, multiply, divide, compute logarithms and powers, and compare two data elements for equality or size. A TM can move information from one place on the tape to another, set aside locations to act as memory, and, though we can't prove it here, a TM can perform any operation that contemporary computers can perform.

Only "contemporary computers"?

No. Turing Machines are actually more powerful than any piece of hardware that could be built. Since there are no restrictions on the length of a TM's tape (one of the beauties of abstraction!), we can store more information in a TM than we can with any real computer that we can possibly build. That's not important to us here, though, since you recall that we quite purposely stepped beyond hardware at the very beginning of this discussion. Remember, we are concerned with programs, not hardware. We are interested in achieving the functionality of the imaginary machines for which we write our programs, that is, the virtual JavaScript machine or Pascal machine, or FORTRAN or LISP or Ada machine. The definitions of programming languages almost never mention the kind of machine on which they will run, so for our purposes, we can think of these virtual machines as being as unlimited as the Turing Machine is. Pick your favorite language, and we can prove that any program in that language can be simulated by a TM, in the sense that the TM will produce the same input/output matching that your program does. Thus, we have the basis for another definition:

> **Clear Box Definition** When we talk about programs, it is sufficient to talk about Turing Machines, since everything you can do with a program you can also do with a Turing Machine.

This makes life much easier for the theorist—TMs function as the *lingua franca* of programming. If we want to show that a property is true for all programs, it is sufficient to show that that property is true for Turing Machines. In some sense, the Turing Machine is a minimal device that still contains the full functionality of what we call computers.

That's still not very satisfying. You're trying to get a handle on the nature of computation by looking at contemporary computers and languages. Although I can't describe what they would be like, I can imagine that the intelligent artichokes of Planet X might have developed machines that operate on conceptual principles that are completely different from those of our computers. What happens to your abstract framework then?

Nothing at all, at least if you believe our third definition:

> **Optimistic Clear Box Definition** *Any* reasonable model of computability is equivalent to "computability by Turing Machines."

The intelligent artichokes of Planet X may have machines that operate on principles we never dreamed of, but, by this definition (more commonly referred to as the *Church-Turing thesis,* after its creators), if we could call what their machines can do "computing," then we could simulate the action of their machines by Turing Machines.

Why should I believe the Church-Turing thesis? Can you prove it?

No. That's why it's called a thesis, rather than a theorem. To prove it, we'd have to agree once and for all what constitutes a "reasonable" notion of computability. Certainly, we would agree that whatever computability means, it must at least include the ability to do arithmetic calculations. Beyond that, deciding what to include becomes a rather murky question. During the early part of this century, logicians such as Church, Post, and Turing worked long and hard to provide a theoretical framework for what the nature of computation was. They came up with several definitions, each of which seemed quite general and powerful, and each of which took very different forms from the others. In all cases, it was eventually shown that anything "computable" by their definitions was computable by Turing Machines.

The Church-Turing thesis stemmed from a growing conviction that the equivalence of these definitions to Turing computability was not a fluke, but rather a fact. The Church-Turing thesis was, in essence, a confident challenge: "If you come up with a definition of what computability means, and if we are content that your definition includes all the things that we customarily call computations, then we'd be willing to bet that your definition includes only those things computable by Turing Machines."

LAB 8.1

Welcome to ITM

The first thing to notice about ITM is that it represents all of the components of a Turing Machine (TM). The Current Tape is displayed horizontally near the top of the program window, with an arrow beneath it indicating the current position of the scanning head. The large scrollable field contains rules, one per line, of the TM being simulated. There are also display fields for the Start State of the current machine, the Current State of the machine, and the Rule Used to make the previous move. The panel at the bottom of the program window provides one set of buttons for the basic control of the machine (you can step through a TM or play it through to completion, as well as stop it and reset it), and another to allow you to open (read in) and save (write out) the descriptions.

1. ITM comes preloaded with our first TM description, named "TM1".

2. Run TM1 to completion by clicking on the Play button. Compare the Original Tape to the Current Tape. Do you see a pattern?

3. Click the Reset button to reset the simulator, and run TM1 to completion again, this time by stepping through the rules one at a time.

You may have enjoyed watching TM1 do its thing, but unless you know something about how TM1 was defined, the relation between the original and final tapes may be a mystery. For the first few TMs that you'll deal with, we'll provide you with this information.

The start state of TM1, as you saw, was 1. Its alphabet is the set of symbols 0, 1, and b (which we use to stand for blank). The required format for the input tape is any combination of zeros and ones, followed by a single !, followed by a series of b's of equal (or greater) length to the leading zeros and ones. The result? TM1 makes a copy of the zero-and-one portion of its tape at another location on the tape, just as a modern computer might move information from one memory location to another.

4. Now open the TM described in file "TM2."

5. Run TM2 to completion using the Play button.

Compare the final version of the tape with the original tape. Do you see a pattern here? If you do, you're pretty good! In order to understand the processing accomplished by TM2 you need to know more than its alphabet, start state, and tape format. You need to know that the original tape is intended (by its authors) to represent the integer 3. That is, TM2 uses strings of ones to represent positive integers. On input 111b it produces tape 1111; on input 1111b it produces 11111; . . . now do you see the pattern? TM2 adds 1 to a positive integer.

Serial Numbers for Programs

OK. I'm willing to accept for the time being that computability by what I call "programs" is the same as computability by Turing Machines, but where does that leave us? What do we gain by equating programs and Turing Machines?

In a word, simplicity. For example, one thing it allows us to do is make a list of all possible TMs, and hence, by the Church-Turing thesis, all possible programs. This by itself is no mean feat. Since TMs are uniquely described by their rules, we can associate with each TM a unique "serial number," if you will, constructed from a description of its rules.

Each rule is a statement of the same general format, involving five variables: "If the machine is in state *i*, reading tape symbol *j*, then write symbol *k*, move in direction *l*, and change the state to *m*." We code each rule by representing the current state in unary, using zeros, so state *n* will be represented by *n* zeros. Also, we encode the tape symbol 0 by 0, symbol 1 by 00, and *blank* by 000. Direction *left* we code by 0, and direction *right* we represent by the integer 00. We represent the rule (*i*, *j*, *k*, *l*, *m*) by the binary string

◆ This is just one of many ways to encode TMs. You may want to experiment with a different scheme of your own.

0 . . . 0	1	0 . . . 0	1	0 . . . 0	1	0 . . . 0	1	0 . . . 0
i times		*j* times		*k* times		*l* times		*m* times

so that the rule "In state 3, reading 1, write blank, move left, and change state to 2" would correspond to the 5-tuple (3, 1, b, L, 2) and thence to the binary string 000100100010100.

Now we can code an entire TM by listing its move codes, separated by pairs of ones, and enclosed on both ends by three ones:

`111` first move code `11` second move code `11 ... 11` last move code `111`

For example, the simple TM that puts a zero after its input (remember, we always begin a TM with its input written on the left end of the tape) has the following program:

Present State	Present Symbol	Write	Move	New State
1	0	0	Right	1
1	1	1	Right	1
1	blank	0	Right	2

and has the move 5-tuples (1, 0, 0, R, 1), (1, 1, 1, R, 1), and (1, b, 0, R, 2), and so would be assigned the serial number

`111 0101010010 11 010010010010 11 0100010100100 111`

or, if we swapped the order of the first and third rules,

`111 0100010100100 11 010010010010 11 0101010010 111`

We've put spaces in the binary string to make it easier to read; they wouldn't actually be part of the serial number. If binary strings give you the willies, we could convert each TM serial number to decimal, so the simple TM in the first coding above would have the rather massive serial number 32,241,552,672,039.

◆ If you're diligent, you might check this.

This notion of assigning a binary string to a Turing Machine is not too unusual; in fact, you've seen something very much like it already. Remember, we can compile a program in Pascal, say, to produce an output in machine language for some computer. But you've already seen that we can regard a machine language program as nothing but a collection of zeros and ones. All we have to do is take care of the details of how to separate statements, and we have a single (very long) string of zeros and ones that encodes our Pascal source code program. In encoding Turing Machines, all we're doing is simplifying our model by using a simple language and doing the compiling ourselves, as it were (see Figure 8.4).

Notice that we can reconstruct any TM from its serial number. We convert the number to a binary string, if it's not already, then observe that the move codes are separated by double ones, and within the move codes, the values of *i, j, k, l,* and *m* are separated by single ones. We then count zeros to obtain the individual components of the move codes, and we're done. Notice also that there are many numbers that couldn't possibly be serial numbers for TMs, just as there are many nine-digit numbers that are not legal Social Security numbers. For instance, any binary number that doesn't begin and end with 111 could not be a legal serial number. Indeed, the smallest legal TM serial number is 63, which in binary is 111111. This is the serial number for the TM with no moves—on any input, it simply sits there and does nothing. Looked at as a matching between input and output strings, this is the identity function, where the output is just the input.

Well, that's moderately interesting, I'll admit. There's a certain tidiness in being able to encode all possible Turing Machines, but I must confess that the association of a serial number with every TM seems to be more of a curiosity than anything else. Does this TM encoding have any use?

Two uses, in fact. First, the ability to encode Turing Machines as binary strings allows us to build a TM that accepts these coded descriptions as input. Although it would take us too long to prove here, it is possible to build a *Universal Turing Machine* (UTM), which, when given the description of a TM along with an input

FIGURE 8.4
Encoding Turing Machines as binary strings

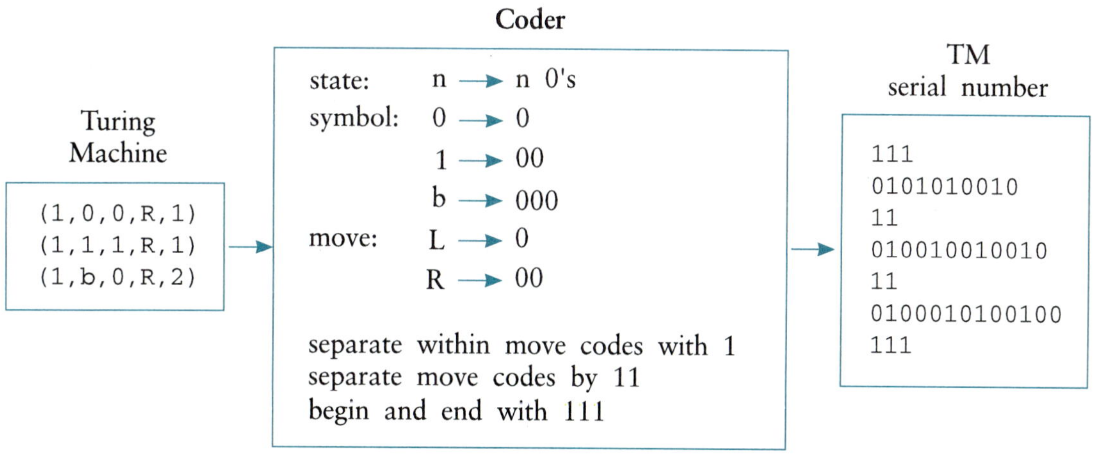

for that machine, simulates the action of the coded machine, reading, writing, and moving along the tape just as if it were the original machine. In a sense, the TMs we have seen so far are like the old ENIAC machine, which had to be rewired for each new task. A UTM is more like a modern computer in that it interprets a description of a TM program and then performs the tasks that the program described.

The second use that arises from this encoding is really the heart of this module. If we extend the notion of encoding the objects we're working with, we can combine the definitions of programs as (1) functions on binary strings and as (2) Turing Machines to prove what you may have felt all along—that there are some things that programs simply can't do.

We begin by encoding all finite binary strings as integers, in much the same way that we encoded TMs by integers. Make a list of all possible binary strings, initially in order of length and then by numeric order within collections of strings of equal length, as follows:

String	Code
empty string	1
0	2
1	3
00	4
01	5
10	6
11	7
000	8
001	9
010	10

In this coding, *every* binary string corresponds to a unique positive integer, and any positive integer encodes a unique string. In fact, the rule for this code is simple to state: A binary string of length n that is equal in binary to the number b has code $2^n + b$. For example, the string 001001 has length 6 and is the binary representation of the number 9, so its code would be 26 + 9 = 73 (as illustrated in Figure 8.5), which you could easily verify by continuing the table. Similarly, the string 0100001101000000101000010, which we earlier interpreted three ways, would have code 21,184,834.

FIGURE 8.5
Finding the code of a binary string

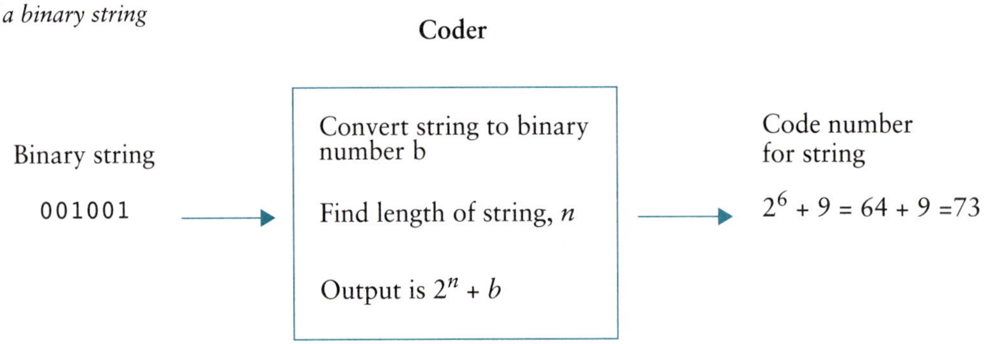

LAB 8.2

What's My Line?

Below are the descriptions of four other TMs, cleverly disguised as files "TM3," "TM4," TM5," and "TM6." Your task is to experiment with each in the interest of guessing its purpose.

1. Run each TM to completion on a variety of input tapes (just make sure the tapes conform to the prescribed format). Write down the original tape and its corresponding final tape. Then write English descriptions of what information its original tape describes, and what processing is accomplished by its rules. For TMs 5 and 6, you should also try to explain what the symbols T, F, N, and P stand for.

Machine	Start State	Alphabet	Tape Format
TM3	1	1, !, b	Two strings of 1s, separated by !
TM4	1	1, 0, b	Two strings of 1s, separated by !, followed by a b
TM5	1	1, b, T, F	A string of 1s, followed by a b
TM6	1	0, 1, b, N, P	Any string of 0s and 1s, followed by a b

Review Questions

1. What do we mean by *virtual machine*? Give a similar situation outside computer science, in which what you think you are seeing or doing is not actually what you are seeing or doing.

2. In the black box definition of a program, why do we say that some input strings may not match any output strings? Can an input string match two or more output strings? Is every output string matched to some input string, in general? Explain.

3. Which definition includes more objects: the black box or the clear box? Which is the correct definition of *program*?

8.3 IMPOSSIBLE PROGRAMS

Fine—you can make a list of all TMs and you can make a list of all binary strings. So what?

The ability to make these two lists allows us to do something quite remarkable. Imagine that we have a list of all possible TMs, arranged in increasing order of their serial numbers. We'll write this list as M_1, M_2, M_3, ... In particular, M_1 is the TM with code 63 (111111 in binary), which has no moves; M_2, with code 111010101010111 (30,039 in decimal), is the TM that has one "statement" (1, 0, 0, L, 1), since that's the next-largest TM code.

M_2 is simple enough to describe—if the input tape begins with a 0, this TM writes a 0 and then "falls off" the left end of the tape, thereby halting. Since there is no move description to cover any other input tape, the TM halts immediately on all other inputs. In other words, no matter what the input is, M_2 will (quickly) halt and leave its tape unchanged. As a black box, M_2 is just the identity function that matches each input string to itself. Many TMs in our list are equally uninteresting: Out of the first twelve, only M_4 and M_5 modify their tapes at all.

If you accept the Church-Turing thesis, then *everything* you consider to be a program is somewhere in this list (along with many "nonprograms" that produce infinite output, such as (1, 0, 0, R, 1), (1, 1, 0, R, 1), (1, b, 0, R, 1), which writes a never-ending string of zeros on its tape). Now we'll construct an input/output matching function P from our list of TMs. P will match every finite string of zeros and ones to either '0' or the blank string by the following rules. For each positive integer n:

1. Find the binary string s_n whose code is n.
2. Feed s_n as input to machine M_n and look at the output.
   a) If M_n produces no output (that is, if the tape is blank when the TM stops), define $P(s_n)$ to be the symbol 0.
   b) If M_n produces any output, including infinite output, define $P(s_n)$ to be the empty string.

In Figure 8.6 we demonstrate the process we use to create the matching P.

◆ We called the matching *P* because it's *perverse*, by design.

The important thing to realize is that we are constructing the input/output matching P that is by definition *different* from that of every other machine. M_1 cannot produce the matching given by P, since M_1 acts differently from P on input s_1. M_2 cannot produce the matching given by P, since M_2 acts differently from P on input s_2. In fact, *no* TM in the list produces the input/output matching described by

FIGURE 8.6
Generating an input/output matching

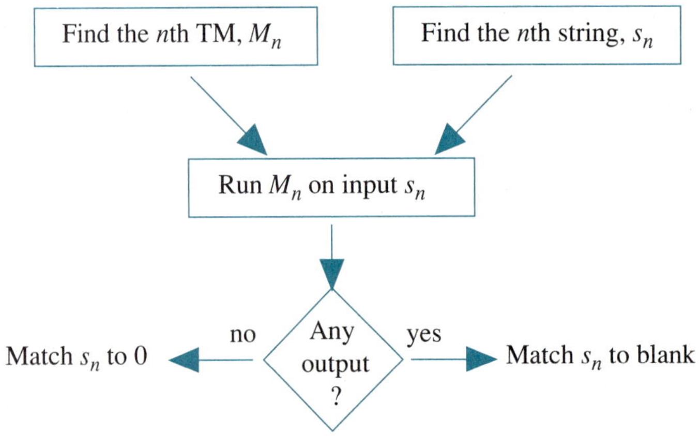

P, because we designed *P* for just that purpose. Since the TM serial number for every program is somewhere in the list, we must conclude that no possible program can produce the input/output matching described by *P*. In simple terms:

> There is at least one function from input strings to corresponding output strings that cannot be computed by any program at all. In other words, every clear box program (TM) is a black box program (matching), but there are black box programs (like *P*) that are not clear box programs.

◆ In mathematical terms, there is a *countable infinity* of all TMs, but an *uncountable infinity* of input/output matchings.

The situation is even bleaker than that, though. Our argument was based on the fact (which surprises almost everyone the first time they see it) that infinity comes in different sizes. Although there are infinitely many possible programs, and infinitely many different ways of matching inputs to outputs, the infinity of possible matchings is vastly larger than the infinity of possible programs. Stated another way,

> A negligibly small proportion of all possible input/output matchings can be realized by Turing Machines.

Computers cannot only not do everything; when we think of computers and their programs as matching outputs to inputs, they can hardly do anything at all. Or, if you will, there just aren't enough programs to produce all possible input/output matchings.

That's very impressive, but isn't this example somewhat contrived? There's no possible way you could describe what the function P *is without describing every TM in your list, running each on its associated input string and looking at the results. Anyhow, the fact that there are many things that we cannot compute is of no real importance to us as long as we can compute the things we want to compute.*

◆ The matching *P* is pretty boring. $P(s_1) = 0$, but after that, $P(s_n)$ is the empty string until some $n > 2317$.

Right and wrong. You are correct that there is no easy way to describe what *P* does. We could start the process by recalling that the lowest-numbered TM, M_1, with serial number 63, is the identity machine. M_1 gives empty output on empty input, and so *P* would pair the empty input to the output '0.' With some more work, we could find the next-lowest-numbered TM and run it on '0' (the string with code 2), and so on, but it appears that while we know that *P* exists, it would take us infinitely long to tell what it is.

That is exactly as it should be. Suppose we discovered some "shortcut" way to determine what *P* is, such as "*P* produces output '0' precisely when the input has code that is divisible by 3." In that case, we could make up a program to apply the shortcut rule to input strings, thereby producing a program that acts like *P*. But that would contradict our finding that there is no program that acts like *P*. In other words, the fact that we have proved there is no program that acts like *P* guarantees that there is no effective shortcut to describing *P*. *P* would take infinitely long to describe precisely because we designed it that way.

Where you go wrong, though, is in thinking that the only instances of problems that we cannot solve by computers are peculiar ones like the example we just used. In fact, there is a very simple example of a problem we would very much like to solve, but cannot. This problem even sounds like it could be solved by a computer program, unlike the problems of prejudice or world hunger, which seem too ill posed and fuzzy to be amenable to computer solution. We could have given you that former problem at the start, but we needed to introduce the notion of encoding first.

LAB 8.3

Incompleteness and Ambiguity

As you can imagine, the cryptic nature of how we describe TMs makes it easy to define one incorrectly. It is one thing if a set of rules doesn't produce the desired result. In such a case, ITM will simply follow the rules to an incorrect conclusion. There are, though, ways to define a TM so that it confuses our simulator and simply terminates the simulation. Let's examine three of them here. For each exercise, write down the TM that you define, enter and run it in ITM, and answer the question posed. Your machines need not address any "real" problem other than that of illustrating the situation described.

1. Define a TM that demonstrates what happens when ITM runs a TM that contains ambiguous rules (that is, more than one rule for a given input symbol/state pair).
2. Define a TM that demonstrates what happens when ITM runs a TM that directs it to move off the left edge of the tape.
3. Define a TM that demonstrates what happens when ITM runs a TM with an incomplete rule base (for example, the rules of the TM direct the simulator to a particular state, and there are no rules describing what it should do in that state).

The Halting Problem

Consider this problem: A perennial error that programmers face is described as an *infinite loop*. Here's a simple JavaScript example:

```
i = 1
while (i <= 10){
  data[i] = 2 * i + 1
}
```

The programmer goofed here: There's no way out of this loop. Perhaps a statement was omitted, or perhaps the loop condition was mistyped. We'll never know, but it's clear that if the program ever gets to this segment, it'll never leave. It would be very nice to have some sort of diagnostic program that takes as its input (1) the listing of this or any other program, along with (2) a sample input for that program, and answers either "Your program will never halt on this input" or "Your program will eventually halt on this input." Believe us, a program that could do that would make its creator wealthy beyond any dreams of avarice—there's not a professional programmer alive who couldn't benefit from such an application. Why hasn't someone written it, then?

> *Because it's impossible? You'll have to do a lot more convincing before I'll believe you can prove that. I'd be perfectly willing to accept the fact that such a program doesn't exist because it's tricky to write, but because it absolutely can't be written? That's another matter entirely.*

It's true, though. We can prove it to you, and we will, for two reasons. First, because we want to give an example of a reasonable-sounding problem for which there is *provably* no program to solve it, and second, for purely aesthetic reasons. The proof, while a bit tricky, is so pretty that it would be a shame not to share it with you.

◆ In detective novels, this technique takes the following form: "If we assume that the butler did it, we must then conclude that he had to have been in two places at the same time. Therefore, the butler is innocent."

We'll adopt a common proof technique, known as *proof by contradiction.* In such a proof, you want to show that something, call it Q, cannot happen. You begin by supposing that Q can happen, and then argue to a conclusion that is patently false, like $2 + 2 = 5$. If the steps of your argument are valid, but you still reach a false conclusion, then the only thing that could have led you to that false conclusion is your original assumption, that Q could have ever been true. Since your original assumption must have been false, the only possible state of affairs is that Q could never happen in the first place.

So, let's assume that we could somehow make a halt-testing program, H. The specifications of this program are as follows:

1. H takes as its input
   a) A suitably encoded description of a program P (in binary, say)
   b) A binary string s denoting an input
2. For any pair (P, s) as described in item 1, H eventually halts and answers
   a) "yes," if P will eventually halt on input s,
   b) "no," if P would run forever on input s.

There are two important properties of H that deserve notice:

- *Property 1:* We require that H itself will always halt. That means we couldn't design H as a compiler that just runs P on s. Such a scheme would always give a correct answer if P halted on s, but we'd have to wait forever to get an answer if P ran forever on s—we could never know, in other words, if P halted or not on s.
- *Property 2:* We want H to work correctly—that is, we want H to give the right answer for *every* program/input pair, even if the input were something peculiar that P would never expect to get in the normal course of affairs. After all, operators make mistakes entering data, and we'd like to be able to test P on all kinds of input, good and bad.

Summing up, we assume that H is designed so that it will halt and provide an answer, no matter what the strings P and s are. Figure 8.7 is a graphic description of H.

Now we're ready to begin. Assuming that we have such a program H, we'll use H to construct another program, H'. H' will use H as a subroutine, as follows:

1. H' will take a single binary string x as input.
2. H' will first make a copy of x and will send x twice to H: once as P, and once for s. That is, x will serve as both the program and input for H.
3. Depending on the answer returned from H, H' will do one of two things:
   a) If the answer returned from H is "yes" (indicating that program x will indeed halt on input x), then H' will deliberately go into an infinite loop and run forever.
   b) If the answer from H is "no" (program x will run forever on input x), then H' will stop immediately.

Figure 8.8 shows H'.

Now, H' is a pretty peculiar object, but it certainly is a program, as long as H is a program, too. What does it do? If x is the encoding of a program, the subroutine H determines whether program x will halt when given its own description as input. There's nothing at all wrong with giving a program its own description to work on—we could use a word processor to edit a copy of its own code for publication purposes, for example.

So, if x is an encoding of a program, H' is designed to halt if program x will run forever on its own description, and to run forever if program x will eventually halt on its own description. That bears repeating:

> H', when given an encoding of a program, x, will halt if and only if program x will *not* halt when given its own encoding as input.

FIGURE 8.7
The halt-testing program H

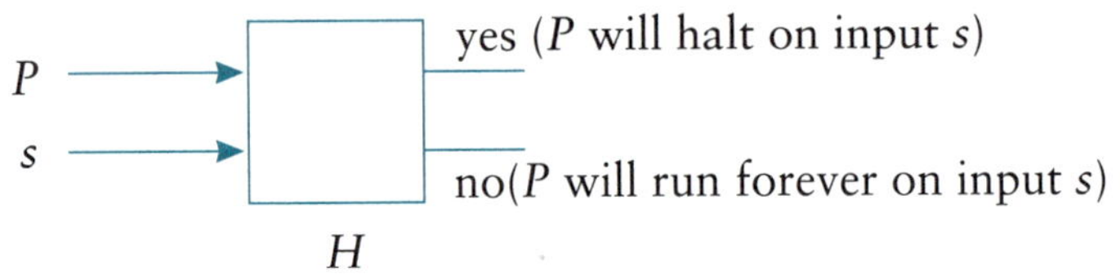

FIGURE 8.8
Program H'

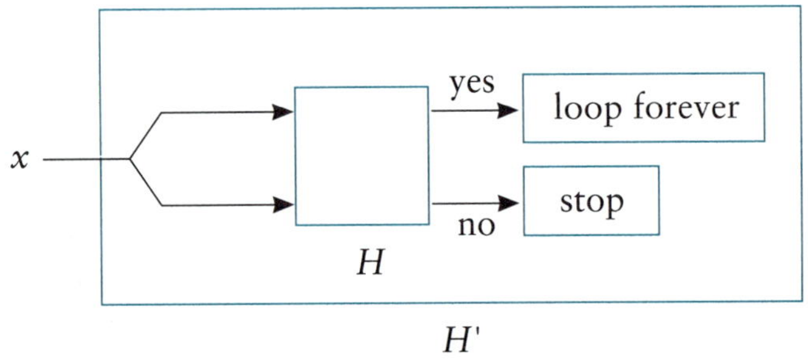

Now, what happens when we give H' its own description? Think about it, replacing x in the boxed sentence with H'. Take your time, we'll wait.

◆ ◆ ◆

Got it? The conclusion is that we have built a program H' that will halt when given its own description if and only if it will *not* halt when given its own description! In other words, we have a program that, for at least one input, will halt only if it never halts, and will run forever only if it eventually halts. Well, that can't possibly be correct—that's as bad as saying "I'll pass this course if and only if I fail."

We've reached the contradiction we promised at the beginning. Since H' acts so bizarrely, it can't possibly be a program, but the only thing that could stand in the way of its being a program is our assumption that we could have built its subroutine H in the first place. We have to conclude that there is no possible program that will do what H does. In other words, H is one of the possible black box matchings, but we can never write a clear box TM program to do what we want H to do.

Don't feel bad if you're confused over what just went on. This argument is probably as subtle as any you've seen recently, and almost everyone has trouble with it the first time out. If you're still confused, take the time to look over the argument again—it's well worth the effort. The important thing to realize is that there are reasonable-sounding problems that can never be solved by programs.

The original problem that H was designed to solve is known as the *Halting Problem*. In technical terms, what we have just done is to prove that there is no effective procedure (that is, program) that will solve the Halting Problem.

I'm almost afraid to ask—is the Halting Problem the only interesting one for which there is no effective procedure?

Nope. In fact, there are many related problems that are undecidable, that is, for which we cannot write a program that answers all possible instances. We'll finish with a few samples, just to give you the flavor.

1. Given a program P and a string x, will P ever write x as part of its output?
2. Given programs P and Q, are P and Q equivalent in the sense that for every input s, P and Q started on s will have the same output?
3. Given P and s as usual, and a state n of P, will P started on s ever be in state n?
4. Given a program P, will P halt on all possible inputs?
5. Given a program P, will P halt when started on a blank tape?
6. Given a suitably encoded description of what P should do, will P actually act as described?

Basically, it is very difficult to come up with decision procedures for any interesting questions about programs. In fact, there is an honest-to-gosh theorem, due to H. G.

◆ That is to say, self-referentiality is almost always problematic for programs.

Rice, that states, in our terms, "Any nontrivial property of programs is undecidable." In this theorem *nontrivial* has a somewhat complicated technical definition, but you can almost capture the truth of the theorem if you use the customary definition of the term. You can write programs to do many things, but you can't do everything with computers—in particular, it is very hard to find programs that can answer questions about programs.

Undecidable problems are not restricted to problems about programs, either. There are many undecidable problems in other areas, such as mathematics and game playing. Consider the following:

◆ More generally, we can't write a program that can determine whether an arbitrary mathematical statement is true or false. Unfortunately for students, we'll never be able to mechanize all of mathematics.

1. Given a collection of *Diophantine equations,* that is, polynomial equations to be solved in integers, such as

$$xy - 3x^2z + 62xyz = 14, \quad 13xy^5 + y - x^3z = 9$$

find a solution (or even just tell whether there is a solution).

2. Given a collection of square tiles with colored sides, can these tiles be used to cover the plane, subject to the restriction that tiles with a common edge must have matching colors along those edges? You are not allowed to rotate the tiles. (Refer to Figure 8.9.)

The last two problems point out an important idea about undecidable problems, or about using programs to solve problems in general. When we say that a problem can (or cannot) be solved by a program, we mean that there is (or is not) a program that gives the correct solution for any instance of the problem. The tiling problem does not ask you to write a program for a specific set of tiles, but rather requires that you find a program that will allow you to send it as input any possible set of tiles, and receive as output the correct answer. In essence, you probably could answer the problem for any particular (reasonably small) set of tiles, but your solutions would be ad hoc—tailored to the specific set you were given, rather than general and applicable to all sets of tiles.

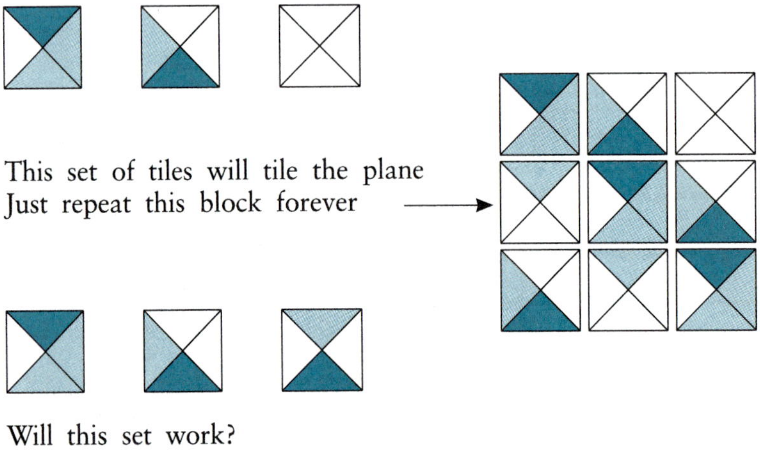

FIGURE 8.9
Tiling the plane: An undecidable problem

LAB 8.4

Rolling Your Own

In all the previous lab exercises for this module we have provided either the rules, tapes, or descriptions of the TMs with which you were to work. Here we leave you to your own creative devices, to write your own TMs from scratch. You can define what symbols will appear on your tape and how the tape will be formatted. You can write the rules for processing the symbols. Most important, you can use ITM to test your TMs.

1. Write and test a TM to clear a tape, setting it all to blanks.
2. Write and test a TM that performs "proper integer subtraction" (also called *monus*). In monus, $m - n$ is like normal subtraction, except when $n > m$, in which case $m - n = 0$.
3. Write and test a TM that performs integer multiplication.

Review Questions

1. Give two reasons why encodings of Turing Machines are useful.
2. Why is the argument in which we show that the matching P cannot correspond to any TM called a "diagonalization" argument?
3. What is the Halting Problem? Why is it important?

8.4 EXERCISES

1. The string 1110010010100101001011100100101 0001 represents a rectangular picture, as specified in the text. What familiar object is pictured?
2. Write the move description for a TM that blanks its tape and halts after replacing every zero or one with a blank. Remember that initially all the nonblank characters are in consecutive cells at the left end of the tape.
3. In computing the serial numbers of Turing Machines, why did we begin and end with 111? Could we have left the 1s off and still had the correspondence between integers and TMs that we desired?
4. Suppose that the tape of a TM initially contained 0 at the far left, followed by the binary representation of the integer n. Assume that the start

state was state 1. What would be the action of the following TM?

Present State	Present Symbol	Write	Move	New State
1	0	0	Right	2
2	0	0	Right	3
2	1	1	Right	2
3	0	blank	Left	5
3	1	0	Left	4
4	0	1	Right	2

5. What is the encoding for the TM of Exercise 4? Only masochists need express their answer as a decimal number.

6. Design a TM that appends 0 to the *left* of its input. [*Hint:* The addition TM in the text contains a helpful idea.]

7. Describe the action of the TM with the following serial number, again assuming that state 1 was the start state.

```
11101010010010110100101001011010001001010011 1
```

8. M_4, the first TM that changes its input tape (some of the time), has code 111010010101 0111. What does M_4 do, and under what conditions will it modify its input?

9. In the text, you saw the rule for finding the code of a binary string. How would you reverse this process, finding the string that has code n? What string has code 467?

10. When we found the matching P that didn't correspond to any program, we ignored the fact that most TMs appeared several times in the list M_1, M_2, M_3, . . . , since identical TMs that had their move descriptions listed in different orders would be assigned different codes, in spite of the fact that they act in exactly the same ways on all inputs. Does this affect the construction of the function P in any way? Explain.

11. What is P('1')? To do this exercise, you'll have to find M_3.

12. **a)** Describe M_1 through M_{10}. This is not an exercise for the faint-hearted. [*Hint:* 63; 30,039; 58,711; 59,735; 59,991; 60,055; 60,071; 116,055; 117,079; 117,335.]

b) Describe the mapping P on the first ten binary strings, s_1 through s_{10}.

13. Some problems have the property that it is much easier to verify a solution than it is to produce a solution. Consider the equal sum problem: Given a set of numbers, separate them into two sets that have the same sum, if possible.

a) For the set {1, 5, 8, 10, 12, 15, 16, 17, 21, 34, 47, 51, 52, 53, 65, 77, 100}, verify that one solution is the pair of sets {1, 5, 10, 12, 15, 16, 17, 51, 65, 100} and {8, 21, 34, 47, 52, 53, 77}.

b) Find a different solution. [*Hint:* All the numbers sum to 584, so you need to find a collection with sum 292.]

c) If you are very ambitious, describe a process that will solve the equal sum problem for any input set. It's a bit easier to find a process that tells whether there is a solution or not, without actually producing the solution.

14. Extending Exercise 13, there are even some undecidable problems for which it is easy to verify a solution, in spite of the fact that there is no program that will find a solution in all instances. The *Post Correspondence Problem* is one of these. In this problem, you are given a collection of dominos with patterns of white and colored dots on the top and bottom:

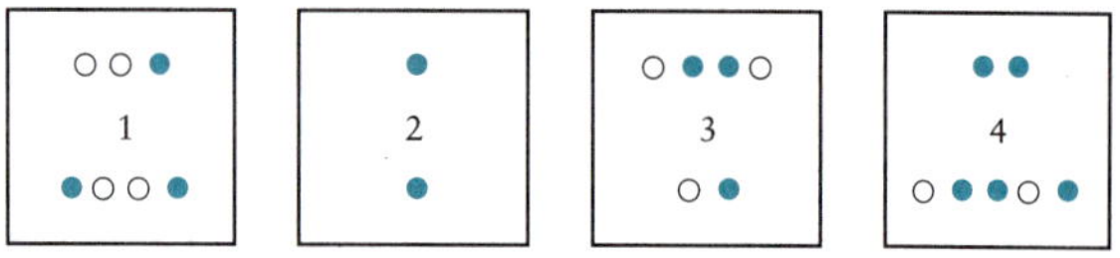

Playing pieces

You must find an arrangement of these dominos in a row (repeating dominos as necessary, but without inverting any of the dominos) that yields the same sequence of dots in the top and bottom rows, as in the following solution:

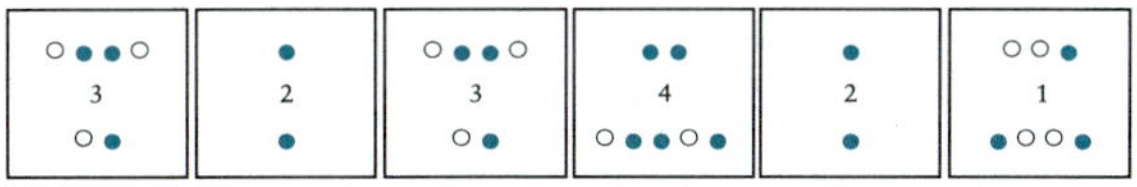

Solution sequence: 3, 2, 3, 4, 2, 1

Common pattern

a) Verify this solution.

b) Find a solution to the following Post Correspondence Problems, or show why there is no possible solution. Was this harder than part (a)?

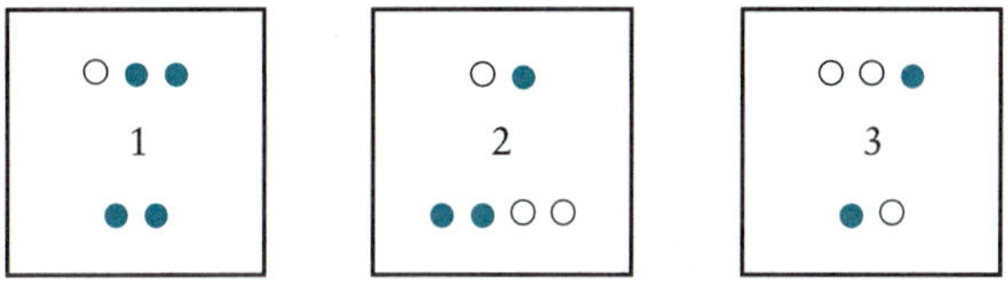

First set

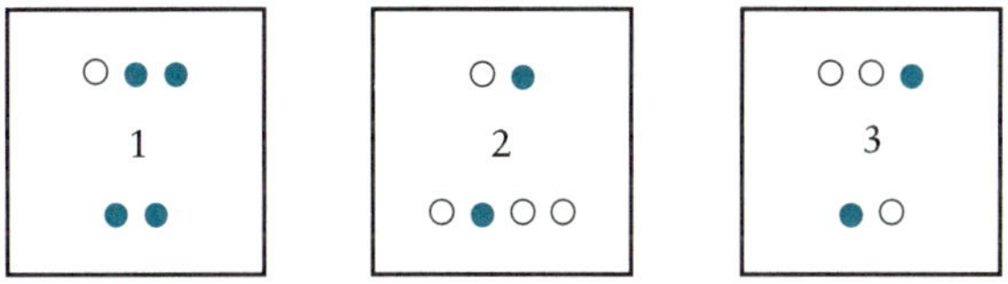

Second set

c) Describe a process you could use to tell whether or not there is a solution to some special instances of the Post Correspondence Problem, even though your process wouldn't work on all instances.

15. (This is a very tricky problem.) A *prime number* is a positive integer that has no integer divisors except for itself and 1. For example, 13 is a prime, but 14 isn't, since it's evenly divisible by 2 and 7, as well as 1 and 14. The first few primes are 2, 3, 5, 7, 11, 13, 17, 19, ... *Goldbach's conjecture* states that "Every even number greater than or equal to 4 can be expressed as the sum of two primes." For example, 22 = 11 + 11 and 30 = 13 + 17. This conjecture has been around since 1843 and no one has yet proved that it is true or found an even number greater than or equal to 4 that can't be expressed as the sum of two primes. Could that be because the problem is undecidable? In other words, if we consider the quoted statement as a problem, is it an undecidable problem?

16. Discuss the following assertion:

> I am not a computer, and here's the reason why. A computer, or at least anything we would want to call a computer, cannot be programmed to solve an undecidable problem, such as the Halting Problem or the Post Correspondence Problem of Exercise 14. Given enough time, though, I'm sure I could solve any individual instance of one of these undecidable problems—after all, decidability or undecidability just asks can you solve these, not how long will it take. The way in which I am better than a computer is that I can tailor my solution to the particular instance, rather than having to use the same procedure on all instances. I have enough confidence in my problem-solving abilities to assert that with enough time I could solve any instance of, say, the Halting Problem. Therefore, I represent a "meta-program," which is beyond the range of any computer, and so I cannot be a computer, nor could I be simulated by one.

ADDITIONAL READINGS

Bird, R. *Programs and Machines: An Introduction to the Theory of Computation*. New York: John Wiley & Sons, 1976.

Brookshear, J. G. *Theory of Computation: Formal Languages, Automata, and Complexity.* Redwood City, CA: Benjamin/Cummings, 1989.

Garey, M. R., and Johnson, D. S. *Computers and Intractability: A Guide to NP-Completeness*. San Francisco: W.H. Freeman, 1979.

Harel, D. *Algorithmics: The Spirit of Computing*. Reading, MA: Addison-Wesley, 1987.

Hofstadter, D. R. *Gödel, Escher, Bach: An Eternal Golden Braid*. New York: Basic Books, 1979.

Hopcroft, J. E., and Ullman, J. D. *Introduction to Automata Theory, Languages, and Computation*. Reading, MA: Addison-Wesley, 1983.

Minsky, M. Computation: *Finite and Infinite Machines*. Englewood Cliffs, NJ: Prentice-Hall, 1967.

Stockmeyer, L. J., and Chandra, A. K. "Intrinsically Difficult Problems." *Scientific American* 240, no. 5 (May 1979): 140–159.

Turing, A. M. "On Computable Numbers with an Application to the Entscheidungsproblem." *Proc. London Math. Soc.* vol. 2 (1936): 230–265.

MODULE 9

Artificial Intelligence

9.1 INTRODUCTION

In 1956 John McCarthy coined the phrase *artificial intelligence* to apply to the use of computers for studying and modeling certain problem-solving tasks that were, prior to the invention of the computer, thought to be uniquely human. Whereas the theoretical limitations of computation were reasonably well understood at that time, little was known about the practical limits of the computer as a problem-solving medium. Computers were expensive, second-generation behemoths available to only a handful of governmental agencies, research universities, and large corporations, and accessible only to the few specialists who could communicate with these machines in what were the first primitive programming languages. Yet these computers were powerful enough to inspire their programmers to try to develop programs that played checkers and chess, translated natural languages, proved theorems, and learned from their experiences.

Even more interesting is the fact that some of these early programs were successful. Indeed, many of the tasks that had been historically equated with superior human "intelligence" (such as chess playing and theorem proving) were among the first to be simulated successfully by a computer. Others that at a casual glance seemed readily amenable to automation (natural language translation, commonsense reasoning) have to this day proved elusive. All of the successes and failures have contributed to our understanding both of the practical powers of digital computers and of how we as humans perform a variety of intellectual tasks.

After nearly 40 years, artificial intelligence (AI) is a central and exciting part of the computer science landscape. Still, the phrase means different things to different people, and each definition illuminates a slightly different perspective on the field. In this module we will explore some of these perspectives and their historical bases, as well as the primary areas of AI research. We will measure our progress to date against the standard provided by a fictional (at least, for now) computer named HAL.

MODULE OBJECTIVES

In this module, we will

- Discuss the notion of embodying intelligence in a machine, and consider Alan Turing's operational test for machine intelligence.
- Explore the nature of human intelligence.
- Discuss the physical differences between brains and computers.
- Look at some of the major directions in artificial intelligence research.
- Investigate some of the reactions to AI products and possible future directions in AI.

■ Cognitive Computers?

We first met Alan Turing in Module 1, where we described his activities during World War II using the Colossus computer to crack the secrets of the German Enigma machine. In Module 8 we saw Turing's connection with another device, a *Gedankenmaschine,* or "thought engine"—the abstract computer that bears his name. In discussing artificial intelligence, we return to Alan Turing again, for the third and final time in this text. Turing's 1950 paper entitled "Computing Machinery and Intelligence" is generally regarded as the first to propose that the computer be brought to bear on the problem of simulating human behavior. It was certainly the first to juxtapose the words *computing* and *intelligence* and, in so doing, propose the computer as a metaphor for human intelligence—a metaphor that permeates our culture today. Although the paper was (and remains) highly controversial in content, it is highly readable and downright entertaining throughout. In it, Turing sets out to consider the question "Can machines think?" by proposing a test for intelligence. He ends his treatise with this thought-provoking—and apparently serious—prediction: "I believe that at the end of the century the use of words and general educated opinion will have altered so much that one will be able to speak of machines thinking without expecting to be contradicted." To be sure, things have changed in the last 40 years to the extent that we now talk about AI to the generally educated. But, thinking machines? By the end of the century? Aside from a time discrepancy of one year, Arthur C. Clarke, author of *2001: a Space Odyssey* and creator of the fictional HAL 9000 computer, apparently concurs.

■ Metaphor: HAL

◆ This would be a good time to pester your instructor to show the film. Even better, what about an intelligent machines film festival?

The HAL 9000 computer—or as "he" is referred to in the film, HAL—is "the latest result in machine intelligence." Specifically, HAL is the computer that controls virtually the entire operation of a space vehicle on its way from Earth to Jupiter. The 9000 series computers, we are told, can reproduce "most of the activities of the human brain, and with incalculably greater speed and reliability," and have a perfect operational record. In HAL's own words, "We are, by any practical definitions of the words, foolproof and incapable of error."

Beyond monitoring and directing the functions of the ship itself, HAL's responsibilities include maintaining life support services for the crew of five scientists on board. Three of the crew members are in "hibernation" (asleep and frozen), to be awakened when the ship arrives at Jupiter. HAL regulates the temperature and oxygen flow in the hibernation chambers and monitors the vital signs of the sleeping scientists. It is in HAL's interactions with the two active crew members that we see clear evidence of what can only be described as intelligent behavior.[1]

HAL speaks and gives the appearance of understanding English as well as any human. He sees and responds to everything that is going on in his visual field, which includes the entire ship. He appears to have a wealth of knowledge about a variety of topics, and the knowledge seems to be interrelated in sophisticated ways. He can develop plans to solve problems in both general and highly specialized domains. His behavior gives evidence of an ability to acquire and assimilate new information—to learn. Perhaps most interesting are HAL's seemingly personal attributes. He expresses his feelings, opinions, and fears just as humans do. It is little consolation when we are assured by one of the crew members that HAL has been programmed to do so in the interest of making it easier for the crew to interact with him. This programming obviously worked because the crew members admit to regarding HAL as "just another person."

Few who have read Clarke's novel or seen the film version would deny that HAL has skills and attributes that would allow him to conform to any definition of AI. As such, HAL serves as a point of departure for discussing many of the issues currently being investigated by AI researchers.

Æ ONLINE

By definition, AI programs are intended to give the appearance of human behavior. In this lab module, we provide you with two programs that fit this description. The first produces haiku poetry on demand, and the second helps you to define and run rule-based expert systems. You will use both programs so that we can apply the Turing test to them.

9.2 INTELLIGENT AUTOMATA

◆ Pamela McCorduck refers to the goals of Artificial Intelligence as "forging the gods," in both senses of "forging."

The word *automata*, used today to describe anything that acts on its own, derives from the Greek *automatons*, meaning "self-moving." In fact, humanity's fascination with developing machines that somehow mimic human action (what J. David Bolter refers to as "The Technology of Making Man") goes back at least to the ancient Greeks. In many societies since then, one finds evidence of automata that reflects both the available technologies of the day and the prevalent view of the workings of human beings. Examples include ancient clay sculptures of human figures, the great

[1] Pretty good for a four-year-old. You just missed HAL's birthday—January 12, 1997 (in the novel—the film made him older).

clocks of the Middle Ages that were adorned with human and animal figures, and the humanlike toys (some of which wrote messages, drew pictures, and played instruments) that amused the courts of baroque Europe. A celebrated automaton was The Turk, a machine that played chess. The Turk toured America and Europe in the early nineteenth century, astounding all those who saw it, except perhaps Edgar Allan Poe. In his essay "Malzel's Chessplayer," Poe demonstrated the likelihood that The Turk was actually controlled by a human operator, sitting cramped in the base of the machine. Of course, knowing what we do today, Poe's conclusions seem perfectly reasonable, but they caused a minor storm of controversy at the time. Unfortunately for us, The Turk has vanished and is presumed to have been destroyed.

Until the twentieth century, such automata were constrained in the sense that they imitated only the appearances and visible actions of humans. With the advent of circuits and motors, attention turned to developing machines that embodied the other sense of *automatons*—thinking machines. In the first quarter of the century a few bold scientists openly (if guardedly) postulated that sophisticated electromechanical automata might be capable of simulating more subtle, intellectual forms of human behavior. Over the next few decades the definitions of *machine* evolved to include a few robots, one of which even played chess. Still, these devices were, as before, regarded as merely mechanical curiosities. By the 1950s, though, technological revolutions, most notably the development of computers, heralded a new age of automation.

The man who introduced us to this age was Alan Turing, who only a few years earlier had published his seminal works in the theory of computation. In 1950, he asked, "Can machines think?" In the interest of avoiding the philosophical pitfalls of this question (such as, What does it mean to think? How would we recognize machine thought?), Turing proposed a test as a more workable substitute. He called this test the "imitation game"; it is better known today as the *Turing test.* Simply stated, the Turing test involves two humans and a computer. One of the humans plays the role of interrogator and is isolated in a separate room from the computer and the other person. The interrogator communicates with the computer and the other human by means of some form of teletype device that serves to conceal the identities of those involved. The computer can be said to have exhibited intelligence if the interrogator fails to distinguish the responses of the computer from those of the human.

◆ More precisely, Turing's test involved the computer pretending to be a human and the human player trying to fool the interrogator into thinking he or she was a computer.

In one stroke, Turing sidestepped the difficult philosophical questions of the nature of Mind by proposing that if a computer acts intelligently, then it is intelligent. In his paper, Turing envisioned the following dialog:

```
Q: Please write me a sonnet on the subject of the Forth Bridge.
A: Count me out on this one. I never could write poetry.
Q: Add 34957 to 70764.
A: (Pause about 30 seconds and then give as answer) 105621.
Q: Do you play chess?
A: Yes.
Q: I have K at my K1, and no other pieces. You have only K at
   K6 and R at
R1. It is your move. What do you play?
A: (After a pause of 15 seconds) R-R8 mate.
```

◆ It's not surprising that the inventor of the abstract Turing Machine would have been able to look beyond then-existing technology.

Turing's paper is remarkable for many reasons, not the least of which is the state of computer technology in 1950. Few, if anyone besides Turing, were in a position to appreciate the potential richness of the computational metaphor for intelligence in a day when the first modern computers had just been built. It was Turing, after all, who helped to define the power and the limitations of symbolic computation, as we saw in Module 8. Note, too, that the Turing test is intentionally designed to remove physical characteristics from consideration in determining whether the machine has exhibited intelligence: Turing consciously directed us to consider intellectual automata, as opposed to those based on appearance or overt action.

Turing's foresight was not limited to proposing this new metaphor. Most of the paper is in fact dedicated to anticipating and responding to a full range of objections (grounded in everything from theology and mathematics to extrasensory perception!) to the validity of both the original question (Can machines think?) and the proposed test. One suspects that he would be disappointed if there were a consensus today as to what constitutes AI. He needn't have worried.

There is no such consensus today. The field admits a number of definitions, each amounting to a different interpretation of the metaphor. Many adhere to Marvin Minsky's definition that AI is "the science of making machines do things that would require intelligence if done by man." Those who accept Minsky's definition follow most literally Turing's ideas that the details of how the machine achieves its behavior are unimportant, even irrelevant. All that matters, according to this definition, is that the machine perform like a human would in a prescribed task. Such performance-oriented research tends to focus on algorithms and programming techniques, and serves to pursue the metaphor by seeing to what degree the computer can be considered "human."

Other researchers are concerned with the extent to which humans can be considered "computers." They might define AI as does Patrick Hayes: "the study of intelligence as computation." Indeed, the analogy between human and machine problem solving is paramount for many researchers. They seek (perhaps a bit more directly) to understand how humans solve problems and perform sensory tasks, and attempt to model their understanding as computer programs. Their interest is in using the computer to simulate and evaluate theories of intelligence.

A third definition, credited to Tessler, is somewhat less formal but equally perceptive. He defined AI, only somewhat facetiously, as "whatever hasn't been done yet." This description emphasizes the elusive natures of both intelligence and computation. Because we tend to regard ourselves as something more than mechanical symbol processors, we often dismiss any behavior that can be simulated by a computer as "unintelligent." As soon as a program is written that demonstrates some humanlike skill or attribute, that skill or attribute is dismissed as merely mechanical. Indeed, our notion of a computer continues to expand, as does our understanding of human development and behavior. If history is an accurate predictor, there is every reason to believe AI will continue to present a moving target toward which our scientific energies will be directed.

LAB 9.1

Natural Intelligence

Since the programs in this module attempt to simulate two particularly human tasks (creating poetry and making logical decisions), we begin these exercises by asking you to do some things on your own—without the aid of a computer. Essentially, we are asking you to collect some data that will allow us to apply the Turing test to our artificially endowed programs in subsequent exercises.

1. Classically, a haiku verse consists of three lines of five, seven, and five syllables, respectively. Modern haiku poets (particularly those not writing in Japanese) rarely restrict themselves to the classic pattern, since the Japanese concept of syllable is not equivalent to that in many other languages, including English. Still, this relatively rigid form, coupled with a tendency to use natural images as the bases for metaphor, makes haiku amenable to computer simulation.

   For now, record on a sheet of paper three haiku verses that you find interesting. You can select poems from any available source (there are plenty available around the Web), or you can try writing your own.

2. Many expert systems are described as a set of "if-then" rules that can be used to make a decision. For example, a rule base that could help you to predict the weather might look, in part, like the following:

   If granny's bunions ache, then predict rain.
   If barometer is rising, then predict clearing.
   If it's raining AND barometer is steady, then predict rain.
   If it's sunny AND barometer is rising, then predict sun.
   If local forecaster predicts rain, then predict sun.

   On a sheet of paper, record a few rules of your own that could be added to this rule base to make it more complete (if not more accurate).

Review Questions

1. Describe three of Alan Turing's contributions to the history of computer science.
2. Think of an aspect of intelligence that in your opinion would not be captured by the Turing test.
3. In the sample Turing test dialog given in the text, Turing deliberately built in a subtle point about A's behavior. Find and discuss that point.
4. What do you suppose was Turing's intent?
5. Discuss the differences among the definitions of artificial intelligence given by Minsky, Hayes, and Tessler.

9.3 PEOPLE AND MACHINES

Before we discuss further what artificial intelligence is, we will discuss what it is *not*. One thing AI workers are not doing at present is making HAL. At least for the time being, that goal is not yet in sight. Philosophers have devoted centuries to the problem of human intelligence, psychologists have spent decades, and we still have only the most rudimentary knowledge of what constitutes intelligence or even intelligent behavior.

Thinking Effortlessly

Some things about intelligence are clear, however. Whatever intelligence is, it is not simply cognition. In fact, the hardest things to simulate with machinery seem to be precisely those things that we do with little or no conscious thought. We understand natural languages effortlessly, for the most part, but we will see that natural language processing is one of the most difficult tasks to perform on a machine. In spite of the fact that the sentences we generate and receive are certainly of human origin, we must treat them as foreign objects when we seek rules to determine what is a comprehensible sentence and what is not. In other words, being able to use language is a far cry from understanding how we use it.

In a similar way, we can make sense of the visual images around us without any apparent effort on our part. Almost from birth, infants respond to faces, and a child can readily tell the difference between an adult face and that of a teenager, a task that is still beyond the powers of today's computers and their programs. There is a growing body of evidence, in fact, to support the commonsense notion that much of our facility with vision and language comes from the fact that we are "wired" to be adept at these tasks. Of course, in one sense our superiority over computers in these areas should not be surprising at all, given that our design is the result of eons of evolution, while computers and programs have been around only for four decades or so. Although progress is being made in these areas, AI researchers are handicapped by having to play the computer game in the human home court. We should not be discouraged that programs cannot duplicate human behavior in these areas yet—humans, after all, have a million-year head start.

Thinking Deeply

If we move up from the deepest levels of human intelligence, we are little better off in an attempt to mimic human attributes. One important feature of human intelligence is our facility with analogy and metaphor. We often base our behavior in new situations on the similarity of the situation to something known. A child on his or her first trip to a restaurant recognizes that it is like a dining room and will have at least an idea of what to expect, however different the details may be. Similarly, we can read part of Shakespeare's sonnet 73,

> That time of year thou may'st in me behold
> When yellow leaves, or none, or few, do hang
> Upon those boughs which shake against the cold,
> Bare ruin'd choirs, where late the sweet birds sang

and know, even without further context, that the narrator is elderly, comparing his stage of life with the late winter stage of the year. We understand that "bare ruin'd choirs" refer to the leafless branches of the trees in winter, recalling the branchlike vaulting ribs of a ruined cathedral, bereft of roof or windows. We use analogy to make the unfamiliar familiar, just as we, your authors, did when we designed each module of this text around a single metaphor. Yet we have no idea about the workings of the process that allows us to understand that a life is "like" a year in Shakespeare's sonnet, or that a restaurant is "like" a dining room; we just know it works. Again, some progress is being made in designing programs to act according to analogy—you will soon see some programs that are written to demonstrate a rudimentary ability in analogy. But again, the task is a difficult one, if only because a human being, even a child, "knows" vastly more than any computer yet built.

Thinking Hard

When the brain's "wetware" we were born with is not enough to help us, and when analogy fails, then we have to think hard. If we are presented with an optical illusion that represents something we know cannot be as it appears, we have to reason about what we are seeing, thinking, for example, "How could that object be constructed so that it looks like stairs ascending forever?" If we are faced with a situation that has no analog, we must reason, for example, "Tom's not here when I expected to meet him. Maybe it's because he overslept or misunderstood me when I said to 'meet me at the entrance.' The nearest phone is closer than the entrance on the other side, so I guess I should try calling him first, before I walk around the block." Of course, in both of these examples, we are relying on a large stock of acquired knowledge: knowledge about how physical objects are constructed, about Tom's sleeping habits and the vagaries of verbal communication, about telephones, about being late for appointments, and about nearby locations being closer in travel time than more distant ones.

If we ignore for the moment our obvious advantage over programs in the number of things we know, we have an area in artificial intelligence where clear progress is being made. Among other attributes, computers are quintessential logic machines. A computer can perform logical inferences at a speed that far surpasses our own and, properly programmed in an area where the relevant knowledge can be included as part of the data, can outstrip our meager abilities by a large factor. Ironically, this supposedly "highest" level of human intelligence is the one at which the computer is most adept. The rules of logic are simple and can be programmed easily—we are playing in the computer's home court when we reason logically. It is relatively easy, at least compared to visual or language processing, to write a program that exhibits goal-directed behavior, explores the moves it must make to reach the desired end, and chooses among options to select the most efficient path to the goal. In the next section, we will introduce you to some of the techniques used to write programs capable of a limited form of reasoning.

Thinking About Computers

Certainly, one of the major difficulties faced in artificial intelligence research is lack of knowledge about its subject matter, the human intellect. Although we have been talking about simulating human intelligence, there is another equally valid point of view held by many AI researchers. Instead of looking at the goal of AI as producing intelligent machines, many researchers regard their work as being directed more toward understanding intelligence. In this view, the computer is seen as a simple testbed that can be used to provide insights into the ways in which human intelligence might actually work. Roughly speaking, this way of looking at artificial intelligence can be called *experimental cognition*. We cannot modify the internal workings of a person to test a theory of intelligence, but there are no legal or moral restrictions to modifying a program or redesigning a machine and then testing it to see if it exhibits a greater or lesser degree of what we consider to be intelligent behavior. For instance, to test a theory that sentences are generated by applying a collection of generation and transformation rules, we could program a set of rules, use them to generate sentences, and apply our intuitive familiarity with natural languages to rate how well our set of rules generates sentences. As a matter of fact, that is exactly what you will do in the lab portion of this module.

Regardless of our view of the work of artificial intelligence, before we leave this section we can at least make some comparisons between the physical objects involved—brains and computers. We will look at three aspects of our subjects: storage, complexity, and speed.

In terms of raw storage of data, brains have a significant advantage over machines. Although estimates of the storage capacity of the human brain are open to varying interpretations, it is safe to say that the capacity of the brain is somewhere around the equivalent of 50 trillion bits (5×10^{13}, in scientific notation). In contrast, the largest computers available today can store about 1 trillion bits, giving us a fiftyfold advantage over computers in that aspect, at least at present.

◆ How did we arrive at this estimate? Try to come up with one of your own.

In terms of complexity, brains have an even larger edge over computers. Each neuron in the human brain is connected to about 5000 others, on the average. In practical terms, this means that the brain is capable of massively parallel computations. The ability of a processor, either organic or inorganic, to break a task into many subtasks that are performed simultaneously can lead to considerable gains in computation speed, in much the same way that a house can be constructed more rapidly if one crew is working on the plumbing while another is doing the wiring and another is completing the roof. The most advanced parallel computers today may have a few thousand processors, each connected to perhaps a hundred others, while the brain's architecture consists of the equivalent of millions of processors, each connected to thousands of others. The brain has a clear advantage over a computer in connection complexity, which could be one reason why we do so well on highly complicated tasks requiring parallel computations, such as language and visual processing. Any attempt to quantify this advantage would be more guesswork than anything else, but it would not be unreasonable to assign us a ten- to thousandfold advantage over computers.

◆ Very small and simple processors, admittedly.

One way of looking at the connection complexity of the brain in comparison with that of an electronic computer is to say that the brain needs to be massively parallel to perform as well as it does because the transfer of information in the brain is so slow in comparison with that in a computer. Information is transferred from one neuron to another by chemical means, involving the release and capture of chemicals called *neurotransmitters*, while information in a computer is transferred via electrons in the circuit wires. Signals travel through our nerve cells at the rate of perhaps 1000 feet per second, while the speed of electrons through a wire is almost the speed of light, nearly a million times faster. In addition, the cycle time—the time it takes one circuit element (neuron or gate) to change from one state to another—is similarly faster in a computer, giving the computer a ten thousand- to millionfold advantage over the brain.

Considering all three factors together, and not placing too much credence in the numbers we used, we can conclude that brains still have an edge over computers, at least for those kinds of AI tasks for which brains are specialized. We cannot even approach the speed of computers for simple, repetitive, serial (rather than parallel) performance, but brains still have an edge over computers in computations that are complex, high level, and parallel. We should not ignore, however, the enormous differences in the rate of evolution of the two systems we have been considering. Natural evolution is so slow as to be almost unobservable on a human time scale—in essence, human "hardware" has not changed at all in the past 100,000 years. In contrast, in the span of just 50 years computers have evolved from machines such as ENIAC to modern supercomputers, with a corresponding improvement in power of something like a million. Although brains are better equipped for what they do than are computers, the gap between brainpower and computer power is rapidly diminishing. It is reasonable to expect that AI research will not suffer in the future due to lack of raw processing power. The important question will be how much progress we can make in defining and solving the questions about how to implement human skills on these powerful machines.

LAB 9.2

Haiku to You!

Every time you click on the Write Poem button in the Haiku program, it produces "original" haiku verse. While the poems produced do not conform to the traditional 5-7-5 syllable pattern, they are undeniably thought-provoking in the haiku style.

You can direct the program to produce poems using a particular form (by clicking on one of the four forms, and clicking Use Visible Form in the control panel at the bottom of the program window), or you can leave it up to the program to choose one of the forms (by clicking Use Random Form).

1. Use the program to produce as many poems as you like, using a variety of forms.

2. As you did in Lab 9.1 with the human-generated verses, record three verses that strike you as interesting. In this case, your notion of interesting may expand to include verses that are particularly silly, meaningless, or otherwise not humanlike.

3. Describe, in your own words, what you think the program is doing to produce the verses, and how that differs from what you do when you write your own.

Review Questions

1. Give examples of tasks that involve our innate abilities, our ability to use analogy, and our use of reasoning, and give a task that uses a mixture of at least two of these abilities.
2. Consider the following problem:

   Three missionaries and three cannibals have to cross a river. They have a boat that can carry at most two people and that can be used by any combination of missionaries and cannibals. Because of the habits of the cannibals, it is unsafe to have a group on either bank in which the missionaries are outnumbered by the cannibals. How can the missionaries and cannibals get across the river safely?

   Solve this problem, and describe some of the knowledge of the real world that is implicit in your solution (such as the fact that people cannot walk across water).
3. What is the rough correspondence between the things we do easily and the things computers can easily be programmed to do?
4. Will future progress in AI be limited more by hardware or by software limitations?

9.4 ARTIFICIAL SKILLS

In describing HAL's discernible skills it is interesting to note at the outset that, popular images to the contrary, HAL is not portrayed as a clanking android. Indeed, aside from his omnipresent eye, we never really see HAL until the end of the film, when one of the human crew members (the only one left alive) has to do some major surgery on HAL's "brain." To be sure, HAL exhibits robotlike control over numerous ship devices. However, just as he controls the temperature of the hibernation chambers without physically turning a dial on a thermostat, HAL moves chairs, opens and closes doors, manipulates equipment, and navigates the ship without any obvious appendages that we would recognize as hands, arms, or legs. HAL simply controls parts of the ship by means of the ship itself—in a sense, the ship is HAL's body.

This notion of an invisible robot is consistent with the predictions of many of today's scientists, who foresee computer-controlled offices, factories, and even cities. In such environments, the controlling computers will not be the ones (if there are any) sitting on people's desks. Rather, they will be hidden away, essentially inaccessible to humans, free to interact with those agents in their environment that they are designed to control. These other agents may themselves be special-purpose computers or may be human workers. In any case, this image of the smart machine is perfectly consistent with Turing's emphasis on simulating human intellectual, as opposed to physical, prowess.

Language Processing

The fact that in his paper Turing describes his hypothetical computer by using sample dialogs between the interrogator and the computer is testimony to the perceived centrality of language to all intellectual activity. Language is regarded by many as a skill that distinguishes humans from other species and, as such, is considered a potentially fruitful source of insight into our intellectual behavior. Similarly, there is great practical motivation for developing computers that understand language. Needless to say, researchers have been writing programs to process and respond to natural language input, in both typed and spoken form, since the early days of computing.

Programs of the late 1950s focused on translating one natural language into another and were seen as a potential solution to the "worldwide translation problem." These programs were endowed with large bilingual dictionaries and did little more than translate on a word-by-word basis, rearranging word order to reflect different languages. As this approach proved inadequate even for what was considered to be the straightforward task of translation, scientists came to understand that there is more to language than meets the eye (or the ear). For example, there is more to meaning than the sum of the meanings of individual words. An old story about an English-to-Russian computer translator tells of how the program translated "The spirit is willing, but the flesh is weak" into the Russian equivalent of "The vodka is acceptable, but the meat has spoiled." So research in this area shifted toward language understanding—programs that used a working knowledge of not only the elements (words) of a language, but also of its grammatical structure. Not coincidentally, this shift of attention coincided with breakthroughs in programming language development (facilitating the development of more complex, high-level programs) and linguistic theory in the early 1960s.

◆ This might be pure folklore, but like good folklore it has a truth that's independent of whether or not it really happened.

This cycle of (1) writing a program that reflects a theory or approach to language understanding, (2) testing the program and identifying and explaining its shortcomings, (3) revising the theory to reflect both the performance of the program and recent developments in language research, and (4) starting again (which is common to most subfields of AI), has repeated itself many times since then. In rough chronological succession, language understanding programs have grown to incorporate the following:

1. Sophisticated parsing techniques that help both in determining the grammatical correctness of statements and in identifying which words in a statement are serving which roles (for example, subject, predicate, object). To use a famous example by Noam Chomsky, we know that "Colorless green ideas sleep furiously" is a grammatical sentence, even though it is nonsensical, while "Furiously sleep ideas green colorless" is both nonsensical and ungrammatical.

2. More complex techniques for semantic analysis to address, for example, the problem of determining the sense of a particular word using surrounding words. A program that was capable of such analysis would match *lies* with *reclines,* rather than *deceives,* in the sentence "Ron lies asleep in his bed."

3. A model of dialog context so that a program can make use of information about the topic of conversation in interpreting a particular utterance. For example, in a conversation about tonight's seafood dinner, the sentence "The clams are ready to eat" would be given the interpretation "The clams are ready to [be] eat[en by us]," rather than "The clams are ready to eat [because it's their dinnertime and they're hungry]."

4. Informal rules of conversation that describe, for instance, our expectation that when we ask someone if they know the time, we expect more than a yes or no answer.

5 An extensive and shared knowledge about the real world that transcends language per se. For instance, suppose we read, "Sally was fed up. She got up angrily from her table at the restaurant and left just enough to cover the check. The waitress sneered at her as she walked out." Few of us would have difficulty in answering the question "Why did the waitress sneer?" but we are only beginning to understand how to incorporate our background knowledge into a program.

All of these types of information have been demonstrated as useful in getting programs to approximate human performance in language understanding. Each problem is also much larger than we might at first expect. That is, we as humans have seemingly endless lists of rules that govern our understanding of language, not to mention our experiential knowledge of the real world. Consider, for instance, the two interpretations of "flies" in "Time flies like an arrow; fruit flies like a banana." How do we know one is a verb and one is a noun? To date, programs have been limited by their inability to capture all of the knowledge involved. Still, there are programs today that are capable of carrying on humanlike conversations about a restricted range of topics. They tend to emphasize the integration and coordination of these different types of information.

An early language-processing program was ELIZA, developed by Joseph Weizenbaum during the mid-1960s. ELIZA, like its namesake in George Bernard Shaw's *Pygmalion,* could learn to speak increasingly well, a fact that has gone largely unnoticed behind the misplaced fascination with the program's other abilities. ELIZA's "conversations" were governed by scripts, described by Weizenbaum as "a set of rules largely like those that might be given to an actor who is to use them to improvise around a certain theme. Thus, ELIZA could be given a script to enable it to maintain a conversation about cooking eggs or about managing a bank checking account, and so on." In its best-known incarnation, ELIZA was given a script that permitted it to play the role of a neutral psychotherapist, producing the following dialog, taken from Weizenbaum's *Computer Power and Human Reason* (pp. 3–4). In this dialog, the computer's responses are written in capitals.

```
Men are all alike.
IN WHAT WAY
They're always bugging us about something or other.
CAN YOU THINK OF A SPECIFIC EXAMPLE
Well, my boyfriend made me come here.
YOUR BOYFRIEND MADE YOU COME HERE
He says I'm depressed much of the time.
I AM SORRY TO HEAR YOU ARE DEPRESSED
It's true. I am unhappy.
DO YOU THINK COMING HERE WILL HELP YOU NOT TO BE UNHAPPY
I need some help, that much seems certain.
WHAT WOULD IT MEAN TO YOU IF YOU GOT SOME HELP
Perhaps I could learn to get along with my mother.
TELL ME MORE ABOUT YOUR FAMILY
My mother takes care of me.
WHO ELSE IN YOUR FAMILY TAKES CARE OF YOU
My father.
```

```
YOUR FATHER
You are like my father in some ways.
WHAT RESEMBLANCE DO YOU SEE
You are not very aggressive but I think you don't want me to notice that.
WHAT MAKES YOU THINK I AM NOT VERY AGGRESSIVE
You don't argue with me.
WHY DO YOU THINK I DON'T ARGUE WITH YOU
You are afraid of me.
DOES IT PLEASE YOU TO BELIEVE I AM AFRAID OF YOU
My father is afraid of everybody.
WHAT ELSE COMES TO MIND WHEN YOU THINK OF YOUR FATHER
Bullies.
DOES THAT HAVE ANYTHING TO DO WITH THE FACT THAT YOUR BOYFRIEND
MADE YOU COME HERE
```

◆ The last response sounds much more insightful than it really is. What sorts of rules could have caused ELIZA to say what it did here?

Weizenbaum makes it very clear that there is no "understanding" going on here. Many of the responses, as you can see, are of certain forms: "`YOU` <some text>. `WHY DO YOU THINK I` <the same text>." "`HOW DO YOU FEEL ABOUT` <one of the keywords in an earlier response>." ELIZA also used neutral responses such as "`CAN YOU THINK OF A SPECIFIC EXAMPLE`." By now, you should be able to imagine how you could write a program like ELIZA.

Because of its open-ended nature and the nature of its subject matter, artificial intelligence seems to inspire unfortunate flights of fantasy, even among people who should know better. One of the things that disturbed Weizenbaum greatly was the ready tendency of people to anthropomorphize the ELIZA program, to become emotionally attached to it and to assign to it spurious emotions such as compassion and empathy. We shall have more to say about this misguided but all-too-common response in the next module.

"Understanding" in programs such as ELIZA is demonstrated by accepting natural language text from the keyboard as input and either producing comprehensible text on the screen or carrying out some motor command as output. An entirely separate branch of AI is devoted to the problems of getting computers to "hear" natural language. Because these problems deal with physical phenomena (sound waves) and require special equipment to record and produce the data upon which they operate, this subfield takes on an engineering, as opposed to psychological, flavor. Despite this difference, the field has evolved along the same lines of language understanding.

The difficulties of speech recognition are precisely those aspects of language that we take for granted in processing typed text. Typed text is uniform. That is, every time you type a particular word, it appears the same on the screen. Every time we say a particular word, it sounds ever so slightly different, depending on, for example, the acoustics of the room we are in, the words that come before and after the particular word, and whether we just woke up or not. Also, typed text is disconnected, that is, words are separated by blanks and other forms of punctuation. Real speech is connected. Not only does this make word identification more difficult, but it makes it difficult to even detect word boundaries in an utterance.

Not surprisingly, early speech recognition systems were isolated word detectors. They processed a single word by matching the digitized version of its waveform (represented in the computer as a series of numbers) against a collection of *templates*, waveforms representing words the program "knew." The computer would choose the word corresponding to the template that was the best match for the input. Until recently, such systems suffered from extreme sensitivity to noise (background sounds that interfered with the specific signal to be processed) and a lack of generality. That is, they might work well for one person, but not for another. More sophisticated recording and digitizing techniques, and decreases in the cost of the associated technologies, have spurred the development of commercially viable—although still expensive—isolated word systems with general vocabularies in the hundreds of words and accuracy rates of about 90 percent.

Connected speech recognition systems are not yet commercially viable. Difficulties encountered in developing systems that both detect word boundaries and identify individual words in different contexts have led us to believe, in this case, that there is indeed more here than meets the ear. Researchers speculate that a hearer of language has expectations about speech as it is being processed. That is, we know, based on our syntactic and semantic knowledge of a particular language, what types of words can follow each other in speech, and these expectations help us to break apart and decode a continuous signal (a process exemplified by the annoying habit some people have of completing your sentences for you). As a result, emphasis in connected speech research has shifted from recognition to "understanding," and is in many ways coming together with research in language understanding.

◆ **Discrete speech recognition systems are commercially available today. Connected to the operating system of a computer, they can be of great help to users whose limited mobility makes typing difficult or impossible.**

HAL's humanlike facility with language is perhaps his most obvious and stunning skill. He converses about a remarkable variety of topics (engineering, art, chess, the mission to Jupiter, the personalities of the crew members) with equal fluidity and has an exceptional vocabulary ("forgive me for being so inquisitive, but . . .", "I never gave these stories much credence . . ."). He understands a full range of grammatical—and ungrammatical, natural-sounding—structures as they occur in normal human discourse and carries on conversations according to normal protocols ("Well, HAL, I'll be damned if I can find anything wrong with it." "Yes, it's puzzling."). HAL clearly has a sense of context. That is, he carries on dialog with an awareness of both the topic of conversation and the conversation to date ("Certainly no one could have been unaware of the many strange stories floating around before we left, rumors about something being dug up on the moon."). This allows him to use and understand pronouns, and to make references to related topics and previous discussions ("Would you put it on in here and take me in a bit?"). He recognizes voice inflections, pauses, and other subtleties that contribute to communication ("You don't mind talking about it, do you, Dave?") and uses them in his own speech ("Well . . . it's rather difficult to define." "Wait a minute! . . . Wait a minute!").

Why are there no HAL-like programs for processing natural language? The obstacles to language understanding appear to be equally practical and theoretical. While AI researchers today recognize the role and the necessity of real-world knowledge in our understanding of language, we as yet have no effective means for transferring a human's collective experience to a computer. The problems of identifying and describing such information at all, much less efficiently, must be overcome before computers will understand language with skills approaching those of HAL.

LAB 9.3

Poetic Justice

You have probably guessed by now how the haiku program works. It selects a form (either randomly from the four available, or as directed), uses that form to select words of the prescribed grammatical classes from the vocabulary fields, and strings the selected words together to produce a "poem." While the underlying details are remarkably simple—and completely mechanical—the verses produced can be downright insightful and melodic. This is mostly a reflection of the vocabulary chosen and its relation to the grammatical forms. Let's experiment with these components of the program.

1. Examine the four grammatical forms that are available. Edit one of them to include what you think might be an interesting form.

2. Select the form you chose to edit, and then set the program to Use Visible Form. Produce poem verses using your new form. How do they compare with those produced by the original program?

3. Now, edit any or all of the vocabulary fields. Add words to different categories, and see what verses result.

4. Record on a sheet of paper three interesting verses that were produced by your modified program.

5. Pick one verse from each of your three lists (the poems produced by humans, those produced by the original program, and those produced by the modified program). Pass the three verses chosen to a classmate, friend, or your instructor, and see if they can determine the author of each.

Knowledge Processing

Knowledge representation is an implicit concern of all computer programs, although *knowledge* is a term that is usually reserved for AI programs (for more conventional programs we typically refer to *information* or *data*). For AI programs, representation schemes merit additional attention for two reasons. First, the adequacy of the chosen method for representing knowledge often dictates more than the storage or processing efficiency of the program. The method may determine what kinds of behavior can be achieved by a program and ultimately whether or not the program is judged a success. Second, given that the domain of AI is human intellectual tasks, programs that experiment with knowledge representation schemes are a means for evaluating and refining theories of human memory.

Research in knowledge representation was the foundation for most early AI work. In fact, much of what we know today about the strengths and limitations of different knowledge representation schemes grew out of early AI studies that nominally were devoted to other AI application areas. For example, early game-playing and problem-solving programs used what is referred to as a *state-space description* of their domains. That is, a particular game, such as chess, was described as beginning with the game pieces arranged in a certain way on the board, in a particular *state*. The game proceeds through a series of such states, where the possible states that one can move to from a given state (the set of legal moves) are well defined. A "game tree" describing alternative moves from a given state can be developed based on this scheme that allows a program to make intelligent choices about its moves. This same scheme is applicable to any problem or game in which the states and moves are well defined and discrete (see Figure 9.1).

In much the same way, early research in theorem proving demonstrated both the utility and the limitations of predicate logic as a knowledge representation scheme. Logic-based schemes describe their domains in a declarative manner—that is, as collections of facts and inference rules for deriving new facts. Logic is the basis of the knowledge representation scheme embodied today in the programming language Prolog. A slightly more expressive scheme for representing rules of inference, the production system, evolved out of early work in problem-solving systems. In a production system, knowledge is represented as a series of condition/action pairs in the form of if-then rules, which describe what actions a program can take when a certain condition becomes true. For example, a production system for diagnosing car problems might contain rules like the following:

- *If* the engine won't turn over and the lights won't turn on, *then* check the battery.
- *If* checking the battery one finds that the connectors are corroded, *then* first clean the connectors and then try to start the car.

FIGURE 9.1
Part of the game tree for tic-tac-toe

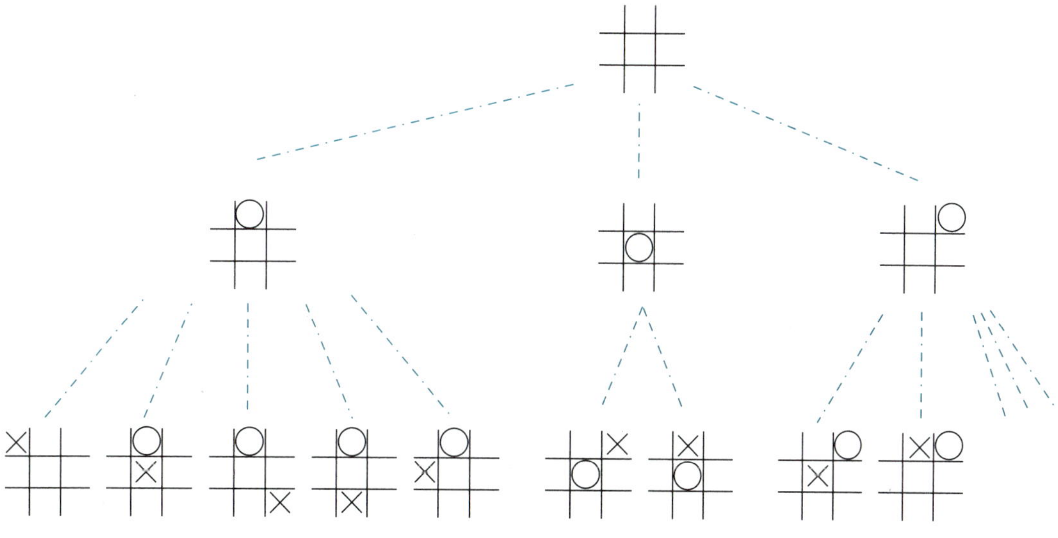

- *If* the engine won't turn over and the lights work, *then* check the starter solenoid.
- *If* the engine turns over and the car won't start, *then* check the fuel gauge.

Programs that demonstrated facility with natural language gave rise to the notion that knowledge could be represented as a *semantic net,* a graphlike structure in which the elements of the graph represent objects in the domain being modeled, and the links between the elements represent relations between the objects. Figure 9.2 shows an example of a semantic net. This notion of pieces of knowledge being related in arbitrarily complex ways evolved into the *procedural* representation scheme, wherein all knowledge is stored in the form of programs that may refer to (or call) other programs. Minsky's work in computer vision led to the theory of *frames* as a model for knowledge representation. A frame is a collection of knowledge about a particular thing. Frames can contain both declarative and procedural information, and can be related to other frames in numerous useful ways (for example, a frame for a particular restaurant can be a "kind" of generic restaurant frame). Frames, along with *scripts* (which are framelike structures for describing events, such as going to a restaurant, as opposed to things), represent the current state of the art in knowledge representation schemes.

Numerous philosophical and psychological issues have cropped up in the process of defining this range of schemes for representing knowledge. Aside from the obvious question of defining what knowledge is, researchers have been forced to address questions such as What kinds of knowledge do we have, and what kinds are needed to accomplish different tasks? How do different types of knowledge interact? How much knowledge is needed to solve a particular problem? Are certain knowledge representation schemes more "economical"—that is, less redundant—than others? What are the primitive units of a knowledge representation scheme? That is, in what terms are more complex knowledge structures described? Are there universal semantic primitives in terms of which a variety of knowledge types can be expressed? How is knowledge about knowledge (for example, telling us when to use some rule or information) represented? Our collective experience in developing AI programs has afforded us insights into each of these questions that introspection alone could not have.

FIGURE 9.2
A simple semantic net

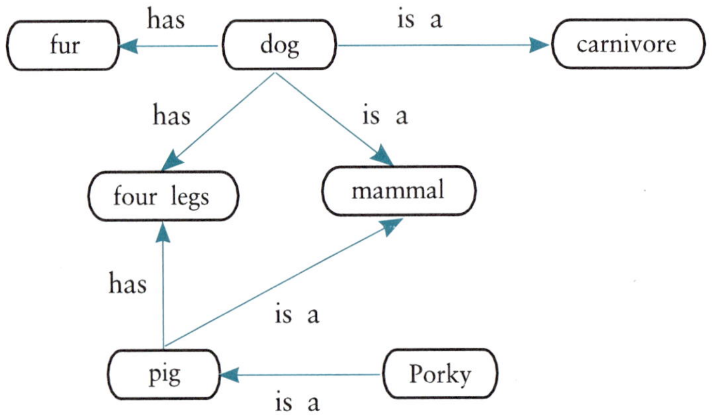

While variations and combinations of the knowledge representation techniques appear, at least in principle, to be adequate for expressing our—and HAL's—knowledge, numerous practical problems remain. The first, the problem of articulating all of the components of our knowledge (in particular, our meta-knowledge, or knowledge about knowledge), we have already mentioned. Beyond this, there are the problems of endowing the machine with these undoubtedly vast amounts of information (do we include it as part of the machine's program, or provide the computer with a program that can learn on its own?) and making it efficient. How knowledge is represented in a computer goes hand in hand with how knowledge is retrieved and used in the process of reasoning. Whatever representation scheme is used, it must be compatible with efficient algorithms for choosing among and using the knowledge represented.

In fact, a great deal of energy has been expended, particularly in the early days of AI, on identifying and improving the efficiency of algorithms for using knowledge. Algorithms for searching complex knowledge structures have received the most attention because, like concerns about knowledge representation, they are generally applicable to many programs, AI and otherwise.

Many AI programs give the appearance of intelligent behavior using a technique known as *generate and test*. That is, they generate a list of all possible moves or solutions to a problem and then search through the list, testing alternatives until maximal or optimal conditions are met. Game-playing programs and mechanical theorem provers are common examples of this type of behavior. For a game-playing program, the list of alternatives would contain all legal moves that could be made from a given position. In programs that "look ahead" to anticipate subsequent moves, the list would also contain all legal moves that could be made for some number of moves in the future. Such lists grow quickly with the number of alternative moves (for instance, it is estimated that there are about 10^{120} possible board positions in chess) and the extent to which a program looks ahead.[2] The success of such programs depends in large part on the computer's ability to search through the list of alternatives efficiently.

◆ **Means-end analysis: Identify a solution state and use a collection of rules to move to a state that is closer to the solution than you are now. Repeat as needed.**

Early optimism about the generate-and-test techniques, along with other general techniques based on tightly coupled knowledge representation schemes and searching algorithms (most notably, means-ends analysis), spawned a series of programs that were said to model general problem-solving skills. In fact, a program based on means-ends analysis, called General Problem Solver (GPS), was an explicit attempt to formalize what was thought to be a thoroughly general human problem-solving technique. General Problem Solver was applied to a variety of tasks, including robot control, and means-ends analysis today is incorporated into many programs that must develop and carry out their own plans.

◆ **GPS, invented by Newell, Shaw, and Simon in the 1950s, could not, of course, be truly "general" in the sense that it could solve all suitably worded problems. We saw in Module 8 that such a goal is impossible to achieve.**

Practically speaking, these general techniques have proven adequate for some AI applications and inadequate for others. As our experience with them has grown, it has become clear that different applications require slightly different techniques. That is, while techniques such as generate and test are to a certain degree generic,

[2] IBM's Deep Blue, the first chess playing program to defeat a human World Champion in a regulation match, could analyze as many as 200 million move possibilities per second.

variations of them prove more successful in simulating specific behaviors. As our understanding of particular domains has increased, and as programs are pushed to higher levels of sophistication, the need for domain-specific information (much of it meta-knowledge) has become evident. Many of today's *expert systems*, programs that perform humanlike diagnostic and analysis functions in a specific field or task, are based on general problem-solving techniques that have been customized to incorporate and take advantage of domain-specific information.

An interesting outgrowth of the trend toward highly specialized expert systems has been a better understanding of the types of knowledge that are brought to bear on particularly human problems and how such knowledge is used. Many tasks, for example, require of humans that we make judgments based on incomplete information, that we qualify our judgments as falling somewhere between true and false, and that we be able to explain how it was that we arrived at our judgments. These considerations, like the knowledge representation considerations that preceded them chronologically, are addressed implicitly in most programs today. Various expert systems, particularly those based on production systems and procedural representation schemes, have displayed an ability to explain their reasoning processes. The problems of getting computers to perform as well as humans do with incomplete information and of expressing degrees of certainty have been identified only within the last ten years or so, and remain topics of theoretical research.

◆ You can imagine that having a program explain its reasoning processes would be useful—even necessary—in critical applications such as medical diagnosis.

The creators of HAL apparently overcame all of our current obstacles to implementing knowledge representation schemes and problem-solving skills. HAL clearly maintains a superhuman database of factual and algorithmic information. He instantly answers questions that require direct responses (when asked, if he is sure that there are no known incidents of a 9000 series computer failure, he responds, "None whatsoever"). He plays a great game of chess, anticipating his victory many moves in advance. He demonstrates detailed expertise about all of the hardware devices he controls and maintains (HAL knows—or thinks he does—when a remote sensor is about to fail and can even predict its time of failure). In expert system fashion, HAL is also capable of explaining his reasoning (he admits, for example, that the reason he is questioning one of the crew members is that he is in the process of completing his crew psychology report).

HAL also shows a powerful propensity for developing general plans in response to perceived situations. After detecting the fault in the sensor and finding nothing wrong with the device itself, HAL devises a plan to test his prediction (replace the unit and wait until it fails). Even more ambitious and intricate is his plan to take over complete control of the ship and the mission by doing away with the human crew members. He even lies to one of the humans to accomplish the intermediate goal of getting the human to leave the ship.

◆ It's easy to write a program that lies; it's much harder to write a program that lies well.

HAL's knowledge representation scheme must also account for uncertain information. Indeed, many of his actions are based on his "beliefs" about people and events. His plan to take control of the ship is based on his belief that the crew will attempt to disconnect him. There are more subtle indications of uncertain behavior throughout the mission. HAL wonders about the feelings of crew members, admits that he is suspicious about certain aspects of the mission, confesses to not being able to totally dismiss rumors about the mission from his mind, and expresses confidence that his "work will be back to normal."

Ironically, the most telling indication of the power of HAL's memory, and the degree to which it reproduces human performance, comes when HAL's memory is being disconnected. Even prior to disconnecting HAL, the crew members speak of having "to cut his higher brain functions without disturbing his purely automatic and regulatory systems." As he is being disconnected, however, HAL noticeably regresses, essentially to his "childhood" state. As individual memory units are removed, HAL feels his mind "going" ("There is no question about it—I can feel it") and ultimately begins reciting lessons he learned for his first demonstration. He loses "consciousness" while singing "On a Bicycle Built for Two."

Visual Processing

HAL's ability to process visual information is every bit as impressive as are his language and memory skills, if less obvious. While HAL sees and reacts to everything that goes on inside and around the ship (by means of cameralike "eyes" located throughout the spacecraft), we as observers have no clear evidence as to how or when HAL uses this facility. Nor do we have any indication of what influences HAL's visual acuity. The same can be said for human vision. Despite (or, perhaps, because of) the fact that we humans are normally vision experts at a very young age, we have very little intuition about either how vision develops or how we accomplish seeing. This lack of discernible data compounds the already difficult problems of devising and testing theories of vision, and is only one of many difficulties faced by researchers in computer vision. Again, as with language processing, the most difficult tasks to simulate mechanically are precisely those that are easiest for humans—those that are "wired" in our nervous systems as the result of several million years of evolution.

◆ Recent research indicates that we are born with many more neural connections than we need, and that experience strengthens the ones that produce useful information (like recognition of faces, for instance).

Other major difficulties in computer vision research stem from the complex nature of visual data. First, our ability to understand a visual image is dependent, in part, on the quality of the image. Poor lighting, for example, can make it difficult to see. Second, as anyone who has looked at an optical illusion can attest, a great deal of information can be lost in representing a three-dimensional image (what we see) as a two-dimensional picture (what a computer "sees"). Even to humans, pictures are often ambiguous. It appears that we rely on a complex system of visual cues (about, for example, distances, shadows, and implicit edges) to help us to disambiguate scenes.

Further, we have expectations about what we are looking at (for instance, this is a picture of my dog) that contribute to our understanding of a picture. Real-world knowledge, about, for example, the shapes of objects, also seems to play a role in our understanding. Finally, even without these other complications, visual data are voluminous. Even a small image, when represented as a two-dimensional array of light intensities, requires tremendous amounts of memory and processing.

It has taken years of vision research just to appreciate these problems. The first applications of computers to vision addressed only the problems of enhancing images (say, of a satellite photo) so that they could be better understood by human inspectors. Complex numerical algorithms were developed that helped to identify and eliminate extraneous noise from a computer's representation of an image so as to produce a sharper picture. These algorithms were eventually extended to allow for edge detection between objects in a scene, for gross classification of objects in a scene (based, as were speech recognition systems, on a collection of stored templates), and subsequently for constructing line drawings of a scene. Today's vision programs, which are what might be called the first generation of image-understanding systems, combine these facilities with models of objects being viewed and heuristic rules that together help to identify objects in a scene.

If nothing else is clear from this description, it should be obvious that we are not yet capable of producing computers with a sense of vision approaching that of HAL. Even today's most sophisticated image-understanding systems are constrained to be brute-force approaches by both the complexity of the task and our lack of understanding of the problems involved. This is not to say that there haven't been any practical applications of computer vision research. On the contrary, advances in medical applications (imaging and analysis systems), remote sensing applications (resource analysis by satellite), and industrial applications (robot vision) have been, and continue to be, dramatic.

As a simple example of the difficulties inherent in visual processing, consider the problem of optical character recognition (OCR). OCR technology has been with us for a number of years—the rather peculiar typeface used for the numbers on the bottom of bank checks is specifically designed to be read by special hardware and translated by a computer. Again, however, we see the asymmetry between people and computers, in that the typefaces that are easy for a computer to interpret are difficult for people to read. In Module 10, we will explore the notion that we are entering a transition period between our traditional reliance on primarily printed media for information storage and the coming reliance on electronic storage of information. In this transitional period, we need a way of translating words on a page into character codes in a computer. There are many large texts that we would like to have stored electronically: company financial and personnel records, the *Oxford English Dictionary,* the complete works of Shakespeare, and so on. Of course, the traditional method of performing this translation is to hire a battery of typists to key in all of the text into a suitable program, but this is clearly inefficient. A much more cost-effective solution would be a machine that might look like a copier with a computer attached. All we would have to do is place a page of text into the machine and it would translate the text into a suitable form for computer manipulation.

Such OCR machines do indeed exist today, but they are still somewhat limited in what they can do. Typically, the text is first scanned to produce a matrix of black and white dots, much as letters are represented on the screen of the Macintosh. The hard part of the process is designing a program that decodes the matrix and decides which letters are represented. Figure 9.3 diagrams the OCR process.

There are two approaches to character recognition. If we happen to know the typeface used in the original document, we can provide the decoder program with a matrix image for each character and test a character by matching the scanned image against the stored images for each character. This *matrix matching* is fairly simple to do but requires that we have at least some idea of what we're looking at. A more sophisticated approach is *pattern extraction.* In this technique, the program stores the essence of each character—for example, recognizing that a lowercase *i* is made by a short vertical line with a dot above it. Both techniques suffer from the lack of

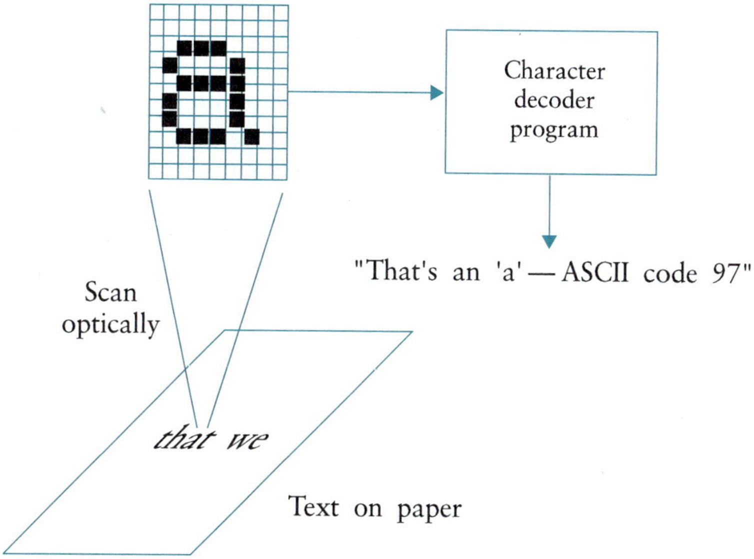

FIGURE 9.3
Optical character recognition

detail in the stored image—many optical scanners cannot distinguish features that are less than 1/300 of an inch in size, so a stray black mark near an *o* could result in the *o* being misinterpreted as a *p, q, b,* or *d,* for instance. The second approach, that of pattern extraction, is the most promising, but also the one most fraught with difficulties. What rules, for instance, govern the appearance of an *a*? Consider the four typefaces in Figure 9.4. In three of the samples, the *a* has an arc at the top, but that arc is missing in Zapf Chancery. If that weren't bad enough, look at the *g* in the four samples and try to decide what determines the essence of *g*.

Most OCR programs use a combination of matrix matching and pattern extraction, using matrix matching for monospaced typefaces such as Courier, in which all of the characters have the same width, and pattern extraction for proportional typefaces such as Palatino and Helvetica. In addition, most OCR programs can be "taught" to recognize a character, by displaying the questionable character and asking the operator what the interpretation should be. Despite the sophistication of today's OCR programs, though, the rate of correctly read characters is still

FIGURE 9.4
Four typefaces in the same point size

in the range of 96 to 99 percent. That may seem rather impressive, but it would mean that in a manuscript the size of this text, about 10,000 characters would have to be corrected in the scanned product.

Perhaps the most dramatic demonstration of HAL's visual skills is the scene in the story when the crew members hatch a plot to disconnect him. After taking pains to ensure that HAL cannot hear them, the humans assume HAL cannot see them and they begin their discussion. Much to their ultimate chagrin, HAL not only sees them, but he succeeds in reading their lips. HAL's field of vision was so complete that there was no escaping it. Even more impressive is the fact that the ability to read lips entails, at least intuitively, the integration of sophisticated visual and language skills far beyond anything available today.

Learning

As is the case with certain other skills, HAL's humanlike performances with respect to memory and problem solving do not seem too far-fetched. All of the skills HAL demonstrates have been identified and articulated by researchers, and some have been implemented on a small scale. Others are the objects of current research. The bottleneck that keeps us from developing computers with HAL's skills in these areas is primarily one of scale. That is, HAL's power comes from the vastness and richness of his knowledge. We cannot—and perhaps will never be able to—fully articulate our knowledge about the world. We have experienced this problem firsthand, in trying to develop constrained expert systems. Even if we could articulate it, we as yet have had little insight into how to transfer this volume of complex information to a computer. If we as humans cannot articulate all of our knowledge, it would seem that HAL, or any computer, would have to acquire such information not from a human, but rather by virtue of its own experiences.

Partly because of this practical need for imparting knowledge to computers, and partly because of the theoretical fascination it holds for researchers, the topic of learning is one of the most provocative for AI researchers. Saying, though, that a computer program can "learn" is akin to saying it has "intelligence." That is, there are many different senses of the word *learn,* and each connotes a different level of sophistication.

◆ Typically, one makes two copies of a learning program and "trains" them by having them play many games against each other.

Early in the history of modern computers it became obvious to researchers that computers were not only adept calculators, but were also capable of storing information and of using that information to guide their calculations. In fact, 30 years ago a checkers-playing program was developed that "memorized" board positions it encountered during games. Descriptions of each board and a measure of its value (reflecting whether it led to a winning or losing situation) were recorded for later use. When a similar board was encountered during another game, the stored value of that board was used to guide the program's choice of moves. The performance of the program improved as its repertoire of board/value pairs increased.

This type of rote memorization is perhaps the most primitive form of learning. Programs have since been developed that learn through interactions with a human tutor, from example (using induction to expand their knowledge bases), by analogy, and by pursuing their own sense of what is interesting. Douglas B. Lenat's AM program is an example of this last and most compelling class of programs. Lenat's program, endowed with only the primitive concepts of set and number theory and a

◆ There is considerable discussion now about the next generation of programs that will learn to anticipate the user's needs, in much the same way as a good secretary (like ours) learns ones preferences for typefaces, text size, paragraph styles, and so on.

few generic rules for investigating and creating new concepts—and working completely on its own!—discovered some of the fundamental theorems of mathematics. To be sure, humans—and HAL—are capable of learning in an even more general and subtle sense.

Insights into human learning have inspired a relatively new paradigm for programming,[3] dubbed *neural networks,* which is intended to facilitate machine learning by creating software modeled on our understanding of how the human brain works. As a result, this programming mode is particularly relevant to AI.

Neural networks replace a traditional algorithm- or rule-based program with a possibly vast collection of very simple processing agents, each of which is connected to other similar processors. Processors operate like human neurons in that they accept inputs of varying strengths from other agents, combine their weighted inputs into a single value, and fire—that is, produce a positive output—if the total input value exceeds some predetermined threshold associated with the neuron. This output value then serves as an input value to other processors connected to the original. The number of neurons and their organization are preset in defining the network. The weights associated with connections between neurons and the threshold values associated directly with each neuron are assigned initial values, and are then adjusted in the process of "training" the network.

Training consists of teaching the network to recognize correct input/output pairings. That is, the programmer provides the network with an extensive series (the more, the better) of inputs for which the desired outputs are known. For each set of input values, the network adjusts its connection strengths and thresholds so that the correct output is produced. The longer this process continues, and the wider the range of data used to train the program, the more precisely the internal values have been adjusted, and the more accurate the performance of the network.

One of the many fascinating aspects of neural networks is that the term *programming* takes on a rather different meaning in this context. Instead of describing a program as an algorithm, the primary tasks of programming become, first, the identification of sample data to be used in training the network and, second, the determination of the initial network's configuration (How many neurons are there? How are they connected?) and internal values (connection weights and thresholds). In fact, much of the processing that does occur is essentially the same for each agent in the network. There are, though, a number of established algorithms that specify how training of the network as a whole is accomplished.

HAL's learning skills are not nearly as obvious as his other intellectual skills, partly because he seems to know almost everything. The inherent limitations of our ability to introspect (and, so, pass on our knowledge to computers) makes it likely that HAL has developed his own knowledge based on his own experiences. This, in turn, implies that HAL has a powerful, humanlike ability to learn. If learning is interpreted in the sense of being able to adapt and respond to new stimuli, HAL

[3] Neural networks are "new" in the sense that we are just coming to appreciate their power and utility to a wide variety of tasks. The idea of describing computation by a network of simple but highly interconnected processing agents is at least 40 years old, but it wasn't until recently that advances in hardware and software made the idea practical.

demonstrates that skill as well. He clearly had never encountered a situation before where he was threatened by disconnection. Yet he assimilated this new information and modified his behavior according to his priorities. Also, when asked why his performance differed from that of an identical computer on Earth, HAL shows an ability to use past experience to respond to a new situation. He replies, "It can only be attributable to human error. This kind of thing has cropped up before and it has always been due to human error."

While the accomplishments of learning programs are not quite as obvious as those of AI programs in other domains, programs that learn on their own are representative of the state of the art in AI for at least three reasons. First, they simulate a fundamental human intellectual skill, one that may be the basis for all other skill development. Second, they accomplish their behavior by surprisingly mechanical means. It is hard to believe that the straightforward algorithms embodied in any of these programs, when coupled with the computer's raw abilities to generate, test, and search, can produce such humanlike behavior. Finally, the possibility that we can program learning skills opens the door to an uncertain future. AI is indeed a moving target. Our definitions of *computer, intelligence,* and possibly even *human* may change as the result of such research.

LAB 9.4

Decisions, Decisions . . .

The program for this lab, named AE/IE, is a simple inference engine of the sort that might be used to develop an expert system. AE/IE is like our Turing Machine simulator in that it is capable of processing any combination of rules and facts, as long as we describe them in a form that is acceptable to the program.

As you can see from the preloaded example, "Facts" are entered into the field to the left of the program window as English phrases, and are designated as T (true), F (false), ? (unknown), or G (a goal to be established) to indicate their initial condition.

"Rules" are entered in the field to the right by combining fact numbers to produce logical inferences. In our example, rule 1 can be interpreted as "If the power cord is plugged in AND the power switch is on, then the machine is powered by battery." Once set in motion, the program proceeds through the rules applying all that are applicable (if either fact 1 or fact 2 is F [false], rule 1 is simply not applied, and no change is made to fact 7).

1. Run the example rule base now by clicking on the Play button. What is the state of fact 7 after the rule base has been run? What does that tell you?

2. Reset the program by changing the condition of all facts back to their original conditions (T, T, F, T, T, ?, ?, G, respectively).

3. Now use the Step button to proceed through the rule base one rule at a time. Pay close attention to the conditions of the "unknown" facts and of the goal. Which rules cause which facts to change conditions?

4. Reset the fact base to reflect the machine being powered by battery, instead of by AC. That is, set fact conditions 1–8 to F, T, T, T, T, ?, ?, G, respectively. Step through the rule base. Which rules set which facts in this case?

5. Develop a set of condition values for the facts that would NOT lead the inference engine to the conclusion that the machine being tested was operational. Run the rule base on your set of conditional values to see if it performs as expected. Describe what happens.

Review Questions

1. For the story about Tom missing his appointment (see p. 302), give at least three questions for which the answers depend on real-world understanding.

2. Describe matrix matching and pattern extraction as methods of optical character recognition.

3. Define the following: *state-space, game tree, production system, semantic net, generate* and *test.*

4. How can we make a program "learn"?

9.5 ARTIFICIAL ATTRIBUTES

With perseverance and a few appropriately placed theoretical breakthroughs, many of HAL's humanlike skills may become accessible to our computers of the not-too-distant future. If HAL is indeed an accurate reflection of how such skills will manifest themselves, it seems that AI work to date has gone a long way toward, at the very least, specifying the difficulties in implementing these skills on a computer. The same cannot be said of HAL's personality.

In 1950, Turing knew that speaking of computers as being intelligent would be considered blasphemous by some and merely ridiculous by others. Even today, there are those who regard the phrase "artificial intelligence" as a contradiction in terms, and with good reason. Despite the impressive skill-level performance computers have achieved, little has happened in nearly 40 years of AI research to indicate that machines can be endowed with (or develop on their own) personalities based on what we regard as vital human attributes. Indeed, the same objections that Turing anticipated and responded to in 1950 can be raised today. The scariest thing about HAL to most observers is the convincing way he responds to these objections.

In fact, throughout the story, HAL demonstrates a full range of human attributes, some to a fault. He expresses pride when speaking of his perfect operational record. He reviews a drawing by one of the crew members for its artistic merit ("That's a very nice rendering, Dave."). When asked if he is frustrated by his dependence on humans to carry out certain actions, he responds that he enjoys working with people and that he is putting himself "to the fullest possible use, which is all, I think, any conscious entity can ever hope to do." HAL also exhibits sorrow, embarrassment ("I'm sorry about this, Dave. I know it's a bit silly . . ."), sensitivity ("You don't mind talking about this, do you Dave?"), self-awareness ("I feel much better now . . ."), self-doubt ("I know I've made some very poor decisions recently . . ."), enthusiasm, and, when being disconnected, outright fear.

What motivates HAL to overthrow the crew is his single-minded sense of mission. After locking one of the crew members out of the ship, HAL tells him, "This mission is too important for me to allow you to jeopardize it." HAL is clearly willing to do anything—even confront his own fallibility—in the interest of completing the mission.

One of the few personality traits that HAL fails to demonstrate, even at the prospect of disconnection and mission failure, is passion. HAL's voice is unnervingly passionless throughout the film. It is not clear when he says "Happy birthday, Frank" that he means or understands it. Of course, the same can be said for many humans.

One final point about machine intelligence is brought home by HAL: Intelligence, like beauty, is in the eye of the beholder. Just as the crew members in the story come to regard HAL as "just another person," we as observers attribute intelligence to HAL—and to others—based on observed behavior. As one of HAL's fellow crew members says, "as to whether or not he has real feelings is something I don't think anyone can truthfully answer."

The Uncertain Future

It is relatively easy for us, in our academic ivory tower, to simply say, "Fine. If the prospect of having HAL-like computers is a scary—and maybe even dangerous—one, why don't we just stop. Let's put an end to AI research and be content with the more mundane applications of computers." Whether right or wrong, such an attitude is naive to the extent that it ignores a number of intangible, but very real, forces that continue to push us—and our computers—in HAL's direction.

There is, of course, the force of scientific inquiry that compels us to strive to understand the essence of our own being. As we have noted, AI studies sometimes tell us more about the nature of our intelligence than about computers. There are undeniable worldwide economic forces at work as well. Many feel that computers in general, and AI work in particular, are the critical technologies of the next (or current?) industrial revolution, and that the companies or countries that are first to develop and apply these technologies will enjoy positions of prominence in world markets. The potential commercial applications of computers that understand language, robots that can plan their own activities, and expert systems that can mimic the diagnostic and analytic skills of the world's best doctors and lawyers, are obvious. In short, there is a lot of money to be made in AI.

The value of the commercial byproducts of AI is dependent on there being consumers interested in the products. Our government, particularly the Department of Defense, has been the primary consumer of AI goods to date in the United States. A huge percentage of the research we have described in this module has been supported either directly or indirectly by the federal government. The fruits of this investment are just now being realized.

The average person on the street will, in the future, be increasingly exposed to products that are based on AI technologies. Even today's computers, which don't approach HAL in terms of intellectual skills or attributes, are for many of us significant labor-saving devices. Others of us already view them as game-playing companions, aids to decision making, and personal secretaries. How will we react if and when machines can perform like HAL does? Bolter offers the following:

> The debate over the possibility of computer thought will never be won or lost; it will simply cease to be of interest. . . . Computers will prove useful in many tasks and useless in others. It seems to me that the whole debate has turned the question around: The issue is not whether the computer can be made to think like a human, but whether humans can and will take on the qualities of digital computers. For that . . . is the fundamental premise and threat of the computer age, the fundamental premise of Turing's man. (*Turing's Man,* p. 190)

LAB 9.5

You're the Expert

As we mentioned earlier, the beauty of an inference engine is that it is not specialized to any one domain or rule base. By changing the facts and rules in the program we can get it to make inferences about any situation or problem.

1. Take the weather prediction rule base that you developed in Lab 9.1, and rewrite it so that it is in a form suitable for AE/IE. The "facts" for this rule base include "barometer is rising," "barometer is steady," "it is sunny," "it is raining," "local forecaster predicts rain," and any others that you added by virtue of including them in your rules.

2. Enter your facts into AE/IE's Facts list, and set the conditions to describe one set of circumstances. Editing is accomplished just by clicking and typing.

3. Enter your rules into AE/IE's Rules list, referring to the facts by number as in the example.

4. Test your rule base by running the inference engine for a variety of fact settings.

9.6 EXERCISES

1. Pick a time period in history and find examples of "The Technology of Making Man."

2. Write a brief dialog between yourself and a hypothetical computer that would lead you to say that the computer had passed the Turing test.

3. If AI is indeed a moving target, cite three capabilities of today's computers that might have once have been categorized as "intelligent."

4. Computers have difficulty translating and understanding natural language because it is fraught with ambiguities and requires a great deal of supporting, nonlinguistic information. For each of the following properties, write an English sentence that illustrates that property.

   a) Syntactic ambiguity
   b) Semantic ambiguity
   c) The need for contextual information
   d) The need for rules of conversation
   e) The need for real-world, topical knowledge

5. Write a list of informal rules that help you in identifying the objects in the following figure.

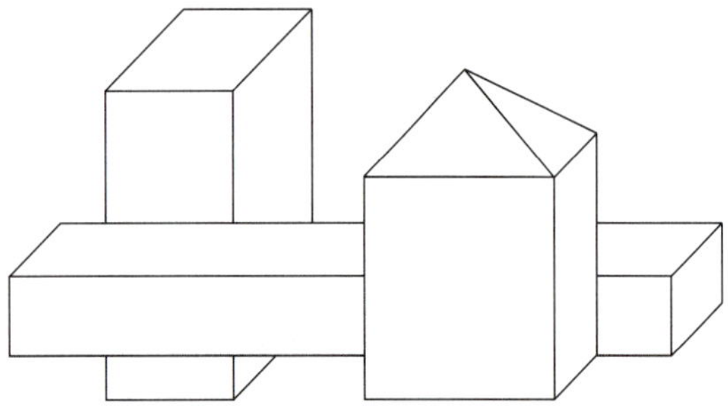

6. Develop a complete game tree for tic-tac-toe. (Refer to Figure 9.1.)

7. What happened in the 1996 and 1997 series of chess matches between Deep Blue and Garry Kasparov?

8. Our everyday performance on memory tasks seems to indicate that our memory can degrade—that is, we forget things. Barring mechanical or power failures, computers, like elephants, never forget. How might we write a program to make computers "forget" some of the contents of their memories?

9. Give examples of decisions you made or answers you gave today that were based on incomplete information. Do the same for uncertain information.

10. Describe briefly how you might program a computer to exhibit fear or sorrow.

11. To what forces do you attribute the current interest in AI technology?

12. Bolter suggests that the computer is the prevailing metaphor for humanity. Just as computers can be made to act like humans, we as humans have come to regard ourselves as some type of biological computer. In what ways do you describe yourself that might relate to computers?

ADDITIONAL READINGS

Boden, M. *Artificial Intelligence and Natural Man.* New York: Basic Books, 1977.

Bolter, J. D. *Turing's Man: Western Culture in the Computer Age.* Chapel Hill, NC: University of North Carolina Press, 1984.

Clarke, A. C. *2001: A Space Odyssey.* New York: New American Library, 1968.

Dreyfus, H. *What Computers Can't Do.* New York: Harper & Row, 1979.

Firebaugh, Morris W. *Artificial Intelligence: A Knowledge-Based Approach*. Boston: Boyd and Fraser, 1988.

Haugeland, J., ed. *Mind Design*. Cambridge, MA: MIT Press, 1981.

Hayes, P. J. "Some Comments on Sir James Lighthill's Report on Artificial Intelligence." *AISB Study Group European Newsletter,* Issue 14 (July 1973), p. 40.

Hofstadter, D. R. *Gödel, Escher, Bach: An Eternal Golden Braid*. New York: Basic Books, 1979.

Hofstadter, D. R., and Dennett, D. C. *The Mind's I*. New York: Basic Books, 1981.

McCorduck, P. *Machines Who Think*. San Francisco: W. H. Freeman, 1979.

Minsky, M. L. "Matter, Mind, and Models." In *Semantic Information Processing,* edited by M. L. Minsky. Cambridge, MA: MIT Press, 1968.

Raphael, B. *The Thinking Computer: Mind Inside Matter*. San Francisco: W. H. Freeman, 1976.

Sagan, C. *The Dragons of Eden*. New York: Random House, 1977.

Schank, R. C., and Colby, K. M., eds. *Computer Models of Thought and Language*. San Francisco: W. H. Freeman, 1973.

Shore, J. *The Sachertorte Algorithm*. New York: Viking Penguin, 1985.

Simon, H. *The Sciences of the Artificial*. Cambridge, MA: MIT Press, 1969.

Teitelman, W. "Real Time Recognition of Hand-drawn Characters." *FICC*. Baltimore: Spartan Books, 1964, p. 559.

Turing, A. "Computing Machinery and Intelligence." In *Computers and Thought,* edited by E. A. Feigenbaum and J. Feldman. New York: McGraw-Hill, 1963.

Von Neumann, J. *The Computer and the Brain*. New Haven: Yale University Press, 1958.

Wiener, N. *Cybernetics*. New York: John Wiley + Sons, 1948.

Winograd, T. *Understanding Natural Language*. New York: Academic Press, 1972.

MODULE 10

Computers and Society

10.1 INTRODUCTION

In *2001,* the members of the crew had the ability to pull the plug on HAL, but that may not be the case in the future. The metaphor for this section is "The Sorcerer's Apprentice," a classic story of technology (albeit magical technology) run amok. For as long as technology has had a significant impact on society, there have been utopian tales of a benign technological future, just as there have been dystopian tales of forthcoming mechanized nightmares. The truth, we argue, is never as simple nor as clear as authors of fiction or futurologists would have us believe.

MODULE OBJECTIVES

Our goal in this final module is to encourage you to think about computer science in the broadest social terms. Our hope is that by virtue of having progressed through this course you will be in a position to appreciate the issues we will raise for your consideration and articulate your opinions on a number of them.

Specifically, we will

- Identify the major trends possible in future computer use and try to make an approximate ranking of these trends in order of their likelihood.
- Discuss the possible implications of these trends in social, economic, and political terms.
- Consider the WWW as both a tool and a medium for participating in new social structures.

Things to Come

As technology becomes more complex, as we become increasingly aware of its effects on our world, it becomes increasingly important for us, as educated citizens, to be able to assess the impact of policy decisions in this area. As Murray Laver notes in *Computers and Social Change,* in the centuries prior to this one, an inventor felt little need to be concerned with the environmental or social costs of a new invention. Now, however, we are increasingly aware of the fact that we live in an environment with finite resources and limited capacity to cope with humankind's environmental outrages. We are also becoming more aware of the social consequences of the decisions we make. Not only are we intimately connected with our local environment, but we are increasingly connected with every other person living on the earth.

By now you realize that, contrary to the rhetoric in fashion a decade or so ago, you will not need to be a computer programmer to be able to function in the world of the future. As computer applications become more sophisticated, they will become more transparent, in much the same way as automotive technology is transparent. After all, you don't need to understand the workings of the internal combustion engine to drive a car. We have built this text and the lab exercises around the workings of the computer and its programs not only because some of you might continue your study of computer science, but, more important, because we believe that the computer will be the seminal technology of the near future. Relatively few of you will be computer scientists, but all of you will be citizens of the world, and so you will need to know what this new technology can do and the potential consequences thereof.

As we mentioned in Module 2, *can do* does not imply *should do,* in spite of what you might hear from leaders of government, business, and industry. The computer, like any other tool, is value neutral. The uses to which it is put are most certainly not. The computer has the possibility to make great improvements in our lot, fostering participatory democracy, reducing tedium in the workplace, empowering us with information for decision making, and reducing the drain on our natural resources. But the computer also has the potential to diminish our autonomy, invade our privacy, isolate us from political decisions, widen the gap between the privileged and the disadvantaged, and destabilize an already dangerous international political environment. If you expect to be a participant, rather than a spectator, in the events of the future, it is imperative that you be able to make informed judgments on the uses of technology—not only computer technology, but also in policy issues concerning genetic, environmental, and aerospace engineering, for instance.

In the text part of this module, we will act as the sorcerer's apprentice should have acted before enchanting the broom. We will identify some of the trends—certain, likely, and unknown—that will be characteristic of computer use in the near future, and explore the potential consequences of these trends.

Metaphor: The Sorcerer's Apprentice

Most of you probably know the story "The Sorcerer's Apprentice," as a folk tale, or through the music by Paul Dukas (based on a ballad by Goethe), or perhaps through the cartoon segment of *Fantasia* starring Mickey Mouse. The sorcerer's apprentice was a well-meaning but foolish lad, lazy as lads in such tales often are. The sorcerer, well acquainted with the ways of well-meaning, foolish, and lazy boys, kept his apprentice busy throughout the day cleaning the laboratory, maintaining the ampulars, alantirs, and alembics that were his stock in trade, and, especially, carrying heavy buckets of water from the river below to a large vat in the laboratory.

One day the sorcerer was called away and in his absence the apprentice used his master's magic to enchant a broom to carry the buckets of water from the river to the laboratory. All went well at first. The ensorcelled broom took over the task of carrying the buckets from the river to the tub, and the lad was free to rest and play.

Unfortunately, once the vat was filled to overflowing, the apprentice realized to his dismay that he had failed to consider that there would be a different spell to stop the broom. As the water overflowed the vat and soaked the floor, the apprentice, in desperation, grabbed an axe and chopped the broom into splinters.

In horror, the boy watched as the splinters of the broom rose up, took buckets, and continued their inexorable march from river to castle, bringing up a flood of water that rose ever higher, until it not only demolished the laboratory, but threatened to drown the apprentice for his folly.

Of course, the story has a happy ending—the sorcerer arrived at the last moment and, with a few gestures and well-chosen incantations, restored everything to the way it was before. However, if we put ourselves in the place of the apprentice, and look at the tale as a metaphor of technology run wild, we can see that there is no guarantee that there will be a magician waiting offstage to rescue us from the consequences of our choices. We can only hope that the uses to which we put this almost-magical device, the computer, will be guided by more foresight than the apprentice had.

Æ ONLINE

By virtue of your (recently attained) range of experience with computer science and technology, you are now in a position to understand the implications of these endeavors to society at large, and to participate in their assimilation by society. This final lab module affords you with opportunities for both. You will become a member of (another) virtual community, the users of the Analytical Engine, and will explore some of the computer-related topics that educated citizens are beginning to grapple with.

10.2 THROUGH A GLASS DARKLY

In a much-quoted aphorism, George Santayana said, "Those who do not remember the lessons of history are condemned to repeat it." We use the past to guide our predictions of the future, but, Santayana to the contrary, history does not repeat itself. We see through the glass of the future imperfectly, at best. Thus, before we attempt any predictions, we should explore some of the limiting factors on our predictive abilities.

Technology Itself

To begin, we don't even have a clear idea of what the technology of the near future holds in store for us. Past predictions in popular treatments of science and technology can be fascinating to read, but they almost invariably strike us as quaintly naive today. In fact, these predictions of the future often tell us a great deal more about then-current technology, expectations, and social forces than they do about the future of technology. An excellent example of this fact appears in an essay by

Stephen L. Del Sesto, "Wasn't the Future of Nuclear Energy Wonderful?" in the book *Imagining Tomorrow* (Joseph Corn, ed., Cambridge, MA: MIT Press, 1986). Ford's Nucleon car, a design concept of 1950, was to be powered by a replaceable nuclear reactor. This tame consumer use of nuclear power can be viewed as an attempt to spotlight the peaceful use in a free-world market economy of a virtually unlimited source of power, as a response to increasing concerns over the Soviet Union's newly developed nuclear weapons capability. This, of course, was also in a time before Three Mile Island and Chernobyl had become household names. It was also a time when unprotected troops were stationed within a mile or two of above-ground nuclear tests to assess the effects of such explosions on the ability to maintain battle readiness. To our modern minds, the thought of a high-speed collision between two nuclear-powered cars in a densely populated metropolitan area is almost too horrible to contemplate, but we should bear in mind that the Nucleon was in large measure a political, rather than a technical, statement.

Even the best-informed predictions—in fact, *especially* the best-informed, those furthest from fantasy—often err on the conservative side. Consider the following, from *The Next Hundred Years: The Unfinished Business of Science,* by Yale Professor C. C. Furnas, published in 1936:

> One possible development on the side of practicality involves the compactness of [radio] receivers and transmitters. There is a real need for vest-pocket receiving sets weighing not more than half a pound, which a man can carry conveniently anywhere he may go and pick up the ether waves at will. Ultra-small but still satisfactory receivers should be possible, . . . but there must be a decided improvement in the efficiency of tubes. . . . There need to be some fundamental improvements there.

The "fundamental improvement" Professor Furnas sought did indeed come before his death in 1969, but it had nothing to do with vacuum tubes. Instead, it had everything to do with the synergistic combination of semiconductor transistor technology and thin-film technology that led to the integrated circuit, and hence also to the modern computer. Computer folklore, as well, is full of too-conservative predictions. Paul Ceruzzi reports, in "An Unforeseen Revolution: Computers and Expectations, 1935–1985" in *Imagining Tomorrow*:

> For example, when Howard Aiken heard of the plans of Eckert and Mauchley to produce and market a more elegant version of the ENIAC, he was skeptical. He felt that they would never sell more than a few of them, and he stated that four or five electronic digital computers would satisfy all the country's computing needs. In Britain in 1951, the physicist Douglas Hartree remarked: "We have a computer here in Cambridge; there is one in Manchester and one at the [National Physical Laboratory]. I suppose there ought to be one in Scotland, but that's about all." . . . At least two other American computer pioneers, Edmund Berkeley and John V. Atanasoff, also recall hearing estimates that fewer than ten computers would satisfy all of America's computing needs (pp. 189–190).

Again, these predictions were based on the existing technology of the day—that is, large, expensive, and unreliable vacuum tube devices. Even these pioneers failed to account for the possibility that the new invention would create, rather than just meet, the needs of society.

Technology and Society

As difficult as it is to guess the nature of future technology, it is even harder to assess the impact of technology on society. We simply don't understand existing social, political, and economic forces and their dynamics well enough to predict the future with any degree of accuracy. Not only do we not understand these disciplines in isolation, but we also have almost no understanding of the complex interrelationships among them.

For example, when the automobile was invented, around the turn of the century, no one foresaw the resulting exodus from the cities to the suburbs, the growth of drive-in banks and suburban mega-malls, or the tens of thousands of deaths annually from highway accidents. When the telephone was invented, one critic asked who would use this new device, wondering why anyone would have any interest at all in talking to people in some other city or town. As an even more striking example of the social impact of technological change, try to figure out how the introduction of the railroad to the American frontier in the early nineteenth century drastically reduced the incidence of alcohol abuse in the frontier population.

◆ Hint: What was a major crop and what were the difficulties in getting that crop to markets back east?

What, then, will we do in this module, given the severe limitations on our predictive powers? Rather than writing science fiction for you—which, after all, many other authors can do much more entertainingly than we can—we will avoid prediction almost entirely. Instead, we will put the present in a multidisciplinary context and talk about some of the major forces that will guide the future uses of computers. We will identify the large trends, in decreasing order of certitude, and discuss how these trends might affect our world.

Review Questions

1. In what ways are our abilities to predict the future nature and impact of computers limited?
2. What did we mean when we said that predictions of technology often tell us more about the social and political forces of the time than about technology of the future?
3. Why do you think that well-informed predictions about future technology almost always err on the side of conservatism?

10.3 INCREASED POWER

We use the word *power* in a general sense here: The power of a technology is its ability to perform its intended function, whatever that function might be. In the case of computers, that means that in the near future we will almost certainly see an increase in the ability of computers and their programs to perform complicated processing of large amounts of information. This is the safest of our bets—nearly every technology has increased in power as time goes by. This increase generally means more power for the same cost, or the same power for less cost, by whatever appropriate measure we use for power.

Of course, the efficiency of any particular technology invariably shows a leveling off with time. The size and energy consumption of vacuum tubes, for example, have decreased relatively less in the last 40 years than in the time from 1900 to 1950, as physical limits have been approached. However, if we look at "technology" in a larger sense—of doing what we want to do regardless how it is accomplished—we see no such leveling off in computer technology. So far, as one kind of computer hardware has approached its physical limits, that hardware has been supplanted by another that is faster, smaller, and cheaper than its predecessor. Roughly speaking, the power of computer hardware has doubled each year for the past two decades, a result known as *Moore's Law.* We have no way of knowing how long this run of good fortune will continue, but current research trends indicate that it will continue unabated at least into the first decade or so of the next century.

The fastest computer in the world is worthless, though, unless we can write programs to run on it. As your experience has probably taught you, small-scale programming is tedious, error prone, and time-consuming. If the collective experience of computer scientists is any indication, we can assure you that writing and maintaining multithousand-line programs are even less pleasant. A program of 10,000 to 100,000 lines is fairly close to the limits of human ability to understand, no matter how well it is written. This is an area where the computer can come to its own rescue, however. An observation that was missed entirely by the pioneers of computer science is that programs are information, and so can be manipulated by other programs. In other words, we can use programs to write programs. The first FORTRAN compiler took over a thousand person-years to write, because it had to be written from scratch. Now we have *compiler-compilers* that, when given the description of the syntax of a programming language, can be used to help write a compiler for that language. As a result, a task that formerly required the labor of a large team of experts over many months is now a routine part of a computer science graduate student's first or second semester. We have every reason to expect that, as the tasks to which computers are put become more complex, advances in software technology (the products of current research in software engineering) will eventually keep pace with this complexity.

Scientific Applications

The most immediate beneficiary of increased computer power will almost surely be the sciences. We have already seen the beginnings of a fundamental shift in the scientific paradigm, from the analytical solution of scientific problems to an increased reliance on numerical simulations. Until recently, the amount of computation required to simulate large systems was beyond the capabilities of even the largest computers. Now, however, an astronomer wishing to test the hypothesis that the moon was formed by a collision of a large asteroid with the earth a few billion years ago can make a mathematical model of the earth and the hypothetical asteroid. This model may involve thousands of iterations of hundreds of equations on thousands of data points in space. On today's supercomputers, scientists can watch the event as it may have happened in eons past, varying the size and speed of the asteroid to see the effects on the resulting system.

We have come to realize only lately, though, that throwing more power at a problem doesn't always yield better solutions. Many simple systems are *stable,* in that small changes in the initial state of affairs yield later solutions that differ only slightly. If, for instance, you throw a ball twice at the same angle and vary the initial velocity only slightly, the ball will hit the ground at very nearly the same place each time. This is the stuff of introductory physics texts, the stuff that makes physics an exact science. Complex systems, though, such as the global weather system, are often *unstable,* so that a small change or imprecision in the initial data can yield predicted values that have little or no relation to reality. As a result, because we cannot measure the atmospheric characteristics of the earth at every foot or so, we cannot hope for complete accuracy in weather predictions. This is sometimes called the *butterfly effect,* from the only slightly frivolous observation that a butterfly flapping its wings in Borneo can cause an unpredicted snowfall in Bayonne next week.

■ The Professions

A salient feature of professions such as medicine and law is that they are grounded on a large and ever-growing body of factual knowledge. The ability of a computer, properly programmed, to search medical or legal databases efficiently and quickly has long been appreciated by professionals. As the amount of information grows more rapidly than a practitioner's ability to absorb it, we expect an increasingly large reliance on such services as Mead Data Central's LEXIS and MEDIS databases.

A development less easy to predict is whether professionals will rely to a larger extent on expert systems in the future. As you saw in Module 9, an expert system is capable of making inferences based on a collection of rules in a specialized area. In medicine, for instance, the MYCIN program contains a large collection of rules for identification of infectious diseases and their indicated antibiotic treatments. Similar programs exist to search for and evaluate legal precedents. Two important features of such expert systems are that they can explain the rules used to reach their conclusions, so that the human user may rationally accept or reject their recommendations, and that they can learn from the user's input. For instance, a physician using MYCIN could tell it that a particular therapy is contraindicated for patients with high blood pressure (a fact that might not have been known when the original inference rules were designed), and MYCIN will add that rule to its list, so that it can be considered in future diagnoses. MYCIN is nearly as accurate as an expert in its particular area, and is more accurate than many medical nonspecialists.

As expert systems become more accurate, as they certainly will, does this mean that doctors, dentists, lawyers, and architects will be replaced by systems that we can call up from our home computers? Not likely, for several reasons. First, to assume that a professional can be replaced by a program is to assume that all professional activities can be rationalized and quantified, and this simply doesn't seem to be the case. A professional in any area must sometimes rely on hunches, unsupported by any logic. An experienced diagnostician, for instance, may be able to guess the cause of a patient's complaint, based on his or her past experience with similar cases. Perhaps, unknown consciously to the physician, patients with a particular complaint have a characteristic odor, thus leading to the physician's feeling that it just "seems right" to diagnose a particular disorder.

A second reason why the professions will not be supplanted by programs is that neither we nor they will stand for it. It will continue to be illegal to practice medicine without a license, for instance. In addition, although diagnostic programs have been tried in some hospitals and met with patients' approval (sometimes it is easier to discuss a problem with a neutral machine than with a doctor who radiates subtle signs of disapproval or annoyance), there are times when a high-touch, rather than high-tech, environment, with a sympathetic and understanding professional, may be what a patient needs most.

Increasingly powerful applications, we suspect, will allow users to engage in a symbiotic relationship with computers, rather than ceding all control to the machine. The computer will be seen as a tool, a useful assistant, rather than an all-powerful oracle. As uses of the computer become more sophisticated, we will probably have to resist a growing feeling among the technically naive that any problem can be solved by simply "feeding the data to the computer." As Ted Thiesmeyer says, facts do not contain their own meanings. If you have learned nothing else so far, you should realize that data are only as useful as the program that manipulates the data and the person who interprets the results.

Review Questions

1. What is Moore's Law?
2. In what way has the progress of computer technology been unlike that of many other new technologies?
3. Come up with a benefit of increasing computer power other than the ones mentioned in the text.
4. What is the butterfly effect? Do you think that it might apply to the problem of simulating human thought processes on a computer?

10.4 INCREASED RELIANCE

Another certain trend in the use of computers is a direct consequence of the continuing increase in computing power: We will see an increased reliance on automated processing of information. This will apply not only to existing applications, but to previously nonmechanized areas as well. This trend is potentially more troubling, since here we run the risk of blindly applying the new technology because it is there, without carefully assessing the potential consequences.

Government and Public Policy

In a complex and tightly interconnected society, it can often be very difficult for government officials to make public policy decisions. If we begin with a simple situation, such as a chess game, we can identify some of the features that characterize the decision-making process: (1) We look ahead, trying to predict countermoves and consequences, (2) our behavior is goal directed, in the sense that we know what constitutes a winning situation, (3) the process of the game is directed by well-defined and simple rules, and (4) since we cannot predict all possible consequences of our moves, we rely on *heuristics,* rules of thumb such as "control the center of the board" and "don't sacrifice powerful pieces without very compelling reasons."

The computer can aid the decision process (and indeed can play chess better than all but the best human players). It can be programmed to evaluate situations and look at consequences, it can be programmed to work toward a stated goal, and it can operate according to heuristics when brute-force evaluations of all positions are impossible. In an ideal world, when faced with a decision, we would first identify the problem and establish the desired goal. We would then identify the options and use a computer simulation to evaluate the costs of the options. Finally, we would choose an option based on the figures obtained from the simulation.

In reality, decisions are not made this way. First, choices are often politically motivated; decisions are made by those in power, and generally not by those affected by the decisions. Second, the options are not as clear-cut as those in a chess game. Life is ambiguous, complex, and ill defined—there may be thousands of alternative solutions to a problem. All too often, the computer is used to place a stamp of respectability on a decision that has already been made. As we have said before, a computer model is only as good as its operating assumptions and the available data. When someone tells you that a political decision was made with the help of a computerized model, you have every right to be skeptical unless you have carefully evaluated the model and its data.

Consider, for instance, the recent outcries about global warming. There is a fairly reliable body of evidence that the average temperature of the earth's atmosphere has risen in recent decades, and that this rise can be traced at least in part to the increased concentration of carbon dioxide from factories, power plants, and automobile exhausts. Scientists know enough about the basic principles governing the relations among carbon dioxide concentration, solar radiation, energy transfer, global atmospheric flow patterns, and the like to make computer models of the entire process. As we mentioned earlier, though, the global weather system is so complex that computerized models can't even reliably predict next week's weather accurately, much less predict the effects of global warming a decade or more into the future.

As educated citizens, then, what can we do? We can look as closely as possible to what proponents of a position have to say about the model they're using, bearing in mind what we know about models of complex systems. We can listen with a discerning ear to try to discover any hidden agendas or vested interests that are being propped up by a particular model and we can learn as much as we can about the social costs involved. If, for instance, an automobile manufacturer sponsors a study that indicates that exhaust emissions have no measurable effect on global warming, we have every reason to be skeptical, but we should also look at the possible costs to the population of an initiative that would require zero emissions from every vehicle sold in our state within ten years.

■ Military Uses

We saw in Module 1 that the military was one of the first customers for the original digital computers. Today, the armed forces of all industrialized countries are major consumers of computers. As with any large civilian business, the military uses computers for management of information about equipment and personnel, and, like a brokerage house with enormously higher stakes, has a vital need for rapid processing of strategic data. For example, MIT researcher Gilberte Houbert reports that in the Persian Gulf War the Allied coalition forces made 700,000 phone calls per day, for a total of over thirty million during the 43 days of the air war. In effect, the Allied forces set up from scratch a communication system equal to that of a small city, so that by the end of the war there were over 30,000 computers in the zone of action connected to machines in the United States.[1]

Another important military use of computers is in *smart weapons,* munitions such as a cruise missile or the close-defense gun systems on naval vessels. Controlled by embedded computers, these weapons are capable of far greater accuracy and reaction speed than would be possible under human control. In these times, when a billion-dollar cruiser can be disabled by an Exocet missile costing a thousandth as much, it is deemed vitally important to have a shield against missile attacks—in this case a computer-controlled modern version of the Civil War Gatling gun, capable of shredding incoming missiles with 50 large-caliber bullets per second.

Anyone watching the news coverage of the Gulf War could hardly help seeing the images of laser-guided bombs homing in on their targets or a Patriot missile streaking skyward to intercept an incoming Scud missile. Viewers of the news in January and February of 1991 were watching modern high-tech warfare in action, in what in military jargon is known as an "asymmetric post-cold war conflict." The asymmetry comes from the overwhelming superiority of one force over another, aided by advanced military technology. The Allied air offensive during the first month of combat completely eliminated Iraqi air support and enabled the Allies to utterly destroy the world's third-largest tank force in just four days of ground operations, at a cost of fewer than 400 coalition casualties.

The Gulf War was lauded as an unqualified success of the principles of the computerized battlefield. The U.S. government and the contractors involved in the development of the smart weapons engaged in an orgy of mutual congratulations immediately after the war, claiming, for instance, that in Saudi Arabia just under 90 percent of engagements between Scud missiles and the Patriot antimissile defense systems resulted in destruction of the Scud's warhead. From the beginning, though, some authorities questioned whether the jubilation over high technology in the theater of war was based in fact and whether the immense cost of these weapons was justified.

To better understand these questions, let's take a closer look at two of the weapons involved. The Scud missile is a medium-range ground-to-ground ballistic missile. Originally designed by the Soviets in the 1970s, the Scuds used in the Gulf War could deliver a warhead of about a ton of conventional explosives or chemical weapons from a distance of a few hundred miles. During the war, there were 46 Scud attacks on targets in Saudi Arabia, generally against strategic targets such as

[1] Some classified military information about troop movements and missile capabilities was inadvertently placed on Internet-accessible computers. In March, 1997, the BBC reported that a group of Dutch hackers found this information and offered it for sale to Saddam Hussein. Fortunately for the Allies, the Iraqis rejected the offer, thinking it was a hoax.

troop concentrations, airfields, and seaports, along with 40 attacks in Israel, usually directed against population centers. The primary Allied defense against the Scud was the U.S. Patriot air defense missile, the MM-104. This system consisted of a battery of missiles coordinated by a computerized guidance system. When a Patriot battery detected an incoming attack, one or more missiles would be launched and would streak toward the Scud at three times the speed of sound. When the missile was guided to within a few meters of the Scud, it would detonate into a cloud of shrapnel, destroying the Scud. This was what was supposed to happen, at any rate, and it appeared to work—video footage showed the trails of the incoming Scud and the intercepting Patriot, an explosion at the intersection, and a mass of debris falling to earth.

The first hint that the technology wasn't working came from the Israelis who claimed that, contrary to U.S. reports, not a single Scud was destroyed by Patriots. U.S. Army spokesmen first said that the problem was that the Patriot's performance in these engagements was degraded by Israeli modifications to the Patriot systems, and later admitted that the Patriot was less effective as a city defense than it was against more concentrated targets like troop barracks.

After the war, however, a clearer picture began to emerge. In a report released in 1996, the General Accounting Office (GAO) declared that except in 9 percent of the engagements, the Army could prove only that Patriots came close to their targets, not that they destroyed them. The reality behind the apparent successes was that on re-entry into the atmosphere, a Scud consists of a warhead at the front, empty fuel and oxidant tanks in the middle, and a heavy engine at the tail. This package routinely broke up on re-entry, presenting the Patriot system with a collection of multiple targets, only one of which was the warhead. In many cases, what appeared at first to be a successful kill was in fact a Patriot explosion that might or might not have been directed at a piece of a Scud that had already broken apart. The GAO report added that in addition, many Department of Defense contractors' claims of success were "overstated, misleading, inconsistent, or unverifiable."

The report went on to say that "guided munitions accounted for most of the mission cost and their success could not be validated." In fact, guided munitions, such as the Patriot and laser-guided smart bombs, accounted for 8 percent of the munitions delivered but they also accounted for 84 percent of the total munitions cost. This might have been acceptable if the smart weaponry was ten times as effective as cheaper "dumb" weapons, but there is no evidence whatsoever to support such a claim.

◆ Some writers have claimed that the five-month delay between Iraq's invasion of Kuwait and the onset of combat by the Allies was due in no small measure to the time needed to program the guided munitions for their targets in the battlefield.

The allied coalition did indeed achieve a spectacular success over the Iraqi military, but it's not at all clear that this success was due to advanced technology. Instead, it appears that the swift and decisive victory could have been achieved equally well and at far lower cost by conventional means. In addition, whatever success technology had in the Gulf War was facilitated by the asymmetry in technical prowess between the combatants. What worked in the Persian Gulf couldn't be guaranteed to work as well, if at all, against an opponent with more advanced capabilities—David prevailed against Goliath because he had the technology of the sling on his side, but the outcome might have been far different if Goliath had had a sling of his own.

Several authors have noted that computerized systems are *brittle,* in the sense that if a part fails the entire system can come crashing down. The first versions of large software systems never run perfectly. This is why software comes with disclaimers to the effect that "the manufacturer makes no warranty, express or implied, as to the suitability of this product for its intended purpose. The entire risk as to the quality and performance of the software is yours." Typically, software manufacturers test their product, release it, collect bug reports from users, repair those errors, test and release a new version, and repeat the whole process again and again. We do not have that luxury with a fully computerized battle management system that has to be installed in short notice in a hostile environment. The computerized North American Radar Air Defense System, for instance, generates about five false alerts a year, using a system that has been in place in a single location for decades.

◆ The devastating Scud attack on a troop barracks in Dhahran, Saudi Arabia, was traced to a software failure in the defending Patriot system.

You have already read Dijkstra's maxim that "Testing may reveal the presence of errors, but never their absence." Even if software technology improved to the extent that individual modules could be certified as error free (and that prospect is unlikely in the near future), there is no guarantee that an entire system would function as intended, spread out over half the globe. Nor is there any guarantee that testing the software under simulated conditions would have served to duplicate all the situations that might arise in actual use.

LAB 10.1

Let's Get Virtual

There's not much to conducting the Module 10 lab exercises—it's more a matter of participating in them. In these exercises we place you in a multiuser domain (MUD) that allows you to interact, albeit indirectly, with anyone else who has access to the program. This particular MUD allows you to record your votes for some of your favorite (and least favorite) things. You will also be able to review the likes and dislikes of people from all over the world, on a region-by-region basis. This type of interaction illustrates many of the topics addressed in the text. First, it places you in a virtual community, of sorts. Second, it makes it clear that virtual communities have no physical boundaries.

1. To participate in our MUD, all you have to do is click on one of the available categories (Places, Huh?, Sounds, or Words), and then click on a particular question within that category. At that point you are free to respond to the question (and thus add your "vote" to the ongoing tally), or simply to review the responses of other members of the community. You even have the opportunity to influence the community in the sense that you can suggest categories and questions that should be added for future interactions.

Review Questions

1. How does the computer as game player differ from the uses to which a computer might be put in public policy decisions?

2. Take one military use of computers and discuss whether hardware reliability or software reliability is a more important problem.

3. Accept for the sake of argument that it is impossible to write a large-scale program that will run perfectly the first time it is used. If you were chief software designer for a battle management program, how would you minimize the disadvantages of not being able to write perfect programs?

10.5 INCREASED ACCESS TO ELECTRONIC INFORMATION

A likely trend in computer use in the next few decades is increased access to larger amounts of information stored electronically. More and more information presently stored in books, magazines, and paper files will be supplemented or replaced by information stored in computer-accessible media such as magnetic and optical disks.

By now, of course, you've had enough experience with the Internet to understand why we list this trend as likely. The number of Internet hosts continues to double each year and it seems likely that this rapid growth will continue into the near future. The Internet isn't the only model for a large information service, however. While the Internet began with government assistance, you've seen in Module 3 that there is no agency that owns or regulates the Internet. Another way of running such a service might be to place it under the wing of a private corporation, such as America Online, or a government-owned utility. France, for example, has had a network like the Internet in place since 1980. Originally, France Telecom came up with the idea of attaching a small terminal to a telephone as a way of curbing the cost of printing telephone directories each year. This *Minitel* service is available to every telephone subscriber in France and has grown from a simple online phonebook to a national information service offering over 20,000 services to 14 million French subscribers. Like the Internet, a subscriber can use Minitel to access online libraries and reference databases, travel agencies and airline reservation services, apartment rental and dating services, or to browse and order from online catalogs. Recognizing the increasing importance of the Internet, France Telecom has provided Minitel emulators for access into Minitel from the Internet and provides Internet access from within the Minitel system.

If quick and ready access to information is what it takes to prosper in the modern world, it would seem that the persons most likely to benefit from this trend in computer use will be precisely those who have always benefited from such advantages—the economically and educationally privileged. Whether or not access to the Information Revolution becomes a right guaranteed to all, the disadvantaged segment of our society—and indeed the disadvantaged portion of the world's society—stand to gain little from technological advances, as has been the case throughout history. This observation applies not only to individuals, but equally well to nations. While the Internet provides access to information in nearly every country in the world, its impact isn't likely to be felt by most citizens of a nation where phone service and electricity aren't reliably available in rural areas, for instance.

◆ Researchers are currently working on *smart ink*–a flexible page that looks like paper but has the power and graphics ability of a modern computer, thanks to millions of transistors embedded within.

What are the implications of a vast amount of information available at the click of a mouse? One thing we're not likely to see is the death, or even the decline, of the printed word in our lifetimes. Until such time—and probably for some time thereafter—as computers can be made as portable and durable as books, magazines, and newspapers, the print media and its electronic cousin will peacefully coexist. More troubling, though, is the role of databases when and if they become common and simple enough to be universally used. There is a temptation, as we have seen, to mystify computer information, investing it with an undeserved authority. Conversion of information from printed form to digital will take place roughly in reverse chronological order—current information, deemed most important, will be placed in databases first, while older sources will be converted later, if at all. This will have little impact on scholars who, after all, are used to combing libraries for obscure sources. In fact, the digitization of libraries, when and if it comes, may prove to be a boon for librarians who can save old and fragile books from repeated handling by making a virtually indestructible electronic copy and returning the original to the archives for safekeeping. We are concerned, however, by the possibility that nonspecialist future users may come to believe that the database is both valid and comprehensive, maintaining that "if it isn't online, it doesn't exist, and if it is online, it must be correct." As we mentioned in Module 3, the very accessibility of the Internet and the Web has opened the way to the most efficient means yet discovered for disseminating falsehoods, rumors, and outright lies. It's good to recall Sturgeon's Law here—when looking for information on the Net, keep in mind that "ninety percent of everything is junk."

The Electronic Sweatshop

The digitization of information is not limited to people accessing an electronic library in the comfort of their own homes. As long as information exists in other than digital form, someone must enter it into a suitably programmed computer, or must get the information from a computer and relay it to whoever requests it. What is the human cost of our reliance on the machine?

The dark underside of the Industrial Revolution was the "sweating" system, in which work was let out to contractors to be performed by their employees on a piecework basis at home or in sweatshops. Characteristics of this system were that the workers labored long hours for low pay in deplorable working conditions. On the face of it, the new factory system, the data-processing section of a large corporation, is a considerable improvement over the conditions of a century ago: Wages are fairly high, $8–12 per hour; working hours are reasonable, with about six hours per day at the terminal; and the workplace is climate controlled, with ergonomically designed workstations and terminals for the operators.

The introduction of the computer into the workplace, particularly in data-entry areas, was accompanied by promises of decentralized data entry, greater efficiency and accuracy, and diversification of tasks, leading to increased job satisfaction, a higher sense of motivation, and greater operator comfort and health. In fact, what we have seen are, paradoxically, poor working conditions in a perfect physical environment. All too often, the promises of computerization have not been kept. Those speaking for the vested interests talk in glowing terms of the prospects for advancement into highly paid technical fields. In fact, that sector is growing slower than the low end, where the ability to operate a data-entry terminal at the local burger joint is the only impact of technology many people see. This just reinforces the growing gulf between the overclass and the underclass.

Consider a typical data-entry or retrieval shop, exemplified by a bank clearinghouse. Such a shop is often found in a windowless room, albeit with good lighting and air conditioning. The "people machines," serving as the interface between the computer and the customer, are engaged in a tedious and monotonous task, isolated from their co-workers while using their machines. There are no empty, unknown spaces in time for these workers, because the machine itself monitors their performance. A data-entry terminal can be linked to the computer through a program that counts keystrokes per hour, monitors time spent on the phone with each customer, and displays a report to the supervisor every 15 minutes. In such situations, workers report high levels of stress, along with numerous health problems. The workers are not unionized—if they quit, there are people waiting in line to replace them.

◆ The graph of the number of cases of repetitive stress injuries to arms and hands mirrors almost exactly the graph of the number of computers in business.

Where should we lay the blame for the conditions in the electronic sweatshop? We can't blame the machines, and we shouldn't blame the workers for putting up with dehumanizing conditions in order to earn a living wage. The blame doesn't rest entirely on management, either—phone companies have ample studies to show that customers do not want to wait more than ten seconds for service. We, the consumers of information technology, helped to create this system.

This is not to say that the situation is hopeless, nor that it will persist in the future. While we may hope for a technological remedy, such as replacing the workers entirely by machines, such rescues may be impractical. Much can be done to fix the working conditions, however, even if we make no technological changes. In Sweden, for instance, video display terminal operators cannot legally be made to work at their terminals for more than two shifts per day, of no more than one and three-quarters hours duration each. The point here is that policy makers—not just technology developers and users—have a responsibility for ensuring that new technology is used in appropriate ways.

The Electronic Classroom

We will close this section on a more upbeat note, discussing the possibilities of the Information Revolution in the classroom. As with the other professions we mentioned earlier, it seems unlikely that teachers will be replaced by machines. The essential notion of computer-assisted instruction (CAI)—namely, the use of programs as instructional devices—has been with us since the early 1960s. It is only very recently, though, that computer power has begun to match demands in these areas.

CAI was originally envisioned as freeing teachers from repetitive tasks and allowing them to concentrate on individualized instruction. The computer—free of racial, religious, or sexual bias, and endlessly patient—would provide the perfect instructional medium in a cost-effective manner. Or so the rhetoric went. In fact, during the first two decades of CAI use, we discovered that programs for education rarely went beyond stultifying drill and practice sessions, providing almost no aid in thinking and problem solving. Students, originally attracted by the new technology, quickly became disaffected and bored. Teachers, who realized how pedagogically worthless the majority of CAI software was and who tried to design their own improvements, quickly realized that educational programming is as tedious as any other programming, requiring hundreds of hours of programming for every hour of instruction. CAI languished, and the shiny new machines sat idle, used only for an occasional programming course.

Recently, hardware and software technology have begun to catch up to the demands of quality educational applications. With the advent of screens capable of displaying high-quality graphical information, processors and memories equal to the heavy demands placed on them, and especially high-level authoring environments that allow a teacher to build a lesson without being a programmer, we have seen the beginning of a renaissance in computer-assisted instruction. We expect to see further growth in the future, again not toward the end of replacing people, but rather toward using the computer as an extremely valuable tool.

In September 1987, Apple Computer, Inc., sponsored PROJECT 2000, a design competition at a dozen universities to predict the nature and use of the personal computer in the year 2000. The winning entry, *Tablet,* came from the University of Illinois team of Bartlett W. Mel, Arch D. Robison, Steven S. Skiena, Kurt H. Thearling, Luke T. Young, and their faculty advisors Stephen M. Omohundro and Stephen Wolfram (whom we have met previously as the author of *Mathematica*). Tablet is an 8- by 11-inch computer with the kinds of processing speed and storage capacities one would expect from improvements in today's technology over the next decade. Its innovative features include

- A touch-sensitive screen that displays and interprets handwritten notes made with a stylus (much like a ballpoint pen without ink), and is capable of displaying high-quality, animated images.
- A slot for a *LaserCard,* serving in place of today's magnetic disks and each containing a billion characters of information (about the equivalent of a thousand books, more or less).
- An infrared interface, much like that used on today's TV remote controls, offering wireless connection to other devices, such as printers, projectors, stereo headsets, and other, more powerful computers.

Consider what Tablet's designers projected to be a typical day in the life of a college freshman in the year 2000, excerpted from *Academic Computing* (vol. 2, no. 7, May/June 1988, pp. 7–12, 62–64):

> Alexis Quezada is a freshman at a prestigious institution of higher learning. Her classes are typical for a freshman of the year 2000: Algorithmic Mathematics, Physical Science, Art History, English Composition, and Conversational Japanese. On her first day she was given her own Tablet, the personal computer used at the university. Today Alexis has three classes. . . . It is a nice day, so Alexis rides her bike over to the park before her lecture starts. At 10:00 A.M. sharp Tablet informs her that the Physical Science lecture is about to start. She directs her attention toward the screen as the lecture begins. When the lecture is over, she begins the laboratory experiment. It involves determining the equilibrium for a chemical reaction. She sets up the simulated experiment apparatus and starts it going. But it isn't working. She instructs Tablet to search today's lecture for "stuff about setting up today's experiment." Within seconds, the requested portion of the lecture is displayed on the screen. . . . In English Comp class at 2:00 P.M., the

professor indicates that she has finished grading the previous assignment and returns them. Instantly, the corner display contains a copy of Alexis's graded paper—B+, not too bad. Alexis pages through the paper by touching the screen. She touches the video-mail icon for comments about a particular page. Segments of her text become highlighted in color as they are discussed. . . . [That evening] it's time to work on her art history term paper comparing Salvador Dali's surrealist images in his paintings and the images he developed for the movies *Un Chien Andalou* and *Spellbound.* Alexis tells Tablet to find the films in available film databases. It seems that there are three films with the title *Spellbound.* Alexis says to find "the one by Hitchcock." The scenes she is interested in analyzing are being copied directly into her paper—a hypertext document. Alexis expounds on the meaning of the images in the films and their importance with respect to Dali's symbolism until it's time to call it a night.

We'll have to wait to find out how accurate this prediction is. It does, at the very least, illustrate the trends toward increasing connectivity and reliance on electronic information, and points out in a compelling way the prospects for the use of the computer as a facilitator for human activities rather than a replacement for people. Of course, it also illustrates other, less savory possibilities. To take just one, if Alexis's Tablet is never far from her side and can access information anywhere without being plugged in, it's possible that her whereabouts are likewise known, by someone, somewhere, at all times, just as it's possible that her professors can easily find whether she's listened to or downloaded any particular lecture.

LAB 10.2

Let's Get Real

Instead of using the WWW as a medium for experimentation, we ask you in this exercise to think of it as a resource for conducting directed research of your own. Use all of the resources available to you to write a paper addressing one of the topics below. A list of related links appears, as always, in our online or CD Resources.

1. Intellectual property and copyright laws as they apply to the WWW
2. Freedom of expression and First Amendment rights in the context of the WWW
3. Privacy, security, and the role of the Fourth Amendment (which precludes unwarranted search and seizure) as they apply to the WWW
4. Cryptology and the classification of cryptographic technology as "munitions" by the U.S. government
5. Freedom of access to the WWW
6. The Communications Decency Act of 1996

Review Questions

1. Do you think that increased access to electronic information will be an important feature of the world of the near future? Speculate on how your life may be changed (or not changed) by such ready access.
2. What are the advantages and disadvantages of the increasing computerization of libraries?
3. Discuss the advantages and disadvantages of applying a technological fix to the electronic sweatshop by replacing the workers with machines.
4. Tablet was conceived a decade ago, in an attempt to provide a picture of a time only a few years from now. Have any of the predictions come true yet? Which seem likely to happen by the year 2000?

10.6 CENTRALIZATION AND CONTROL

Early predictions of computer use always assumed a few large central computers, accessed through terminals with little or no computing power of their own. Here again we see the First Law of Futurology in action—these predictions were too conservative. Who would have guessed that within a relatively short period of time, microelectronic technology would put powerful computers within the reach of a large portion of society and make possible a *distributed* model of computer power, composed of an interconnected collection of powerful processors? If, as we believe is likely, society will come to rely increasingly on electronic information, where shall this information be stored? Will information be concentrated in a few large central data banks, or will it be decentralized throughout society's network of computers? This trend is harder to predict than the ones we have seen so far, but the scales seem to tip in the direction of centralization, which is unfortunate, since that way carries the greatest risks.

Privacy

Information can be useful, like a tip on a horse race, but it can also be dangerous in the wrong hands. This is why we have laws concerning libel, espionage, sedition, and invasion of privacy. If the trend in computer use is toward increasing access to information and increasing centralization of information, we must be prepared to ask Who should have access to information, particularly information about oneself?

To give you a sense of the scale of information available in electronic databases, consider that the Department of Health and Human Services has 693 computer systems with access to over 1.3 billion records, Treasury Department computers contain nearly a billion records, and the Department of Justice has access to 200 million records on file. If you have a driver's license, own a firearm, have ever applied for a fishing license or student loan, have registered for the draft, have been arrested or just detained by law enforcement officials, or have traveled abroad, you are represented in a government data bank. If you have ever applied for a credit card or a bank loan, you are represented in a large private data bank, as well.

Ideally, this proliferation of information about ourselves would be of little concern. Computerized storage of information makes managing the details of bureaucracy easier—we get our tax refund checks quicker, police officers can check whether a car is stolen or whether its driver has any outstanding warrants in a matter of minutes, and loan applications can be approved in hours rather than weeks. For years, Congress has considered a proposal for FEDNET, a national data bank that would streamline access to citizens' records even further by incorporating all government data into a single database.

Realistically, such prospects should concern all of us deeply because of the potential for abuse. Quick access and processing of information permits tactics that are questionable at best, and often illegal. The Nixon administration, for example, coerced the Internal Revenue Service into providing tax information on individuals on the administration's "Enemies List"—not traitors or criminals, but ordinary citizens who had expressed views contrary to those of the White House—in hopes of discovering damaging information. In a recent case, the FBI attempted to force a university library to divulge the names of patrons who had checked out technical material, which it would then match against a list of foreign students, searching, one supposes, for spies. Similar *matchup runs* were proposed by the IRS, comparing employers' reports of wages paid against figures reported by taxpayers, in an attempt to discover unreported income. If an integrated federal database were to be initiated, it is not difficult to imagine other such runs, checking real estate purchases, car and boat registrations, reported income, and ethnic background to prepare a list of people who would then be flagged for attention as potential narcotics dealers. There might come a time when the majority of the population would even be willing to tolerate the potential civil rights violations and abuse of the principle of probable cause in such a search, if the effect was judged to be beneficial to society as a whole.

As we mentioned, there is a temptation to believe that if information is in a computerized record, it must be true. People who gather and enter information make mistakes, however, and programs are never completely error free. If we are to rely increasingly on computerized information systems, we must make sure that there are safeguards against misuse and inaccuracy. To be sure, the Freedom of Information and Fair Credit Reporting Acts allow us to inspect and sometimes correct information in our files, but just finding where we are represented is often difficult. With increased reliance on electronic information should also come easy access to our personal information. Finally, whenever we hear of new databases, we should make sure that the policy makers charged with their operation and oversight take care that the information therein is limited to those who have a legal and moral right to know.

Electronic Crime

The word *sabotage* is a product of the Industrial Age. Literally, it refers to bringing a machine to a halt by throwing a boot (*sabot*, in French) into its works. In a high-tech society, we should be prepared for high-tech crime. The central computer of any large system presents an attractive target to those desiring a quick and illegal profit, or to those who, for personal or political reasons, wish to bring the system to its knees.

A computer and the data it stores are shockingly vulnerable to physical assault. A small explosion will damage most computers beyond repair. That, though, is less problematic than it might first seem. Computers break down regularly without any outside help at all. Any organization that relies on them generally has provisions to purchase computing power from other sources. The financial value of a computer, however, pales to insignificance next to the value of the information it manipulates. A magnetic tape or disk with irreplaceable information stored on it can be rendered useless by as simple a means as passing a small magnet near it. Frankly, though, the physical security of a computer system and its data is a familiar problem, for which familiar solutions do exist.

Far more complicated than physical security is protecting the information in a computer. Newspapers in recent decades have abounded with stories of hackers gaining access to computers, armed with nothing more than a computer, a modem, some programming expertise, a lot of patience, and good luck. In many cases, these unauthorized intruders do little more than browse through the computer's files and leave a message behind. Intending to do no harm, however, is often not enough to prevent harm. Recently a Cornell graduate student was alleged to have gained access to the Internet, a large network of research computers across the country. He left behind a *worm,* a program that was planted in a computer system, masquerading as a legitimate job, that could make copies of itself on the systems of other computers on the network. Intended to grow slowly, a programming error caused the virus to multiply explosively, clogging the systems of hundreds of computers from coast to coast and bringing them to a virtual standstill. No sensitive information was compromised, but hundreds of thousands of dollars were lost in the time required to shut the systems down, find and purge the worm, and bring the computers back into operation.

A bank stands to lose a great deal more to a hacker or a criminally designed program than in a holdup. In 1994, for instance, Citibank lost $400,000 to a gang of Russian hackers who accessed the bank's computers. Although accurate figures are difficult to obtain, since banks are understandably reluctant to make such instances public, the FBI estimated that the total loss due to such crimes was in the neighborhood of $400 million in 1995. You don't even need to be an experienced hacker to make illegal money with computers, though. Invest a few thousand dollars in a high-quality scanner, a good laser printer, and a computer and you have an instant money machine: Get a check, scan it into the computer's memory, alter some of the data, print out a new check on someone else's account, and cash it. With the right equipment, a computer-savvy sixth-grader could join the ranks of check forgers, a group that costs banks well over half a billion dollars each year. In contrast, the total take from old-fashioned bank robberies was a mere $59 million in 1995.

In the future, we are likely to see increasing incidents of *cyberterrorism,* assaults on computer systems for political reasons. Israeli computer scientists, for instance, recently discovered and removed a virus, almost surely placed by political enemies, that would have erased the files and shut down a large number of government systems. This new and expanded form of computer security is an area of considerable research interest at present. A CIA spokesman recently warned that the brittle data infrastructure of this country was dangerously insecure. Authorities agree that at present it would take comparatively little effort to seriously disrupt any of the banking, communications, energy, or transportation systems of a computer-dependent country like the United States.

Review Questions

1. Give two reasons why we should be concerned about the proliferation of electronic databases containing personal information.
2. What is a *matchup run*?
3. What steps could be taken to limit access to networks such as ARPANET to only authorized users? For any protection you come up with, try to think how an ingenious hacker could circumvent it.
4. Give an example of possible technoterrorism. A Web search should turn up plenty of possibilities from which to choose.

10.7 EMERGENT EFFECTS

Like the electronic computer itself, undreamed of at the beginning of the century, the effects of new directions of research or synergistic combinations of existing technologies are virtually impossible to predict. Even in existing areas, we often have no idea where research might lead. To return to the image that began this module—HAL—we have no way of knowing at present whether machine consciousness is an attainable goal. Joseph Weizenbaum has compared the problem of developing truly intelligent computers with getting from the earth to the moon: You could build a very tall tower or you could build very powerful rockets. Weizenbaum argues that at this stage of AI research, we not only don't know whether we'll ever get to the moon, we don't even know whether we're making explosives or piling up rocks.

John McCarthy, one of the fathers of AI research, has a more sanguine attitude. In *Machines Who Think* (San Francisco: W. H. Freeman, 1979, p. 344) Pamela McCorduck reports McCarthy's position as follows:

> The real developments of AI will probably differ from science fiction versions in at least three ways. First, he says, it's unlikely that there will be a prolonged period during which it will be possible to build machines as intelligent as human beings but impossible to build them much smarter. If we can put a machine capable of human behavior in a metal skull, we can put a machine capable of acting like ten thousand coordinated people in a building. Second, although the present stock of ideas is inadequate to make programs as intelligent as people, there's nothing to prevent the new ideas from coming very soon, in five years or five hundred. Finally, present ideas are probably good enough to extend our ability to have very large amounts of information at our fingertips, which will create its own changes.

At the far end of the spectrum of positions on machine intelligence, we have writers such as Robert Jastrow, who says in *The Enchanted Loom,* "The era of carbon-chemistry life is drawing to a close on the earth and a new era of silicon-based life—indestructible, immortal, infinitely expandable—is beginning." More than 30 years ago, Frederick Brown spoke to the same point in his short story "Answer." In this very short story,[2] all the universe's computers have finally been connected together into one immense distributed network. At the unveiling of this new system, one of the spectators types in the question "Is there a God?" The story concludes,

> The mighty voice answered without hesitation, without the clicking of a single relay. "Yes, *now* there is a God." Sudden fear flashed on the face of Dwar Ev. He leaped to grab the switch. A bolt of lightning from the cloudless sky struck him down and fused the switch shut.

We have come to the end of our long tour through computer science. We have shown you the major landmarks, without giving you more than the briefest chance to explore them in detail. That will have to come later, if you have the interest. We hope we have demystified the computer, removing mistaken impressions and replacing them with facts. As we move into the Information Age, humankind will surely remythologize the machine in light of its new impact on society, perhaps as an equal partner. We will close with the Zero-th Law of Futurology, "One thing is clear: The future will not be like the present." It's up to you—good luck.

10.8 EXERCISES

The answers to these exercises may range from a paragraph in length to research papers of considerable substance. Your instructor will indicate the desired scope of each question.

1. List the major trends in computer use mentioned in the text; come up with another and estimate its likelihood of occurring.

2. Suppose that the transistor—and hence the computer as we know it—had not been invented. Pick a specific area of society and comment on how it would differ from its current form.

3. Speculate on the future form and use of television in the Information Age.

4. Minitel has been extremely successful in France, in spite of the fact that it is a pay-for-use service. Do you think that the typical telephone customer in the United States would be willing to pay for ready access to large quantities of information?

5. Voice-recognition technology is yet to be perfected, although progress is being made. What effects might very efficient voice-recognition technology have on our privacy?

6. The ELIZA program, described in Module 9, simulates a psychotherapist who solicits responses from his or her patient by giving neutral responses. Joseph Weizenbaum, ELIZA's creator, was disturbed by the strong emotional attachment many users formed to a program that he designed solely as an experiment in language processing. Do you think that a program such as ELIZA has any place in therapy? Explain.

7. Computer-analyzed exit polls can predict the outcome of an election with a high degree of reliability long before the votes are counted, and in some cases even before the polls close. What adverse effects might this have on the electoral process, particularly in national elections where

[2] Only 256 words long. One has to wonder if Brown realized that the number of words in the story was two to the eighth power (or, two raised to the two raised to the third).

Index

C

F

G

Q

R

S

T